It Happened in Southern Illinois

SHAWNEE CLASSICS

A Series of Classic Regional Reprints for the Midwest

John W. Allen

It Happened in Southern Illinois

SOUTHERN ILLINOIS UNIVERSITY PRESS
Carbondale

All rights reserved. First edition published 1968. Southern Illinois University
Press paperback edition 2010
Printed in the United States of America

22 21 20 19   5 4 3 2

Library of Congress Cataloging-in-Publication Data
    Allen, John W.
    It happened in southern Illinois / John W. Allen. — Southern Illinois
    University Press pbk. ed.
        p. cm.
    Originally published: Carbondale : Area Services, Southern Illinois
    University, © 1968.
    Includes index.

    ISBN-13: 978-0-8093-2968-7 (pbk. : alk. paper)
    ISBN-10: 0-8093-2968-9 (pbk. : alk. paper)
    ISBN-13: 978-0-8093-8566-9 (ebook)
    ISBN-10: 0-8093-8566-X (ebook)

    1. Illinois—History. I. Title.

    F541.A42 2010
    977.3—dc22   2009046364

Printed on recycled paper ♺

Contents

List of Illustrations

John W. Allen:
A Personal Word

PLEASURE AND PRIVILEGE enough for anyone. That's what it was to have been invited to write the Foreword for John W. Allen's first collection of newspaper columns on folkways and regional history, *Legends & Lore of Southern Illinois*.

To enjoy a second chance at riding high on John's capacious coattails is just too good to be true. Yet here it is. So let Allahen be praised!

I allowed at the outset of the first of these journalistic harvest homes, more than five years ago, that John Allen and his handiwork needed no official presentation. That statement was completely true. But if it was so before John's first book was published, it is far more the case now that *Legends & Lore* has gone into three printings, totaling in excess of 17,000 copies. For in that time many thousands more people have met its kindly, rugged, tireless author in person or on the printed page or both.

Since I used up nearly all the dictionary's adjectives of adulation in the first Foreword, what confronts me now is doubly not a theory but a reality. What can I say in this second tribute to my friend and exemplar that will not be repetitious of the first? After considerable head scratching, I figure there are two things that I can do.

Because of its subject, I can recommend the first Foreword without reservation of any kind. I can urge all new readers of the book at hand to go back and con as "basic biography" what I said about John Allen on that earlier get-together in print. Even if I did write it—and partly just for that reason— the first Foreword told a lot about John Willis Allen: about his origin and background, about his birth in a log cabin and his early years on a pioneer farm down in Hamilton County, about the family moves during his boyhood, about his fascinating life and its countless good works. These are the personal facts that almost any reader would have had a hard time pulling out of John Allen himself with a six-horse hitch.

Second thing I can do, and it follows right after the first, is just as much in order. I can see to it that the John Allen record is brought up-to-date. This is what I now proceed to do.

If we were to ask John what has happened to him in the half decade since *Legends & Lore* brought him fame—and I hope at least a becomingly modest measure of fortune, too—he doubtless would say with that bit of a drawl, "Well, not much." Then if we pressed him, he probably would tell us that he had just been plodding along in what used to be called the even tenor of the way.

At this writing, dogwood blossom time, 1968, John is roughly midway through his eighty-first year. He claims he has slowed down some, but no one else can notice it.

What he is really getting at is that he has had two or three hospital sessions in recent years. But it ought to be obvious to everyone that these were arranged so John could see what being in a hospital was like. He had called on plenty of friends, but he had missed out on the hospital experience himself and he was just plain curious. Naturally he has won each and every hospital decision.

Also John found time to try on for size a major automobile wreck. He butted out both sides of the windshield of a Volkswagon camper. This left him with skinned shins and one black eye and a vehicle that fared considerably worse. If this also was a new and broadening experience, and John holds that it was, he has put it down as one that does not require repetition. He has learned all he needs to know firsthand about auto wrecks.

Partly to keep his muscles flexed, John helped dismantle the Aydelott double log house, built out of the surrounding timber in Saline County in 1848. Then for good measure, and his purpose all along, he joined in reconstructing this frontier dwelling and its accompanying barn on the grounds of the Saline County Historical Society at Harrisburg. But John had an extra special reason for seeing that this job was done right. Why? Because he says that so far as he has been able to find out, the Aydelott barn contains the only original threshing floor still existing in the whole nation. John agrees that this takes in a lot of territory, but then a fairish number of states, starting with Hawaii and Alaska and working east, never saw a threshing floor. And anyway, who among us knows enough threshing floors to argue with John Allen about how many originals are left? In his fourscore years, John has seen the pioneer culture pretty much vanish from his region. So he was not going to stand by with his hands in his pockets when he could help save its last threshing floor from destruction.

New honors have not just come John's way. They have literally swept over and around him, with John there in the midst of them like a rock in a river filled with rushing water after a gully-washing spring rain.

McKendree College honored itself by conferring on him an honorary Doctor of Laws degree. The Southern Illinois University Alumni Association chose him for its Alumni Achievement Award and before that called him up for its Distinguished Service Award. In 1966 the editors and publishers of Southern Illinois, through their S. I. E. A., gave John its "Headliner of the Year" citation.

No one was appointed more fittingly to the Illinois Sesquicentennial Committee. This distinction brought John a handsome official certificate signed and sealed by Governor Otto Kerner and pledging to its recipient "all the rights and emoluments thereof." John is pretty well up on the rights, but he will welcome suggestions as to how he may best go about collecting his fair share of the emoluments.

One job as a presiding officer John must have performed with extraordinary relish. That was when he served as president of the Carbondale Memorial Day Association at the very time of the one hundredth anniversary of the first community-wide decoration of the graves of the Civil War dead. The inspiration and leadership for that act of esteem came from Jackson County's own General John Alexander Logan. This brought together a pair of Johns who would have had a great how-to-do swapping stories and anecdotes if the wheel of fortune had thrown them into "Little Egypt" in the same generation. John A. might have been the more dashing horseman, but John W. would have outpointed him as sparring partner for Heavyweight Champion Gene Tunney.

If you happen to ask John how long it takes to read *Legends & Lore* out loud, he can tell you right off. It uses up a full eight-hour day with extra time for lunch. He found that out when a ladies' organization to aid the blind asked him to read his book onto tape so it could be circulated to people who cannot see.

A high point for John since the appearance of *Legends & Lore* was reuniting with his World War I buddies of the Second Division at Miami, Florida. Among the veterans who made it back along with John was a 1919 classmate in the postwar educational program held at the University of London. He was the first of the group John had seen since they all checked out at the end of classes a mere forty-eight years earlier.

But then John touched a whole series of high points when, thanks to his own bright idea, he armed himself with Washington press credentials from the Sparta *News-Plaindealer*. As easy as pie John found himself among the pundits at two White House press conferences and several others conducted by Cabinet officers. And on that January day when the presidential oath was administered in 1965, a warmly-coated John W. Allen was on the spot, in a seat reserved for him and no one else.

When John is on his Washington prowls, he headquarters at the home of his son, Robert Allen, who is the Soviet Union Specialist in the Library of Congress. Since Son Robert goes off on his own official forays to Moscow and Leningrad, Father John may wind up with the run of a Washington house.

John has found that tracking down something he wants to know more about in the National Capital is not too much different from following out a trail in the Ozark upland deep in the tip end of Southern Illinois. The main thing, John counsels us, is to get on the right track at the start and then stay on it all the way.

Come New Year's Eve and John still is apt to turn up at Prairie du Rocher. He has missed *La Guiannée* a few times in recent years, but his attendance average must be just about the next best to that of the most faithful natives. When the night arrives for those merry fiddlers and the singing bands under the winter stars and flowing eggnog bowls that decorate the holiday tables, there is just one town in all the world for John. Let's all make a date now to meet "The Old Rascal," as S.I.U. President Delyte W. Morris affectionately calls him, on next December 31, and troop door-to-door about Prairie du Rocher. That is the only way to know how much fun you have been missing all these years.

Now a twist but only a bit of one. So far everything has been for or about John Allen. Now I am going to insert a couple of paragraphs on my own hook. In the Illinois 150th Anniversary Newspaper Supplement, circulated Sunday, February 4, 1968, by some thirty-five Illinois dailies, I wrote a piece entitled "Triangle on a Point." I wanted Southern Illinois' crossroads, hamlets, and country villages, no less than its cities and towns, to have their own place in the sun. To that end I managed to find ways to pack more than a hundred place names into my short text.

But I did not ever quite get it said that these were only a representative fraction of the places I might have included, that "Little Egypt's" persons and things, too, could be long extended. For example, I did not mention the Old Stone Face or the Old Slave House, or the Old Bethel Church in the Lemen Settlement that was a station in the Underground Railroad. I failed to include the Elsah of Frederick Oakes Sylvester, poet-painter of the Mississippi. I did not pay honor due to the Sign of the Silver Horse, the private press of Hal and Violet Trovillion, that brought international distinction to Herrin over many years.

Somehow my reference to colleges omitted Captain Benjamin Godfrey's Monticello, where my mother was graduated in 1893, and The Principia, whose chapel spire atop the wind-carved palisades can be seen for miles up and down the Great River. There should have been notice for the Mermaid Tavern at Lebanon where Dickens wrote out some of his American notes, and for the Main Street in Sparta as the location for the 1968 Academy Award Best Motion Picture of the Year, "In the Heat of the Night."

How could there be any account of Southern Illinois without the United Mine Workers and the Progressive Miners of America and their struggles, and life and death in the coal fields? Or without sports figures like Collinsville's Art Fletcher, the strong-chinned, hard-playing shortstop of McGraw's New York Giants? Or lots more?

And so my gratitude for this digression which was not too much of a digression after all. I did not leave Southern Illinois and everything I said was related in one way or another to John. Now back to him.

Turn down that bright lamp. Still better turn it out altogether. Put another crab apple log on the fire and the firelight will be enough for all the seeing we need to do. Slip off your shoes, loosen your belt, settle back into your most comfortable chair. In short, make yourself easy. For we are going to sit a while. The Old Rascal, or if you prefer a more accurate description also used in public, "The Best Friend Southern Illinois Ever Had," is going to talk with us about important things.

John, the floor is yours for as long as you want. If you don't mind a suggestion first tell us about some of the interesting people you have met up with, "Mother" Jones, Dr. Anna Bigsby, the Illinois teacher who became a legend, and others that pop into your mind. Then swing over into Christmas superstitions, owl calls, beekeepers, and such like. Take us to Cave-in-Rock, Old Shawneetown, the American Bottom, and Bloody Island and go on from there. Remember that you don't believe in ghosts but that you are afraid of them.

Your throat may get a mite dry so here's a pitcher of chilled home-pressed cider to wet your whistle now and again.

We're all listening, John.

IRVING DILLIARD

Paw Paw Hill, Collinsville, Illinois
Dogwood Blossom Time, 1968

Preface

THIS TITLE, "It Happened in Southern Illinois," like its predecessor, "Legends & Lore of Southern Illinois," is a random recording of the lore, legends, and sometimes odd beliefs, practices, and happenings that comprise the very down-to-earth records of this region since the French came 295 years ago. There also are mentions, somewhat aside, to the Indians who lived here ten thousand years prior to the coming of the French.

Failure to acknowledge the many encouragements, helps, and constructive criticisms from those connected with Southern Illinois University, as well as from those who have lived in the declining years of the era encompassed, would be amiss.

And, once again, acknowledgments would be grossly incomplete without an expression of appreciation for the competent and careful help in correcting, arranging, typing, and retyping by students. They also have served to keep alive an abiding faith in the basic goodness, competency, and sincerity of youth.

J. W. A.

Carbondale, Illinois
June, 1968

xvii

It Happened in Southern Illinois

Chapter 1

Individuals

🌼 *SOUTHERN ILLINOIS HAS A STORIED BACKGROUND*

Our "egypt" has played a prominent part in the efforts of several European countries to build empires in North America. It was into this region, early known as the Illinois Country, that the French came as early as 1673. Explorers came to discover and to seek riches in a new country. Missionaries sought to spread the beliefs and practices of Christianity among the natives. These were followed by the *coureur de bois,* a strange and lonely band of wilderness wanderers and clandestine traders. Next came those known as *voyageurs* who were authorized or licensed Indian traders; they in turn were followed by settlers. These French settlements prospered and the culture of France flourished at isolated spots in the vast forest—places such as Cahokia, Kaskaskia, Vincennes, and Prairie du Rocher. Both the French settlers and the Indians were happy.

In 1763 Britain defeated France in war, the lilies of France were hauled down, and French hope for empire in Illinois ended. It was back and forth across this section that George Rogers Clark and his intrepid band marched, countermarched, and fought to accomplish the incredible in 1778–1779 to hold the Northwest Territory. This marked the end of British rule here and doubtlessly decided the ultimate extent of our nation. The success of Clark's expedition enabled the colonists to push our western boundary beyond the Allegheny Mountains.

It was to the site of present-day Wood River in Illinois that Meriwether Lewis and William Clark, the brother of George Rogers Clark, came in 1803 to organize and equip an expedition to explore the Louisiana Territory, recently bought from France.

3

French, British, and colonial Indian traders in turn came to the Illinois Country to barter their trinkets, toys, pots, firearms, and "firewater" to the Indians for furs. Men of the Illinois Country later played an important part in crushing Indian resistance to the settlement of the whites.

Illinois has known some great Indian leaders such as Pontiac, Tecumseh, and Black Hawk, along with men of fame like LaSalle, Joliet, and Tonti. Southern Illinois saw the coming of the Catholic fathers more than 250 years ago.

William Morrison's first group of traders set out from Kaskaskia, now vanished, to go on trading trips to Santa Fe and to establish the Santa Fe Trail, whose story is large in our nation's history.

Some written records, and others not written, linger to tell of the hazards that often lay along early trails. The names of Potts' Tavern, Digbytown, Goshen Road, Miles Trace, and Fords Ferry Road suggest many stories. Stories of its river pirates, brigands, robbers, and folk figures are many. Log houses, log barns, and early farm buildings await an opportunity to tell their stories to those with ears that listen properly.

The romance of the Western Waters lingers along the bordering rivers. It was from southern Illinois that literally millions went west. At Cairo, once the world's greatest river port, military forces were collected and campaigns launched that cut the Confederacy in twain. The state has imported and exported men who have done much to shape the nation's course.

Southern Illinois surely has something that appeals to almost anyone.

🎖 THE LEGEND OF DR. ANNA BIGSBY

WHEN ASSETS ARE MEASURED by dollars, Hardin County in southern Illinois is among the poorer ones in the state. If legendary and romantic figures be the unit of measure, it is among the state's richer counties.

Its early story is filled with roistering boatmen, river pirates, counterfeiters, strong men, feuders, killers, highwaymen, bullies, braggarts, and a variety of brigands. There also were those less frequently publicized, whose first purpose was to do good.

Perhaps no other earlier settled area along the Ohio can claim more half-real, half-mythical characters. Each of these began as a real individual around whom legend gathered. Sometimes it becomes difficult to separate the real from the legendary.

Most of Hardin County's misty figures were men. Only a few were women. Among its legendary women, perhaps Dr. Anna Bigsby is the most widely and kindly remembered one.

When Anna was about sixteen years old she came from Philadelphia to Illinois in a covered wagon with her parents, Norman and Catherine Pierce. Her father appears to have been an ambitious, industrious, upright, and respected man. Her mother was an intelligent, kindly, and helpful woman—among those considered better educated by standards of that day.

Before coming to Illinois, Anna received the educational advantages that her years permitted. She continued to study under her mother's guidance and help, and became a teacher.

Anna was fearless and capable. After coming to Illinois, legend, apparently reliable, relates that she killed a man who attacked her. Grown to womanhood, Anna returned to Philadelphia and studied medicine. When her studies were completed she returned to Illinois and began to practice her profession. She also taught school, not an unusual combination of jobs, and engaged in church work. She shortly was married to Isaac Hobbs, son of a neighboring farmer.

Dr. Anna's medical practice extended over a wide area. It took her on many lonely trips through night and storm over woodland trails. She was successful beyond the average. Because of her skill, kindliness, and sincerity, she was respected by all and affectionately referred to as "Doctor Anna."

There were some, however, who considered her promotion of schools as too high-toned and feared the influence of the church which she supported.

Legend quickly began to grow about Dr. Anna. One story tells of the deadly milksick that often appeared during the late summer and early autumn. At such times it took a number of human lives and caused the death of nonmilking cattle. No one knew either its cause or its remedy.

The superstitious believed that it came from a magic poison scattered by witches. There was some talk of dealing out summary punishment to those suspected. Doctor Anna did not believe the witch theory. She suspected that it was caused by some plant the cattle ate and accordingly made observations to determine the plant responsible. Legend tells us that she was helped by a Shawnee Indian squaw who knew a plant that produced like symptoms upon people.

According to the legend, Doctor Anna's inquiry and investigation indicated that the white snake root plant, which the Shawnee squaw pointed out, was the culprit. Since then, its guilt has been definitely

proven. Once suspected, men went into the woods, seeking and destroy-
ing the plant. The malady of milksick subsided. A few years ago, a
farmer and his son living in Hardin County were observed digging out
some clusters of the offending plant.

At about the time when milksick was the most prevalent, Anna's husband died of pneumonia. Some years later she was married to Eson
(pronounced Ason) Bigsby, who turned out to be a timber thief associated with other lawbreakers. Tradition tells us that he married Anna
because he thought she had money. To gain possession of her savings, a
persistent story relates that he, with the help of others, seized her as she
was going to visit a patient, bound her with chains, pushed her off a
cliff, and set fire to the woods. According to the story, however, she
lodged in a tree, and a rain came to put out the fire. Dr. Anna succeeded
in freeing herself from her bonds and climbed down.

A cave beside Rock Creek in Hooven Hollow, still known as the
Doctor Anna Bigsby Cave, is the legendary hiding place of her money.
It is along this bluff in the vicinity of the cave that an occasional
traveler with a vivid imagination reports seeing weird lights. The lights
are supposed to guide the spirit of Doctor Anna as it goes about to safeguard her treasure.

The legend of Doctor Anna Bigsby is indeed a strange one. There are
enough written records to establish her as a very real person whose descendants still live in the vicinity. There is enough of legend and
imagery to cast a strange aura about her. Her full story is told in a book
called *Ballads From the Bluffs,* published some years ago by E. N. Hall
of Elizabethtown.

❧ *LAST LAWSUIT OF ABRAHAM LINCOLN*

"Prowling" has some unpleasant connotations; nevertheless it is an
enjoyable pastime. A recent visit to the Alton Residence Center of
Southern Illinois University gave opportunity to indulge that pleasure.
The minutes of the faculty meetings of Shurtleff College more than a
hundred years ago were made accessible.

Several pages of the minutes tell of faculty action to regulate the
conduct of students. It immediately becomes apparent that boys were
boys, even then. Some of them, the records declare, drank, swore, played
cards, and attended dances. One youth was charged with being rude,

and another with prevarication. A few insisted upon belonging to both literary societies and were dismissed from college.

Some of the century-old entries proved of more than passing interest. It was from the faculty's action concerning one student, William Baker Gilbert, that there arose the last lawsuit in which Abraham Lincoln appeared as counsel.

William was the son of a prosperous Missouri farmer who lived just across the Mississippi from Kaskaskia and farmed four thousand acres. Young William's grandfather was David J. Baker, prominent Alton attorney and former senator from Illinois. Young Gilbert, a student at Shurtleff in June, 1856, met with seven other students in the room of his friend, S. S. Boone, to duly observe the term's ending. He served as one of the committee sent out to procure "wine and brandy." Making use of the refreshments procured, the students observed the occasion with considerable hilarity.

Their activities did not pass unnoticed. The faculty met on June 13 to investigate. The evidence apparently was conclusive, and all were adjudged guilty. Of Williams it is said, "No one mentioned any circumstance that might tend to palliate his offense." The records of this meeting made by Mr. Oscar Howes, secretary of the faculty and teacher of classical languages and literature, also indicate that some "had drank lager bier" at other times.

All were placed on probation until the end of the first term of the coming year. They also were to be "publicly admonished on Tuesday morning in the chapel." Further developments induced the faculty to meet and modify the penalties of Gilbert and one other student. Because of "the degree of penitence manifested by Mr. Gilbert and apparent determination to conduct himself properly in the future," his period of probation was reduced to one month. The other student, because of his "downright falsehood," was resuspended for one year and required to leave the college immediately.

With these items on his record Gilbert was on his way back to Shurtleff after the Christmas vacation in 1856. He stopped in St. Louis over the New Year to visit his classmate and fellow probationer named Boone. Together they went to an art exhibit and a reception given by Mr. Chouteau. At the reception a Negro butler, using a silver ladle, dispensed punch from a large silver bowl. Young Gilbert, who figuratively "didn't know the gun was loaded," drained his glass and smiled his appreciation. Only then did he look up and see Mr. Read, the president of Shurtleff, watching him.

Back at Shurtleff, things began to happen. At a series of faculty meetings held on January 8 and 9, 1857, a thorough investigation was made concerning drinking by students. Each one accused was called before the faculty and given opportunity "to mention any circumstance that might tend to palliate his offense." The result of it all was that Gilbert, among others, was suspended from the college for one year. The next day a petition signed by a majority of the student body was presented to the faculty asking that Gilbert be allowed to remain in school. The faculty refused to relent, and Gilbert accordingly left school but continued his studies in his grandfather's law office under arrangements with St. Paul's College at Palmyra, Missouri.

William's father and grandfather were much dissatisfied with the treatment accorded the youth and began action against Shurtleff in the U.S. Circuit Court at Springfield. Abraham Lincoln was employed as their attorney. John M. Palmer represented the college. Through various delays the case did not come to trial until June, 1860, after Lincoln had received the Republican nomination as candidate for the presidency.

According to an account given by Mr. Palmer many years later, the court proceedings were brief. The judge is reported to have said, "Mr. Lincoln, I'll argue this case for you. You have too much on your hands already. You haven't any case." The judge then explained the law and its application. "Well," said Lincoln with a smile, "don't you want to hear me make a speech?" The judge said, "No." Palmer continued, "Thus the last case that Lincoln tried, he—well he didn't try it at all."

Lest someone worry about the wayward young Gilbert, he continued at another college where he received both the bachelor's and master's degrees and graduated from Harvard Law School. Admitted to practice, he became a very successful attorney.

🏵 *LINCOLN'S MOTHER*

EACH FEBRUARY MILLIONS of people pause to observe Abraham Lincoln's birth date. The thoughts of many doubtlessly dwell upon his greatness while some think sympathetically of the rugged pioneer boyhood that was his. No one who has spent a winter in a chinked log cabin or just one chilly and blustery night in a rudely constructed half-faced camp can easily forget the experience. But this was the way of life of the Lincoln family, and his young years were years of physical hardship and meager living.

Measured by another standard, however, the boy Abraham was rich.

Any boy at any time who has an intelligent, capable, and affectionate mother is never poor. One with two such mothers is rich indeed, and Lincoln was so blessed. Nancy Hanks Lincoln, his blood mother, was the first of these. The second was Sarah Bush (Johnson) Lincoln who lived beyond the death of her illustrious stepson, and thus her story is more fully known than is that of his real mother.

Nancy Hanks Lincoln died before the boy was ten years old, and her recorded history is brief. Enough remains, however, to indicate that she was a wonderful mother. The lasting influence she exerted over her son was great; perhaps it was the force that shaped his destiny. Of her effect on his whole life Lincoln said in his later years, "All that I am or hope to be, I owe to my angel mother. Blessings on her memory."

Even so, some morbid-minded persons, using flimsy and often the more spurious appearing evidence—along with an occasional phrase out of context—would defame her.

Nancy Hanks was the daughter of Joseph and Lucy Hanks. She is indicated by the order of listing on her father's will as the youngest of several children. Her name appears few times in contemporary records. One of these is the marriage bond filed by Thomas Lincoln; another is the record of their marriage by the Reverend Jesse Head at Beechland, Kentucky, on June 12, 1806. Her name and signature, appearing on a few legal documents, show that she wrote a clear and legible hand.

Tradition relates that she received a fair education, considerably above the average for girls at that time. Tradition also holds that it was she who gave her son the most help in his learning to read. All records indicate that she was cheerful in disposition, genial, kindly, and was a devout Christian.

It was this woman who went—perhaps not reluctantly even with a full knowledge of the trials that lay ahead—with Thomas Lincoln and the children to settle in the wilderness of Indiana near Gentryville in the winter of 1816. It was there that Thomas Lincoln built his first home in the state, a half-faced camp of poles that was heated by a log fire on its open side. In this they spent the remainder of the winter, completing a better cabin in the spring.

There were many hazards to pioneer life. To the usual ones there was added that of the mysterious milksick in the fall of 1818. Nancy Hanks Lincoln contracted the malady and died in October. Her body was carried to a knoll in the lonely forest a short way from the cabin and buried; the grave was marked by rough unlettered stones. A few other burials were made there before the cemetery at Pigeon Creek became the one commonly used.

The little cluster of graves near the Lincoln cabin site remained abandoned, neglected, and all but forgotten for a long interval. Finally, one of the Studebaker brothers of wagon, buggy, and automobile fame, decided to mark the grave of Lincoln's mother. To determine its location, three survivors among those who had attended the funeral were brought back. All agreed that her's was one of three pioneer mothers buried side by side, but one insisted that it was the grave farthest north while a second thought it was the center one, and the third believed it was either the southern or center one. The center one, accordingly, was marked.

The story of the grave's location was told by a very old man who, as a youth, had driven the carriage of Studebaker, and others come to locate the mother's grave, from the railway station to the lonely burial place in the woodland. My meeting with him occurred more than thirty years afterwards when the governor of Indiana and a commission were there to plan part of the improvements that one sees now. The old gentleman was there at the behest of the governor to supply bits of firsthand information.

The Indiana homesite stirs the imagination and helps one to visualize Lincoln's early environment and more fully comprehend the influence that Nancy Hanks Lincoln had on one of America's truly great men. The site is a must for those who would follow the Lincoln Trail.

🌸 ONE ARTIST PAINTED A SMILING LINCOLN

It has been far more than a hundred years since Abraham Lincoln's name became a prominent one over America. Since Lincoln's death more has been written about him than about any other man who ever lived, unless it be about the apostle Paul.

Perhaps no other man's name calls forth a clearer mental image with more people. The most familiar image is one of a tall, gaunt man with a seamed and careworn face, and with sad but kindly and trusting eyes. A portrait, therefore, that shows him smiling is unusual.

One of the three known likenesses that show Lincoln with a smile was found in the library of Shurtleff College, that now is the Alton branch of Southern Illinois University. This portrait of Lincoln was painted in August, 1860, during the presidential campaign. This was before he, at the suggestion of little Grace Bedell, grew a beard. It is one of three paintings made by the same artist, Albert Johnson Conant. According to a letter written by the artist, and now among other materials relating to this portrait gathered by Dr. Alfred G. Harris, formerly with Shurtleff but now with the Alton Residence Center, this is the first of the three portraits he painted.

Conant, the son of a carpenter-house painter, was born on a farm in Massachusetts in 1815. From childhood he showed artistic talent in his sketches and painted portraits of those about him. His formal education, aside from art, was somewhat thorough. He earned both the bachelor of arts and master's degrees. In art, however, he was self-taught.

In 1857 Conant came to St. Louis where he established the Western Academy of Art in 1860. With the coming of the Civil War the academy closed. In addition to his recognition as an artist, Conant was a distinguished and competent archeologist and scientist. He wrote *Archeology of the Missouri Valley* and *Footprints of a Vanished Race*. The latter dealt with the Illinois mounds. He also wrote *My Acquaintance With Lincoln* and some poetry. Conant was curator of the University of Missouri for eight years and founder of that institution's noted School of Mines and Metallurgy at Rolla, where he served as director for three years.

In the summer of 1860, after Lincoln had been nominated as the presidential candidate of the Republican party, many artists sought opportunity to paint his portrait. Conant, the leading portrait painter of St. Louis, was one of those given the privilege.

In July and August of 1860 he made trips to Springfield where Lincoln posed for him. On his first trip Conant found Lincoln in conference and was asked to await its ending. From the place where he sat in an adjoining room the artist had opportunity to observe Lincoln. He noted the easy smile on Lincoln's face as he talked with the group and decided that he would portray Lincoln with smiling face.

The completed portrait met the ready approval of Mrs. Lincoln who said, "That is excellent; that is the way he looks when he has his friends about him." Conant made three copies of this "Smiling Lincoln." One hangs in the library at Shurtleff. Another is in the possession of Mrs. C. Conant Smith of New York, and the third is in the A. Smith Cochran Historical Collection in Yonkers.

After the portrait at Shurtleff was painted, it was exhibited in the Baptist Church in St. Louis and at a fair opened by the Prince of Wales in St. Louis. Dr. Read, then president of Shurtleff College, saw the painting and wanted it for his college. At the request of Dr. Read, Conant brought it to Alton to use in illustrating a lecture he gave there. After the lecture Dr. Read secured subscriptions amounting to $125 toward the purchase of the picture. The actual amount paid Conant is not definitely known. Suffice it to say, Shurtleff obtained the painting.

After being brought to Shurtleff, it was on display for a number of years. Then it was taken down, rolled up, and stored behind a stairway where it was found in the early 1890's covered with dust and grime. We are told that it was carefully cleaned and oiled and that subscriptions were taken to properly frame it. It then hung in the college chapel until taken to its present place on the south wall of the library. Not being an artist, we hesitate to evaluate the portrait. We do know that this full face, beardless portrait is distinctive and intrigues those who see it.

Another interesting Lincoln portrait, made during the same summer, hangs in the office of the Alton *Telegraph*. It also shows a beardless, sad-eyed Lincoln with the calm dignity so universally portrayed.

🌸 *A GRANDMOTHER'S NOTES*

"Virtue hath its rewards," and so does rummaging. The latter again proved to be true when the writer called at the home of Mrs. Jane Culbertson in Effingham recently. In fact, it was twice true. Mrs. Culbertson produced first a diary of a soldier in the Mexican War and, secondly, a collection of notes left by her grandmother, Mrs. Mary Tennery.

Mrs. Tennery, nee Mary Allsop, was born in Belper, Derbyshire, England, and came with the family to Effingham County while still a girl. Her notes are interesting for the events they briefly describe, and also for the fleeting glimpses they give of earlier customs and beliefs which now are gone. Some afford interesting historical sidelights, including two having to do with the Slater brothers who built the first successful clothmaking mill in America.

Grandmother Tennery, whose own grandmother was a sister of the Slater brothers, says the oft repeated story that the American mill was built from "plans recorded in memory only" is not altogether correct. She says that the brothers brought drawings with them, concealed in the heavy soles of four pairs of boots, two pairs worn and two carried as spares.

Her notes also tell that resentment ran high against the Slater brothers in England for their part in building the American mill. She reports that enemies there contrived and built a death-trap, boxed it, and sent it to the brothers here. When they were opening the box, one of them observed that pistols had been arranged to fire when a certain board was removed. The brothers simply stood out of line and removed the board by remote control. The pistols fired but injured no one.

The notes of Grandmother Tennery tell how the long-handled brass bedwarmer was used to remove the chill from cold beds in the winter. One can almost see live coals being placed in the covered pan of the warmer before it was passed beneath the covers of the bed.

She tells of the English practice of changing from winter to summer-weight clothing at Easter, even though an Easter squall might be in the wind at the time. The parallel practice in America took place on May first, which also was the day when children began to go barefoot. Some oldsters may recall the feeling of fresh air that greeted both body and feet on that day.

Her notes also tell of the way in which leeches were used to reduce bruises in both England and here. She describes how they were used in treating her younger brother, who had come away second best from a frenzied round of fisticuffs. Perhaps the story can best be told by quotes from her notes.

"His face was black and blue from bruises and his eyes were almost swollen shut. We went down to the drugstore and got some leeches, a long flat worm like a fishworm. Grandmother had the maid place them on the bruised parts and leave them there until they were gorged with blood. They were then taken off and laid on a large plate and sprinkled with salt that caused them to throw up the blood. They were then washed with lukewarm water and replaced on the wound." After use, they were returned to the druggist, and his fee of two pence for their use was paid.

She writes about an epidemic of smallpox in their community in Effingham County and of the manner in which the children's hands were balled in cotton so that they could not scratch and scar their faces.

Her notes also tell of a time, shortly after her mother's death, when the father was away and they lived for a spell on corn bread and pumpkin, often with no meat and no salt. Even now the reader sympathizes with them and reacts pleasantly upon learning that her brothers succeeded in trapping some prairie hens and that a kindly neighbor sent his boys with some salt. Her brothers also worked for a neighbor and were paid with a hog that another man helped them butcher.

The hardships she describes evidently were not crushing. She tells of the cherished china ornaments, sea shells, and mementos kept on a shelf above her mother's gay, life-sized portrait against the log wall, as she remembered it lighted by the glow from the fireplace. She tells of the Dutch oven, the trundle beds, the yard with its "many bright pink roses," of the country school, of the first Sunday school, and of an early Children's Day.

She says that their home later became the social center of the community, one where parents were willing to have their youngsters go. As time passed, they became a prosperous and respected family.

These and other glimpses of a hundred and more years ago make the life of the common folk more real.

Much interesting material of this nature yet lies, often forgotten, in old trunks, in closets, and in attics.

✿ *JOHNNY APPLESEED*

A SIGN, "Historical Marker Ahead," beside a highway always seems to make my Chevrolet slow down or come to a complete stop. Almost automatically it turns off the road to follow arrows pointing toward some interesting spot off the main line of travel.

Among the places where such stops were made were at the Indian battlefield of Fallen Timbers, at Old Towne, and at the ruined remnants of the early canal alongside the Maumee River. Then there was the Johnny Appleseed Memorial Park behind the stadium at Fort Wayne, Indiana, followed a bit later by the Tippecanoe battlefield where men from Illinois went to help defeat the Indians near present-day Lafayette, Indiana, on November 7, 1811. Last visited place of the day was the study of General Lew Wallace at Crawfordsville where he completed *Ben Hur.*

All were interesting, but the Johnny Appleseed burial place had a particular appeal because of childhood memories of a giant apple tree. The old tree, the largest one I remember, stood just north of the line between Saline and Hamilton Counties beside a branch of the Goshen Road that led from Shawneetown toward the Land of Goshen, where Edwardsville was established later. There were a few other dying and decaying trunks and high stumps with broken limbs that showed where an early orchard had been. This tree was the only bearing one left. Its yellow fruit was wonderful—if memory, tinged with a boyish appetite, can be trusted.

According to traditions in the Wilson family, on whose farm the tree was located, these were Johnny Appleseed trees that had been planted there by that eccentric wanderer, whose real name was John Chapman. No documentary evidence has been found as proof of this story, but I want to believe it; it is in keeping with the practices of the patron saint of American nurserymen.

Chapman was a familiar figure along the early roadways and trails of the Old Northwest. On many of these journeys, it is known that he carried bags of appleseeds acquired from early cider mills as far distant as Pennsylvania and planted a few of them in return for food and lodging. All this makes the story more plausible.

His constant travels far and wide, and his habit of establishing nurseries and planting seeds at temporary stops, coupled with his marked eccentricities, made John Chapman one of America's greatest folk figures. He is known to have gone about at one time wearing his tin sauce pan for a hat. The earliest known artist's sketch of him shows this unusual headgear. His clothing was crude and scant, and he almost always went barefoot, even in freezing weather. He would camp wherever night overtook him. Chapman was a most self-sufficient traveler and could cope with almost any situation. He was widely known and highly regarded by the Indians.

There are some who would have you believe he was a simpleminded, unlearned pauper. This hardly could have been true. It is known that he was a fluent speaker and a clever conversationalist, and he is often mentioned as a most gifted and pleasing reader. Chapman was a follower of Swedenborg, and the records of Swedenborgians indicate he was a capable apostle of that order. An account of his missionary work appeared in an English newspaper as early as 1811.

He surely was not a pauper. There are records of nineteen nurseries he established and references pointing to others. He held twenty tracts of land when he died, along with some personal property. It appeared once that he might have become a successful land speculator. There are reasons to believe that he held additional lands scattered over Ohio and Indiana of which his administrator found no records.

John Chapman was the son of a Revolutionary War captain. He was born at Leominster, Massachusetts, on September 26, 1774. He died at the home of a man named Richard Worth at Fort Wayne, Indiana, in 1845, and was buried on a narrow ridge in the David Archer Cemetery beside the St. Joseph River. His burial must have been simple indeed. The administrator's records show: "Expense of sickness, ten dollars; Expense for laying him out, three dollars and forty cents; Expense of coffin to Samuel Flutter, six dollars, March 17, 1845."

The six-by-eight grave plot is enclosed by an iron fence placed there by the Indiana Horticultural Society many years ago. A simple unshaped granite boulder with a portion of one side smoothed has the outline of an apple inscribed. It gives his real name, John Chapman, with the date of his birth and death, then, "Johnny Appleseed. He lived for others."

Ever since, his tall gaunt figure has plodded across the pages of folk-lore.

❦ *THE BOY OF BATTLE FORD*

IT IS NOT DIFFICULT in almost any part of Illinois to find books that tell about the locality or about the people who have lived there. Many of these books were written by those who lived in the region. Frequently, they were published locally. Among such books, *The Boy of Battle Ford* meets both the conditions named. It is the autobiography of the Reverend W. S. Blackman, once a prominent churchman of Saline County, and was published by the Egyptian Printing Press Company at Marion in 1906.

Blackman's book is written with heavy religious overtones, and is interesting for that reason to those who enjoy reading religious literature. It is interesting to the general reader for its accuracy and the vivid manner in which the sixty-six year old author tells of those who first came to settle in the region.

His story begins in 1840 near the point where an Indian trail crossed the south fork of Saline River about a mile from the present town of Mitchellsville. This crossing was called Battle Ford because two Indian tribes once fought there. The crude and lonely one-room log cabin in which Blackman was born stood near the Ford in one of the more sparsely settled parts of the region later included in Saline County.

The life of the Blackman family was not an easy one. Among the boy's earliest memories are those of the death of his father with winter fever—which we know as pneumonia. The family was poor and, to make matters worse, the father had signed a bond for someone. This took all their property except one mare, a cow, a few sheep, some small shoats, and a few articles of household furnishings. We are assured that the value of their entire property would not have amounted to fifty dollars.

Their cabin he calls a pen. Its floor with wide cracks was made of puncheons. The doors were on wooden hinges. Cooking was done at a fireplace. A small plot of cotton was grown. The cotton, wool from a few sheep, and deer skins were made into clothing. He tells us that his clothing, and that of the family, was most often a single, Mother Hubbard kind of long skirted shirt, dyed with maple bark, walnut hulls, or copperas. Crude shoes were fashioned in the home for the worst part of winter.

That the country was wild is evident from the fact that wolves still were common. He tells of their invading the family's small pasture and killing some of the sheep. The survivors fled to the dwelling in the corner of the field. The dogs charged the wolves as they feasted on sheep that they had killed; in turn, the dogs were chased to the house by the wolves who promptly returned to their kill, only to be charged by the dogs once more. The frightened family looked on all this through cracks in the cabin walls. No one dared go outside. Blackman makes the reader sense the terror of the mother and youngsters.

Blackman tells of finding large rattlesnakes. Deer still were common. There were a few bears and panthers, and wildcats often were heard. Wild turkey were seen frequently. Fish were bountiful and squirrels a nuisance.

For bread the Blackmans depended solely upon corn grown in their small, fenced clearing among the deadened trees. In fact, young Blackman recalls that he knew no other bread until he was about six years old. At that time he had the fever. When he was recovering, Mrs. Cole, a Negro woman living a few miles away, came to see him and brought him his first biscuit. This he remembered to be as delicious as cake.

He tells that there were no matches and that fire was started by using a piece of flint and steel to strike sparks. By another method a string and a spinning wheel did the job. (He doesn't say how.) The straw hats he knew were made in the homes, as was practically all clothing, including wedding dresses.

Sick people were bled. Water was doled out by the spoonful to fevered patients. Calomel was a common remedy for almost everything. People often were salivated by it. Many persons believed firmly in witches, a man in the moon, and many, many signs. Blackman did not condemn these odd beliefs but rejoiced that education and common sense were gaining ground.

He received a fiddle as a youth and hid it in a hollow tree where he was clearing ground. Chopping and practicing by turns he became an adept old-time fiddler, and kept up his playing for forty years.

In childhood he saw men meet near the Blackman home on muster day. He tells of neighbors who went to the Mexican War. Rough and tumble fights were common, sometimes including eye gouging and biting. Bullies are mentioned along with the fate they met.

Adding a few weeks here and there, Blackman accumulated about a year of schooling. However, he read much and studied to become a rather literate man. He taught school and expressed a belief that he could have rendered a great service if he had continued to do so. He later was county superintendent of schools. When the Civil War came along, Blackman served his country well. After the war, he entered the ministry and preached for forty years.

Blackman lived an interesting life during an interesting period, and his story reveals glimpses of a way of life then common. If the reader can find a copy of *The Boy of Battle Ford,* it doubtlessly will be read with interest because it is good Americana.

The writer has vivid and pleasing youthful memories of the Reverend Blackman.

🎖 MOUNT OLIVE AND "MOTHER" JONES

OCTOBER 12 IS OBSERVED over America as Columbus Day. In the town of Mount Olive, about eighteen miles south of Carlinville in Macoupin County, it is doubly observed. It is Columbus Day, but it is also the anniversary of a significant date in the bitter and sometimes bloody struggle between coal miners and operators in Illinois.

The second observance centers in Miners Cemetery at the northwestern limits of Mount Olive. A decreasing number go each year to this ordered and well-kept little burying ground with its many strange names, but here is one of labor's great shrines in America. It was on October 12, 1898, that a number of men were killed in a gun battle between armed guards and the organized miners who sought to halt the importation of nonunion men to operate the mine at Virden. Some of the miners killed in the clash were brought to Mount Olive for burial.

The dedication of the monument commemorating this event on October 12, 1936, drew forty thousand persons. Others prominent in the early effort to organize mine workers were also brought here for burial. Among these were English-born "General" Alexander Bradley (1866–1918) and Irish-born Mary Harris Jones (1830–1930), better known during the last fifty years of her life as "Mother" Jones.

It was the "General" who, spurning all attempts to be bribed, was responsible for the unionization of southern Illinois miners in 1897. It was for his leadership in this work that he was given the title of "General." His grave is identified by a dignified marker saying, "Erected by Sub. Dists. 5, 6, 7 and District 12 to the memory of General A. Bradley."

"Mother" Jones, born Mary Harris and brought to this country when she was five years old, received a better education than the average immigrant child. Until the death of her husband and three children, all in 1867, she was a housewife, teacher, and dressmaker. After that she gave her untiring efforts to the cause of labor, especially to the miners. "Mother" Jones was a born crusader with a great sense of the dramatic. Wherever conflict was greatest, she would be found addressing miners, or leading their wives armed with brooms and mops in a parade of protest. She even led a parade of children into New York as a demonstration against child labor.

"Mother" Jones remains one of the most forceful and picturesque figures in the labor movement of America. In appearance Clarence Darrow described her as "a little old woman in a black bonnet with a high falsetto voice, and a handsome face framed in curly white hair and lightened by kindly gray eyes." She was fearless and aggressive. When she died at one hundred, she was buried at her request in Miners Cemetery at Mt. Olive.

Her grave in front of the impressive monument and shaft, "Dedicated October 12, 1936, to Mary 'Mother' Jones, 'General' Alexander Bradley and the Martyrs of the Virden Riot of 1898," is marked with a simple bronze plate. On this is recorded " 'Mother' Jones, May 1, 1830–November 30, 1930. She gave her life to the cause of labor, Her blessed soul to Heaven, God's finger touched her and now she sleeps." Beside "Mother" Jones's grave, two on either side, are markers for miners who lost their lives at Virden; a bronze on the shaft says, "We count it death to falter, not to die." Perhaps this expresses the flaming zeal of those who led the miners' crusades.

It may all appear sentimental to some who stop to visit the small cemetery. Others will be reminded of the days when miners worked long days for a small wage, a time when the stretcher at the mine's bottom was a pit car drawn along over a rough track by a mule, and when the ambulance at the top was a manure cart. There was no workmen's compensation, and the miner's labor was a commodity which the mine operator could take or leave when and as he chose.

A pause at Mount Olive, just off Highway 66, to visit one of America's outstanding shrines of labor is a worthwhile experience for the thoughtful.

❧ LONG-TIME PARTNERS

THE AUTHOR'S ACQUAINTANCE with two Benton Attorneys, Thomas J. Layman and William B. Johnson, began more than two decades ago. Now a call in their town seems incomplete without a stop at their office.

A recent visit was made on February 5, and the scene was much the same as it was on the first visit twenty years ago. It was just another day being added to the more than fifteen thousand that these partners have sat there together.

In one way, however, this February 5 was a day apart. It marked the completion of exactly forty-nine years of an unbroken law partnership. On the morrow they would begin the fiftieth year of an association that began on February 6, 1911. It was then that young attorney Johnson, who had recently been licensed to practice in Illinois, took over a spot in the office of Layman, who already had been practicing six years. It was the beginning of a law partnership that is now said to be the oldest unbroken one in Illinois.

The office of these interesting partners is on the second floor of a building across the street and southwest of the courthouse. Moreover, it is in the same rooms where the partnership began. Some of their present furniture and fittings likewise have served since that beginning. Their law library, many volumes of which are older than the partnership, is shelved in cases along the walls, in others in the hallway and in an adjoining room. Numerous volumes lie in ordered disarray on a long center table. Diplomas, licenses, portraits, and school groups a good lifetime old are hanging in the office, too. One photograph shows the 1904 class of Southern Illinois University.

Any stranger, however well acquainted he might be with the usual arrangement of law libraries, could have difficulty in locating a desired volume, but not they. "It's right where it has been for forty years." In some cases it is true that their law books and commentaries have become infiltrated with county histories and other assorted Americana. You may find *Chitty on Pleadings* alongside the *Bloody Vendetta*.

All the history to be gleaned in their office is not written. Both men alike are members of prominent early families of their county and take pride in that fact. Perhaps no other two men know as much of the lore, legend, and historical background of their county as they. Certainly, no others can relate it so interestingly. The easy and pointed style of their telling is unique. It is a living misfortune that more of their knowing is not being recorded.

The clatter, stress, tension, and hurry of many offices is not part of theirs. This may be illustrated by one incident when the partners had just begun to tell an account of pioneer horse racing. The horses were being "brought to the line" as a client entered. He was greeted promptly and courteously and asked, "Are you going to be in town a while?" Upon an affirmative reply he was asked to return in thirty minutes. He readily agreed and did so—just at the conclusion of the story about John A. Logan's riding Walnut Cracker in one of the region's wildest races.

These partners illustrate the fact that men do not have to think exactly alike to get along well together. Each is a devoted churchman: Johnson is an active member of the Primitive Baptist Church, and Layman is a member of the First Baptist Church in Benton that recently honored him for his services as clerk of the church for fifty years. Layman is a practicing Republican while Johnson has remained an active Democrat. Neither has been known to question his partner's political privileges nor to even intimate that the other's beliefs were "crazy." Layman has also served three terms as county judge.

Each has a nice home and lives graciously. Both the Laymans and Johnsons have been married considerably over fifty years. Throughout these years the wives have remained steadfast friends and associates. Either husband, given the least opportunity, begins to eulogize his wife. They are indeed a genial foursome.

Evidence of the trust in which each of these men holds the other is shown by a remark made by one during the other's absence. He said, "So far as I have ever known, nothing that one has said to the other in confidence here has been betrayed." In slightly different words, the other echoed the same sentiment. Not a bad average for fifty-odd years.

These partners do not even keep books on each other. During one previous visit, a client came in and paid his fee. The partner present took the payment and made an entry in a daybook lying on the table. He then separated the money into two lots, put one of them in his pocket, and rolled the other into a bundle which was laid aside. When the absent partner shortly returned he was told, "Jim came in and paid his bill. Here's your part of it."

Bits of poetry, apt sayings, and passages of scriptures and good literature are not wasted on them. If you falter in an attempt to quote, one of them will most likely be able to help you.

To those with a measure of imagination, a visit to the law office of Layman and Johnson affords an ideal setting from which one may envision the lawyers and law offices of legend.

JOHN MESSINGER AT CLINTON HILL

THE WRITER HAS an abiding tendency to stop and read historical markers. A recent rewarding digression accordingly was made at the northeast edge of Belleville near the end of Lebanon Avenue. An arrow points to a small painted marker that is easily overlooked unless one looks closely. A simple legend on the small marker says, "John Messinger Memorial."

Our recent visit was not the first time the writer has paused at the memorial. But this time it was a pleasant spring morning, just the kind of day on which to visit a site of historical interest. So the writer drove about two miles north to Clinton Hill, where Messinger—one of the most gifted, versatile, and capable men of the territorial and early statehood days of Illinois—lived and where he is buried.

John Messinger was born at West Stockbridge, Massachusetts, in 1771. In 1783 the family moved to Vermont where young John received a good education for that day. He showed a particular aptitude for mathematics. In Vermont he became a teacher, carpenter, builder, millwright, and successful farmer. He was married to Anne Lyon, a daughter of Colonel Matthew Lyon, a newspaper publisher much prosecuted for violation of the Alien and Sedition Laws.

In 1799 Colonel Lyon and his family, including Messinger, floated down the Ohio from Pittsburgh on flatboats and settled in Kentucky near the mouth of the Cumberland River. There Colonel Lyon became an active slave trader. This did not please Messinger or another son-in-law, Dr. George Cadwell. They accordingly moved to Illinois in 1802. Messinger first settled near New Design in Monroe County where he operated a gristmill on Rockhouse Creek east of the settlement. In 1806 he moved to Clinton Hill, in the vicinity of the present memorial, and lived there until his death in 1846.

Messinger was a man of many talents and great energy. He exerted a wide influence in the state's early days. He was by turns a teacher, farmer, millwright, carpenter, cabinetmaker, cartographer, and public official. He was rated by many as the most profound mathematician and best land surveyor in the state. He and another man, Philip Creamer, turned to the making of surveyors' compasses which were ranked with the best in America.

In 1821 he published *A Manual or Handbook of Practical Surveying,* a widely used text. He taught mathematics in John Mason Peck's academy at nearby Rock Spring.

There are no records to indicate that Messinger deliberately sought political office. Nevertheless, he was elected to represent St. Clair County in the Indiana Territorial Legislature and became one of the leaders in the movement to establish Illinois as a separate territory.

He surveyed much of Madison and St. Clair counties and the military tract between the Illinois and Mississippi rivers. He was the representative of Illinois on the staff appointed to establish the line separating Illinois and Wisconsin; he did the astronomical observations and calculations on which the work was based.

When the time came to form a constitution for the proposed state of Illinois, Messinger was one of the men chosen for that task. His name appears on many of the more important committees appointed, including the one that approved the final form of the constitution to be submitted. Later, Messinger was elected to the first general assembly from St. Clair County, and was made the first speaker of the Illinois House of Representatives.

In earlier times it was common to say of someone, "He is a jack of all trades." When he did a bungling job, the designation was amended to say, "He is a jack of all trades and good at none." Concerning John Messinger one apparently could say, "He was a jack of all trades and superior in each." He was not only very capable in all his many endeavors, but he was also a man of established ideals.

A side trip to the John Messinger Memorial and the reading of the legends seen there will prove interesting to those passing that way. It also will go far to convince the thoughtful visitor that some brilliant men lived then.

❧ WILLIAM BARCLAY "BAT" MASTERSON

A LISTING OF NOTED GUNMEN and peace officers who made and shot their way to fame during the days of the roaring West would be incomplete without the name of William Barclay "Bat" Masterson, an Illinois boy who emigrated with his family to the vicinity of Wichita, Kansas, in 1871. Although volumes have been written about Bat's exploits after his arrival in Kansas, little is known of his Illinois boyhood.

Bat was born in Illinois on November 23, 1853. Legend and tradition among surviving kinsmen say he was born near Golden Gate in eastern Wayne County where a number of Mastersons still live. While he still was a youth the family moved to Kansas. In the fall of their first year there, Bat and his brother joined a party going to Fort Dodge to hunt buffalo. After his venture as a buffalo hunter Bat returned to Dodge City where he, with a partner, took a subcontract to grade a mile of roadbed for the Atchison, Topeka, and Santa Fe Railroad. The mile graded was the first one extending west from the military reservation. Front Street, for many years one of the most storied in all America, lay alongside the mile they graded. The general contractor from whom Bat and his brother had subcontracted failed to pay them. Later, seeing the contractor on a passing train, Bat very unceremoniously hauled him off and collected in full at the point of a pistol. This action seems to have launched the long and checkered career of one of the West's most colorful characters.

For the next thirty-one years Bat was a prominent figure in the roaring West. He was, by turn, buffalo hunter, railroad contractor, Indian fighter, military scout and messenger for General Miles, teamster and bull whacker, town marshal, sheriff of Ford County, professional gambler, prankster, faro dealer, and, along with Wyatt Earp, another Illinois-born boy, a deacon in Reverend Wright's Union Church.

In 1874 Bat was at Adobe Walls, a trading post in the northern end of the Texas panhandle, when several hundred Indians made an unsuccessful attack upon twenty-six traders and hunters gathered there. As one of its spirited defenders, Bat was commended for his coolness and bravery. He next became a scout and messenger for General Miles. After this, he returned to Dodge City to serve as deputy town marshal.

In 1876 he resigned and joined the gold rush to Deadwood. After a few months Bat returned to Dodge City with an established reputation as a skilled and daring gunman. Since it was then a custom to select a gunman to deal with gunmen, Bat was elected sheriff of Ford County in November, 1877, at the age of twenty-four.

He was immediately successful. Early in 1878, a few weeks after taking office, Bat learned that Dave Rudabaugh, a notorious operator, had committed a robbery in another Kansas county and was in flight toward Texas. Bat took a small posse and went to a cattle camp outside his county, but on the trail along which he thought the robbers would flee. When Rudabaugh and his half-frozen men appeared during a raging blizzard, Bat captured him without firing a shot. Numerous other captures of noted gunmen followed. Bat's star was in its ascendancy.

Shortly afterwards, Bat's brother Edward, marshal of Dodge City, was killed while trying to subdue two drunken cowboys. Bat arrived at almost the same instant and shot his brother's killers. The whole episode was over in a very few seconds. As information concerning such incidents spread, so did fear, admiration, and hatred turn toward the young sheriff. Legend began to gather about his name.

In personal appearance Bat was striking. He was six feet tall, weighed about 180 pounds, was well proportioned, and graceful in his movements. His hair reached to his shoulders and he wore a sweeping mustache. His eyes were a pale, cold blue that many termed expression-less, but were considered typical of the successful gunman and gambler.

His suits were in the latest style, being, it is said, even more striking than those of Wild Bill Hickok. He wore a Prince Albert coat and a pearl gray bowler with the finest of handmade boots. He often carried a gold handled cane which had been awarded to him for being the most popular man in town. Always tastefully dressed, Bat never appeared in public without his trusted revolvers.

One admirer who knew Bat well characterized him as "fearless, but no trouble maker, a gentleman by instinct, of pleasant manners, and mild until aroused, then for God's sake look out. There is nothing low about him. He is high toned and broadminded, cool and brave."

Bat was loyal to his friends and was liked by many eminent men among whom was Theodore Roosevelt who offered to have him appointed U.S. Marshal for Arizona. Bat declined saying, "If I took it, inside a year I'd have to kill some fool boy who wanted to gain a reputation by killing me."

In 1902 Bat left a somewhat subdued West and went to New York City to spend his remaining nineteen years as a writer and sports editor with the Morning Telegraph.

When he moved to New York, President Roosevelt again offered him an appointment as deputy U.S. Marshal, which Bat accepted. Two years later he resigned because he said that it interfered with his chosen work.

Most of the noted gunmen and peace officers of the Old West became casualties of their own professions. Bat Masterson died quietly, pen in hand, at his desk in New York City on October 25, 1921, far removed from the scenes and incidents that had made him famous.

🏵 *JAMES BUTLER "WILD BILL" HICKOK*

ILLINOIS EXPORTED another young man who attracted much attention in the field of law enforcement. It seems that being born in Illinois somehow offered a better than average start toward such a career, often a brief one, as a law officer of the Old West. A noted legendary figure of the hectic West was an Illinois boy, James Butler ("Wild Bill") Hickok.

Hickok was born in LaSalle County, Illinois, on May 27, 1837. A marker beside United States Highway 52 near the town of Troy Grove indicates the site. Like that of Masterson, little is known about Hickok's boyhood beyond the fact that he was one of the best marksmen in that part of Illinois. Tradition tells us that he was industrious, peaceably inclined, and a willing worker.

When eighteen years old, Hickok made his way to Leavenworth, Kansas, became a member of a Free State movement and joined the forces of General Jim Lane, serving as one of the General's bodyguards. When nineteen years old he was chosen constable of Monticello Township and it is recorded that he served in that office faithfully and efficiently. Records also indicate that he pre-empted land, and thereby indicated his intention to become a farmer. As a member of the Free State forces and as constable, Hickok became acquainted with violence. No record has been found, however, that his reputation as a gunman had then begun.

In 1859, at twenty-two, Hickok became a wagon and stage driver on the Santa Fe Trail. In late 1860 at Raton Pass he barely survived being mauled by a bear which he finally killed with his bowie knife. When he could be moved Hickok was taken to Kansas City for medical care. Afterwards he was transferred to a station at Rock Creek on the Oregon Trail in Jefferson County, Nebraska.

David McCanles, manager at Rock Creek station, promptly indicated a dislike for Hickok, made him a stable hand, and nicknamed him Duck Bill. McCanles also engaged in horseplay and roughly wrestled the still weakened Hickok about. Hickok naturally resented McCanles's treatment but was physically unable to retaliate. The resentment thus aroused undoubtedly contributed to a later clash between the two. This clash resulted in McCanles's death on July 12, 1861. His killing of McCanles apparently launched Hickok on a career that led him to become one of the West's most noted two-gun men.

With the coming of the Civil War, Hickok took service in the Union forces and was made a wagonmaster out of Fort Leavenworth. It was while serving as a wagonmaster at Independence, Missouri, that an incident occurred to give him his special name. A woman in the crowd watching Hickok pass by shouted, "Great for you, Wild Bill." The name stuck and James Butler Hickok was known thereafter as Wild Bill.

Wild Bill soon was transferred to the Union forces at Springfield, Missouri, where he served as scout and spy. His performances and escapes at times appeared almost miraculous. They clearly indicated his cleverness, daring, and prompt and discriminating snap judgment.

After the war Wild Bill, already with a great reputation as a gunman, became a U.S. Deputy Marshal operating about Fort Riley. He next became an Indian scout, guide, and messenger working for Generals Hancock, Sheridan, and Custer. He also served as sheriff and town marshal at different places. In 1869 he became marshal in Hays City, Kansas, then considered the toughest town on the border. He did his work there well while adding to his reputation as a gunman.

Leaving Hays City, Wild Bill became marshal at Abilene, where he took the place of the recently slain marshal, Thomas J. Smith, known in legend as Bear River Tom, perhaps the greatest bare-knuckled marshal the West knew. In Abilene Wild Bill established headquarters at the Alamo, a noted saloon and gambling house. Having an office there not only gave Wild Bill opportunity to gather information concerning incidents and persons but also to ply his regular trade, that of a professional gambler. As marshal he often patrolled the streets of Abilene armed with his two revolvers and a sawed-off shot gun. His stay there added to his reputation that already had become fabulous.

In Abilene he presented the unusual spectacle of one man, by courage and skill, holding all the lawless elements of the border at bay. In the execution of his task he added several notches to his gun.

In 1872–1873 Wild Bill toured the East with the William F. "Buffalo Bill" Cody show. Little interested in the life of a showman, Hickok returned to the West and became town marshal at Deadwood, Dakota Territory. He was murdered there by Jack McCall while playing poker on August 2, 1876. The hand he held when shot, two aces and two eights, has ever since been known as the "dead man's hand."

In appearance Wild Bill was striking. He was six feet tall, well built, and almost pantherish in his movements. He was always well dressed, altogether a fascinating man. There was nothing about him to suggest the bully. It is said that he never killed except in self-defense or in the line of duty. Despite all this, at his death his revolver bore seventy-two notches, none of which were for Indians.

AN ILLINOIS BOY AND THE WILD WEST

One writer, speaking of the noted sheriffs, marshals, and deputies of the Old West, said, "They shot their way to heaven," a destination with which all did not agree. That writer then gave the names of some that attained a kind of immortality by the firearms route. Included among these were three former Illinois boys—"Bat" Masterson, "Wild Bill" Hickok, and Wyatt Earp. If there is to be a hall of fame for two-gun men, none of these three could well be excluded. Whether it be considered glory or embarrassment, they definitely contributed.

Something already has been said about Masterson and Hickok. Presently, much is being heard and seen of the third one, Wyatt Earp, who, with his good friend Doc Holliday, once more madly rides and shoots it out by way of television.

Wyatt Berry Stapp Earp, for he really did have that long name, was born on a farm at the edge of Monmouth in Warren County on March 19, 1848. He was of Scotch descent and from a family that had come to America and had lived on the frontier for 175 years. It might somewhat accurately be said that pioneering was in the Earp blood.

When Wyatt was still a child, his family moved to Iowa and in 1864 moved from there to San Bernadino, California. It was on this long journey that young Earp, then seventeen years old, drove an ox wagon and helped to drive away any Indians encountered. This was his first taste of the real West, and he liked it.

At San Bernadino, Wyatt got a job as driver of a stage that made a daily round trip of 120 miles between that town and Los Angeles. Changing teams and driving wildly, Earp did the stint in about twelve hours. For the skilled way in which he handled this job, Earp came to be numbered among the best of drivers.

Six feet tall, slender, straight, wiry, agile, and well poised, Wyatt was an attractive personality. One discerning observer said, "The handsomest and best mannered man in Wichita." He was always tastefully and well dressed. Like Bat Masterson, Wyatt was a gambler, gunman, and railroad contractor, and much interested in prize fighting, being a rather competent two-fisted fighter himself.

After some success as a contractor, but perhaps more as a gambler, Earp returned to Illinois in 1868, apparently to study law in the office of his grandfather at Monmouth. There he met and married a local girl who died within a few weeks. Wyatt, deeply grieved, soon became dissatisfied in Illinois and returned to the West where he led a truly dangerous life as long as the Old West lived.

One can hardly name a noted gunman of those roaring days without finding him in some way associated with Earp. He "rode shotgun" for Wells Fargo Express, operated a gambling house, played for high stakes, and served with Bat Masterson as a deacon in the church. He owned and raced horses, hunted buffalo, engaged in many a gunfight, prospected for gold and silver, and staked many claims.

In 1883 Earp paid his last visit to Dodge City, the scene of many of his most noted exploits. He retained an active interest in boxing. This was shown on December 2, 1896, when he climbed into the prize ring wearing his celebrated Ned Buntline Special .45 to referee the famous Bob Fitzsimmons-Tom Sharkey championship fight. In 1897 he joined the Alaska gold rush.

Few men have shown, over many years, more of what could be called "cold nerve." There was little of the theatrical or dramatic about him. Earp calmly calculated his risks, drew quickly, and, with his deadly aim, seldom missed. The most boisterous towns, camps, and corrals of the untamed West knew Earp. Ellsworth, Tombstone, Deadwood, Dodge City, and many others contribute to his legend.

The last years of Earp and Masterson were somewhat alike. Each left the West he had helped to tame and ended his days in peace, Bat in New York and Wyatt in Los Angeles where he died on January 18, 1929—more than seven years after Bat Masterson's passing and sixty-five years after he first had become a part of the roaring West. By then, the Old West, which he had done so much to create, had practically vanished.

❀ AN UNUSUAL MAN AND HIS STRANGE CAR

SOUTHERN ILLINOIS HAS had its full quota of unusual and interesting men. On a list of such persons for the Alton area one should include the name of James Semple*, descended from a prominent family in Scotland.

Semple was born in Green County, Kentucky, in 1798. His opportunities for an education were meager. He was fortunate, however, in having an uncle, a graduate of Princeton, to capably guide his educational efforts. At sixteen Semple enlisted in the Kentucky militia and served under General Jackson in the closing months of the second war with Britain. He became the ensign of his company and was entrusted with important tasks.

In 1819 he married and moved to Chariton, Missouri, where he engaged in business and studied law. From Chariton he wrote to his mother that he had a law library of 130 volumes, then a large one for a student to have. While at Chariton he freed the one slave given him as

---

* See *Legends & Lore,* p. 357.

an inheritance. His feelings on slavery may easily be inferred by this entry on the freedom papers files. He wrote, "This is the only slave I ever owned or ever will own."

After a few years Semple moved to Madison County, Illinois. In 1833 he was elected to the lower house of the Illinois legislature and served six terms, three of them as Speaker of the House. In that position he apparently used his full powers to promote internal improvements so popular at that time. He was influential in bringing two locomotives from New York by sea and river to Meredosia, about 1843, for use on the Meredosia-Springfield road. These two locomotives were several hundred miles from shops properly equipped to care for them. Men available to make repairs had training about like that of a good country blacksmith. In such a situation both locomotives fell into bad repair and soon were replaced with mules. Four mules often were hitched in tandem and walked the center path between the rails. One of the discarded locomotives was given to Semple, who had been elected a United States senator from Illinois. This he proposed for another use.

From a study of locomotives received, Semple had arrived at a bold new course. He would devise a train that could use existing highways or, lacking such, could travel across the unfenced prairies. He accordingly brought the locomotive he had been given to Alton and began the construction of a queer transportation device.

Adapting the locomotive to suit his purposes, he arranged gears that would drive the rear wheels of a huge wagon-like prairie schooner. To keep his contrivance from miring in marshy places, he equipped it with wheels about six feet in diameter, each with treads three feet wide. Traction was improved by bolting wooden lugs across the broad flat rims of these wheels. This was completed and ready for trial in the later summer of 1847. It had attracted wide attention. A reporter from the Boston *Courier*, J. H. Buckingham, came to write about it. Though he did not see the car and did not await its trial, he ridiculed it. The Alton *Telegraph* defended it and insisted that condemnation should come only after thorough trials. Semple himself held high hopes of success; he wrote to a friend in the summer of 1847, "If my car succeeds I can float along, if not I shall go to Oregon in 1847."

In September all was in readiness and Semple's land craft, with much clashing, hissing, clanging, and rattling, rolled out of the shed at Semple Town between Alton and Upper Alton and began its trip to Springfield. The first part of its course lay over the plank road to Edwardsville. The receptions given to Semple's car varied. Delegations from some villages even asked him to take it around instead of through their towns.

Progress, though slow and noisy and requiring frequent stops for adjustments, appears to have been fairly satisfactory until it started across the prairie from Carlinville on the last leg of its journey toward Springfield. A short way south of Springfield a mishap, fatal to the locomotive, occurred when one of the wheels dropped into a hole and an axle was broken. Semple decided to abandon the car where it stood. It remained there for many years rusting away and being pointed out to strangers as "Semple's Folly." Though it failed to fulfill his hopes, Semple's contrivance embodied several features found in the first automobiles in Illinois.

James Semple was a man of varied interests. He was by turns a merchant, politician, public official, lawyer, and a soldier who attained the rank of brigadier general. He was chargé d'affaires at Bogota in South America, author of a history of South America and another of Mexico, nonconformist, dreamer, promoter, and inventor. He also is known to have been active in the founding of three Illinois towns, Highland, Elsah, and Tamaroa. As United States senator and governmental representative, he exerted considerable influence in foreign affairs.

❧ THROUGH GRAND CANYON WITH A ONE-ARMED ILLINOISAN

EVEN A CASUAL LOOK at the Colorado River from almost any point along the rim of the gorge known as the Grand Canyon is enough to reduce anyone's yearning to make a boat trip down the stream. Such observation, however, did not have that effect upon a daring, one-armed Civil War major named John Wesley Powell, one-time resident of Bloomington and of Carbondale. The audacity of his plan should intrigue anyone.

A long-time interest in the major's trip was revived a few days ago when a volume, entitled *Scrapbook of John Wesley Powell,* was found in the rare book section of the Congressional Library at Washington. This book consists of newspaper and magazine articles with some marginal notes by Frederick S. Dellenbaugh, one of the last two survivors of the party that made the journey down the river ninety-nine years ago. The book of clippings was given to the Library by a Clyde Eddy on September 5, 1922. Though the book is somewhat disorganized, it affords some interesting glimpses of the venture.

The stouthearted major, who had lost an arm in the Civil War, asked for and was authorized to organize and conduct an expedition down the length of the canyon, through which the river tumbles and roars for several hundred miles. Powell gathered twenty men from the vicinity of Bloomington. He had the four boats he needed made in Chicago and shipped to a point near that from which he would begin his journey. The smallest of these was the *Emma Dean,* sixteen feet long, which was to serve as a kind of flagship for Powell. Three larger boats, each twenty-one feet long, completed his fleet. They were named "Kitty Clyde's Sister," "Maid of the Canyon," and "No Name." Each was in the charge of a competent boatman. One of these, named W. H. Powell, had served as captain of Company B, Third Illinois Artillery, during the recently ended conflict. There are no indications in the scrapbook that he was related to Major Powell.

The men and their four boats set out from the place recorded as Green River City on May 24, 1869. Practically every one living within the area came to see them off on what all considered a highly dangerous mission. Major Powell, in the sixteen-foot *Emma Dean,* led the way.

Difficulties began almost as soon as the journey began. Many times it was necessary to tie long ropes to the boats and lower them through rapids and over smaller falls, while the men carried their supplies around the dangerous points. Powell wisely distributed his goods in such a manner that the loss of one boat would not be fatal to the venture and perhaps to the men.

In spite of all due care, one of the boats was broken to pieces on the rocks soon after the journey started, and the cargo it carried was lost. Powell records that this boat carried most of his writing paper and that records were kept thereafter on paper sheets intended for use in pressing plant specimens. Some of their tools and instruments also went under, but duplicates carried in other boats kept the loss from being felt too greatly.

In a very short time after the party disappeared down the river, stories and rumors began to circulate. It was reported that all had perished. One man named Risdon, who apparently had been connected with the venture in its earlier stages or in some manner had intimate knowledge of it, appeared and claimed that he was the sole survivor of the group. He carried this report to the governor of Illinois. He even went about lecturing on the grim manner in which the disaster had come about.

As it turned out the "lost" expedition really was not lost. On August 27, 1869, it appeared at the lower end of the canyon. The expedition's success marked the first time on record that men had completed a trip through the gorge, which is at places a mile deep. They had found much of scientific interest.

Powell was hailed as a great explorer, and deservedly so. He remained in the West for several years to study Indian life. His writings and lectures made him well known to many. Even until now, few have duplicated the feat of the one-armed artillery major from Illinois in conquering the river.

Until a few years ago, the walls of a room that the major occupied for a while on West Main Street in Carbondale remained covered with many interesting maps that he had plastered there, several being of his own making.

🌿 *AARON BURR'S GREAT SCHEME*

SOMEONE POINTED TO an encircled February 6, the birth date of Aaron Burr, and jokingly asked, "Has that anything to do with southern Illinois?" The answer was "Certainly."

Casual checking shows that several places and some names of individuals prominent in the region's story are associated with Burr and the bewildering activities in which he engaged. After all, his great scheme almost happened next door.

Generally called the "Burr Conspiracy," this daring plan apparently began in Washington during the winter of 1804–1805 when Burr and General James Wilkinson spent much time together. Burr was then vice-president. Wilkinson, who soon was to take active command of the Army of the West at Fort Massac (Cantonment Wilkinsonville) near Metropolis in Massac County, was ranking general of the army. Each had served as captain under Benedict Arnold in the campaign against Montreal. Both alike were masters of intrigue, equally self-seeking, unscrupulous, and ambitious. Many wonder whether they, being as they were, should be called co-conspirators or rival conspirators.

There definitely was conspiracy, still much shrouded in mystery. No one seems to know its details and objectives. Some say it was to separate the western territories and out of them form a new nation. Others say that it was to conquer Mexico, set up an empire there, and enthrone Burr's brilliant daughter, Theodosia, as its queen. It may have included all these and more. Anyway, it was a magnificent plan.

Wherever it may have begun, the plan became active when Burr came down the Ohio in May, 1805. Stopping at Louisville, he went to Nashville, Tennessee. There he visited from May 29 to June 3 with General Andrew Jackson. Leaving there in a boat that Jackson provided, Burr reached Wilkinson's headquarters at Fort Massac on June 6. He and

Wilkinson remained in close conference for four days. Burr then departed for New Orleans on a "handsome" barge that Wilkinson furnished and manned with a sergeant and ten enlisted men. Wilkinson gave Burr letters of introduction to men along the way and in New Orleans. There are many reasons to believe that it was at these Fort Massac conferences that the details and objectives of the plan were determined.

Burr returned from New Orleans over the Natchez Trace through Nashville, Louisville, and Vincennes, Indiana, to St. Louis for added conferences. From St. Louis he went to Vincennes and met William Henry Harrison, Governor of Indiana Territory, that then included Illinois. Through the remaining part of 1805 and the first half of 1806, Burr was busy enlisting the cooperation of others and obtaining financial support. In early August he began his second trip to the West. He stopped at Pittsburgh to contract for supplies and enlist recruits. On August 27 he was at Blennerhassett's Island where he contracted for fifteen large flatboats of shallow draft.

From Louisville, another stop, he again went to see General Jackson. Believing Burr's story that he was organizing forces to repel an impending Spanish attack, Jackson, who commanded the Tennessee militia, pledged three regiments of troops and issued orders that they be placed in readiness. A few days later Burr wrote to William Henry Harrison at Vincennes. He enclosed a copy of Jackson's order and asked that Governor Harrison take similar action. Leaving Nashville on October 6, Burr moved toward Louisville where he contracted for additional supplies and equipment and enlisted men along the way.

Troubles now began to beset him. Among those seeking to expose his real objectives was a Joseph M. Street who then was editing a Kentucky newspaper but later was to become a promiment citizen and official at Shawneetown in Illinois. As a result of Street's publications, Burr was called into court at Frankfort where his leading defense counsel was Henry Clay. Found "not guilty," he returned to Nashville and went to call upon Jackson. His reception at the Hermitage was cool. He was not invited to stay for the night, a somewhat rare occurrence at that time. In the evening Jackson returned home and went to make a formal call upon Burr at the tavern where he had gone. Jackson apparently wished to have Burr explain some of his actions. Burr's explanation did not allay Jackson's mistrust.

Burr left Nashville a few days later and on December 26 was at Cumberland Island, a short way below Lusk's Ferry, which is now Golconda. A man named Blennerhassett, who had stopped for a few days at Shawneetown, was assembling the expedition at Cumberland Island. Burr addressed his men there but did not reveal a definite destination nor the purpose of the venture.

The ten assembled craft left the island and reached Fort Massac in the evening of December 29 where they were tied to trees just below the fort. Captain Bissell, then in command at Fort Massac, sent Sergeant Dunbaugh to greet Burr and to offer any needed assistance. The next morning Bissell visited Burr and invited him to the captain's quarters.

It appears that Bissell either did not yet suspect Burr's real motives or was acting under General Wilkinson's direction. He accordingly "loaned" Sergeant Dunbaugh to Burr for ten days.

Before nightfall of December 30, 1806, Burr left Massac and went on his way to New Orleans. On January 4, five days after Burr left Fort Massac, a request came from General Jackson to seize and hold him, but he was far down the river.

On the basis of these incidents, perhaps southern Illinois should share some of any dubious fringe benefits arising from the Burr Conspiracy.

🌑 *LEE'S SUCCESS AND FAILURE*

THE CIVIL WAR gave America two colossal figures. Named in order of their birth, Robert E. Lee and Abraham Lincoln represent more clearly than any other two men the idealism of the South and the North.

So great is the influence they wielded that their actions and utterances are studied for guidance in a much changed world today, and their records are searched for statements or decisions that can be cited as approval of proposed present-day decisions.

Securely and justifiably enshrined in the affections of millions, these two men offer some strange contrasts. Lee was a member of one of America's most illustrious families. His father was Henry "Light Horse Harry" Lee, daring and capable cavalry commander of the American Revolution and a cherished friend of George Washington. An earlier Lee served as Royal Governor of Virginia, the only native-born American to do so. The Lee family played a long and prominent part in colonial affairs.

It was into this background that Robert Edward Lee was born in a Virginia plantation mansion on January 19, 1807. It was a home of luxury and distinction. Figuratively, it could well be said that he was "born to the purple." One would naturally assume that for such a child a world of opportunity and promise lay ahead.

Lincoln's story is well known. He was born in a crude Kentucky log cabin, to a little known but respectable family. There was no background to faintly indicate that greatness might be ahead.

From these very different beginnings, the two youngsters were destined to grow up and become the leaders of a divided nation. Lincoln was to achieve great success and to die when it was attained. Lee was, after many years of outstanding service, to meet ultimate and complete military collapse. Strange to say, he was to do this without losing a high regard that amounted almost to adoration of a people whose cause he championed to defeat.

The world regularly proclaims the successful military leader and tends to forget those who are failures. The case of Robert E. Lee is an outstanding exception. Those he led never wavered in their affections, loyalty, and high regard for him. The stature of the man seems not to have suffered because he was defeated.

As the years passed, even those who opposed him came to recognize his simple greatness. Once the military issue was decided, Lee readily accepted the generous terms of surrender set by Grant and expressed appreciation for their liberality. He urged his men to "return to your homes, plant your crops and obey the laws." When proclamation extending amnesty and pardon to most of those who had taken an active part in the rebellion was made, Lee made written request to President Johnson asking that he be included among those to whom amnesty was extended. The rights he asked for never were restored, and Lee died a prisoner of war on parole. In addition he was indicted for treason but never was brought to trial.

At the war's end, Lee returned to Richmond. He could not go to his former home at Arlington for it had been sold for taxes in 1864. These taxes, plus penalties, amounted to $144.11. Some contend that the sale for taxes was irregular, and this appears to have been practically acknowledged by the national government when, in 1884, it paid the heirs $150,000 to obtain clear title.

In September, 1865, after refusing offers that carried assurance of greater financial rewards, Lee went to Lexington, Virginia, to become president of Washington College, now Washington and Lee University.

In 1866 he established a comprehensive School of Law and Equity. In 1867, a Students' Business School which offered courses in practical and theoretical journalism was introduced; these were the first such courses offered on the college level in America. Plans for courses in agriculture also took form in the same year. Such actions indicate that

Lee was a rather bold progressive educator. Enrollment at the college rapidly increased with students coming from twenty-six states.

A candid study of his life clearly shows Lee's greatness of mind, a greatness that all can acknowledge without detracting from the greatness of any others. Thomas Nelson Page, in paying tribute to him, said, "His monument is in the adoration of the South; his shrine is in every Southern heart." One has only to wander through the South today to know that Robert E. Lee is still the greatest name in the South.

🏵 *A FIGHTING IRISHMAN*

THE NAME OF Michael K. Lawler, a Gallatin County farmer, would be high on any list of the colorful figures that southern Illinois sent to the Civil War. Born in County Kildare, Ireland, in 1814, Lawler came with his parents to America in 1816 and to Gallatin County in 1819. In September, 1837, he was married to a daughter of John Crenshaw, builder of the Old Slave House and operator of the salt works at Nigger Spring.

Records indicate that Lawler was a reasonably prosperous farmer. He also was interested in other businesses including contracting for and selling merchandise. Lawler showed an early interest in public affairs. He was leader of a group known as the Vigilantes, formed to oppose the Regulators who had organized to "regulate" the activities of Negroes, both free and bound.

In 1841 Lawler organized a company of Illinois militia and was commissioned as its captain. Some think that he hoped to use these troops to suppress the Regulators. Just one year later, he was commissioned a brigadier general in the Illinois militia, but it was hardly more than a title.

When the Mexican War began, Lawler recruited Company G of the Third Regiment, Illinois Volunteers, which was sent by steamer to New Orleans and on to Mexico. Sketchy records show that their most deadly conflicts were with reptiles, dysentery, fever, measles, and mosquitos rather than with the Mexicans. At the end of the war, Lawler returned to his farm in Gallatin County.

Lawler began to recruit troops again as soon as Sumter was fired upon. His regiment, which became the Eighteenth Illinois, was taken into service at Camp Douglas near Anna in May, 1861, by U. S. Grant, who was then a captain. Shortly afterwards, this regiment, with Lawler as colonel, was moved to the Mound City shipyards and then to Cairo, from whence it took part in several expeditions.

Though the colonel had much enthusiasm for the military, he appears at first to have lacked knowledge concerning army practices as well as ability to organize and discipline. Captain D. H. Brush, who later was to become colonel of the regiment, said of Lawler in a journal he kept that "the bump of order is very slightly developed in his cranium."

Whatever may have been the reasons, Lawler maintained a sorry standard of discipline, though perhaps not much worse than that of other volunteer regiments commanded by other colonels who were equipped with little beyond ambition.

Lawler's mistakes, omissions, and indiscretions came to sharp attention when one of the enlisted men of Captain Cruse's Company G shot and killed a comrade at about 2:00 A.M. on September 30, 1861. Ordinarily such an offense would have been dealt with promptly by a court martial. Instead, Lawler tried to turn the case over to civil authorities. They, fearing that all soldier witnesses would be gone before court would convene three months later, refused to accept responsibility.

Lawler then turned the offender over to his company for trial and judgment. A jury of twelve men was selected, and a trial (more of a kangaroo court) was held. The accused was adjudged guilty of murder and accordingly sentenced to death. The convicted man was hanged in the woods just north of town at 8:01 on the morning of October 2. Just or unjust, the affair at least had the virtue of promptness.

This did not end Lawler's troubles, but rather tended to consolidate them. A number of charges were filed against him, and he was brought before a court martial. He was found guilty of several items on a long list of charges and sentenced to dismissal from the army, but General Halleck reviewed the findings of the military court and set them aside. Colonel Lawler was restored to duty on January 8 and told to "resume his sword."

Lawler proved to be a fighting officer and went on to win distinction. For gallantry in action he was made a brigade commander. He led wild attacks at numerous places and was severely wounded at Donelson. No one questioned his bravery nor the alacrity with which he grasped a chance to strike effectively. His whole philosophy may be summed up in his advice: "If you see a head, hit it." General Grant said of him, "When it comes to just plain hard fighting, I would rather trust Old Mike Lawler than any of them."

Lawler was an enormous man; some said he weighed about three hundred pounds. He dressed informally, wearing a checked blue shirt and blue woolen trousers tucked into high-topped boots. A gilt band on his white hat was about the only mark to indicate he was an officer.

Lawler left the service on August 11, 1865. He died at his home near Equality on July 26, 1882, and a monument was dedicated to him in Equality on September 25, 1913. A simple marker is at his grave in Hickory Hill Cemetery a short way from the place where State Routes 1 and 13 cross east of Equality. It bears the familiar three-letter inscription, R.I.P.

THE LIFE AND WORKS OF F. F. JOHNSON, M.D.

OCCASIONALLY, EARLY CITIZENS, more ambitious and literate than the average, felt the urge to write books. A sizable proportion of these works took the form of autobiographies. Remnants of such productions are found lying among other papers in attics, in smokehouses, and in old trunks. Others were published in book form.

One of the more interesting published autobiographies of a somewhat unusual man is entitled *The Life and Works of F.F. Johnson, M.D., Stonefort, Illinois, U.S.A.* Interest in this book increases when one observes that it was printed by the Turner Publishing Company, likewise of Stonefort, Illinois, U.S.A. This publishing company was really only one individual, James W. Turner, who combined writing, editing, printing, and binding books with teaching school, founding an academy, and sundry other activities to make up a useful life. Turner himself was the author of two books.

The Life and Works of F.F. Johnson, M.D. is somewhat sketchy. Nevertheless, it often clearly and pointedly tells of incidents in the life of a citizen of "Egypt" around the time of the Civil War.

Johnson's was a life of many ventures that he records out of a sure memory. He tells interestingly of preschool days and of roaring sessions of a "blab" school, similar to those of southern Illinois, in Lebanon, Tennessee. A portion of his account tells how he was hauled up when a small boy and brutally whipped in order to scare some older boys. Something in his story written sixty years after the incident leaves a conviction that the resentment he still expressed was justified.

Johnson, from childhood, seems always to have been at work, and he was a willing worker. At one time, he tells us, he was a ragwheel boy at his father's watermill on the creek near Lebanon, Tennessee. When sufficiently advanced to attend an academy, Johnson apparently thought nothing of walking to one or the other of two schools, sixteen or twenty miles away. He would walk to school on Monday morning, board there during the week, and walk home after the close of school on Friday.

When he was nineteen, F. F. and his father made a trip to Illinois looking for a place to settle. They came in a carryall, a combination of a buggy and a light wagon. Their motive power was Ben, the faithful family nag, that made the two hundred mile trip from Lebanon, Tennessee, to Raleigh, Illinois, several times before the family finally came to locate near Bethel Creek Church, northwest of Raleigh.

On his first journey, Johnson tells us that he saw his first telegraph line and a large steamboat. He tells of crossing the river at Ford's Ferry and of the great flights of passenger pigeons he saw, and he laments the fact that in 1890 they were gone. When the end of their travel day came, they "took up for the night." On this first trip, Johnson walked more than half the distance in "no-heel" shoes that the local cobbler had made to his special order. Regarding high heels he said, "Seventy-five years hence high heels will be considered a relic of Barbarism." He erred.

Coming by way of Benton they stopped to visit some former Tennessee neighbors and saw prairie sod being broken with a plow that turned a furrow three feet wide and required six yokes of oxen to draw it. Corn planted in this inverted sod did not require cultivation the first year.

In the spring of 1855, F. F. and his brother Joe, along with Ben and the carryall, came to locate near Raleigh, reaching there at "10 A.M. on April 5, 1855." They moved into a double log house with a stick and clay chimney and "kept bach" in one room. F. F. taught a school of thirty-five pupils in the other while Joe cultivated the farm.

These Tennessee boys were popular socially. They attended Bethel Creek Church. In the first winter after their coming to Illinois, F. F. engaged in a friendly snowballing game and noted that a "Minerva" was constantly hurling pellets at him. They were married the next summer.

Then followed clerking in a store, studying medicine in the office of Dr. V. Rathbone, and attending a medical school in Kentucky and in Philadelphia, at that time the medical center of America. After this he returned to teach and practice his profession at Raleigh.

When the Civil War came, he enlisted and became an assistant surgeon. He helped to dig "graves"—we call them foxholes—to sleep in on freezing nights. A teetotaler, he carried canteens of whiskey and gave drinks to men trying to haul mired cannon out of the mud with long ropes. He also complained bitterly of deplorable conditions in the Cairo hospitals.

After the war he returned to Saline County, practiced medicine, kept a drug store, taught, served two terms as county superintendent of schools, was ordained to the ministry, became a staunch advocate of keeping the seventh day of the week as Sabbath, and wrote rules of health and rules for care of the sickroom.

Death came to this interesting character shortly after 1890.

🌼 *AN ILLINOIS TEACHER*

M ILLIONS GO THROUGH LIFE practically unnoted, but others attract more than passing attention by doing something, good or bad, beyond the ordinary. Two former Illinoisans, both teachers, are typical examples. Moreover, each literally rode to prominence on horseback. Each is outstanding for the unusual role he played in the Civil War.

One was Benjamin Henry Grierson, brilliant and daring cavalry commander, who rose from the rank of private to that of Major General of Volunteers. The other was William Clarke Quantrill, romantic and controversial figure and most notorious of all guerrillas. He was the capable and heartless leader of a band that waged a war that paid little heed to accepted rules. He gave no quarter nor asked any. Each of these men paused for a time in Illinois, one on his way to abiding fame and the other to equally enduring notoriety.

The writer's interest in Quantrill dates from boyhood when he took plowpoints to the shop and admiringly watched them sharpened by John Taylor Lemay who had his smithy in Broughton. First interest was aroused by a story that "Uncle" Taylor told about the first horse he ever shod unassisted, but closely supervised. This incident occurred in the early days of 1865, shortly after Quantrill and thirty-three of his horsemen had been forced to flee from hiding places in his Missouri-Arkansas-Texas-Kansas domain.

They were heading east, perhaps to Virginia. On their way Quantrill stopped at the shop of the elder Lemay, John Taylor's father, in Tennessee and demanded that his horse be shod. The shop's owner was not there. The only one present was fourteen-year-old Taylor, who regularly helped his father at assorted jobs about the shop. Quantrill told young Lemay to shoe his horse and, with drawn pistol, seated himself to supervise the job. The boy was told he would be shot if he lamed the animal. Judging from his past record of wanton killings the guerrilla leader doubtless would have made good his threat, but the job was completed by the youngster without striking the quick.

A few weeks later, in March, 1865, John Taylor Lemay enlisted in the Union army. He was discharged the following June—still only fourteen years old—the youngest Civil War veteran personally known by the author. But, back to Quantrill.

William Clarke Quantrill was born at Canal Dover, Ohio, on July 31, 1837, and lived there until he was about seventeen years old. His father was a teacher in an academy or high school. Perhaps because of this, young Quantrill received an education somewhat above the average for that locality and time. At sixteen he began teaching school in Canal Dover and in nearby country schools. Later, he left home to teach, first at Mendota, Illinois, and then in Kansas.

Before he was long in Kansas, however, he was in trouble of various sorts. He was accused of stealing food, blankets, and horses. He took oxen from a man he disliked, yoked them together, and chained them to a tree deep in the woods where they almost starved before he was forced at gunpoint to lead the owner to them. He became a gambler of note. Quantrill soon entered into the strife and conflict over slavery that then raged along the Kansas border. In this contest he betrayed a group of men, supposedly his friends, by leading them into an ambush that cost some their lives.

At the outbreak of the Civil War, Quantrill joined the Southern cause. For the next four years, his was a hectic life. Never with more than 450 men, seldom with as many as 250, he struck terror into the hearts of thousands over a wide territory in the Missouri-Kansas-Arkansas borderlands. A mere list of his doings would fill a page. Among the places they attacked was the town of Lawrence, Kansas, which Quantrill particularly disliked.

Their attack there was typical of many others, only on a larger scale. On August 19, 1863, Quantrill rode with 294 men from the farm of Captain Perdee in Johnson County, Missouri, toward his objective. One hundred four regular Confederate troops joined his group on the way, making a total of 450 men. In two days they reached Lawrence after numerous killings and much destruction along the way. His force halted on the outskirts of the sleeping town in the early morning of Friday, August 21. Then, shooting to right and left, they dashed from their gathering place into the town, being instructed to "Kill every man big enough to carry a gun."

The massacre that followed was without equal in the Civil War, perhaps in no other American war. To show their contempt for the Union, they tied national flags to their horses' tails. Saloons were broken into and soon many of Quantrill's men were wildly drunk. They chased and shot men like rabbits. Some were beaten to death with pistols and muskets. Others were killed with knives or bayonets. At nine o'clock, the carnage was ended with 150 men and boys dead. Not one raider had been killed. At nightfall of August 22, the raiders were back in Missouri and disbanded. Their only casualty was one man who had stayed behind in Lawrence and was shot by an Indian.

There literally were a hundred similar raids on a smaller scale. They continued until the War's end. Perhaps no area in the nation suffered so severely and continuously as the region where Quantrill operated.

A recent book, *Gray Ghosts of the Confederacy,* tells the story well, as does *Civil War on the Western Border.*

❧ A MAN WHO HAS BECOME A LEGEND

IT IS NOT OFTEN THAT a man becomes a legend within his own lifetime. It is less often that he attains such distinction because of a life of usefulness. Both conditions, however, have been applicable in the case of Dr. Andy Hall of Mt. Vernon, but the process has taken many years.

Andy Hall was born on a farm southwest of McLeansboro ninety-six years ago, at a time when the last echoes of Civil War cannonading were dying away. His father, a successful farmer, was an officer in the Union army.

Andy tells of some dry summers that came about 1880 when pasturage was scant. During those unusually dry seasons his father sent a herd of cattle into the lowlands at the head of Rector Creek or into Pond Creek bottoms, both in southern Hamilton County, to feed on the swamp grass there. Andy, then "a chunk of a boy," would be sent in charge of them.

It is interesting to hear him recount the experiences that he and another boy, younger still, met while camping at a shelter contrived beside some watering place where the cattle could be "bedded down" at night. He tells of being awakened at about dawn each day by the clanging of the cowbell worn by the leader of the herd.

He tells of the manner in which the ears of the cattle were notched, cropped, slanted, forked, and cut with overbits and underbits to mark them as his father's property.

Andy evidently liked farming and planned to be a farmer. About that time, however, a certain insect pest changed his thinking. In the mid-1880's there were some chinch bug years, years when these now infrequent pests came by uncounted millions to kill corn and wheat. This experience convinced the young farmer that the practice of medicine would be better than farming. He accordingly enrolled in the medical school of Northwestern University and was graduated with the class of 1890, in time to establish an office at Mt. Vernon in the fall of that year. In a short time the name of "Doc Andy" became a familiar one in Mt. Vernon and the vicinity. After seventy years, it still is so. Until three years ago he was active in the practice of his profession.

In the intervening years he did many things in addition to going about the country on horseback, in a top buggy, and later in an automobile. After a long lifetime of active practice he retired to the large frame house that has been home for many years and here he lives surrounded by memories, medallions, medals, citations, and engrossed evidences of honors that have come to him. There are letters from those to whom he has done some simple kindnesses as well as from a president of the United States and those high in the councils of medicine.

The walls also carry photographs of the doctor and his three sons who are physicians, one of whom is a retired major general in the U.S. Air Corps. There is a photograph of his wife who lived until six years ago and to whom the doctor gives high praise for raising the family so well.

There is a photograph of Major Andy as regimental surgeon in the Spanish-American War. In another he appears as a somewhat "fierce mustachio" in the medical corps during the Philippine Insurrection; he tramped jungle trails with General Funston and others of note in that unpleasant episode.

Doc Andy tells of the trips along dim trails through jungles at night to some isolated military post in the interior. He tells of evacuating the sick and the wounded by the use of litters and carriers, or carts drawn by water buffalo, in great outrigger log canoes, and on steamers with cabins of steel plate built abovedeck to protect those aboard against attack by snipers hidden in the forest beside the stream.

During World War I, Dr. Andy once more saw service in the U.S. Army Medical Corps. When World War II came, Dr. Andy was adjudged too old to assign to active service. He served, however, as a member of the board to whom those taking exception to the rulings of the local draft board made appeal. He has served his country well.

Almost a century has failed to dull Dr. Andy's zest for living or his interest in people. Tolerant and kindly, but with marked convictions, he sits in his large comfortable home reading, listening to good music, and writing accounts of some incident of which he alone has had firsthand experience. From time to time he records on tape a radio program of particular interest and replays it.

He attends church, basketball games, and various community events. In summer he works in his garden and among his flowers. Last summer he grew sweet corn, perhaps thinking back to the crawling hosts of bugs that came to destroy his fields of corn and sent him to study medicine.

🏵 *MOTHER BICKERDYKE*

OUR CIVIL WAR has been a favorite subject for books, news articles, and endless speeches. They have told of the military grand strategy and political activities of the great and the near-great whose successes and failures have been recounted. Some of the books, articles, and talks have been concerned with the weary, hungry, footsore, and homesick private soldiers—steadily marching over dusty roads through the heat of summer and over muddy ones through the storms of winter toward another clash of arms.

Relatively little has been written, however, about the women who followed in the wake of conflict to nurse and care for the sick and those wounded in battle. Perhaps Illinois, with its numerous surviving letters, diaries, journals, and contemporary accounts set down by those directly concerned, has been as negligent as any other state in this matter. It may be even more so since story has it that the last surviving Civil War nurse was living in White County within the memory of many. Illinois furnished one of the most capable and devoted members of the Corps of Union Nurses, Mary Ann Bickerdyke, a legendary figure known for a hundred years as "Mother Bickerdyke."

The army career of this woman, born in Knox County, Ohio, in 1817, strangely had its beginning in Knox County, Illinois, in the summer of 1861. A powerful army for the invasion of the South was being gathered hastily at Cairo. These men were poorly housed, ill-fed, and scantily equipped. Sanitary arrangements and medical care were crude. Typhoid, dysentery, pneumonia, measles, and malaria were rife. Hundreds of these troops were dying without ever having known battle.

This was the situation when Pastor Edward Beecher, brother of Henry Ward Beecher and of Harriet Beecher Stowe, came to the pulpit of his Congregational Church at Galesburg on a summer day in 1861 to conduct the regular Sunday services. After the opening hymn, the Reverend Beecher stated that instead of the usual passage of scripture, he would read a letter written by a Galesburg man. The letter graphically and forcefully told of the fearful situation in the army camp at Cairo, where five hundred Galesburg men had been sent. Some already had died and their bodies had been returned to Galesburg for burial.

Instead of the usual Sabbath Day sermon, the service quickly became a business session of the church. All bemoaned the conditions existing in the camp and agreed that they should do whatever they could to remedy them. They accordingly decided to send supplies for the Galesburg men at Cairo. They also would send someone to see that the supplies were properly distributed and used.

The first and only name suggested was that of Mary Ann Bickerdyke, nee Mary Ann Ball, a forty-four year old widow with two young sons. After being chosen, Mrs. Bickerdyke was called upon for a statement. Declaring herself no speechmaker, she briefly stated, "It will be a hard job . . . All right. I'm used to hard jobs. All I ask is that you look after my boys. This is the Lord's work you're asking me to do and I'll do it." Moreover, she did. It is difficult to conceive that a better choice could have been made.

Not much is known about Mary Ann Ball's girlhood beyond the fact that she grew up in a community adjoining that in which William T. Sherman lived his boyhood. Mary Ann grew to be a strong, husky, plainspoken, kindly woman, one endowed with daring, sound judgment, and boundless energy. At thirty years of age she married Robert Bickerdyke, an accomplished musician and artist, and moved with him to Galesburg, Illinois, where he died.

Evidence of formal education is lacking. Apparently she did have some training as a nurse and was acquainted with the practices of the "botanic physician." Whatever her training, she was a firm believer in proper diet, cleanliness, and fresh air.

Shortly after her selection by the people of Galesburg, Mrs. Bickerdyke went to Cairo and to four years of ceaseless conflict with antiquated army regulations, with jealous and too often incompetent medical help, and sometimes with those plainly vindictive.

Through it all she drove her relentless way always a devoted champion of the ailing and wounded soldiers. Thousands knew her, loved her, and called her "Mother Bickerdyke." She followed the commands of Grant and Sherman, both of whom defended and sustained her.

After the war had ended she returned to Galesburg, later going to Kansas and then to California. She traveled widely over the country, always seeking to help those with whom she had once served.

The autumn of 1901 found her back in Knox County, Ohio, her

childhood home, where she died on November 8, honored and beloved by the entire nation—north and south. She was buried in Galesburg where a monument on the public square does her honor.

A book written by Nina Brown Baker, entitled *Cyclone in Calico,* tells her story and of the trying conditions under which she did her great work.

❧ JOSIAH NICKOLSON'S CIVIL WAR STORY

MORE THAN A HUNDRED years ago our War Between the States began. In this conflict, more than two and a half million men in blue and gray were engaged in fearful combat for four years. It was almost a brother-against-brother conflict with all the viciousness that such struggles bring.

Some older persons will remember the wavering ranks of survivors they once saw marching along on Decoration Day or at soldiers' reunions. Now such can only be memories for the last surviving veteran of that conflict has passed on.

The stories of their exploits have been written and rewritten, until many of these tales have been worn threadbare. There does remain, however, a body of materials and attachments which are not generally known. These are the diaries, letters, journals, recorded reminiscenses, and the personal and family papers of the men who actually bore the brunt of the war. These personal recollections and recordings of the soldiers themselves—which often had been dismissed as trivia—have now gained the regard of more learned historians. They help us to realize clearly that the Civil War was filled, as wars always are, with "blood, sweat and tears," mud, lice, cold, hunger, loneliness, sorrow, death, and grievous wounds.

One of the strangest wounds was that, or rather those, suffered by Josiah Nickolson of Eddyville in Pope County. The military record of Nickolson in the National Archives goes far to support the story that follows. Very old persons who knew him furnished additional evidence. I have found nothing to make me doubt his strange story and shall let him tell it in bits taken from a copy of a longer account he wrote at Eddyville in July, 1905, forty-one years after the event.

"I was with a squad . . . so sorely pressed that everyone but myself was killed or captured. I lay concealed day and night till I became so hungry that I went in search of foods at all hazards. I saw a man go into the barnyard but I went directly to the house. The landlady was clearing the table. That was on June 15, just five days since I had eaten anything. I told her I was very hungry. She gave me all I could eat. The man volunteered to watch while I ate. I never tasted anything better."

"I then started on and came to two little boys working in a field [then] crossed over to go through it. Six Rebs came and inquired. The boys pointed (to me) and the soldiers commanded me to stop. They lost sight of me, then went for bloodhounds. The dogs soon brought me to a stand. I tried to surrender but a musket ball went through my uplifted hand. . . ."

"They made me march all day in the rain. I held my hand under my hatbrim. The water ran off on my wounded hand and reduced the fever. . . . It became cool and pale. They took me to Holly Springs, Mississippi, and put me in prison."

"The next day two guerillas pried the door down and took me away. We had not gone far when Jack Cook shot me in the back of the head, low enough to miss the brain and far enough to one side to miss the spinal cord. . . . [The ball] lodged above the roof of my mouth. After I was on the ground he shot me through the head . . . just in front of one ear and out in front of the other. . . . I had not lost consciousness. . . . They dragged me by the feet and threw me into a thicket. . . . Hood pointed his pistol against my forehead and pulled the trigger. The cap burst but the ball did not leave the pistol."

"Two little boys seeing the trail of blood went for their father. The good man took me to his home and cared for me. They were kind. He was a minister of the gospel. That family cared for me four weeks. . . . Then six Confederates took me to the guardhouse. I was then taken to Jackson, Mississippi, for exchange. On August 4, I met my regiment."

Twenty-one years after the experience, Nickolson relates, he sneezed violently and the lodged bullet was freed from the roof of his mouth. According to local accounts he carried it as a souvenir the remainder of his life.

Chapter 2

Folklore

🏵 *STRANGE BELIEFS ABOUT BIRDS*

THE PASSENGER PIGEON which Illinois pioneers saw by the millions has disappeared. The heath hen, once common in the northeastern states, is extinct. The prairie chicken which once boomed in endless numbers here is now rare in Illinois. Unless a movement now underway to provide the prairie chicken better opportunities to survive is successful, it, too, will disappear from the state. Other birds like the Carolina parakeet, several waterfowl, and some of the woodpeckers are seldom seen.

Except for sparrows and starlings, birds are not so plentiful as those who love them would wish. With their decrease in numbers, the folklore about them likewise has dwindled. There once was much of this lore, some of it very old and worldwide. "A little bird told me" is a centuries-old answer to the question, "Where did you hear that?" Perhaps little birds still tell things but it has been a long time since the expression has been heard. A superstitious belief that birds carried news and gave it to a favored few is at least two thousand years old. Allusions to it appear in the Bible, in the Koran of the Mohammedans, in the writings of Whittier, Shakespeare, Longfellow, and others.

Oldsters will recall some of the strange beliefs that were associated with birds. They may remember that a bird pecking at a window was tapping to tell of approaching misfortune. They may also recall the legend they learned in school that told them how the robin came by his red breast. They heard that the cawing of the crow foretold rain, just as the owl's hooting did. The call of the yellow-billed cuckoo was equally reliable, along with the night crowing of roosters. Many a person has had a kind of shivery feeling when a woodpecker settled on the house and began to

49

tap out his signals of coming ill fortune. About the only thing that could be worse was to have a dove alight on the comb of the house and begin its mournful cooing.

All knew that the sight of the first bluebird in spring brought good luck, just as did the first glimpse of a redbird. The plaintive notes of the pewee foretold a mood in keeping with them. It is remembered, too, that bluejays were missing on Fridays, since they had gone to visit the devil and carry him a grain of sand; though no one knew why. It was heard over and over that a crow could be taught to talk if its tongue were slit. (It is true that a crow can learn to talk somewhat like a parrot, but slitting its tongue certainly does not help in the least.) Peacocks cried when it was going to rain, many believed. They were beautiful to see as they strutted out-of-doors, but ill fortune came when their Argus-eyed feathers were brought indoors. Sometimes there was a man or woman "as proud as a peacock."

Bats, not birds, but mammals, came in for their place in the lore of birds. One coming into the room through an open door or window brought sure misfortune. (I still have a firepoker used to fell one such rash invader about 1893.) Bats also were thought to bring bedbugs. "Blind as a bat" was a common expression, but no one suspected then that they used reflected sound, radar fashion, to guide them in their erratic flights. Bats and witches were and still are closely associated.

Turkeys and Thanksgiving are an American tradition. Watching a turkey to its nest in spring was a sly game. Once the hidden nest was found, the eggs had to be removed with a spoon or raked out with a stick that was thrown away from the nest. One egg had to be left in the nest, otherwise the turkey would not continue to use it. Guinea fowls were accorded the same treatment.

Scarecrows made of crossed sticks draped with flop hats or bonnets and bits of old clothes were supposed to ward away marauding crows, blackbirds, and hawks. Faith in their effectiveness is somewhat shattered when one sees a blackbird perched on such a contrivance.

There was a tradition that crows sometimes held court and tried an outlaw member. Trial or no trial, they had some noisy sessions. If the first call of the whippoorwill in the spring came near the front of the house, a death could be expected. A man with "misery in his couplin's," upon hearing the first call, could turn a somersault and secure welcome relief. A man making his last plea or flimsy explanation was often "singing his swan song."

We wonder if it still is the belief of children that it is good luck to see and "stamp" a robin and make a wish. Does particularly good fortune come to the one who sees and stamps a hundred robins come spring? Do youngsters still believe it is very bad luck to kill one? Do some children and adults alike believe that spring and robins come together?

Do some still believe that when the first robin is seen the beholder can sit down, remove a shoe—the left we believe—and find a hair colored like those of his future mate? Are the stories of how the robin came by his red breast still told to children? Is it still a sign of good luck for a robin to build near the house? Or, if a robin sings under the same window on three successive mornings, does it still mean distress and sorrow will befall the home?

Are bluebirds still the harbingers of happiness? Does seeing one in the morning presage a fair day? Do crows generally forecast a storm, rain, and general misfortune? Can one still call to the buzzard soaring high overhead, "Sail to the east, sail to the west, sail to the one I love the best" and have it swerve away in the proper direction? Is buzzard grease really good for rheumatism?

Do the cooings of doves, or white doves coming to clutter about a house, forebode death? Does hearing the first coo of a dove as one goes uphill mean good fortune, and hearing the same as one goes downhill mean misfortune? Will the hearer be going, figuratively, downhill all the year? Is it true that sweethearts live in the direction from which the first coo of a dove is heard in the spring?

Is it good luck to have a woodpecker nest near the house, and is it time to plant corn when he comes? Does his pecking on the house mean misfortune for someone living there? Does it mean headaches if a woman tosses out her combings and the birds use the hair to build a nest? Does the hair remaining on the comber's head become tangled when the birds weave the hair they take into a nest? Can birds be caught by sprinkling salt on their tails? Do birds singing in the rain mean a fair day on the morrow? Is it bad luck for a bird to enter a house unless it leaves by the same way?

An evening spent musing over strange discarded beliefs is a harmless way to relax and to wonder just what is "superstition" today.

❦ CHRISTMAS SUPERSTITIONS

A MASS OF superstitions and proverbs have become associated with Christmas, superstitions that relate to subjects that vary from ashes through luck to weather. Since weather was always present and frequently discussed, some of the superstitions connecting it with Christmas come to mind.

According to one weather superstition, one may easily know the number of snows due to fall during the winter. To do this, one need only note the date of the first snow and count the intervening days until Christmas. This method gives a second chance to those who have neglected to count the foggy mornings in August. Each is about equally reliable. If there is a white Christmas, there will be a green Easter and a good crop year with plenty of fruit, particularly of peaches. If a south wind blows on Christmas Day, so much the better. Should Christmas be green, Easter will be white, spring late, and crops not so good. An icy season between Christmas and New Year also means a good crop year.

A reliable method of foretelling rainfall during each coming month was by the use of a dozen onions. It should be remembered that the ritual was enacted between eleven o'clock and midnight on Christmas Eve in the following manner.

The onions were cut across near the top, and depressions hollowed out. They were then placed on a table or shelf in an east-west line. Then beginning with January they were named in the order of the months. An equal amount of salt was placed in each of the hollowed tops.

No one could go near the onions until the following morning, when the amount of water in each depression indicated the relative rainfall for its corresponding month. Those who neglected to use the onion method could obtain equally reliable information by observing the weather of the first twelve days of the year. Each day was thought to indicate the weather for its corresponding month.

Snow or its absence at Christmas also indicated the general health in store for the coming months. A white Christmas meant a "lean graveyard" while a green one meant a "fat graveyard."

Good luck could be had throughout the year by tying a head of cabbage to the ceiling and sticking nails in it on Christmas Day.

A number of superstitions related to animals. Cows were said to kneel at midnight on Christmas Eve, but woe unto the one who tried to watch them. An Indiana folklorist relates that a woman who attempted to snoop suffered a mild stroke and lost her voice for several weeks.

Animals could understand what was said to them on Christmas Eve and in turn could talk to the spirits at midnight. A child born on Christmas Day could also see and talk with spirits. The crowing of a rooster at night foretold misfortune unless it happened at the season of

Christmas. Ill fortune surely was in store for anyone who killed a fly on Christmas Day or for those who left their green decorations up beyond January first.

If someone had a dog and wished to guard it against hydrophobia, he had only to feed the pet some silver filings on buttered bread. This should be done on Christmas Eve. If, in the Christmas rush, the owner failed to get it done, equally good results could be had by carrying out the process on New Year's Eve or, having neglected both, the Eve of Epiphany was equally suitable. A superstition that came to Illinois from Germany offered farmers assurance that their livestock would be safe from the spells of witches during the coming year if the stables were cleaned between Christmas and the New Year.

If a bewildered maiden would know her future mate, she had only to put a wishbone over the door. The first eligible man who passed beneath it would be that mate. This same maiden might also go to the henhouse after dark and knock on the door three times. If a rooster crowed she would wed before the end of the coming year. Bees hummed a tune at midnight of the twenty-fourth.

There were certain tasks that should not be done at Christmas. Ashes were not to be removed on Christmas, and no woman was to sew or knit between Christmas and the fourth day of the new year. With the ever-present needs to knit and sew by hand, women merited a rest from those tasks.

Good fortune would be yours throughout the year if you were the first to greet those you met with a shouted "Merry Christmas." At least one superstition offered a means of escape to a boy. If he took a bath on Christmas Day, he would stay clean all the year. Some may have doubted this, but boys seemed to believe it.

These are not nearly all the superstitions connected with the day. There are many others fully as queer. Space remains for one more, however. Anyone wishing to know the number of gifts to be received had only to count the white specks in his or her fingernails.

❧ SOME OWLS COME CALLING

DURING THE SNOWBOUND days of last winter, several bags of cracked grain were scattered on the crusted snow for hungry birds. Twenty-three varieties of birds came to eat and be counted. Now another species has come to the large sycamore behind the garage in the dead of night and announced its presence. These latest arrivals are a pair of horned owls. Perhaps they are the same ones who have been coming at irregular intervals for the past ten years, for owls live long lives.

The hoots of these night birds sound eerie at any time. When they light in the tree, they give their usual blasts of "whoo-whoo's," then settle down to carry on what sounds like a conversation—consisting of smaller and less familiar cries, shrieks, wails, hisses, snores, meows, cluckings, snappings, grunts, groans, and other indescribable mutterings.

The noises made by these visitors bring back memories of some strange beliefs once circulated about owls. According to southern Illinois lore, their hootings around the time of midnight indicate that rain will be coming soon. As dawn approaches, the hoots increasingly indicate approaching misfortune, which will be greater when two hoots come together.

Hootings in summer daytime foretell rain. In winter they warn against approaching cold spells. If the daytime calls come from the woodlands along the creek, expect a heavy rain. If they come from the timber on high hills, the sign seems to reverse itself; a long dry spell is indicated. Hootings, day or night, near and behind the house, warn of an approaching death in the family. Cries near the front of the house may indicate either a birth or a death. Whether the owl hootings bring warnings of good or bad fortune, they assure the angler that fish are ready to bite.

If one wishes to guard against the ills of the owl's hootings, it may be done in any one of several ways. They may be silenced by removing the left shoe and turning it upside down. Both shoes may be removed and crossed. An iron shovel or a poker may be placed in the fire and allowed to heat. A brass kettle may be turned upside down, or a hatpin may be hung down the chimney of a kerosene burning lamp to heat. Knots may be tied in corners of handkerchiefs or in apron strings with equally good effect.

A farmer's chickens may be guarded by placing a flint rock on the fire to "draw up their claws." Another way to safeguard the poultry is to mount the blade of a scythe on a post beside the henhouse door where the owl will stop to look the situation over, that is, to case the joint. It should be mounted on a slant to be most effective. The owl's takeoff from the sharp edge of the blade is supposed to cut the tendons in his toes.

Many owl beliefs are worldwide and very old. Some may be traced back to ancient Greece where the owl was associated with Athena, their goddess of wisdom and learning. Owls then were considered birds of good omen. It was about this time that the "wise old owl" term first came into use. When evil days and attendant misfortunes came to Greece, the owls simply kept on hooting. The significance of owl hootings were reversed in meaning. The earlier Romans thought the call could be either good or bad, then only bad. They foretold defeat in battle and even Caesar's death.

Whatever he does, the hearer must not mimic the sound of the owl; that surely brings misfortune. Indians thought that the owl was the embodiment of a returned soul come to bring a message. Some Seminole Indians even now whistle the hooting owl. If he hoots again, his warning is not for the whistler.

Association once thought to exist between owls and wisdom has not vanished. Statuary and cartoons of college life often show owls. Daniel Chester French's Alma Mater statue on the campus of Columbia University shows an owl, and students there sometimes wear pins bearing an owlet as a lucky piece.

The belief that one who would see well at night could do so by carrying the dried eye of an owl in a bag has been found in Illinois. There is much more owl lore for those who would like to gather it. And those who have not heard the resounding calls of the great horned owls and the quavering call of the screech owl have missed something.

🌿 FOLKLORE ABOUT THE LEFT HAND

LEFT-HANDED PERSONS, numbering about one in eighteen, are disadvantaged in a right-handed world. Even so, being left-handed now may not be so plaguing as it used to be. Along with the physical inconveniences, there once was a belief that being left-handed was an indication that something was wrong with a person. Indications of strange earlier beliefs have come down to the present time in lingering bits of lore still found in southern Illinois.

Earlier peoples looked upon left-handers as untrustworthy. Some thought them in league with the devil. One expression was that such persons owed the evil one three days of labor. The left-handed pioneer owed the devil a hundred black gum rails. Considering the difficulty of splitting that wood, it was an obligation impossible to meet.

In many languages the word for "left" also carries the suggestion of treachery, insincerity, danger, or evil. Today those who advocate social, economic, or political views not commonly accepted often are designated as "left-wingers" and are held suspect or outrightly condemned.

The left hand long has received special attention. Plutarch had Roman boys hold their bread in their left hands. Moslems pet their dogs, unclean animals, with their left hands. In primitive races where magic is brewed, the "doctor's" left is his performing hand. The gambler who wishes to be lucky should pick up cards with his left hand. Luck is changed in a dice game when the one rolling changes to the left hand. If salt is spilled, a bad omen, the ill effects can be averted by picking up a bit of the spilled salt with the left fingers and tossing it over the right shoulder.

All have heard of an itching palm and money. In lore it was the left palm that really mattered. When this one itched, it was a sign that the person would come into money—the greater the itch, the more money. This sign could be strengthened if the person spat in the itching palm and rubbed it on unvarnished wood or his buttocks. "Rub it on wood, all will be good." In the event that money was not directly forthcoming it meant that employment soon would be available. At the very least it indicated the early arrival of company.

The left hand also had other powers of prophecy and effect. A choking child could be relieved by raising its left hand above its head. Turpentine on the left palm and on the sole of the left foot would relieve a child's spasm. An adult could wear a brass ring on the middle finger of the left hand and thus ward off rheumatism. A string tied about the little finger of the left hand would stop nosebleed. If eggs were placed under a setting hen with the left hand, more of the chicks hatched would be pullets.

It was unlucky to hold a worm in the left hand while baiting a hook. Pins should be picked up or removed from clothing with the left hand, and a pin was best received from another's left hand by your own left. If one must drown a kitten, it should be thrown into the water with the left hand to avoid the inevitable seven years of bad luck.

Those women who would sign with the devil and thereby become witches had only to draw blood from the left little finger or from between the thumb and forefinger of that same hand.

Children seem to be born ambidextrous—that is with the ability (or inability) to use either hand equally well. Just why they become right-handed or left-handed is not fully explained. Folklore, however, does suggest reasons. Sons of a left-handed mother will be left-handed. Laying a child on its left side before it is a year old will make it left-handed just the same as placing its left arm first into the sleeve of a garment or putting its left sock on first.

It once was believed that if a left-handed pupil was required to write with the other hand it would cause stuttering. Some think left-handers are clumsy, but left-handed Leonardo da Vinci did a creditable job painting the *Mona Lisa*. What baseball manager would not welcome a good southpaw pitcher? Almost any football coach would willingly import a good left-handed running passer, even from as far away as Australia. So, being left-handed is not all bad, even though such people may also be left-footed and left-eyed.

🏵 *APPLE TIME*

PERHAPS APPLES COME nearest to being the universal fruit. In the opinion of many, the "forbidden fruit" in Eden was an apple. Later, some golden apples caused a maid of ancient Greece to lose a classic foot race.

When white men came to America they brought the apple with them, and it soon became the land's most important fruit. Since then, it has always been grown extensively in Illinois and doubtless will remain our great fruit crop.

During the centuries that man has grown apples, a great and varied body of folklore has gathered about them. That some bits of this lore survive was brought sharply to attention a few days ago when some youngsters were found "popping" apple seeds.

Though the practice is old, these devotees had gone modern. Instead of a lid on the hot kitchen stove or a hot stone on the fireplace hearth, they were using an electric iron turned upside down and supported on the rim of a stewer. Despite the changed apparatus, however, it is safe to conclude that the results in either case would be equally reliable.

The procedure remains the same. Three or five seeds from a fresh apple are given names and placed on the griddle. The first seed that pops indicates to the youngster performing this rite the one who loves him most.

It was surprising to find the old practice still in use. Seeing it brought to mind other forgotten bits of apple lore, which easily contains a hundred or more items. Some of those current in southern Illinois are given here.

Beginning with a seasonal approach, if sleet covered the trees with ice in February, there would be a good apple crop. It was believed that such a sleet would retard the blooming of the trees until danger from freezing was past. Even if freezing occurred, it would do no harm if it came in the "light of the moon" when it was believed that frosts do not kill.

When apple blossoms appeared, farmers said that melons, pumpkins, and beans should be planted. After this, things moved along in their natural course until the apples were large enough to tempt children's appetites. According to the same lore there would be fewer stomach-aches if the apples were dipped in salt. Above all, cows had to be removed from pasturing in the orchard; if they were allowed to eat the green apples they would surely "go dry."

As the season advanced, the uses of apples increased. When time came for them to be eaten by others than children and cows, they were often peeled. If the peeler succeeded in removing the entire peel without breaking it, someone loved him or her. If this peel were tossed backward over the left shoulder, it would fall to form the initial of the lover. To learn if someone was to become your mate, an apple could be named and cut apart; if the seeds numbered exactly twelve, it meant a wedding.

Seeds from an apple afforded other glimpses into the future. Counting the seeds off, one could chant the following ditty: "One I love, Two I love, Three I love I say, Four I love with all my heart, Five I cast away," and so forth, step by step, until "Twelve they marry." There were additional rhymes to take care of additional seeds, but they are forgotten now. Seeds also yielded other prophecies, such as the number of children to be expected or the direction in which a lover lived.

❦ MISTER GROUNDHOG, CHAMPION SLEEPER

ACCORDING TO AN old superstition some queer kind of built-in alarm clock sounds off in early February, and the deepest sleeper in southern Illinois, perhaps in all the nation, awakens. According to general belief, this should occur at eleven o'clock in the forenoon of February second. At that time this champion sleeper is supposed to awaken, crawl to the doorway of his home, make meteorological observations, and form a decision.

If the recently awakened one finds the sun shining enough to cast a shadow, he returns to his bed for another brief nap of six weeks. By this little gesture he informs us that much winter weather is yet to come, that spring will be late, and that the crop year will be unfavorable. If he can see no shadow, he stumbles around, yawns, and perhaps scratches his head in order to shake off the grogginess resulting from his long sleep.

He then goes out to look for something to eat and to find his lady friend. When he does so, spring is just around the corner, and the crop year will be a good one.

The sleeper mentioned, by proper name, is *Marmota monax,* also known as a marmot, woodchuck, groundhog, or whistling pig. To some persons well acquainted with him, the name is shortened to "chuck." Whatever the name given him, he is America's champion long-distance sleeper. Some insist that he also is about our laziest animal. Both friends and detractors assign him at least two distinctive traits. First he is an industrious individual that digs and keeps a clean and well-ordered burrow. Secondly, he is almost constantly eating.

He spends his summer feasting. By the time cold weather arrives he is miserably fat and decides to reduce by sleeping it off. For about three weeks he nods and dozes for a day or two at a time. Apparently liking these "cat naps," he settles down in his bedroom, well below the frost line, and curls himself into a ball with his nose protected by his hind legs and tail. Evidently having no troubled conscience, he goes into a profound sleep that often lasts three or four months.

Raccoons, skunks, bears, and badgers sleep long and well. None of these, however, rival the endurance record of the groundhog. Specimens of groundhogs in their deepest sleep have been dug from their burrow bedrooms and had their pulse, respiration, and temperature taken. The groundhog's pulse, normally eighty to ninety a minute, has been found slowed down to no more than five, with a breathing rate of about twelve per hour and temperature as low as thirty-eight degrees. Prodding and rolling him about matters little; he really is sleepy. With the arrival of spring a mysterious force begins to stir. Perhaps it is hunger, since the fatter and better fed ones sleep longest.

No one seems to know just how he came to be looked upon as a weather forecaster, nor why the second day of February, long known as Candlemas Day, was assigned to him. Perhaps the old, widely held superstition that the weather for the next six weeks or two months could be determined from that of Candlemas Day helped some. That is shown by the following old English rhyme:

> If Candlemas Day be dry and fair,
> The half of winter's to come and mair,
> If Candlemas Day be wet and foul,
> The half of winter's gone at Yule.

There once were some who insisted that February 14 was Groundhog Day. This controversy was definitely settled for one state when the Missouri Legislature passed a resolution designating the second day of the month as the proper one. There is no mention that groundhogs were informed.

Shortly after 1900 a group of merry chaps about Quarryville in Lancaster County, Pennsylvania, organized the Slumbering Groundhog Lodge. Each year it is the custom of this group to don silk hats, take canes in hand, and go into the fields to discover and make observations concerning Mr. Marmota Monax. When a burrow is found, signal is given, and all gather about it. After careful inspection and note taking, the group return to the village to properly evaluate and interpret their findings and to celebrate.

After twenty years of such "research" they report that the shadow, no-shadow method had been found accurate eight times, inaccurate seven times, and inconclusive five times.

Despite poisons, traps, gas, and natural enemies, the groundhog population holds up well. His thick tough hide makes excellent shoestrings, now little in demand. Native craftsmen rate leather made of groundhog skins without equal for bottoming chairs. Those to whom the idea of eating the meat of the groundhog is not repellent think it is excellent, even comparable to chicken.

🌸 READING PALMS OR BUMPS

ONCE UPON A TIME Gypsy caravans, perhaps leading a few extra horses, roamed the southern Illinois countryside. They made baskets and willow furniture, traded horses, tinkered, and told fortunes. Fortune-tellers again came in for attention when a stop was made last summer at Red Hills State Park about midway between Lawrenceville and Olney. A motorized band of Gypsies was encamped there. Instead of the distinctive horse-drawn vehicles used by such universal vagrants some sixty years ago, these Gypsies were traveling by automobiles, including Cadillacs and Chryslers. Several were towing nice trailers.

No sooner was a stop made than a woman left the group to make her approach, voicing assurance that for a silver coin she would tell my fortune. With a feeling of daring, not enough however to part with a dollar, a two-bit piece was produced with which to properly "cross the palm." Holding my left hand, she began by muttering something about a "long and interesting life line." It was not clear whether she was alluding to the past or the future. Happy is the thought that the life line was long and interesting. The invitation to contribute another fifty cents and have a full reading was declined.

She then wished to "bless" a one-cent coin that was among the pocket rubble exposed in looking for the quarter. In order that the copper coin would bring the greatest measure of good luck, she insisted that it be placed securely "in your wallet, if you have one, and allowed to remain there nine days." As the coin was being properly stowed away—where it still is—she asked for the privilege of blessing the paper money she saw. This brought to mind stories of others who had money blessed in like manner, only to find it had disappeared. The offer was declined. Apparently losing interest at this point, the fortune-teller left.

The foregoing was by the Gypsy fortune-telling formula that has been followed in English America since as early as 1701, perhaps even earlier than that in American territories then under Spanish or French control.

Some older persons will recall the picturesque Gypsy bands that once roved the southern Illinois countryside. They were indeed a motley group. A visit to one of their evening campfires always was interesting. Especially was this interesting when members of the group sang, played the violin, told stories, danced, or shouted at each other in a queerly intoned manner.

When most people think of fortune-tellers, they generally think of Gypsies. They, however, were not the only ones practicing that craft. Another group was the once common phrenologists. Their "science" began about 1790 with the thinking of a German medical student named Gall. Phrenologists contended that there were thirty-seven faculties of the mind. Each was located at a particular point in the brain. Charts accordingly were prepared to show the location of each of these areas. It only remained then to measure the protrusions and depressions of the skull to determine the extent to which an individual had been endowed with a particular trait. This measuring was done with instruments or by feeling the "bumps," or other irregularities of the skull.

A magazine of national circulation, *The Phrenological Journal,* was published. Literally hundreds of books and pamphlets also appeared. Many charts showing the human head with markings to indicate the location of various faculties were printed. These still are found among collections of old papers. The book collections of old-time physicians often contain a text or two on the subject.

All this is not strange. When the "science" of phrenology first was introduced in America, it received wide acclaim. A number of American universities showed a very friendly attitude toward it, Harvard being among them.

The practice of phrenology continued until after 1900. It was in that year that the writer first learned of it when a "graduate phrenologist" came to Broughton on a Saturday afternoon and gave at least one public "reading." The subject of the reading was a well-known neighbor. On the same afternoon one prominent farmer is said to have given five dollars for the phrenologist's written report of the findings revealed from a careful feeling of his son's head. The so-called expert prophecies were excellent but the son failed to fulfill them. Many of those present apparently believed that the practitioner could make a reliable analysis of a subject's traits and capacities by the shape of his skull.

After all, the group of farmers standing beside the general store should not be censured too severely for their unwarranted belief in the abilities of the performer. Horace Greeley defended phrenologists. Bernard Baruch is said to have consulted one before deciding upon his career. One wonders if either Greeley or Baruch could have been influenced by a phrenologist.

🏵 SUPERSTITIONS ABOUT MONEY

THE WORLD IS full of collectors. The objects they gather include almost everything from acorns and buttons to yo-yos and zithers. Whatever is collected, each hobbyist seems to cherish it. Some collect money and apparently are made happy.

Having tried with little success to collect the circulating medium, the writer decided instead to collect superstitions about it. They are easy to come by and cost nothing. Also, they may be passed about without fear of loss. To date about two hundred bits of money lore have come to hand.

It has been found that money superstitions also are associated with many other objects. Some of these are the moon and stars, foods, moles, warts, and whippoorwills. If your pocketbook is empty when you see the new moon, it will be empty during that moon. Should it be full, the reverse will be just as true. Any misfortune threatening from the new moon-flat pocketbook combination can easily be offset by seeing a shooting star and saying "money, money, money" before the star ceases to blaze. Good fortune is doubly sure if one has a piece of money in his hand when the star appears and repeats the magic words before it vanishes.

Pins also may foretell the turn money affairs will take. One who finds a pin with point toward him will inherit money. If the point is away, he will pay money out. A hairpin found in the morning and hung up will bring good fortune.

Charms from plants and animals may foretell money trends. Find a four-leafed clover and you will inherit money. If it is collected on a grave, the inheritance will be greater. A small bag of red pepper worn about the neck brings financial good fortune. Many men have carried a buckeye, a bit of oyster shell, the breast bone of a sparrow, or a rabbit's left hind foot to assure money luck.

Eating some foods brings money. A dried herring at midnight on New Year's Eve gives assurance that you will have money all the year. If one does not like dried herring, equally good results are assured by eating hogshead, cabbage, sauerkraut, or white beans. Many insist that the cabbage is more effective if the cabbage is cooked and then quartered. The white beans should be eaten with hogshead. Onion skins should always be burned, never thrown into the garbage pail, if one expects to have money. Foods that swell when cooked, like dried apples, should be prepared on New Year's Day.

Bubbles that arise on pools of water during a shower indicate that money is to be expected. Bubbles on a cup of coffee indicate the number of dollars that one may expect. In order to assure receipt of the money, the bubbles must be counted. They also are considered more effective if swallowed before they burst. Should they be broken by the drinker's attempt to take the bubbles into his mouth he will lose that number of dollars.

Dreams and money are closely associated. Dream of a turkey and you will receive a large sum of money. Dream of an orchard, the moon, a spider spinning a web, an umbrella, or of cracking and eating walnuts and you will receive a large sum of money. Dreaming of paper money means that news of a death will be received or that the dreamer will lose money. A dream of shabby shoes likewise indicates a loss of money.

One must not give a friend a sharp-edged cutting tool. It will sever their friendship unless the donor is given a penny in exchange. (Now the writer knows, a lifetime later, why he lost a girl friend to whom he gave a manicure set in 1910. She never gave the necessary penny in return.)

All know that wide hands indicate ability to earn money. An itching left palm means that its possessor will be receiving money; an itching right palm means that it will be paid out.

Every child knows that if a freshly pulled tooth is placed under the pillow some money will be found in its place the next morning.

The financial fortunes of a newly born babe may be assured if its first visitor gives it a dime. Should the baby clutch and hold the money in its hand, it will grow up to be rich.

It is unlucky to receive a two-dollar bill unless a corner is torn off.

Mutilated corners show this superstition still is prevalent. And then, when did you last receive a two-dollar bill?

✿ BEEKEEPERS AND LORE ABOUT BEES

ANY CURIOUS PERSON wandering across southern Illinois can easily find something of interest. For instance, on a warm spring day he may see a beekeeper, often an elderly man, leisurely working among his stands in a sunny backyard. One may be tempted to stop and chat. Beekeepers like their bees and almost always are pleased to talk about them, especially if the visitor is not panicked by a bee seemingly on an exploratory cruise.

An old keeper may tell how he once placed bee bait in the woodland, left it a day or two, then returned to watch visiting bees take cargo and start on a lightly wavering beeline for the high hollow of a tree.

When observations were made from two or more stations, and the vicinity where the beelines converged could be determined, it was not too difficult to find the swarm. If done early in the season, May or June, the tree could be cut and the bees placed in a hive, sometimes only a short section of a hollow log set on a section of broad planks and covered with another section held in place with a stone weight. Small notches at the bottom of the log allowed bees to enter and leave the hive.

If the tree was not cut and the bees placed in a new hive it would be marked with a large X and left until autumn, when it would be cut and the bees sacrificed for the stored honey. It was considered plain stealing to cut a tree another man had marked.

Talking with beekeepers, one quickly finds that there is a great body of rapidly vanishing lore about bees and honey. From bits of this it is learned that a weather-bee relationship is summed up in the old saying, "When bees fly far, weather will be fair."

Conversation easily and naturally turned to ways of preventing stings. These included a hot bath and a rinse in strong salt water or the wearing of well-smoked clothing or the indulgence of a vile pipe. Always one had to keep calm and stay out of flight lanes. Sometimes mosquito netting was worn about the face. Trousers might be tucked in and wrist bands tied. Some keepers, however, worked with no other defense than the regular smoker carries in one hand.

A person who was stung by a bee could lessen the pain with a gob of plain cold mud, preferably compounded with peppermint leaves. Even better was a mixture of yellow clay and vinegar. Raw meat lessened pain and swelling. A quid of tobacco bound over the sting was an accepted remedy. If the beeman did not chew tobacco he simply smeared the wound with honey or with ear wax.

Bees also provided medical remedies. An entire swarm—honey, comb, old bees, young bees, grubs—could be stewed together in a broth that would cure kidney disease. For hundreds of years bee stings have been a standard remedy for rheumatism, neuritis, and arthritis. This treatment should begin with two stings, the number being increased at intervals until benefits come. This must be an effective remedy, for the writer has seen just one unannounced sting limber up a chronic rheumatic.

For several hundred years honey has been recognized as a fine remedy for coughs, colds, croup, and the childhood malady of whooping cough. It was mixed with lemon juice and sniffed up the nose for catarrh. A standard cold remedy was one part honey, one part linseed oil, and one part whiskey. A child took one teaspoonful three times daily; adults took it by the tablespoonful. Juice of elderberries mixed with honey expelled roundworms. Resin and honey made a salve good for sores, and especially for burns and scalds. Peach tree bark, honey, and alum were combined for sore mouth. A poultice of crushed carrots and honey would draw out thorns and splinters.

In many European countries it is still the belief that unless bees are told of the death of their master, they will leave, die, or quit making honey. In some places bits of crepe were fastened to the hives. The Irish also told their secrets to the bees. After all, bees long were considered messengers of the gods.

Lincoln said in one of his talks, "A drop of honey catches more flies than a gallon of gall." Others have said: "Honey is sweet, but bees sting;" "A bee sucks honey from the bitterest plant;" "He that shares honey with a bear has the least of it;" "It is dear honey that is licked off a thorn."

Some consider it better to barter for bees than to buy them. The value of a free swarm varies with the season.

> A swarm of bees in May is worth a load of hay.
> A swarm in June is worth a silver spoon.
> But a swarm in July is not worth a fly.

Lest it be forgotten, honey and honeymoons are associated, and politicians still get bees in their bonnets. There also are other ways to be stung.

❦ *THIS "EGYPT" AND THAT EGYPT*

NUMEROUS FOLK SAYINGS, superstitions, and practices observed in southern Illinois are very, very old. These bits of lore occasionally may be traced back through thousands of years to a vanished civilization. Hundreds of odd beliefs and superstitions have doubtlessly been forgotten, but other hundreds have survived, being passed along by word of mouth from ancient peoples to those living now.

An incident to illustrate this occurred late on a blustery, near-zero night in the almost empty Illinois Central passenger station at Chicago. Two men came into the waiting room bearing a pair of long ladders hinged together at one end. They spread the hinged ladders to form an A and began preparations to replace some burned-out ceiling lights.

Before either workman had actually mounted a ladder to begin the job, another man, distinctly a foreigner, hurriedly entered the room and started down the aisle that the ladders spanned. He halted abruptly, turned aside, and walked around and between seats to pass on his way.

Seating himself nearby, this "Egyptian" from southern Illinois and that other one from the Nile fell to talking. Somehow the talk turned to ladders. Each observed how others passing along the aisle had halted as he had done, and had turned aside.

Not mentioning my observation that he had walked aside to avoid passing under the ladders, I remarked that many people avoid passing beneath a ladder, thinking that such action indicates approaching misfortune. It was learned, as I suspected by his action, that his people held a similar belief. He also remarked that though he really didn't think it did so, he just kept on walking around them. Asked how long the custom had been followed, he replied with "always."

The gentleman from the Nile seemed well versed in the folk beliefs and practices of his country. Though he did not appear to be particularly influenced by the folklore of his people he was pleased to talk of their ages-old beliefs and customs. Comparing notes, it was found that many of the half-remembered bits of lore in our Egypt were part of the ancient lore of his Egypt.

He was interested in the account of how our Egypt had acquired its name but was somewhat vague on the story of Joseph and his brethren and of "going down into Egypt for corn." He was interested in our place names of Thebes, Karnak, Cairo, and Memphis.

From him it was learned that the "eyes" in peacock feathers exercised evil influences in the valley of the Nile five thousand years ago just as they now do here. The ancient Egyptians also believed that the cry of a peacock beneath a window foretold misfortune somewhat like the wailing of our banshee. Both beliefs linger here.

Egyptians of long ago uttered phrases of praise or implored blessings when they sneezed. Today we often hear the sneezer or someone nearby say "gesundheit." In the spring, the beginning of their new year, they had observances that featured eggs—we have Easter. Swallows, they thought, buried themselves in mud for the winter. Until bird migrations were understood, some here also thought so. "The goose that laid the golden egg" possibly was their bird god that laid the sun.

Women then used pencils to shape their brows and emphasize eye shape. Lips were painted red to prevent chapping or the entrance of evil spirits. The custom persists but the objectives are different.

The list could go on and on. If Greece, Rome, and other nations of the ancient world were included, many more bits of our folklore would prove to be thousands of years old.

SUPERSTITIONS ABOUT FOODS

A STORY GOES that the poet Oliver Wendell Holmes, of rare good humor, was asked if he believed in ghosts. His prompt answer was, "No, I do not believe in ghosts," to which he added in a softer voice, "but I'd be afraid of them." Many persons have a similar attitude toward superstitions. They deny being superstitious, yet they cite and pass along many baseless beliefs.

That foods come in for their share of strange beliefs and practices was recently illustrated by incidents associated with the dining table on a recent New Year's Day. A head of cabbage had been cut into sections and cooked, one portion being for each one present. We were told that eating one portion of a cabbage so prepared would bring the diner good luck through the coming year.

The group at the dining table was able to assemble a number of other queer superstitions, some of which once were firm beliefs. It was learned that fish is a good brain food, but not any better than cherries.

Those not already knowing were told that good-tasting food when spilled would spot a garment and that ill-tasting food would not do so. Spilling sugar, as well as salt, warned one of approaching ill fortune. In the case of spilled sugar, no measure to counter its ill effect was forthcoming.

Bread came in for numerous strange beliefs. If a piece of bread is held in the mouth, one can peel onions without shedding tears. Even a bit of bread attached to the end of the knife being used will assure dry eyes. Eating burned bread or bread crumbs was warranted to give one the ability to whistle. This question, however, remains: will eating burned bread or bread crumbs reinvest even an octogenarian's ability to whistle to his dog? If bread crusts are eaten, cheeks will be rosy. Men eating much bread have hairy chests. If the diner breaks bread into crumbs at the table, he will know poverty. Two persons must not hold a piece of bread to break it, and one must not break bread against the plate held by another.

If bread falls butter-down, which it seems generally to do, a hungry visitor is coming. The same is just as true if you take bread while you have bread. Misfortune awaits the one who takes the last piece of bread from a plate. That would appear to be in conflict with the saying that if the bread is eaten the morrow will be a fair day. If that last piece be a biscuit, the one taking it is privileged to kiss the cook. A woman who cuts thick slices of bread will be a good stepmother. Whether sliced thick or thin, slicing is not to be done while the loaf is hot. If a loaf breaks while being sliced, it bodes ill.

The foregoing superstitions about bread are old ones. A new one is that hot cross buns for Easter, if soaked in water, thoroughly dried, and carefully wrapped, assure abiding good luck. It was then recalled that if a piece of dry bread be placed upon the lid of the stewer used in cooking cabbage, no odor will arise.

It seemed that the bits of superstition tossed about would have no ending. It was learned that drinking well water will make one tall, just the same as eating bananas. If hands are crossed by two persons as they reach for food, they will quarrel. If tea leaves float, company is coming. Cream in hot tea will sicken you. Drinking tomato juice will sober a drunken person. Drinking water rapidly will make you fat, but you can reduce weight by eating rhubarb and lemon. When pineapple is eaten for dessert, food is not so fattening. A listing of the effects upon the offspring of an expectant mother's craving for particular foods would fill a page.

One wonders how all these strange beliefs first began. We know of the origin of only one that gained rather wide local circulation. You must not eat a dish of ice cream and bananas together. A man in our community did so and was dead within a few minutes of "acute indigestion." A physician hastily summoned called it a heart attack. Despite this ominous superstition, daring youngsters continue to eat banana-splits and somehow survive.

🌿 *RANDOM BITS OF HORSEY FOLKLORE*

MEN, HORSES, AND dogs have been closely associated for ages, and great collections of superstitions, strange beliefs, and other odd bits of folklore about both these favorite companions of man have been passed about. Since dogs still are numerous, the lore relating to them has not dwindled so greatly, but horses are becoming more scarce, and the lore about them is passing from circulation.

A few bits from the items of that vanishing lore are given here. Many of these items will be familiar to oldsters and may suggest others. A prominent segment of that lore is related to horseshoes. Other bits of it concern the harness, trappings, and behavior of horses.

The horseshoe long has been a symbol of good fortune among many peoples. Jews, Moslems, and Christians alike have considered it a lucky emblem for about as long as horseshoes have been known.

It has been almost universally beneficial to find a cast-off shoe, especially if the open end of the shoe was pointed toward the finder, or, even better, if the shoe contained several nails. If the open end of the shoe was away from the finder, misfortune could be warded off by picking it up by one heel, spitting on it, and hurling it over the left shoulder.

The finding of a mule shoe meant misfortune which could easily be avoided, too, by the spitting and hurling process. Undoubtedly there were bits of lore connected with ox shoes but the oxen have been gone so long that the ox lore also has more nearly vanished.

A horseshoe fastened above a doorway of a home assured good luck if the open end was placed upward. Above the doorway of a barn it offered the owner assurance that his livestock would not be bewitched. The open-end-up position is said to have been effective because St. Dustan, the patron saint of blacksmiths, once had the devil within his power and drew from him a solemn promise to stay away from places thus guarded. In North England, there is a saying, "May the horseshoe never be pulled from your doorway." (I hope the one is not torn from the front of my trailer.)

Sixty years or more ago a great number of men chewed tobacco. A favorite brand of plug tobacco was Horseshoe, marked by a glistening small tin horseshoe which boys treasured highly and carried about in their pockets or fastened to the lapels of their jackets. They were good trading items.

To assure good luck for the coming year one had only to sleep with a horseshoe under the pillow on the night of New Year's Eve. The slender, tapering, sharply pointed nails used to fasten shoes to the horse's hoof, also were considered emblems of good luck, particularly so if they were bent into rings and worn. Boys "mooched" these nails from blacksmiths until some started charging one cent a nail for them. Boys with spare pennies considered the nails worth the price.

A great deal of horse lore already has vanished. Children no longer stamp their feet for good luck when they see a white horse. No longer is it known that a child under one year of age can have its health and well-being assured through the coming year by being passed through a horse collar. Few realize that a horsehair placed in a bottle or barrel of rainwater will become a hair snake, and that those from a gray horse change more quickly and surely.

It seems that farmers do not now know that a nail that has pierced the foot of a horse within the line of the quick should be burned, driven into wood, or greased and laid up in some safe place.

Few have heard that a stocking-footed horse may bring either good or bad luck to an owner, depending upon which feet are stockinged. People no longer believe that evil spirits may be kept away by shiny or tinkling ornaments and bells on harness. Horse blankets are rare, while saddle-bags and sidesaddles are curios. No one seems to know that horses romping about in the pasture portend a coming change in weather or that the same is true when they stand with their backs to chilly winds. During boyhood some farmers and livery stable keepers had a goat, a spotted pony, or a spotted dog in his horse barn to keep witches away. Sometimes there were bunches of pennyroyal to drive away flies.

Test your own horse sense with the following questions. Do men who start out to trade horses still come home with only the bridle? Will a twelve-inch length of alder stem placed in the drinking trough give the horse a mottled coat? How came the expression, a political dark horse? Do headless horsemen still prowl lonely roads on great black steeds? Is a horse worth a hundred dollars for each time it rolls over? Do fishing smacks still have horseshoes nailed to their masts like Nelson had on the mast of the *Victory* at Trafalgar?

Finally, how many beliefs cherished today will be equally as laughable a hundred years from now?

🌸 CATS AND MAN

Dogs, cats, and man have been associated for thousands of years. A recently published book entitled *God Had a Dog* is attracting attention. It tells of the long, friendly relationship between dogs and men and recites bits of the great mass of legend and strange beliefs associated with "man's best friend."

At about the same time this book appeared, a magazine article told about 197 mummified cats being found in the basement of the British Museum in London. They had been stored there for years, and forgotten. The article gave rise to the question: "Why hasn't someone written a book about cats, similar to the book about dogs?" Perhaps that has been done and the book has not come to attention. There certainly would be no shortage of material.

Cats and people have been living together for ages and vast amounts of cat lore have accumulated about this animal that has lived with man but has "walked by himself."

According to evidence found by those excavating in the ruins of ancient civilizations, the association of cats and people began in Egypt six thousand or more years ago. The story pieced together indicates ancient Egypt had a plague of mice that threatened to destroy the never-too-plentiful grain supply. Native African cats, running wild in the hills along the borders of the settled regions, discovered this wonderful food supply and moved in. The cats increased but the mice decreased until a kind of working balance came. The grateful Egyptians came to hold cats in regard.

Both the cat and man seem to have quickly adopted each other, with one basic difference. Cats continued to walk their lonely way while man deified the animal.

It became a custom for each Egyptian of high station to have his favorite cat killed, mummified, and buried with him. The cat often was accompanied by a supply of preserved mice, in case it needed food. It was a collection of these mummified cats that had been found stored in the basement of the museum.

These ancient cats of the Nile Valley appear to have been the source of the familiar housecat of today. Carried on vessels by their owners, many cats took shore leave on strange soil and found new protectors.

Since the Egyptians looked upon the cat as something divine, it was only natural that they closely observed its behavior and attached significance to it. In this way the great body of strange beliefs about the cat began.

Even in that far-off time the blood of the cat was thought to have strange qualities. A member of a group visiting the Louvre in Paris in 1919 asked Dr. Breasted, the great Egyptologist from the University of Chicago, how it was that the colors of inks used by the Egyptians remained so bright after more than five thousand years. He said research indicated Egyptians ground colored stones to powder and mixed it with plasma from cats' blood to make their inks. Whether the mixture had anything to do with it or not, the colors remained bright.

Strange beliefs concerning the powers of cats still linger. It was a common belief less than a hundred years ago that a few drops of blood taken from the snipped ear or clipped tail of a black cat and rubbed over the inflamed area was a specific for erysipelas. And many persons have heard it said that a cat has seven lives—the more credulous say nine. All know that killing a cat will bring ill fortune and a black cat crossing the path is a sure sign of bad luck.

There were many remedies to halt the misfortunes occasioned by the black cat in the pathway. The walker could return to his starting point, pause briefly, and start out again. Or, he might stop, take nine steps backward, then proceed. Those in a hurry might risk stopping, spitting on the ground, and continuing their journey.

Regardless of the color, cats could foretell weather. If the house tabby sat with its back to the wind, cold weather was on the way. If it frisked about the yard and scurried up trees, a storm was approaching. If it ate grass, rain was expected. If paper boots were tied on the cat's paws, it would dance itself to death. Childhood memory recalls that cats treated so did perform strange antics until their boots came off.

Company was expected to come from the direction in which a cat looked after it had washed its face.

This could go an endlessly. About three hundred of these cat beliefs have been collected from Illinois folklore. If one is not too busy at something better, it is amusing to catalog these and other odd beliefs, all the while remembering that many persons once firmly believed them.

❦ WITH A FEW GRAINS OF SALT

THINGS WHICH HAVE been used by people for centuries naturally have gathered much lore about them. A recent incident clearly brought this to mind.

A lady attending a semiformal dinner upset the salt shaker in front of her plate, spilling some of its contents. With a fleeting expression that looked somewhat like fear, she reached to pick up a few spilled grains. These she tossed over her left shoulder with an obvious look of satisfaction because misfortune thus was averted.

Apparently all those sitting nearby knew of the old ritual to be followed in such situations and were not at all surprised at her actions.

Responses to a casual remark by one of the diners drew comment to indicate that most of those present would have acted much the same.

As with many another superstitious practice that still is followed, no one indicated a basic belief in the salt-tossing custom. But this little incident served to turn the table chitchat to other half-forgotten signs, warnings, and proverbs about salt. Borrowing a bit of figurative speech, it could be said that the conversation became "salty."

One person wondered why the spilled salt grains should be thrown over the left shoulder. The questioning one did not know that those who began the practice long ago fully believed the devil lurked to the left and that he could be driven away with the tossed salt. Another diner, this time of Norwegian origin, assured all present that tragedy can just as well be averted by tossing the spilled grains on a hot stove. This salt belief also was a common one in New England.

It seems that once it was the general feeling that a tear of sorrow would be shed for each grain of salt spilled. Some would toss the salt over the left shoulder into the eye of the devil and cause him to shed any forthcoming tears. Others would have the hot stove dry the tears before they came.

A number of other beliefs regarding salt were brought out and reviewed. Everyone recalled a childish belief that one could capture a bird by sprinkling salt on its tail. As a five-year-old the writer emptied his mother's salt shaker in such an attempt—no bird but a stern warning. This method for taking birds has been found mentioned in writings as early as 1580. Another contributor assured all that the first thing moved into a new home should be a salt supply.

The writer remembers two competent businessmen who built a new and spacious brick store with an accompanying warehouse into which they moved the first of their stock of goods, a carload of salt. All present at the dinner had heard that it was well to give a neighbor salt, but that it was dire misfortune if one "brought home what he borrowed." One had heard that some salt should be taken along when a newborn child made its first trip out of the home.

The queer beliefs described here are only a few of those that once were current. There was the belief that salt could be used to fortell the weather; if a small mound of salt softened and melted during the night, rain could be expected. There may be something to this, for high humidity would cause the salt to absorb more atmospheric moisture.

Once it was a practice to invite one with whom a friendship would be sealed to "come take salt with me." Before the Bible was written, oaths were taken on salt. Marco Polo found the Chinese using salt for money.

The soldiers of Rome and even some of our earlier ones, like the soldiers of the American Revolution, received part of their pay in salt. From this practice comes the word salary and the still-current expression, "He is not worth his salt." The politician often is said to go up salt river when defeated. Misers are said to "salt their money down."

Some other bits of salt lore: salt and bread make cheeks red; a table without salt makes a mouth without saliva; housewives must sprinkle a bit of salt in their churns to make the butter come. There once was the belief that salt sprinkled about the house kept evil persons away. Salt sprinkled in the tracks of an undesirable departing guest would hinder his return.

There is quite a bit of diversion to be found in the mass of folklore that survives concerning salt. Much of it will be found to be of Egyptian origin and thousands of years old.

Literature of the frontier is sprinkled with references to salt and salt licks. Prices of salt in old estate settlements show that it was high in price, five bushels of salt bringing forty pounds sterling in 1787.

Some people have "salted" their money away, which is not a bad practice. Pliny, in 79 A.D., suggested that things be taken "with a grain of salt." Perhaps that is true of this salt lore.

Indians

🏵 AN ANCIENT EMBLEM

THE SWASTIKA is about as old as any emblem devised by man. It has been a prominent symbol for thousands of years and in many places over the world. It has been found in the remnants of ancient cultures on all the continents except Australia. Thus, it should not be altogether strange that this early form of the cross once more should come to notice.

This time it is being painted on walls and sidewalks in several places in Europe, and even in America. Along with it there often are anti-Semitic slogans like those which appeared during Hitler's rise.

The swastika is not a stranger in Illinois. During several hundred years—just how many no one seems to know—it has decorated Illinois rock walls and ledges at different places. Despite the fact that these markings were here long before the coming of white men, comparatively few know their location or go to look at them.

The curious can visit and see swastikas and other Indian carvings, called petroglyphs, at two reasonably convenient places. One group that includes an assortment of markings is on the bluff at the west side of Big Hill a short way north of Trestle Hollow. These carvings can be visited on foot from a turnout at the top of the west bluff. The starting place for the tramp is reached over a gravel road that begins on Route 3 about a mile south of Gorham spur. The second collection is about one-fourth mile east of Fountain Bluff, under an overhang at the north end of Big Hill. Either group can be reached with reasonable effort, and the going is not bad.

These carvings, like similar ones found at other places over America, are definitely the work of Indians. Later living Indians, however, appear about as puzzled by them as do whites and often ascribe to them mysterious origins. Many meanings have been attached to the swastika. It has been considered the emblem of the sun, of the "new fire," of the four points of the compass, of the "wheel of life," and of a prayer wheel. In other countries it was the mark of the Buddha, of Apollo, of Thor, or of Quetzalcoatl in Aztec mythology.

In China, India, Japan, and among some tribes of American Indians, where ancient religious rituals still are practiced, the swastika has a solemn meaning. Medicine men in some of our Indian tribes even yet employ the old emblem in their rites.

In shape and proportion all swastikas are much alike. They are made of right angle crosses with the ends of the arms turned. Those glorified by Hitler had the arms bent clockwise. On Big Hill they are turned counterclockwise. These turns at the end of the arms are evidently remnants of an earlier circle that enclosed the cross. Some such emblems still are found. It is related that the direction of the bend in the arms of the cross came in China a thousand years ago when they reversed the direction in which prayer wheels were rotated.

It is indeed a long way, both in time and space, from the ancient swastikas of China, India, and old Egypt to those of our "Egypt." When one goes and looks at those carved here hundreds of years ago, he wonders by what course they came out of the past to appear on the rock walls and ledges of southern Illinois.

🏵 *WHITESIDE'S STATION*

FEW MOTORISTS DRIVING over Highway 3 south of Columbia know that they pass within a stone's throw of the site where Whiteside's Station, a palisade fort, stood on the west side of the roadway and north of the branch during the War of 1812.

This defense center was on the south brow of the hill two miles south of Columbia.

It is not strange that people pass the location unnoticed. Little is left to indicate that a fort was ever there. In fact, only a shallow pit and a small pile of shaped stones that mark the spot of the powder magazine are all that was found on a recent visit. Within memory the pit was deeper, and the stones were part of a wall in the shelter of which cattle stood on wintry days.

Toward the bottom of the hill southwest from the magazine site is a flowing spring now walled by a large section of vitrified tile. This spring was the station's water supply.

There were a number of defense posts like this one in Illinois until the close of the second war with Britain. Looking carefully over the site helps one to realize that there actually was a time when settlers really needed such forts.

Fifty or more such stations appeared in southern Illinois. They were erected to guard against unfriendly Indians, then common in the region. In addition to these posts, erected primarily as defense centers, there were many log houses whose walls had loopholes that made them into family-sized forts.

The typical blockhouse was a sturdy, two-story one of heavy hewn logs closely fitted. Corners were carefully trimmed, and the outside walls were smooth so that those attacking could not climb them. The upper floor was extended about three feet on all sides beyond the lower one. Holes cut through the floor of this projection enabled those within to fire down upon any attackers who succeeded in reaching the walls below.

The upper floor walls were pierced with narrow slits or loopholes through which the defenders could see and fire upon an approaching enemy. Without cannons, which Indians never had, the advantages definitely were with the defenders. When supplied with sufficient water, food, powder, and lead, a small group could hold off a superior force armed with rifles. Women and children would help during an attack by loading and passing rifles to the men firing from the loopholes.

Sometimes a single blockhouse would be surrounded by a palisade. In other cases a rectangular stockade would have blockhouses placed at its corners. This arrangement allowed defenders to fire down the sides of the long walls. Smaller forts had two blockhouses placed at diagonal corners. The more pretentious forts had blockhouses at each of the four corners.

The stockade walls or palisades were made of upright closely fitted logs set in a ditch and having dirt tamped firmly about their bases. These walls, sometimes fifteen feet high, were pierced at regular intervals by loopholes placed high enough to prevent outsiders from seeing or firing at those inside. Near each loophole there would be a block or platform on which a defender could mount to peer out and fire upon an enemy. This same arrangement was frequent in blockhouses. The outside of these openings were not more than two or three inches wide, thus offering the smallest target for attackers. The openings widened toward the inside, thus allowing defenders to shift rifles and cover a wider range. Loopholes also provided rests for rifles and thus made aim more accurate.

Lone blockhouses or family forts could afford protection to only a small number. They did, however, offer convenient and more immediate refuge. Stockades and stations generally had wells or springs to furnish water, and sheds to hold feed for livestock. Supplied with food and sufficient ammunition, larger stations deterred any but the strongest attacking parties. Whiteside's was among the stronger defense stations in southern Illinois.

William Whiteside, who gave name to the station, had grown up on the Carolina frontier in an area of almost constant Indian conflict. After taking a prominent part in the battle against the British at King's Mountain, Whiteside moved westward and reached Illinois in 1782. He immediately became an outstanding leader against the Indians. There are many accounts of the exploits he and his sons performed over the years. The mere mention of his name strengthened the courage of settlers. It likewise aroused dread in the hearts of the Indians.

Fragments of history that linger about this fort are interesting. Numerous stories of Indian depredations and retaliations by the white settlers reveal the deadliness of the conflict.

🏵 *WAR BLUFF, AN INDIAN FORT*

ABOUT A DOZEN ruins in southern Illinois are known as Indian "forts," or "pounds." * The site of each is marked by traces and remnants of a once thick and head-high stone wall. Some of the stones in them weigh two hundred pounds or more. When it is known that much of this stone was carried from stream beds, fifty to one hundred feet below the bluff top, one realizes the great amount of labor that went into their building.

Part of these walls was hauled away by early settlers having use for the stone. Other walls have been partially dismantled, seemingly by those who only wanted to see the stones roll downhill. Even so, enough of the ruins remain to show that these walls once must have been impressive.

All viewing the ruins do not agree upon the purpose for which they were built. Some believe they were intended as places to which a tribe of Indians could retreat when enemies came to attack them. Others express a belief that they were used as enclosures or "pounds" into which deer, elk,

---

* See *Legends & Lore*, pp. 102–4.

and buffalo could be driven and held, a kind of cold storage for meat on foot. They could have served either purpose.

Perhaps the best known and most visited one of these ruins, because it can be reached conveniently, is the one in Giant City State Park at Makanda. A second one that can be seen by walking only a few yards is at Pounds Hollow, beside the marked blacktop road that leads west from Illinois Highway 1, about four miles south of the Saline River bridge. Combined with this one is a nice lake, picnic and fishing facilities, and a narrow wooded valley with precipitous walls.

About ten other "forts" have been identified in southern Illinois. Among these is one only occasionally mentioned and seldom visited. This one, about a half mile across a field from a seldom traveled but passable country road, is known as War Bluff. To those who go looking for it, it is a mile and a half due east from Raum, or rather from where Raum once was. Likewise it could be located as a mile west and one and a half miles south from the village of Lusk, only Lusk also chose to vanish. It is six and a half miles due north of Golconda.

War Bluff is about the most interesting one of its kind. Its walls, though toppled somewhat, are the best preserved, and its area is large enough to give the visitor's imagination room to function. There are fragments of records and a stock of legends, lore, and tradition to add interest.

According to traditional accounts this was a place to which the Indians retreated and were besieged by white men about 1800. According to the same story, the Indians escaped by way of a secret crevice that led downward through the rocks and out at the face of the bluff. The story relates that their escape was led by a white girl who lived with them.

War Bluff also has its "Lovers Leap" on the northwest wall, along with the traditional story. According to this bit of legend, an Indian chief forbade his daughter's marriage to the brave she loved. She and her lover sought to escape but were overtaken at the highest point of the wall. Here their final plea was rejected. Thereupon they turned, clasped hands, and leaped to their death a hundred feet below. True or untrue, as one stands and looks, it is a good story.

Then there is an account of buried treasure. According to a story told by an elderly man who grew up near the fort, a band of Indians led by a squaw came to dig for the treasured bars of gold shortly after 1900, and camped at his father's place. The map they carried showed a cave, the mouth of which had been filled. This entrance was found, cleaned out, and followed to a carving indicated on the map. Likewise, they dug through rubble-filled passages to a second marking. Here, squeezed and closed passages brought confusion. The gold bars were not found.

The Indians despaired and returned to Oklahoma, leaving any treasure still buried at War Bluff. Later visitors with divining rods have likewise failed to locate the gold. Even yet, some visitors knowing the story keep a sharp lookout for any clue that might reveal the location of the hidden bars.

A shelter cave on the west side also has its story. Once it was carefully walled and served as a home for the Sheridan family. Here their son, Thomas, was born. He later served as a county superintendent of schools and became a practicing attorney in Vienna, Johnson County.

Before leaving War Bluff the visitor should pause to look carefully at the stone ruins outside the wall. Perhaps he can decide the use to which they were put. Some have said they were granaries, others that they were sentry posts. One explains that they were advance posts for besiegers and lastly that they mark the burial place of white men killed while besieging the Indians. Perhaps you will come up with a better explanation than either of these. Anyway, put War Bluff down as a place to visit when the days are cool.

❧ THE WORLD'S LARGEST EARTHEN MEMORIAL

Monks' mound, one of a large number of earthen mounds, is in Cahokia Mounds State Park on U.S. Highway 40 west of Collinsville. It is the world's largest man-made earthen memorial and should be visited by every loyal "Egyptian." The story it suggests and partly tells is intriguing.

Centuries before the coming of the French a concentrated Indian population, estimated by some to have been as great as 150,000, lived in the vicinity. They had vanished before white men came, but not until they had built many enduring memorials—for, after all, grass-covered mounds are among the most durable of structures.

The first whites and, for that matter, all later visitors have marveled at the number and size of the mounds these early people left. In size they range from small conical structures fifty feet in diameter and about sixteen feet high, to those four hundred feet in diameter and sixty feet high.

Even larger than these is Monks' Mound—seven hundred feet wide, one thousand feet long, and one hundred feet high, and containing more than a million cubic yards of earth. One observer pondered this for a time, took out pencil and paper, and soon offered the following information: had a sturdy workman been assigned to the task and had he worked ten hours each day in the year, he could have completed this one mound in 5,989 years. If he had been given two thousand helpers, they could have carried the dirt from the nearby pits and completed the job just in time to observe Christmas of their third year—that is if there had been no coffee breaks, strikes, slowdowns, holidays, or weather hindrances. The amount of labor required to dig the necessary dirt out of the nearby pits with mussel shells for shovels and carry it to the mound site in wicker baskets taxes imagination.

Had railways then been available the task still would not have been a small one. Monks' Mound alone would have taken six thousand large cars of dirt, or approximately one hundred trainloads.

The Illinois State Historical Society first began to urge the establishment of a state park to include these mounds in 1900. For the next quarter of a century, the Society, through its Archeological Committee and in cooperation with the Cahokia Mounds Association, kept constantly working toward that objective. In 1925 the State of Illinois began to buy land for the park.

Before the state took possession, a lot of "gophering" had been done, often in a highly unscientific manner by those incompetent to understand the significance or value of their findings. Much of this skimming and spot digging really hindered the work of those more competent. In spite of all this a wealth of fine materials was obtained. A friendly museum in the park has much of it on display. The artifacts indicate that the Indians who built the mounds traded and traveled widely.

Work here pointed to other rich sources in southern Illinois. Perhaps no state in the nation provides a richer and less developed archeological field. Some small operations along the bluffs near Modoc in Randolph County in recent years have demonstrated that significant findings await those who search the promising sites near at hand.

Monks' Mound, the largest of the group, had its name from an exiled band of devout Trappist monks, led by Frs. Urbain and Joseph. They came shortly after 1800 and were given four hundred acres of land by Nicholas Jarrot, who built Jarrot's mansion in Cahokia. In spite of their utmost efforts, they were defeated by malaria and other pestilences. Their property was sold in March, 1813, and they returned to Kentucky.

Cahokia Mission, the oldest church organization in Illinois, was founded near the great mound in May, 1699. It still exists as The Church of the Holy Family at Cahokia.

At first, men were not fully agreed concerning the manner in which the mounds came to be. Some offered the generally accepted explanation that the dirt had been carried from the nearby pits in baskets or bags. Others thought that the mounds were simply portions of an earlier and higher ground that had not been washed away by floods.

Just as the Sphinx has sat brooding over the sands of Egypt for many centuries and posed The Riddle of the Sphinx, so has Monks' Mound looked over another Egypt and likewise posed questions. One standing on or by this mound can easily agree that "Out of this dumb dirt comes a greeting to the present age from a past one."

🌸 THE INSECT WAR AND SHAWNEETOWN

THE NAMES OF places and the manner in which they come by them always are interesting. In tracing backward to find how a place got its name, some interesting little story often is uncovered. An illustration occurs in the case of Shawneetown, Illinois.

It can truthfully be said that the capture of a large grasshopper by two Indian children playing in the Pennsylvania forest contributed to the naming of Shawneetown in Gallatin County, Illinois. All know that the town was named for the Indians who lived around the early trading post which white men had established there. Not many know, however, that a grasshopper started the inter-Indian conflict that caused the Shawnee to leave Pennsylvania and later to settle in the Illinois country.

When white men first came, these Indians lived in the Pennsylvania region, in territory adjoining that occupied by the Delaware. The two tribes were at peace with each other. Their warriors often hunted together and were aligned in defense against any common enemy. Squaws from both tribes joined in gathering food. Their languages were similar and they could talk readily with each other. Their children played together.

One summer day while the women of the two tribes were gathering fruit and the braves were away on a hunting expedition, a trivial incident occurred which greatly affected the history of both tribes. Two of the children, one a Shawnee and the other a Delaware, were playing together and caught a large grasshopper. Both made determined claim to the insect. The quarrel over its possession became bitter, so much so that their mothers became involved. The two contending children and their mothers were joined shortly by other squaws of their respective tribes. The grasshopper had become an important issue.

When the warriors returned from their hunting trip, they divided as their squaws had done. To the grasshopper issue they added the questions of territorial rights and tribal land boundaries. Tensions increased and a clash ensued that caused several deaths. Eventually, a full-scale conflict broke out which is referred to in Indian accounts as "The Insect War." Many were killed. The Shawnee were defeated and forced to retire westward to the valley of the Ohio, leaving the Delaware in control.

The Shawnee continued to move toward the west. Halting in various localities along the way, they left their name. It was during this slow migration that they stopped for a time in southern Illinois, fought with, and defeated the Kaskaskia in a running battle that began at Townmount church near West Frankfort and ended north of Carbondale. From Illinois they continued their halting journey to present-day Oklahoma, where survivors of the tribe now are.

Incidentally, the Delaware, though victorious over the Shawnee in Pennsylvania, fared little better. A few years later, they too were forced to follow the westward course of the Shawnee; many of them crossed Illinois. In the 1840's they were settled in Kansas where they had built dwellings and a church and were operating a ferry across the river southwest of Fort Levenworth during the Mexican War.

If the two Indian children had not captured and quarreled over a grasshopper in Pennsylvania, Shawneetown doubtlessly would have been given another name.

❧ ILLINOIS INDIANS MOVED TO KANSAS

A FEW PEOPLE facetiously say, "Give this land back to the Indians." The majority appear determined to keep it. Whatever their attitude, all southern Illinoisans are agreed that the Indians once inhabiting the region have vanished. Questions as to who they were, how many, just why and how they so quietly disappeared, and even where they went are only partially answered.

It is known that the pitiful remnants of the once powerful Illinois, that took their name from their word, "hileni," meaning a man or human being, left the state shortly after October, 1832, and settled on a reservation in northeastern Kansas where some Illinois Indians already had gone. Before leaving, however, their name had become that of the state.

In 1832 the remaining tribes of the Illinois group—Kaskasia, Peoria, Cahokia, Tamaroa, and Mitchigamie—had dwindled to a total of about sixty lodges or three hundred people. These were located on a small reservation a half mile wide and two miles long near the village of Sand Ridge in Jackson County. On October 27 of that year this group signed a treaty; that is, about a half-dozen Indians signed by mark. This treaty renounced claims to annuities and lands in Illinois. Only one small reservation of 350 acres that had been given to Ellen Ducoigne, daughter of Jean Baptiste Ducoigne, literate chief of the Kaskaskia, was reserved. This tract, shown on government land survey maps, lies in the northern edge of Jackson County.

In return for these cessions of the Indians, the national government assigned them a tract of land ten by fifteen miles, 96,000 acres, in Kansas. A small additional amount of money was given them, part of which was designated as payment for improvements the Indians had made on the lands they released.

A short time after the treaty of 1832 had been signed, the dirty, diseased, hungered, and drink-sodden group left the reservation at Sand Ridge, and started in the care of a man named Worthen for their new homes in Kansas. In Kansas the five remaining tribes of the Illinois Indians were consolidated into one tribe that took the name Peoria. By later treaties these Illinois Indians were joined with other non-Illinois tribes. In this way the Wea and Piankashaw came to be a part of the Peoria (Illinois). In a still later treaty dated February 23, 1867, the Peoria was federated with the Miami, each apparently retaining its own name.

In 1950 there were only 439 Indians that were known as Peoria, the total descendants of the old Illinois tribes plus the Wea and Piankashaw. The familiar tribal names of Kaskasia, Tamaroa, Cahokia, and Mitchigamie, along with at least five other tribes that were listed with the Illinois, were no longer used to designate living Indians. Except as they are referred to in history or have become geographical designations, the names are gone. Without doubt there is not a full-blooded Illinois Indian living today.

Before coming to live together on the Jackson County reservation, the tribes of the Illinois had lived at various places over the state and in Missouri. In 1673, when those representing the French government came to the Illinois country, the Kaskaskia were living in the vicinity of the present-day city of Peoria. The Tamaroa were on the east bank of the

Mississippi about halfway between East St. Louis and Alton. The Peoria lived on the Missouri side of the Mississippi south of Alton. The Cahokia lived in the vicinity of present-day Wood River. The Mitchigamie were much farther south, near the southern tip of the state.

At the height of their power the Illinois could muster a good two thousand braves and were a warlike people. They often fought with the Iroquois, Sioux, Sac, Fox, Shawnee, Chickasaw, and others. In these wars the Illinois sometimes met severe losses. White man's diseases and drink ravaged them. Beset by all these, their numbers steadily decreased. They were preyed upon by traders and were used by the French, English, and even Americans, to their own purposes. The Kaskaskia left their old homes on the upper Illinois on a move toward the far south but stopped near Fort de Chartres. As other Illinois tribes weakened, they likewise gathered about the fort to seek protection. In 1763, ninety years after the height of their power, they could muster much less than half their former strength. Another forty years and they could hardly muster a corporal's guard. By the mid-1830's the last pitiful remnants of the once powerful Indian tribes were gone from the Illinois country.

Their fate is little different from that of other Indian tribes of the eastern United States. The difference to us is that it happened here.

Chapter 4

Landmarks

🌀 *THE VANISHING LANDSCAPE*

A RECENT NEED for the picture of a rail fence sent the writer searching through a collection of photographic negatives to find a suitable one. A good one was finally found. It showed a section of a crumbling fence, bending over the crest of a wooded hill, on a long-abandoned farm in Hardin County. The fence had been placed there before people began to use such fences for ornament. From time to time this fence had been restored and repaired with better rails from other sections of abandoned fences. It stood apart in the lonely woodland, thus allowing any viewer to add his own memories, those needed to complete the picture he wished.

In looking for the rail fence negative, a number of other interesting ones came to light. There were those for houses and barns, smokehouses and corncribs, henhouses, a spring house, a country store, tall tobacco barns, and a blacksmith shop. There were some old schoolhouses and a log privy. Other unusual negatives showed well sweeps and wooden pumps, feed and watering troughs, mounting blocks, and fence stiles, all made of logs. Taken together, the memories they aroused created a feeling of nostalgia and left a realization that many interesting bits of an earlier landscape are gone.

The next day was spent in a long, long ride with a friend driving across the countryside, all the while looking for objects once familiar. Throughout the entire day there were no rail fences seen except two short links used as ornaments. Viewed against the background of a picture-windowed ranch house with built-in garage and television antenna, they just didn't fit.

There were no tall tobacco barns, no fences of pointed pickets, or

86

palings, with stone jars inverted over them (nice places for summer wasp nests). There were no well sweeps with dangling poles and buckets. The last of these seen, still in use, was in the Canadian province of Quebec, in 1958. Before that, it was the one doing service at Uncle Billy Gholson's, still remembered there when Bryan made his first race for the Presidency in 1896. A hooded well house and windlass, as a lawn ornament, was seen east of Mt. Vernon, Illinois, in 1935.

Another place there was an old farmhouse, little changed, which had long ricks of firewood in the backyard. There was no hopper, however, in which to store the wood ashes for soapmaking next spring. In fact, the residents did not even have a smokehouse, a potato hole, or a dinner bell in sight. As night came, no typical yellow glow from the windows told of the presence of kerosene lights.

All day long there wasn't a single top buggy or "surrey with the fringe on top." Except for one pony farm, only three horses were counted—not a single white horse appeared to be "stamped." A few loaded clotheslines were seen but no wash kettles hung on poles above outdoor fires. There was not a single yard gate kept closed by a weight made of odd iron castings or by a couple of discarded plow points or even by a stone. Since there was no gate, there naturally was no discarded length of crosscut saw, turned tooth-down, to keep the hogs from rooting the gate open.

All day long not a single haystack was seen nor the stackpoles around which they once built ricks. There was not a solitary cow wearing a poke yoke to proclaim the fact that she was breachy. No log wagon, two-wheeled cart, log sled, or even a lizard appeared during the day.

Not a house had the once familiar wooden eaves-troughs leading to the cistern with its chain pump. There was not a single threshing machine seen under a barn shed, nor a bull rake, nor a sweep rake, nor a stalk rake, nor an old-time horse-powered, hand-fed, hay baler.

Among the negatives found for buildings none was more interesting than that of the sheepcote mentioned earlier. These long, low buildings of logs were not so rare when many farmers kept sheep and grew their own wool. Sheepcotes invariably faced south, were located on a well drained spot, and were protected from the wintry winds by hills or woodland. Eight or nine feet wide, and as much as forty or sixty feet long, their roofs were sloped both ways. The eave on the open side, generally the south, was only high enough to readily admit a sheep, and was low enough to keep cattle and horses out. They could be termed specialized buildings, and afforded rather cozy shelter for the farm animals for which they were designed. Hogs pastured in the same fenced lands promptly moved in on the sheep. The last remembered sheepcote in southern Illinois was near Pomona in Jackson County about 1943.

It seems strange to speak of a vanishing landscape, but that really is what it is. Older persons will recall other vanished items that have gone so quietly that few have noted their passing.

🏵 OLD HOUSES TELL STORIES

THERE IS AN oft repeated question, "Which came first, the chicken or the egg?" A parallel question, or rather a pair of them, alike, remain unanswered in the writer's mind.

The first one is whether listening to the long-ago recitation of the "A" reading class of a crowded country school taught by a booted and horny-handed but sensitive farmer-teacher left an abiding interest in old buildings and in abandoned homesites. The second question is the first one in reverse: Was it an already acquired tendency to be interested in old places that made the poet Goldsmith's "Deserted Village" so impressive?

Whichever way it may have been, there was pleasure in hearing the older pupils intone the lines that begin with

> Near yonder copse where once the garden smiled
> And still where many a garden flower grows wild . . .

Anyway, old places charm, even though the buildings that once were there must be imagined now.

There are a number of old buildings and abandoned sites in southern Illinois that have their interesting stories. One is the Eddy residence just west of the railway and south of the Shawneetown Community High School. When built in 1828, this sturdy dwelling faced an early-day roadway, one abandoned nearly a century ago. At the time of its building the Eddy House was considered a spacious and somewhat pretentious home. Owned and lived in now by one of Mr. Eddy's descendants, it still is a sturdy, attractive, and well-kept residence, one that seems naturally to arouse the curiosity of passersby.

It may well do so, for many interesting individuals and incidents are associated with the place. First of these, naturally, is Henry Eddy, the man who built it. Born in Pittsfield, Vermont, young Eddy left school to do service in the War of 1812, in which he was wounded. Afterwards, he moved to Pittsburgh, Pennsylvania, where he studied law and learned the printer's trade.

In the late summer of 1818, Eddy entered into a partnership with Peter Kimmel, a practicing printer. With plans to establish a newspaper in

Illinois or Missouri, they purchased type, a printing press, and other necessary equipment, loaded it all on a flatboat and started down the Ohio, presumably on their way to Kaskaskia. Their boat ran aground on a sandbar at Shawneetown. While awaiting a rise in the river that would enable them to refloat their boat, they were "induced" by local business-men to land their equipment and begin publication of *The Illinois Emigrant,* the second newspaper in Illinois. This was in the autumn of 1818.

On May 25, 1820, Kimmel sold his interest in the paper to James Hall, a recent arrival at Shawneetown. Hall, like Eddy, was an attorney from the east. Within a short time he became the district attorney for Gallatin and adjoining counties. Later he became a circuit judge. Hall was an able attorney, a successful businessman, and is known as the region's most accomplished early-day writer.

Hall's writings remain among the best of those that tell the early Illinois story. Within a few years he sold his interest in the paper to Eddy, seemingly because of political differences, and moved to the new state capital at Vandalia. From there he went to Cincinnati, where he was a banker until his death in the early 1860's.

Eddy is recorded as a most competent attorney, a gracious, courteous, and dignified man, but still an active helper at log rollings, barn raisings, and husking bees. Athletically inclined, he is recorded as a good jumper. He often was referred to as a "walking library," a man who read widely and who "never forgot anything." He was an able and persuasive speaker.

Eddy was a member of the second Illinois Legislature and is recorded as the one who introduced and urged the adoption of the resolution to call a convention for the purpose of amending the Illinois constitution in order to make slavery legal in the state.

During Eddy's lifetime his home remained the center of influence in the affairs of southern Illinois and of the state. Interesting events did not end with Eddy's death in 1849. Mrs. Eddy, a daughter of John Marshall who founded the first bank in Illinois Territory in 1818, ably managed the large farm until the fall of 1861, when it became a training camp for Union troops.

Among the units that trained there was the Sixth Illinois Cavalry. This regiment, made up almost entirely of men from the southeastern counties of the state, was commanded by Benjamin Henry Grierson, a music teacher and band director from Jacksonville.

The Eddy place hints at other stories. For instance, the large boat anchor mounted on the front lawn suggests something of the one-time booming river traffic that Shawneetown knew.

🏵 *THE DEVIL'S CLAIM TO REAL ESTATE*

THE DEVIL AND his realm have received their due in Illinois place names, though it is puzzling why he should have been so honored.

Apparently his satanic majesty was popular or feared at Grand Tower in Jackson County where three spots bear his name. The first, a widely known one, is the Devil's Backbone, a rocky ridge alongside the Mississippi just north of the town. It has had that name since the earliest settlement, perhaps because Indians killed a large band of immigrants there in the 1790's.

A second place that has Satan's name attached to it is below the island known as Tower Rock near the Missouri side of the river. At some water stages there is a dangerous eddy at the lower side of this rock. Boatmen called it Devil's Whirlpool and avoided the spot, as small craft still do. Boats and canoes have foundered there.

Jutting into the Mississippi just north of the Devil's Backbone, there is a rocky hill called the Devil's Bake Oven. The shape of the hill does somewhat resemble the old-style outdoor bake oven.

About fifteen miles east of his Grand Tower claims, the devil has his name applied to a table-topped rock column in Giant City State Park. This formation, known as the Devil's Stand Table, is near the place where the roadway from Little Grassy Lake enters the park. The top of his stand table is so near the top of the cliff that those with a full measure of confidence and a reasonable amount of jump can skip across the gap and stand upon the table top. Should anyone wish to sit at the table, however, it would be necessary to bring along a stool at least fifty feet high.

Another place named for the devil is about three miles east of the park, where the dam for Devil's Kitchen Lake is being completed. The name here first was applied to a deep pool in the rocky creek bed and named Devil's Well. This pool held water during the driest of seasons and provided a dependable water supply for campers, hunters, picnickers, and farmers. Those stopping here often built fires and cooked under sheltering ledges of rock until many places were smoked black. It seems that this occasioned the name change to Devil's Kitchen.

East from Devil's Kitchen at Bell Smith Spring in Pope County one finds another object assigned to the devil. This time it is another "backbone" that lies in a fishy looking pool of the rocky creek bed about midway from the Bell Smith Spring to Natural Bridge. In this case the name is Satan's Backbone.

A strange parallel to the Devil's Well already mentioned is found in the gorge of Rock Castle Creek about three miles south of Steeleville in Randolph County. Here, there are two deep holes in the solid rock of the creek bed. One is known as Little Devil's Hole and the other as Big Devil's Hole. Each is located at the foot of a nice waterfall that dwindles during dry spells. On the mossy rocks about each of these pools, and on Lover's Rock between them, many names and initials are carved to show that romance has long blossomed in the canyon, just as the thousands of strangely colored violets now do.

Perhaps mention of two other place names with a profane tinge should be made. One of these is a narrow valley in Union County that answers to the strange name of You Be Damned Hollow. The other is Hell's Half Acre near Petrolia in Lawrence County.

Hell's Half Acre carries an interesting story. Before it was known that an oil pool lay beneath the surface, the owner of a forty-acre tract there contracted to have three brothers clear the land. They built themselves a log cabin on the half-acre corner cut off by an old winding roadway and lived in it while doing their work. Because he was pleased with the finished job and placed small value on the land, the owner gave the brothers a deed to the corner of ground where their cabin was located.

Before long Discovery Well revealed that an oil pool lay beneath the area. Wells were drilled on three tracts that adjoined the mite of ground owned by the brothers, and the law required that offset wells be drilled on their property. Before long they had three producing wells. Drillings on adjoining tracts revealed a second and deeper pool and required more offset wells on the brothers' oil field. At a still deeper level, another pool was found and more offset wells crowded themselves onto the garden-sized plot. With their many wells the brothers became wealthy.

It would be nice if one could say, "They lived happily ever after," but that wasn't true. Indiscreet sales, lavish spending, ill-advised investments, and other errors soon depleted their fortune and left them in penury. This turn of fortune may explain why it is Hell's Half Acre.

🌿 SHAWNEE NATIONAL FOREST

TRAMPING ON WINTER days through the German forests along the Rhine River almost fifty years ago with G. Don Coates was a pleasant experience. It was also a first direct contact with a large, carefully kept woodland. One could easily see that they were raising trees much as other crops are grown, and that their forests were highly regarded and properly protected.

In our country it has been very different. Here the general attitude toward the forest was fairly well summed up in a blunt statement to "log it off and get out." Considering the situation that confronted settlers here, that attitude could well be understood. To the first settlers the forests appeared inexhaustible and almost unconquerable. Across a few hundred miles and about three hundred years of time, men have literally been fighting the forest and have, piece by piece and by great effort, made parts of the forest into farmland. Some of us, youngsters then, had given our boyish efforts to the closing stages of the conflict that had left only remnants of the fine native woodlands of southern Illinois.

Eventually, however, as the trees continued to disappear at an increasing rate, thoughtful people began to voice a plea to "save the forests." The movement gained headway as tracts of timberland were set aside by the National Government and designated as forests. In October, 1933, an area of 801,944 acres was set aside in southern Illinois and named the Shawnee National Forest. Most of the lands included lie in the southeastern part of the state and in the lower counties along the Mississippi. A part of this land, 211,013 acres, was bought by the national government at an average cost of $6.48 an acre and placed under direct management of the U.S. Forest Service.

A small portion of productive and well-kept farms was included in the area of the forest. However, in general, it was a cutover, brushy, farmed out, and often badly eroded area of poor land, much of which already had been abandoned. The CWA, CCC, and other agencies operating as relief agencies during the depression years, were set to work laying out and improving roadways to make the woodlands more accessible. Precautions were taken to prevent and control forest fires. The effects of the fire control efforts are easily seen from the fact that from one thousand forest fires in 1940, the number had dwindled to twenty-two that damaged only 141 acres in 1960.

In cooperation with the State of Illinois and with progressive organizations over the nation, forest tree nurseries were established. Several tree plantations were created, and total planting had reached forty thousand acres in 1951. The next year on 383 acres about a half-million trees were planted. Thirteen thousand additional acres were scheduled for planting.

Shawnee National Forest is one of 154 national forests in the nation. Their combined area is as great as that of all France. The forest in southern Illinois is slowly but surely becoming an asset of great importance to the region. It helps to supply timber to those industries dependent upon it. To best serve that purpose the forest is operated on a continuous production basis. The aim is to have growth and timber harvesting brought into the highest attainable level of balance.

It will thus help meet local, state, and national needs for forest products, and simultaneously help to stabilize local employment. The woodland also provides for outdoor recreation and conservation of forest assets, such as land, water, fish, and wildlife.

Its use for recreational purposes is reflected by some figures for 1960. During that year, 327,140 persons were reported as visitors in Shawnee National Forests. There were 1,700 who came to camp, 50,000 others who came to hunt, and 42,500 who came to fish. Picnickers numbered over 82,000. Additional thousands came to view the interesting scenery the region offers. In the fall a long procession came to view and photograph the fine colors of the autumn woodlands.

Springs, creeks with deep pools, rocky bluffs, Indian campsites, nine natural bridges, a half-million waterfowl, elusive deer, sly wild turkey, and busy beaver are here for the patient and sharp-eyed observer. A rich plant life awaits those interested. Learned geologists and plain "rock hounds" find their rewards. Down numerous byroads one may go to view bits of a countryside that tells how people once lived.

All the while the Shawnee National Forest improves. More trees are planted in the areas owned by the government as well as on privately owned acres. Farmers who wish to make the best use of their woodland are encouraged, advised, and helped. Last year the national forests did their part toward growing enough timber to fully supply increased national demands.

Southern Illinois is fortunate in having the Shawnee National Forest so convenient for enjoyment and use. It has often been said, "You cannot have your cake and eat it too." But it looks almost as if that is being done in this case.

🌼 *NATURAL BRIDGES*

NEARLY EVERYONE has heard of the famous Natural Bridge in Virginia and of those in Utah. Not so many, however, know of such bridges in southern Illinois and comparatively few visit them.

They are fairly common in the area. The writer has visited seven—each reasonably accessible—and he has been told of another which he plans to find. All are alike in that they are stone arches that span valleys. None are so high as the one in Virginia, but two are about the same length.

Perhaps the one most widely known is in the Pomona Natural Bridge picnic area three miles west of Illinois Highway 127 and eight miles south of Murphysboro in Jackson County. A marked gravel roadway leads from the state highway through the village of Pomona to the picnic grounds.

The Pomona bridge is no puny affair. It has a span of ninety feet, approximately the same as that of the one in Virginia. The narrowest part of the Pomona bridge is nine feet and its thinnest section, near the middle, is six feet. The bed of the valley is twenty-five feet below the bottom of the bridge's symmetrical arch. Its proportions are rather pleasing. The little stream that spent a few million years washing away the rocks beneath the bridge is now only a wet-weather stream.

This bridge has been a gathering place for more than a hundred years, as shown by an 1857 date that was dimmed when the sandstone was brushed in an effort to make the carving more legible. Numerous carvings from about 1880 are on the bridge and on nearby beech trees. One visitor, J. P. Murray, was particularly ambitious on October 1, 1887, when he carved his name and the date on both the smooth bark of a beech and on the stone of the bridge.

Romance must have flourished then as now for names and initials appear in pairs. John and Ellen, last names unknown, left theirs there a lifetime ago. Sometimes these pairings are enclosed in tracings that must have been intended to represent hearts.

It is a strangely quiet place, and one can almost hear the silence—often broken by unfamiliar bird calls, a droning airplane overhead, or the rumble of a train across the hills. A few days ago the call of the crow-sized pileated woodpecker and the shrieking of a hawk high above sounded clear in the stillness.

Spring flowers, ferns, lichens, mosses, tulip trees, cedars, redbuds, pines, and fine old beech trees are nearby. Raccoon and deer tracks may be found in the soft earth a short way down the narrow valley.

As one looks at the rough bridge top, he marvels at the daring of a peg-legged man named Frank Hawk who drove his horse and buggy across it. That was before the present good-sized saplings were there to bar the way. Several people are known to have ridden horses across.

Another of the easy-to-visit bridges is on the east side of the railroad tracks behind the Christian Church at the village of Cypress, Johnson County. In one way it is the most impressive of the southern Illinois bridges. It appears so fragile that one wonders just what supports its sixty-foot span that arches thirty feet above the bed of the short valley. It is very slender, no more than two feet wide at its narrowest part, and toward one end it is only about two feet thick. The last two measurements are only estimates; the writer feared to trust himself, the arch, or the slippery rocks in order to make actual measurements. He even felt jittery when he stopped beneath the arch and looked up at it.

Yet, it must be fairly stable, for it has stood as it is now for many years, and countless boys have walked across it to show their daring. One very venturesome lad even rode a bicycle over it. Perhaps the most daring of all those boys, however, would be the one reported to have crossed on the handlebars of the cyclist mentioned.

Fifty years and more ago, the small, twenty-by-thirty-foot church and the modest dwelling just below the bridge were not there. The space they occupy was then a park where reunions, political gatherings, and Sunday school and church picnics were held, and where medicine shows set up shop.

In addition to two other stone arches near Cypress, there is also Bums Cave, an overhanging rock shelter just north of the town beside the railroad right-of-way. At this shelter, in the day of the hobo, it was not unusual to find twenty or more of that wandering gentry gathered there. Very old persons pass along some intriguing bits of information concerning them.

Either Pomona or Cypress offers a fine day's outing.

❦ *CAVE-IN-ROCK*

ALMOST EVERYONE even casually acquainted with the story of Hardin County's noted cave in Cave-in-Rock State Park feels its spell when he visits the spot. Photographers may be flashing bulbs while others clamber noisily over the rocky ledges at the sides of the cave. Groups may be chattering or shouting back and forth as they wander about. All these distractions added together hardly disturb the sphinx-like silence. Any effect they may have is fully counteracted by the occasional lonely cooing of pigeons that come to perch and bow about on the rocky ledges beneath the roof opening that is 150 feet back from the riverside entrance.

From the very first this cave has aroused the admiration, curiosity, and imagination of visitors. Though early river travelers may have heard of the cave, it seems always to have surprised those coming to it the first time. It seems also to have stirred fear in those knowing of the violence that has occurred there. From the first it has been a storied place. In

Indian tradition the cave was the dwelling place of Manitou, an Indian god.

It would be difficult to find another five-acre plot in the Midwest or, so far as that goes, in America, where a more varied or plentiful stock of stories, legends, crimes, and horror accounts are attached. Nor would it be easy to find another storied place where the natural beauty is less changed.

The rugged bluffs and hills along the river are little changed from a thousand years ago. Perhaps there is not a stretch along the river where "Beautiful Ohio" is better justified. It is true that some of the forest has been removed and has grown back a time or two.

The host of river pirates, and the flatboatmen upon whom they preyed, are gone. Likewise the robbers and the robbed, the counterfeiters, the adventurers, the murdered and those that murdered, and many an honest immigrant have passed and left no marks. That is, they left no marks unless one finds a name chiseled by one of them among those that are so plentiful on stones about the entrance. One traveler tells us that "many names" were there in 1795.

The earliest written record of the cave found is that of M. de Lery, a Frenchman, who visited it in 1729. He called it *Caverne dans le Roc* (Cave in the Rock), a name to which it still answers. Many a later traveler mentions the cave.

Before the end of the Revolutionary War, it had become widely known as an Ohio River landmark and was a stopping place for explorers, tradesmen taking cargo to New Orleans, and a rabble of those fleeing the law of the older settled regions. The cave, even then, had begun to gain notoriety and to gather legend.

In present-day parlance it might be said that the cave had its "grand opening" in 1799, that being the year in which Samuel Mason (Meason) came to establish his headquarters. By the riverside, in plain view of those floating down the Ohio toward the New Orleans' market or to find new homes, Mason erected his legendary sign, "Liquor Vault and House of Entertainment."

It immediately became a danger point, the end of the trail for uncautious travelers as well as for many a business venture. Mason, with a reputation for boldness and daring acquired in the Continental Army, soon gathered about him at the cave an assorted group of those, like himself, who had been hampered by law in the older, settled areas, and had come to operate beyond the law. Some say that this marked the beginning of organized crime, brigandage, in America.

Mason really was the first one to make the region of the Hardin

County cave a notorious one, but others who followed added to its grim story. One of the more noted of these was a man named Duff, who is named by some as the one who guided George Rogers Clark from Massac to Kaskaskia. Duff is reputed to have been the first counterfeiter to have headquarters there.

To this cave also came the Harpes, Micajah or "Big" Harpe and Wiley or "Little" Harpe, perhaps America's most notorious killers, both in terms of numbers of crimes and of their brutal executions. About the cave they disposed of a half-dozen or so victims by such methods as tying them, naked, on a blinded horse and lashing it over the high bluff. They even pushed unsuspecting persons off the cliff for no apparent reason. Their wanton cruelty soon repulsed the most hardened hangers-on, and the Harpes moved to other fields.

Mike Fink, legendary "King of the Keelboatmen," "half man and half alligator," noted rifle shot, bully, and a braggart who made great boasts and fulfilled part of them, paused at Cave-in-Rock on his journeyings.

Philip Alston from Henderson County, Kentucky, came here with his broadcloth, lacy ruffles, and bundles of counterfeit money to practice his trade. Later, he left to rob a church in Natchez and move on to Mexico where he became a governmental officer. His son, Peter, was left to carry on.

After Alston came Sturdevant, who took over the counterfeiting franchise, built a blockhouse a few miles downstream, and held sway until driven away by the Regulators—a lawless band formed ostensibly to enforce the law. The site of Ford's Ferry where the notorious Ford's Ferry Road crossed the river is clearly seen from the bluffs at the cave. At one time Ford came to live in Illinois and was overseer of the poor for Cave-in-Rock township.

Today only the natural beauty of the historic spot remains, clothed in mystery. In the hollow silence of the cave that echoes the peaceful cooing of doves, a visitor can let a vivid imagination run riot. He can dream little that will be beyond what actually happened.

🌸 LESSER BLUFFS OF LOESS

No MATTER WHAT highway one may travel, there almost always is some site or object of more than passing interest beside it. Southern Illinois highways have their full share of such places. One of these is the place where high vertical earthen walls stand alongside the newer highway between Belleville and East St. Louis.

The first section is a cut across the sloping side of a hill that leaves about a half mile of continuous high wall on the left. The other section, a short distance beyond, stands where the highway passes through another hill, leaving sheer walls on both sides. In each case, those who pause to look closely at these massive earthen cliffs up to fifty feet high wonder what keeps them from tumbling down.

Those who know tell us that these walls are of loess. It is agreed that they were formed during the period when the great ice sheets that moved over much of Illinois at different times were melting away. That was from ten thousand to twenty thousand years ago, perhaps longer. The great floods originating from the melting ice covered vast areas of the Mississippi flood plain while that stream was busy washing itself a channel through the hills toward the gulf. Water from the melting glaciers carried finely ground materials from the glaciers in suspension. This sediment settled over ground flooded by the waters.

In winter the melting of the ice became slower or ceased entirely. Drainage continued and water receded from much of the flooded land leaving its layers of sediment. The prevailing winds—and they tell us those winds were brisk—were generally from the southwest, as they are now. The winds picked up huge clouds of dust, like the dust storms that came from our droughty prairie lands a few years ago.

Evidently, the results were dust storms of great proportions. As wind moved over Illinois toward the north and east, dust was dropped as a mantle of varying thickness. In some places where the force of the wind was broken more than in others, this deposit of wind-blown dust reached a thickness of many feet. For some reason the region between Belleville and East St. Louis was a favored dumping ground. At some places in the locality mentioned, the deposit of loess reached a depth of about a hundred feet. It is a cross-section of this loess deposit that one sees beside Highway 460.

If one is interested and curious, there is a graveled drive-out and expansive shoulders where those who wish to view the walls more closely may park. Such a visit has its rewards. One first notices the strange vertical flaking of thin earth layers, sometimes more than ten feet tall. He also will see where boys have cut through the base of other flakes, evidently for the fun of seeing them tumble down.

The whole face of the bluff has such an appearance of permanence that people are tempted to carve their names. Many have yielded, and there are a number of carvings so high that one wonders how the lads did the job. Most of the carvings are initials but a few have left their full names. Tom Hulling and Larry Fairchild did so but failed to carve dates. In fact, dates are infrequent. Some initials appear old. The oldest one found was 1951, not bad when one stops to think that the carvings are in ordinary earth.

That romance was not entirely lacking is shown by several pairings of initials. Only Pearl and John, however, left their entire names.

Near the top of the higher portion of the east wall are some holes that are the nesting place of swallows. At some places where the slopes and angles invite, toe and foot notches have been cut, evidently by small boys who were scaling mountains. Some steps appear to have been made in order to carve initials higher. There are one or two sites where picnic fires evidently have been built.

Plant life is gradually taking over. Pokeweed, briar, tall grasses, wild flowers, and weeds are beginning to grow in profusion. These are not so bad since they do not obscure the face of the bluff, but forest trees, also, are beginning to appear—box elders, elms, oaks, maples, and cotton-woods. The writer hopes that these will not be allowed to grow up at the foot of the cliffs and hide the most picturesque earth bluffs in the state.

❧ EBB AND FLOW SPRING

An ebb and flow spring is rare, and thus is an attraction worth seeing, even though the visitor must walk a mile from his parked car to reach it.

One of these is low on the bank of the Ohio River between Cave-in-Rock and Elizabethtown in Hardin County, southern Illinois. In fact it is so low on the bank that it is flooded at higher stages of the river. Leonard Hall in his *Stars Upstream,* a book describing life along a Missouri river, tells us that there are only twenty-three such springs in America.

For those unacquainted with such a phenomenon, ebb and flow springs are those which have a water flow that increases and decreases, or even ceases entirely, at regular intervals. At some springs the elapsed time is several hours, sometimes a day or more. At the Hardin County spring, it is approximately seven minutes and comes with regularity, depending upon the varying rate of the spring's flow. But intermittent springs are not geysers, and their water temperature remains constant.

The visitor naturally begins to wonder when he sees the flow begin its marked decrease; it appears that he came just in time to see the spring run dry. He is even more amazed a few minutes later when a gurgling sound is heard and the water begins to gush again. According to Hall, a large spring of this type on Jack's Fork in the Missouri Ozarks has an estimated flow of a million or more gallons each day, with a time interval of about twenty-four hours. Hardin County's spring is a small one with a daily flow we would guess to be about thirty thousand gallons. One nice feature of the Hardin County spring is the fact that a visitor doesn't have to wait too long to see the cycle completed.

There is something impressive in the behavior of the little spring. It is not strange that until a generation or so ago, reports were heard of the Indians' strange belief that their Great Spirit caused the spring to act so strangely. The best explanation for the ebb and flow of these unusual springs, however, is that an enlarged section of the underground channel serves as a temporary reservoir. The outlet from this pool to the spring would be a passage arched upward and then down to form a siphon. When the water level in the storage space reaches a sufficient height, this siphon begins to operate and drains the stored water. Then the pool refills.

A visit to this Hardin County spring offers additional attractions. There are the nearby weathered bluffs and the narrow flood plain littered with fossil-bearing rock fragments. There are some small caves, about the right size for animal dens or for exploration, out of snake season, by small boys. The fringe of large cedars along the crest of the bluff is a scenic feature, especially outstanding when the woodland is bare. A short way down-river from the Ebb and Flow Spring is Tyner's Spring which has been mentioned as a landmark of the region for a century or more. Interesting ruins of the buildings erected by an early settler are nearby.

If the visitor is interested in plant life, the mile-long tramp from his car parked on the gravel road to the spring is an attractive one. On the narrow flood plain sheltered by bluffs on the north and somewhat tempered by the river on its south, the viewer finds some not too familiar plants. Spring flowers come early, and a botanist could spend pleasant hours and rest between tramps to see the spring as it figuratively shifts gear.

A variety of birds come here, and bird watchers feel rewarded for their visits.

About the only man-made noises one hears are those of passing river craft, the droning of a distant plane, or the faint sounds of a distant farm tractor. A visitor to Ebb and Flow Spring can find just about any degree of loneliness he wishes.

Those wishing to reach this out-of-the-way spot can do so by going out of Cave-in-Rock on the lower or river road leading west. Since there are no markers to show the way, it is best to drive about three miles along this gravel road and then stop to ask some old-timer or boy of the roaming age for directions. Don't give up easily; there are probably a hundred people who have lived within a few miles of it who have never seen the strange spring.

⚜ HOW BLOODY ISLAND CAME BY ITS NAME

About the year 1800 the Mississippi began to deposit a sandbar on the Illinois side, a short distance north of the site of Eads Bridge. In a few years the sandy island was covered with thickets of willow and cottonwood. Thus screened from public gaze, it became a rendezvous for those who would hold illegal boxing matches, gambling sessions, cockfights, or duels. It did very well on each score—becoming notorious for the last one named.

Since one channel of the river then flowed east of the island, there was some question about its ownership. Neither Missouri nor Illinois seemed anxious to assume responsibility for it. Perhaps this no-man's-land status made it more attractive as a "field of honor." Anyway, duelists came, and in numbers.

Most of the duels there attracted only local notice; others enjoyed national attention. One of particular note was between Thomas Hart Benton, later to become famous as United States Senator from Missouri, and Charles Lucas, U.S. Attorney for Missouri Territory. Both were able attorneys and political rivals, and both stood high in public esteem. They often were pitted against each other in court. Benton, becoming incensed at something said by Lucas in a trial, challenged him to duel. Lucas refused, contending that utterances in the practice of his profession required no answer in that manner. Benton persisted in his challenge, however, and Lucas accepted. They met on the wooded island on August 12, 1817. In this encounter Lucas was wounded in the neck and taken from the field.

According to the generally accepted code for dueling, this would have settled the affair but, strange to say, it did not. Within a short time Benton again issued a challenge, and once more Lucas accepted. Their second meeting was on September 27, just over six weeks after their first one. In this second duel, Lucas, then twenty-five years old, was mortally wounded. The later career of Benton is well known.

The island's third much publicized duel was between Thomas C.

Rector, of the surveying Rector family, and Joshua Barton, district attorney for Missouri. Barton had charged Rector's brother, William, with fraud in his work as surveyor general for Missouri, Illinois, and Arkansas. Thomas would defend his brother's reputation. The duel, fought on the afternoon of June 23, 1823, resulted in the death of Barton. The grand jury of St. Clair County indicted Rector for murder, and Governor Coles of Illinois began extradition proceedings, but nothing resulted. Thomas C. Rector was later killed in a brawl.

July 18, 1825, must have been a banner day on the island for it saw two contests. In one Colonel Parkinson was shot through the arm "by a neighbor." In the second performance two men named Mitchell and Waddel exchanged three shots before Mitchell succeeded in shooting Waddel through the body.

One of the most noted duels in the region was fought on the Missouri side of the river by Major Thomas Biddle, U.S. Army Paymaster, and Spencer Pettis, Congressman from Missouri. Biddle, as the one challenged, chose the weapons as pistols and the distance as five paces—he was nearsighted. Standing back to back at the interval agreed upon each whirled at the end of the countdown of One! Two! Three! Fire! and did so. Both were fatally wounded, but they lived long enough to forgive each other. This was on August 27, 1830.

The last duel found recorded for the vicinity was in 1856. In this bout each man fired several rounds before one succeeded in pinking the other near his left knee.

Perhaps General Robert E. Lee should be charged with the disappearance of Bloody Island. It was he, then an army lieutenant, who built jetties that diverted the current toward the Missouri shore. The channel soon silted in and the island became permanently attached to Illinois.

Today one looks down and north from the Eads Bridge upon a peaceful appearing bit of flat land with some railway tracks and warehouses where once was Bloody Island.

MACOUPIN COUNTY'S GREAT COURTHOUSE

THE COURTHOUSE AT Carlinville, in Macoupin County, has a dual attraction for visitors. The structure, itself, and the story of how it was built are equally interesting, and neither is fully understood without the other. Even when both parts of the story are told, some baffling questions remain unanswered.

It all began naturally and simply. An earlier county house that stood on the public square about a block west of the present one obviously was not adequate for the county's offices and records. Therefore, practically no opposition was offered when the county commissioners, in the spring of 1867, arranged for the building of a new courthouse to cost $50,000 and appointed a committee to carry the project through. Until this time the procedure had not been different from that followed in practically every other county in the state.

After this, however, affairs took many unusual turns. First, those entrusted with the building program decided that the original public square was not large enough for the building they proposed, and they accordingly bought the tract of land where the present building is located for about $25,000. They next accepted the sketch and preliminary plans presented by E. E. Meyer, a Philadelphia architect, and employed him for the job. According to the best information available, the architect estimated that the building would cost $150,000.

Details concerning the county capitol were kept somewhat secret. Those outside the inner circle were given no opportunity to inspect the plans, and mild rumblings were heard. When actual construction began, the public was amazed and dumbfounded to see the size of the building indicated by the foundations being laid. Highly vocal courthouse and anticourthouse parties quickly came into being.

In a short time charges and countercharges were being hurled about. Court actions, special state legislation, and political manipulations followed. Charges of collusion, graft, diversion of money and materials, and theft were plentiful. Meanwhile, friendly state legislation that allowed the committee to proceed practically as they chose enabled them to carry on with the building and to complete it in 1870.

When completed, it was far from the $50,000 structure first authorized. In fact, it was a $1,380,500 courthouse. One now looks and wonders whether the original $50,000 authorized would buy one of the eight great columns with pedestal and carving, or even the massive doors.

Completed almost ninety years ago, the Macoupin County Courthouse remains one of the most impressive buildings of its kind in the nation. Its general plan is that of a cross, much like some old cathedral. Its door and window frames are of cast iron, as are its door and window sashes. Its high arched top doors, each of which must weigh a thousand pounds, operate easily if you are in no hurry. The building is almost entirely of metal and stone. The only wooden walls are some "temporary" ones that the visitor somehow wishes had not been built.

The circuit court room with its ornate thirty-two foot ceiling is palatial. The heavy benches with their cast iron armrests are of walnut. (The writer thinks it is butternut.) The stairways with their newel posts, treads, and rails of iron, though not massive, are strong and durable. In fact, the whole building has already acquired an ageless look and appears to calmly and fearlessly face a thousand years. From the ground to the pinnacle, the building is almost two hundred feet high. Its graceful dome is visible long before one reaches the town.

The story of Macoupin County's courthouse should not end without brief mention of a day in July, 1910, when twenty thousand citizens of the county gathered to see the governor of the state burn the last outstanding bond issued to build it. This was forty-three years after the building was begun. People were happy, for the cause of a lifetime of strife was ended.

The people of Macoupin County paid a great price for their courthouse. Perhaps they didn't fare so badly after all if they consider the increased value that has come as unearned increment.

❧ *TRANSPLANTS FROM ANCIENT CHINA*

To THOSE INTERESTED in things botanical, the ancient ginkgo trees with their heart-shaped, queerly veined, silver green leaves that turn gold in the autumn, are appealing. They surely will appeal to those who drive past the residence of Mr. and Mrs. Fred Grieve at 2723 Washington Avenue in Cairo and look at the sturdy ginkgo on the back lawn of the fine old dwelling known as the Dr. Rendleman House, just across the avenue from Magnolia Manor. Both alike are show places of Cairo.

As it is remembered, these trees had been brought from China many years before by a physician returning from a visit there, and are the first ginkgos remembered in southern Illinois. Later they became quite common.

This ancient tree variety first was carried from the East to Europe in 1712, and to America much later. With so much of our land covered with an endless variety of trees, no particular need was felt for another one here. Now, with less woodland, added tree diseases, and increased insect pests, people are looking about for better shade trees. It may be that this strange tree that one botanist calls "the ugly duckling of the tree world" is a partial answer. Anyway, it is fast coming into favor with man, whose companion it has been since his appearance on earth.

In fact, the ginkgo seems to have allied itself with man at an early time, somewhat like geraniums, pigeons, rats, cats, and dogs. It appears to be highly resistant to the smoke, smog, fumes, and contaminations that man supplies.

This ancient tree now is appearing at many places over the United States, particularly in New York City and in Washington, D.C. It would be better perhaps to say that it is reappearing after an absence of a mere ten million years. About that long ago it was a common tree. Fossils, identical with today's trees, are found widely distributed over the world. At a place near Vantage, in the State of Washington, there is an extensive forest of these petrified trees, thanks to a volcanic eruption a few million years ago. It is interesting to see bits of this agatized wood, cut and polished, and to note that its grain is identical with living trees. This petrified forest in a state park near Vantage is one of the largest ones in the world.

The fruit of the ginkgo, borne on the female trees after they are about thirty feet tall, is somewhat like a plum, and has a distinctively unpleasant odor.

The Chinese like the fruit of the tree. When they are ripe, people of our nation's capital often see a tiny Chinese lady, many times a grandmother and a member of the first class of women graduating from a Chinese college, collecting fruits beneath the fertile trees. From these she removes the pulp and dries the nutlike seeds that later are roasted and eaten as a delicacy.

On a recent trip to Cairo some fine specimens were observed. A few other specimens may be seen in our "Egypt," some being on the campus of Southern and two recently planted on the lawn of the writer, who also has passed along some extra ones given him by generous donors.

🌣 FORCED TO CALL OUT, "CALF ROPE!"

I spent a strenuous day recently in and about the village of Cypress in Johnson County. That is, it was strenuous until about two o'clock in the afternoon. At that time, after painfully swallowing all pride, I uttered the defeatist call of "calf rope." As the well-informed know, it simply is a short way of saying, "You win, I give up. I've gone my limit. I can't keep it up any longer."

The admission was made on the fifty-foot-high rocky bluff that borders Snake Hole on the north side of a swampy area of several square miles southeast of the town. Despite the humiliation that came from "calf rope," the day was a treat.

Evidences remain that it was an eventful day. Among these is a left knee that flexes under protest. Also there is a swollen left eye whose lid was used by a disturbed yellow jacket for trial landing, two of them made while both my hands were very busy on a grapevine being used as an elevator to the rocky ledge just above.

Then there are briar scratches and punctures, along with minor cuts, abrasions, bumps, and bruises. In addition, there are some very muddy clothes to soak and some clay-encrusted shoes. Ralph W. Canupp, guide for the day, suffered no apparent damages beyond a very slight sag, wet feet, and a sweaty shirt. Ralph is one of the boys who roamed the Cypress countrysides some forty years ago and who still cherishes it. Given the go-ahead at the beginning of the trip, he led the way and pointed out four natural bridges, with a fifth to check. Caves—real caves—and numerous rock shelters where Indians once lived were visited.

There were a number of waterfalls, mostly the wet-weather kind, and a maze of raccoon tracks along the beds of the branches. There were signs of deer, and there were old house sites where some of the shrubs and flowers that once beautified a dooryard still grew and bloomed. Sunken and overgrown trails led through the woodlands and over the hill to the vanished homes of those who once lived "away back on the west side of that hill."

Caves, rock shelters, Indian campsites, and their carved pictures—petroglyphs—are plentiful. Those who stop to study the petroglyphs go away with many unanswered questions. Did the toes of the "wild" Indian spread as widely as the carvings would seem to indicate? Does it mean anything that the arms of their swastikas are reversed? Why the almost universal use of turkey tracks? Were the pot-like, rounded depressions found on some rock ledges used for cooking with heated stones, to pound grain, seeds, or acorns, or perhaps for all of these purposes? Those interested in the way primitive people lived can find much to ponder.

Many stories cluster about landmarks of the Cypress countryside. One of these concerns the Joe Jones place near West Eden Church. It is the story of an unsolved killing that took place there more than fifty years ago. Jones lived alone and apparently had no enemies. One day he was missing, and neighbors began to look around. They soon found his team of horses, throats cut and dead, on the hill back of his barn. After further search Jones was found a mile or so away, also dead of a slit throat.

No clues were found. Some wonder if a man who died several years later was trying to reveal the secret when he kept mumbling Jones's name as he lay dying. There are a number of somewhat similar stories scattered over southern Illinois.

Chapter 5

Travel

🌳 *A SOUTHERN ILLINOIS TOUR*

THERE IS NO QUARREL with that sage bit of advice, "See America First." To do that in any thorough manner, however, requires more time and funds than many can afford. Since one simply must go somewhere to ease that itching foot why not adapt that bit of advice to read, "First, see your own backyard."

It is not necessary to go far in southern Illinois to find places of interest. A two-hour drive often will allay the wanderlust temporarily, or perhaps, make it worse. Whichever happens, it doesn't cost much in either time or money to try it, and it can be fun. This is to suggest a few short tours in different localities to serve somewhat as trial runs.

The traveler may stop to see all the places suggested or at only those of timely interest. These tours may be taken in either direction. When desirable, one may cut across to shorten the distance and time. Since a trip must begin somewhere, the first one suggested begins at the lookout above Big Kincaid Creek about six miles west of Murphysboro on Route 13.

On this high point one stops to look toward the southwest to the nearby joining of Big Kincaid Creek and Big Muddy River. Kincaid, now a muddy, sluggish, shallow stream, once had a ferry near the site of the present bridge. In very early days flatboats were loaded at the mouth of the Kincaid. William Boon, cousin of Daniel, loaded the first one of record destined for New Orleans in December, 1811, just in time to have it on the Mississippi at the time of the New Madrid earthquake. His boat survived and successfully completed its journey.

About a half mile beyond Kincaid bridge a bronze marker on the south side of the highway points the location of another place of interest, the reservation from whence the last of the Illinois Indians left for Kansas in late 1832. If one wishes to visit the site of the reservation, he may turn on the gravel road that leads south near the end of the bridge and pass through the remnant of Sand Ridge, oldest existing town in Jackson County. There is no need, however, to look for the cotton gin, pioneer store, or tavern for they have been gone for more than a hundred years.

A mile south of the Sand Ridge Road on Highway 3 is the turn-off to Gorham and a region of great interest to both professional and amateur archeologists. It was at Twinhoefel Mound north of Gorham that Irvin Peithmann collected the first material that led to the establishment of the fact that the Hopewell Indian culture once flourished in southern Illinois.

A gravel road leads southwest from the village of Gorham to the north end of Big Hill and on to Fountain Bluff just opposite a farmhouse. Seventy years ago, this area was the best known and most visited picnic area in southern Illinois. Weekend excursion trains were often run to it.

A quarter of a mile to the west past the site of Duncan's water mill on Mill Creek slough is the place where Joseph Duncan, later to become governor of the state, lived in "The White House," that long served as an established landmark for steamboat pilots on the Mississippi. There also was a woodyard here where river craft fueled.

A fourth of a mile back east from Fountain Bluff Hollow and south across the railway tracks and at the base of the bluff is an interesting collection of Indian carvings—perhaps the best in the state. Sad to say, thoughtless visitors have marred some of them.

Back to State Route 3 and south a half mile is a dirt side road leading a short way west and up the hill to the Boone Cemetery, where Benningsen Boone (note addition of an "e" to the earlier spelling), the first white child born in Jackson County, is buried. The low wall about the family plot was built by Benningsen in his old age. He camped at the site while building the wall though his home was only a mile or so to the south.

A half mile south from the Boone Cemetery is a brook flowing from a hollow in the hills. A road leads up the hollow and across the hill to its crest beside the Mississippi. There one may park the car and walk a half mile south along the bluff to find, about halfway down its face, a second set of Indian carvings that some consider fully as interesting as the group near Fountain Bluff.

Coming back down the hill to the pavement and again going a half mile south, the visitor sees the ruins of the Henson House. Tradition which the writer is inclined to believe says that Allen Henson built his house in 1808. To anyone interested in old log houses, a visit to this silent ruin is interesting. On a recent visit a few shaped stones, some yard plants, and decaying timbers could be found.

If the driver turns west on the blacktop road that leads along the south end of Big Hill, he will pass, on the south side of the road, the place where one of Jackson County's three blockhouses stood during the War of 1812. There is no marker to indicate the spot. West from here is the site of an old shipyard that built many barges and at least one steamboat.

One of the state's large coal-fired generating plants is on the river bank near the south end of Big Hill.* Red Town, once the dwelling place of a thousand people when Grand Tower was an important river port, comes next. Only three or four of the dwellings that once sheltered a thousand or more persons still stand.

To the west and near the river there is one of the towers that carries a suspended gas pipeline across the river. The huge rock near the tower is the Devil's Bake Oven, regularly used as navigation guide for steamboats and barges. On and against this rock on its east side are the foundations of a one-time pretentious residence.

South from the Oven there is a second gap where it might be said some vertebrae have been removed. One may pass through this gap in the Devil's Backbone, the site where two furnaces of the once prosperous iron works stood. The remains of several of its coke ovens still are visible. It was at the south end of the Backbone that the greatest recorded Indian massacre in the State of Illinois took place. From this same place an excellent view may be had of Tower Rock or the Rock of the Cross, rich in history and legend.

At the south end of the village the traveler turns east at the site where the third or lower furnace had been when Grand Tower was an iron producing town. It is somewhat painful to see the evidences of a decaying town as one returns to Route 3. Soon he reaches the Big Muddy River at the place where a locomotive fell through the railway bridge and carried its crew to death in the river. After crossing the bridge one may look east and have a wonderful view of the Pine Hills bluff, about three hundred feet high. The road to the right follows along the foot of a three mile long cliff where early spring flowers bloom in season.

---

* See *Legends & Lore*, pp. 313–16.

The journey has only begun. A later drive will take us along that bluff and over Pine Hills.

🏵 *THE VANISHED INTERURBAN*

A PHOTOGRAPH of a horse-drawn Murphysboro streetcar, used before electricity became the motive power, revived old memories recently and suggested a story.

"Ghost tracks" of these cars, made up of sections of railway fills and cuts, are found between Carbondale and Murphysboro, and at a half-dozen other spots in this region. These "ghost tracks" are also seen in sections of pavement which were repaired after abandoned trolley lines were removed. Similar signs are in evidence in the village of Dorris-ville, lying just south of Harrisburg. The patterns left by the pavement repairs still show the location of the erstwhile lines. More such scars and marks appear in the Wamac-Centralia region and in Jonesboro. Additional similar marking may be observed in the Marion-Herrin-Energy-Carterville section where hundreds of miners once rode to their work at the mines.

Excerpts from the Murphysboro trolley rule book prescribed speed limits and set forth rules for the drivers. For instance, the driver was required to collect fares before starting the car into motion. He was admonished not to stop so abruptly nor to start so suddenly as to throw standing passengers about.

There were some half-dozen interurban lines in southern Illinois. Properly named interurban, they were more often referred to as street-cars even when grinding along miles from town. Apparently the first such line, outside those centering in the East St. Louis vicinity, was the one built by the Coal Belt Electric Company, which connected Marion and Herrin and had a branch line from Energy to Carterville. This line opened for business on July 1, 1902. The main line was eight miles long. The Coal Belt carried considerable freight at one time but discontinued this part of its business in 1914. All traffic was discontinued in 1926. After the line was abandoned, some parts of the tracks were used by a steam railway.

A second line, and one of the shortest intercity lines in the state, was that of the Fruit Growers' Refrigeration and Power Company from Anna to Jonesboro. It began at Anna State Hospital and led through the town to Jonesboro. Completed in early 1907, it operated until 1925 when a bus line replaced it. A section of its track remains in use by the Illinois

Central to deliver freight to the state hospital. The cars of this line, supported on four-wheeled trucks near the car's center, furnished a dipping sway in sensation not readily forgotten.

The line at Murphysboro was a venture of the Murphysboro Electric Railway and Light Company. At first, it was a three-mile operation within Murphysboro, but a short time later the system was expanded by private enterprise to Carbondale. This Carbondale line operated until January 26, 1927, when the last car carrying passengers made its trip over the route. Like the others it had become a casualty of the automobile.

The interurban at Cairo was started in 1910. It certainly began with a big name, being called the Cairo-St. Louis Interurban. It operated much of its way over the tracks of steam roads, using those of its own construction only over the streets of Cairo, Mound City, and Mounds. This line was completed in 1919 and abandoned in 1931.

The Eldorado-Carrier Mills venture of the Southern Illinois Railway and Power Company was a fifteen-mile line which passed through Harrisburg where its central offices were located. One of the later roads built was completed in 1913. Its last run was made twenty years later in 1933. Numerous persons who rode it on its first trip also made the last one, out of sentiment. At one time it hauled a considerable amount of freight and enjoyed a good passenger business.

It has not been learned just when the Centralia-Central City line began nor when it finally ceased to operate. It is known that it first began as a line from Centralia to Central City, but, a short time later, the Centralia Traction Company laid an extension south to Wamac.

In addition to those listed above there were several in the East St. Louis area. One of these extended as far south as Waterloo in Monroe County. It discontinued passenger traffic on June 1, 1932, and freight hauling in 1936.

These interurbans came into being at a time when they were much needed. For a short while, they gave promise. Automobiles and hard roads were at hand, however, and spelled doom for the interurbans. Yet, many oldsters will recall with pleasure the grinding, swaying rides they provided.

🌸 *ABOUT LIZARDS*

A woman recently boasted that she had used many means of transportation. The list she gave extended from airplanes to yachts and included camels, elephants, and a water buffalo. She seemed perplexed, however, when asked if she had ever ridden a lizard. Being assured that the question was asked seriously and that it didn't apply to the smallish reptile that darts about fences and stone piles, she asked for an explanation.

The lizard in this case was a transportation device, once in frequent use. Now lizards seem to have scurried away like the little animal for which they were named. They have gone, along with the work in which they were much used, "snaking out" logs.

The last one of our acquaintance was made from the fork of a sturdy hickory tree. It was found in a deserted Jackson County barn in 1944. Its nose, that part extending beyond the fork, had been smoothed and shaped from the main body of the tree. The diagonal runners were the two main limbs of the tree, shaped and smoothed. All in all, it was a very simple device made of just two pieces, the crotch of a tree and one crosspiece. It was particularly well adapted for use over snowy, icy, and slushy grounds and among stumps. It required no prepared roadway.

With the front end of the log chained on top of the crosspiece and the other end trailing, a team of horses or oxen could easily move large and long logs. This was a favorite way to bring in logs to be cut to size on the woodyard for fireplace and stove wood. With the easy to load and use lizard, no hickory near a home suitable for firewood could feel secure—likewise the sweet gums and maples, favorites for cook stoves. These could be sawed or chopped to length on the woodyard, split and corded, or piled to season, all this during idle hours. Farmers jokingly said that firewood warmed them twice, once as they cut it and next as they burned it. A farmer following this practice could soon gather a winter's supply of fuel on his woodyard.

When the roads became snowy and icy a farmer with a low box mounted on a lizard might take the family visiting or to town. Seated on straw or hay and wrapped in blankets they were cozy. It was fun to ride on one of these contrivances and feel the repeated sharp slitherings. Only the driver, with feet planted wide apart and steadied by his hold on the check-lines, dared try standing. Nevertheless, venturesome boys sometimes did so. A lizard could be fun.

Another device somewhat like the lizard was called a mudboat. It was nothing more than the New England stoneboat brought west. It also was at its best during snowy and icy times and was well adapted to swampy and marshy grounds. This boat was made of two heavy crosspieces, often eight by eight inches, and was bottomed by wide two-inch boards or puncheons fastened on by large wooden pegs.

No mudboat has been seen since Mr. Pemberton used one to haul logs to the neighborhood sawmill in 1905.

Another transportation device was the old-time two-wheeled log cart, sometimes having wheels ten feet high. The butt end of a long log could be suspended at the front end beneath the axle and dragged to the railway or rafting yard beside the river. Similar carts with lower wheels had racks built on them for hauling hay, wood, or farm products. The last two-wheeled hay cart remembered was on an English farm between Kenilworth and Stratford-on-Avon. It was part of an animated but awkward runaway. There was no damage beyond some bounced-off heaps of hay to reload.

Every farmer needed a sled or two, for it is doubtful if anything ever has been so well adapted to hauling the common shuck fodder from shocks in the field to the feed lot. Better sleds were made from curved log runners. Others had runners made from two by eights or puncheons. With an attached box and standards fitted to its sides the sled served many purposes.

Sleds also made platforms just the right height against which to incline the scalding barrel at hog-killing time. When wells went dry, sleds were used to haul barrels of water from creeks and ponds to fenced livestock and for tubs on washday. All this was B.T.T. (before trucks and tractors).

A SURREY WITH THE FRINGE ON TOP

A NOTED MUSICAL play, "Oklahoma," was staged in 1942. One of its song hits, "The Surrey With the Fringe on Top," remains popular and is heard on occasion. The other day we listened to a recording of it. The next day a photograph of a real "surrey with the fringe on top" made in Nashville, Illinois, came to hand. The combined effect was to turn thoughts to that once common vehicle that plied pre-automobile roads in southern Illinois. Now, excepting an occasional glimpse of one in some Amish settlement over the country or at some pioneer re-enactment, they are gone. Along with the surrey went its vehicular cousins, the carts and buggies, all to become a part of our vanished landscape.

This disappearance came about so slowly and quietly that few took note of it. People simply looked about one morning and none were to be seen, not even under the few tumbled-down buggy sheds or in surviving carriage houses. Also, there were no longer any livery stables where one could find an array of them for rental purposes. Once there were literally thousands of livery stables. Today, it is doubtful if one survives in all

America. The horse and buggy days definitely are gone. To older persons they remain a one-time institution.

Buggies were considered a necessity as well as a status symbol. Many a young man was proud of his first buggy, and, incidentally, of later ones. Today, an automobile often is thought of as an evidence of accomplishment. Many a high school boy thinks it lifts him from mediocrity and makes him a social asset. Buggies once did that.

A trim, cut-under runabout, neatly striped, moved its owner several rungs up the social ladder. Rubber tires increased the elevation. A buggy with a narrower bed than usual could be counted to add somewhat.

A slender, wrapped, flexible rattan whip with colored bands and a brilliant tassel increased the owner's pride. In summer a flowered linen laprobe was favored. In winter it was a heavy carpet-like one with the figure of an owl, dog, or tiger with great glass eyes. Many owners prized their whips and laprobes so highly that they carried them into church, lest some envious culprit steal them.

There were other trappings to a nice rig. Harness came in for special attention. A narrow collar and thin hames were standard equipment. There always was the blind bridle, apparently designed to prevent any inquisitive horse from spying on the passengers. There was the check or gag rein that held the horse's head cruelly high.

Those wishing to be more fastidious, particularly when roads were not too muddy, used breast harness. In such cases there were no collars and hames. The horse drew the buggy by a broad strap across his breast. Buggy bridles often were highly decorated.

In winter many a considerate driver carried along a blanket to spread over the horse at the end of a brisk drive.

In summer the horse might wear a fly net that even included tasseled ear covers. The mane, foretop, fetlocks, and hairy ears were trimmed to the owner's fancy. Hoofs were carefully trimmed, shod, cleaned, and then greased with wool fat to make them shine.

Names of the buggies once on sale will arouse memories among those older. Some were the Moon, Hudson, Studebaker, and Dexter. Of course there were the aristocrats among buggies, the Brewsters, that sold for as much as $2,500. At one time a serviceable Studebaker could be bought for $89.50 plus another $12.50 for harness. (The name plate off mine is among my souvenirs.)

So far as has been learned there is only one factory still making buggies in America. This one is at Lawrenceburg, Indiana. With its diminished force of aging workmen it turns out about three hundred vehicles a year. All are custom-made; when an order is received the buggy is assembled. There surely are other factories, like perhaps in Amish Pennsylvania.

The standard size of a buggy bed was twenty-three by fifty-six inches. Each had its shiny patent leather dash and whip socket. Accidents naturally occurred and some local blacksmiths became widely known for their skill in making repairs.

In southern Illinois, about 1910, it was said that a factory at Metropolis in Massac County bent more wooden bows for buggy tops than any other place in the world.

🏵 *SOUTHERN ILLINOIS TOUR CONTINUED*

For those who would like "to get away from it all" for an afternoon, or even a whole day, a drive over the gravel roads through the Pine Hill section of Shawnee National Forest is a suggestion. This drive is chosen because of its short length and varied attractions. There is something alongside these few miles of forest roadway to interest each visitor. And too, this is the longest bit of road yet found in southern Illinois where there is not a dwelling or even a rural mailbox to be seen.

This thirteen-mile stretch of road begins when the traveler crosses the railway after turning east of Illinois Highway 3 south of Grand Tower and two miles beyond the bridge over Big Muddy River.

At its beginning a good road passes through a swamp with many strange varieties of plants. Then it turns north beside bluffs some three hundred feet high on one side and swampland on the other.

In the small valleys indenting the face of bluffs about all species of trees native to this end of the state can be found. In season, rare woodland shrubs and plants are to be found in bloom.

The swamp across the roadway from the bluffs is several hundred acres in extent, mostly resulting from the efforts of a colony of beaver that moved in many years ago. Their dam on the west side of the roadway about two miles after crossing the two railways has been there so long and appears so natural that one must look carefully to find it.

A venturesome person who goes a short way along the path on top of the dam, and doesn't fall off, will realize the great amount of work and careful engineering done by this colony of "eager beavers." Careful observation from the dam when foliage is not too dense will reveal some of their huts. The very fortunate and quiet visitor may see one of the inhabitants gliding rapidly and silently through the water. A great spring, choked with water plants, comes from beneath the bluff about a half mile north of the dam and keeps the pond filled. An observer soon is convinced beavers are clever hydraulic engineers.

Parts of building foundations along the bluff side of the roadway and a cemetery in the forest tell that people once lived there. After about two and a half miles of gentle uphill-downhill driving along the bluff from Elm Spring at its south end, the visitor comes to another picnic site at Winter's Pond, where there are countless golden-centered white water lilies. This also must be a great fishing area, if one may judge from the number of fishermen he sees. No statistics concerning fish caught are available.

A roadway atop the Big Muddy River levee leading west from the base of the bluff near Winter's Pond goes back to Highway 3. Those who take it, however, fail to see much of the best that Pine Hills has to offer. It is better to continue and turn to the right toward McCann's Spring Picnic Ground and over a fine example of a hairpin curve to Inspiration Point, about a mile beyond McCann's picnic tables. It is another picnic site. In fact, cooking facilities, picnic tables, waste cans, and toilets are at a half-dozen additional picnic sites along the way. They are presently clean and well kept. The roadway leads onward along the hill crests and "hogbacks" to the south end of the ridge where one finds an east-west gravel road and a farmhouse.

It now has been thirteen miles since the last farmhouse was passed. One has traveled up and downhill all the way through an unbroken forest.

The visitor who hurries past the many picnic areas on the hilltops and jutting bluffs without stopping for a leisurely look misses much. At almost every picnic ground a fine and changed view is to be had, often over many miles. In autumn the range of colors is wonderful and the soft green of spring is not for sneering. As one nears the south end on the hill range he passes the Natural Wildlife Refuge, fenced and set aside as a study area for Southern Illinois University.

Those who are tired here may turn to the right and soon be back on Highway 3. It is better to take the left turn and go about three miles to the concrete bridge over Clear Creek, a stream that is said by those in the know to have real lunkers in it. The gravel road on the west side of Clear Creek leads past wonderful corn and soya bean fields and to another bridge that crosses the creek at Dug Hollow, very near the place where the Cherokee Indians camped and died by hundreds on their forced march from their reservation in the Great Smokies to Oklahoma during the winter of 1838–1839. A short way east of the creek on Highway 146 is a bronze plaque which marks this as a place on the Trail of Tears.

Illinois Highway 146 may be taken west from here to Route 3, but one really shouldn't. Those wishing to continue their journey and return to Route 3 can do so by taking the gravel road leading south from the west end of the bridge. This goes through the Union County Game Refuge. In summer, it will be through great fields of corn, soya beans, barley, wheat, and ladino clover. It is not permissible to sell the grain grown on the refuge, hence it is fed to the waterfowl that gather there in the winter.

In season one may see a hundred thousand wild geese and ducks feeding. Since geese and ducks do not like to eat from piles of grain, their feed is scattered over the fields by using power spreaders. As many as fifteen thousand people have passed over this gravel road during the goose and duck season to see what is literally fields of waterfowl.

When one reaches the woodland near the south end of the refuge, it is not unusual to see young raccoons feeding or playing along the roadway. On the latest trip through this woodland, three baby raccoons and one large and very dark mink were seen.

The gravel road leads onward to Illinois Highway 3. When the distance traveled after leaving the highway south of Big Muddy bridge is totaled, the driver finds he has gone about twenty-five miles.

For those continuing on Route 146 to Jonesboro, there is a bronze marker on the town square that tells of the Lincoln-Douglas debate in 1858 held at the old fairgrounds a half mile north. A lettered stone at the site marks the actual location of the platform they used.

Leaving the site of the debate, the journey continues toward Anna along the street leading past the D. L. Phillips home where Lincoln was a guest. A return is made to Highway 146 near the building that once housed Union Academy, alma mater of Frank Willard, one of America's noted cartoonists and creator of Barney Google. The Anna-Jonesboro High School grounds now include those of the old Academy. These grounds have one of the state's most varied plantings of forest trees in the region. The Union County Hospital grounds adjoin those of the high school.

A short way beyond there is the small but attractive Episcopal chapel with its oversize bell on a support beside the doorway. Nearby is the Anna Public Library, one of the most unusual specimens of architecture in southern Illinois. Plans for this building, whose style is much like that of the Australian capitol at Canberra, were drawn by one of Frank Lloyd Wright's students and reflect the style of that great architect.

A block east of the place where a turn is made north onto Route 51, the Anna Post Office stands on the site where the Kirkpatrick brothers had their pottery, the most noted one that southern Illinois has known. Their products now are collectors' items. They also made millions of the small clay pipes once so widely used. One contract with the Bureau of Indian Affairs called for two million for issue to reservation Indians.

The route north from Anna leads through a great peach growing region. If the journey is made during the blooming season, a picture of the pink hills will provide a pleasant memory. The town of Cobden, five miles north of Anna, is interesting as the place from which the first shipment of fruit under refrigeration was made. Cobden also, for many years, was the largest tomato shipping point in America. The town, first named South Pass, came by its present name when Sir Richard Cobden, the English capitalist who helped greatly in raising funds for the building of the Illinois Central Railroad, visited there.

About five miles north of Cobden, where a paved highway leads east to Giant City State Park, is the site of another pottery, that of John Queen. When compared with the Kirkpatrick pottery, the small one of John Queen was a crude one. At the point where the Giant City road leaves Highway 51 is the well preserved, attractive, and tastefully furnished Wiley-Rosson home, the older portion being built of logs in 1828. So far as has been learned, this is the oldest dwelling still standing in Union County.

Giant City State Park, with its deer pens, Indian fort, attractive lodge, and its "Giant City" with interesting legends, is worth a careful pause or an overnight stay in one of the cabins on the park's highest hill.

Continuing north to Carbondale, the traveler passes Southern Illinois University where he should stop to visit when time allows. A mile north of the University is the crossing of Highways 51 and 13. Three blocks east of the crossing is Woodlawn Cemetery where the first organized community-wide observance of a Memorial Day, which returned veterans directed and in which they participated, was held in 1866.

West out of Carbondale on Highway 13 is the school building, now used as a church, that became the first rural practice school in Illinois. The first (1810) shipping coal mine in Illinois was at the river bank just south of the point where old Highway 13 crosses the Big Muddy at Murphysboro. John A. Logan's birthplace is south of the railway station, a few blocks west of the public square. Three miles west from Murphysboro, near where one sees a row of charcoal ovens, is the site of vanished Brownsville, first county seat of Jackson County and an important town when Illinois became a state. About the only visible evidences of the town remaining are a few wells, some bits of rubble at deserted homesites, and the abandoned cemetery on the top of a nearby hill. No grave marker has been found there bearing a date later than 1846. Don't expect to see the salt works. They have been gone about 150 years.

West of the charcoal ovens on Highway 13 is Kincaid Lookout, where the tour began and now ends.

❧ *GOING DOWN TO CAIRO*

SOMEONE ANSWERED in a singsong voice, "We're going down to Cairo." That started it.

The first geographical notion most of us entertained before going to school was that north was "up" and south was "down." Didn't people go "up to McLeansboro" or "down to Eldorado?" These were the north and south limits of the world that childhood knew.

Then we began a formal education in a one-room school taught at Hardscrabble by Aaron Miller. It quickly became a practice to listen in on the recitations of advanced pupils. In fact, that was the principal method by which a meager stock of information was acquired. This apparently rapt listening received the approval and encouragement of Mr. Miller. By listening, it was learned that north generally was up and south down on the mysterious wall maps.

Mr. Miller combined the growing of fruit trees with teaching. A graduate of Oberlin College in Ohio, he remains distinctive among a host of teachers. In addition to other unusual practices, he encouraged and directed folk dances on hard-packed plots of the school ground and the six-foot long bridge across Duck River.

Among the songs and games popular then were "Little Brown Jug," "Molly Brooks," "Pig in the Parlor," and the ever-remembered one, "Going Down to Cairo." The last name left a store of memories. The manner in which the dancers walked, waltzed, stamped, shuffled, skipped, and tripped about in bewildering patterns confused a small boy; they still do. Through it all the dancers loudly declared, "We're going down to Cairo."

It was not until he was grown-up, however, that the listening tike really went to Cairo. There were wagon ferries to the Kentucky and Missouri shore and a railroad ferry to Bird's Point in Missouri. There were no bridges. Great river steamboats, both side and stern-wheel, were tied to the wharfboats. Skiffs, catboats, and dugouts dotted the banks. The railway stations were crowded with passengers; the platforms were piled with freight and luggage. Large one-horse, two-wheel drays clattered along the streets.

The doors of the Blue Front Restaurant were open day and night just as they had been since the owner first unlocked them years earlier and ceremoniously flung his keys far into the river. Not in more than forty years were the doors ever locked. Other places made similar boasts for there were no closing hours.

The storied Halliday House, that was the St. Charles of Civil War days, still was a deluxe hotel, a great river hostelry of the steamboats' heyday. A fire twenty years ago left only a wing whose stark walls now serve as a billboard, a sad reminder of its one-time glory. Other well-known hotels, banks, stores, office buildings, business places, and several noted saloons stretched along Ohio Street, one of the most widely known avenues of commerce in America.

An observant visitor to Cairo now still finds landmarks of Civil War days standing to tell their story. First among these, perhaps, is Magnolia Manor, built by Charles A. Galiger in 1859 and now a house museum. It is interesting for its architectural features, its thick walls, fine stairway, and frescos.

General Grant visited here when he was stationed at Cairo in the earlier years of the war. When he returned from a trip around the world after being president and came to visit the scenes where his rise to military fame began, he was once more entertained here.

The pretentious residence at 2723 Washington, diagonally across from Magnolia Manor, was built by Captain William P. Halliday in 1865. Its fine magnolias are impressive. It is widely known as the Dr. Rendleman House, after a physician who lived there many years. A small theatre on the third floor was used to stage dramatics by Dr. Rendleman's daughter who later appeared on Broadway.

A house at 604 Twenty-eighth Street, built in 1858, is called the Magnolia because of the fine trees that grow about it. Another, at 703 Walnut Street, is the place where Maud Rittenhouse, an animated young lady, lived and kept a dairy which was written into a best seller in 1939.

"Going Down to Cairo," in fact or in memory, remains an entertaining experience.

❧ ON THE WAY TO OLD SHAWNEETOWN

A LIST OF the points of interest in the Shawneetown vicinity would be a long one. Hence only a partial listing of places reasonably convenient to visit is given and very briefly told about. Because visitors will come by many routes, just as they have done since the town began, no effort will be made to list places in any ordered location of significance.

Since a listing must begin somewhere, this one begins at Nigger Spring, located between the gravel roadway and the Saline River about a half mile west from Route 13 where it crosses the river bridge. At higher river stages its waters cover the spring. At other times it is seen flowing from a silt-filled pool walled with heavy oaken timbers that have been there more than a hundred years. Indians made salt in their earthen pots long before the coming of white men. Stones scorched in Indian campfires, their own bones and those of the animals they used for food, stone implements, broken bits of clay, and shell pots are mixed with ashes and other debris on the slight rises of ground about the spring. In some places these are eight feet deep. It would be interesting to know how many centuries salt making was carried on at the old spring that Andrew Jackson once sought to buy, the one that John Crenshaw, builder of the imposing home on the high hill north of the Saline, last operated.

It was from this spring that the white man's crude pumps forced the brine through pipes made of bored logs to boiling kettles nearer the woodlands that naturally had receded as they were cut away for fuel to fire rows of kettles. Many Negro slaves, rented from their owners in Missouri and Kentucky, were held prisoners and worked here. Some of these were confined in the tiny rooms just under the roof of the Crenshaw residence, widely known as The Old Slave House. According to tradition, the essence of which appears true, those using slaves at the salt works were very harsh and heartless masters. At very best, the lot of the bound black man was a dreadful one. It undoubtedly was all that the expression "back to the salt mine" might imply. Conditions similar to those at Nigger Spring were repeated on a larger scale at Great Half Moon Lick two miles west of Equality.

Much of the Midwest's supply of salt came from these springs, known as the Gallatin Salines. The writer, then a boy of twelve, remembers hearing an old man past ninety years old tell of coming to Equality when a boy and carrying salt back on a packmule to his home in mid-Tennessee. Only fragments lie about now to indicate past importance. Nigger Spring has been abandoned for over a century and Half Moon Lick for more than ninety years.

Those who are hardy and venturesome may go downstream from the highway bridge and visit some rock shelters, called caves, near the riffle in the river. One stock of legend has a noted brigand, John Duff, buried here near his stock of looted gold. Somehow, John forgot to properly mark the location of his buried treasure and left no map.

Those not interested in salt, slaves, or buried treasure can go hunting for mastodon bones in the drainage ditch near the town of Cypress. This is done by probing in the bottom of the ditch with a slender sharpened steel rod until a bone is found and then digging it out. Hundreds of specimens have been gathered in this manner. Failing bones or buried treasure one can drive on toward Shawneetown.

As the age of towns is reckoned, the newer Shawneetown is new indeed. Very few of the buildings generally considered of historical significance in the earlier town were moved intact to the new town. History of the old town came in the form of documents, household furnishings, and assorted artifacts. The most readily seen of these and the ones of enduring value are the county records. These early records are of great interest to those who would know the history of the region. No visitor should leave the courthouse without a long look at the mural, which is on a plaster wall sized with sorghum, in the circuit court room. It highlights much of the locality's history. One wonders if the bell from the old courthouse still rings the opening of court in the new one.

The nice home just south of town and west of the railroad was built by Henry Eddy, early newspaper editor, businessman, attorney, politician, and a man of great influence in the affairs of the early state. It was at this place that a noted cavalry regiment of the Civil War headquartered and trained.

Going west from either the old or new town over gravel roads that merge and continue along the south side of Gold Hill the traveler soon reaches the site of vanished Bowlesville. Only one of its abandoned buildings survives. It once was the hotel, later becoming a farmhouse. Its deeply worn treads and worn handrail lead upstairs to the hotel rooms that still have their numbers above them. The guests have been gone for almost a hundred years. The farm family is gone and the house is falling down.

It was in the Bowlesville schoolhouse that Robert G. Ingersoll is said to have made his first political speech. Two or three other fallen buildings are all that remain of Bowlesville's Log Row and Box Row. Saline Mines, a short way to the west, likewise is no more. These places supplied much of the coal for the United States Naval Yards at Mound City and Cairo and for the Union gunboats on the Western Waters during the Civil War.

The visitors have now reached Old Shawneetown.

Some of the old buildings and sites will be mentioned. The first of these, and the most striking of them all, is on the left of the highway where Route 13 reaches the principal street of the town. This is known as the State Bank Building, placed there in 1837–1839 at a cost of $86,000.

(About forty years later it sold for $6,500.) When completed, it was among the most noted buildings along the Ohio. To those acquainted with good architecture, it is still an impressive and admired building. With its great spread of steps and the massive Doric columns that front it, it is a building of distinction. The five fine columns at its front, made from stone quarried in Pennsylvania and floated to the site on river barges, are adjudged by those competent to do so as among the very best of their kind in America.

The First Bank established here operated for a number of years. After that other banks used the building; the last one left twenty-five or more years ago. Since then it has served various minor purposes, all the while taking on an added look of neglect. Two or three years ago the State of Illinois began a restoration of the noted landmark. It is hoped that this work will be completed and that the restoration will reflect some of its glory of 130 years ago.

About two hundred yards down-river from the State Bank Building is the brick residence that housed the first bank in Illinois Territory. This building was the home of John Marshall, early prominent businessman. He established a bank in one of the rooms of his dwelling after securing a charter for it in December, 1816. The vault he used was made of heavy oak, thickly studded with iron spikes. This strange bank vault now is in the museum of the Chicago Historical Society.

There are numerous other buildings that have historic associations. One of these is the squat brick Methodist Church with its quaint belfry. Built in 1842 the church is well kept, but looks its age. One obvious change shows that the two original front doors have been bricked up, and a center one made. (Someone evidently forgot to tell them that ill fortune could be expected if old doorways were bricked up.) The name of Peter Cartwright is closely associated with the earlier years of the church. Beside the Methodist Church is the residence built by Stephen Rowan in 1830. This building is well preserved and has that calm look that time alone seems able to give. Tradition relates that Abraham Lincoln stopped here on a visit to Shawneetown.

The Posey Building, erected by the sons of General Thomas Posey, stood until recently on the west side of Highway 13, across from the State Bank Building. The last parts of the building remaining are the stone steps that were at the front entrance. They are deeply, very deeply, worn by the tread of those who used them for 125 years. It was in this building that Robert G. Ingersoll, the great agnostic, studied law. John A. Logan had an office here when he was district attorney. Others of note had offices in the building. A book could be written about the Posey Building.

Beside the river and directly in front of the State Bank is the site of the Riverside Hotel, one of the most noted of river hotels during the heyday of steamboating. It sheltered many a noted guest.

One of the most noted ferries across the Ohio operated at Shawneetown for about 150 years, ceasing only when the bridge was completed. At the height of steamboating, Shawneetown was a busy river port, and many a craft tied up at its wharf. Today a few floating fish markets that sell good river fish are seen where packets once stopped.

Almost from its beginning floods have menaced the town. In 1937 a record one caused the removal of most of the town to the hills three miles north of the river. The old and new sections of the town remained connected by a strip of ground thirty feet wide until 1956 when they were separated and became two towns. When Old Shawneetown again became a separate village, it was both the oldest and newest incorporated town in Illinois.

Until a few years ago the battle flag carried by General Posey's troops at the storming of Stony Point was in Shawneetown. It now is in Tulsa, Oklahoma.

The altar in the Catholic Church is of interest. Before being brought to Shawneetown, it was used in the monastery at Wetaug. Before that, it was in an abbey in Europe.

When Lafayette came to visit America fifty years after he had served in the forces that won freedom for the new nation, he stopped at Shawneetown and passed along the calico path strewn with flowers from the steamer to the Rawlings House where the grand reception was held. This event was re-enacted on the hundredth anniversary in 1925. A great-grandson of the 1825 mayor was mayor in 1925.

❦ PROWLING ABOUT OLD CEMETERIES

THE WRITER, WHO FEELS that it does not indicate a morbid interest, likes to stroll about old burying grounds. Almost any one of them will suggest a story or two of human interest. During recent wanderings stops were made at each of four early southern Illinois cemeteries.

Following the habit of stopping to look, a halt was made at the site where an early Primitive Baptist Church stood on Sugar Camp Creek on the blacktop road about three miles east of Ewing in Franklin County. A low, square, sandstone marker at the grave of Lazarus Webb, who died in 1833, tells its story. The man it memorializes settled near the cemetery in 1812 and built the first house on the prairie afterwards named for him. Lazarus, born in Virginia in 1774, had come to Illinois by way of Kentucky where he had remained a short time, at least long enough to court and marry seventeen-year-old Nancy Creek in 1797. On their way to Webb's Prairie the couple stopped for a short time in Saline County. Then they moved to Franklin County where they lived out their lives.

The present marker at the grave of Lazarus Webb was shaped, inscribed, and placed by one of his numerous grandsons, M. N. Webb, in 1894. At that time, shortly before a group of them moved to Idaho, a reunion of the Webb family was held at the church.

There are inscriptions, crudely but sharply cut, on each of the four sides of the Lazarus Webb shaft. The one on the west face is the most interesting, particularly when one considers the fact that the record inscribed extends only to 1894. This inscription tells us that the descendants of Lazarus and Nancy Webb until that date numbered,

> 16 children
> 151 grandchildren
> 816 great grandchildren
> 1,192 great-great grandchildren
> 75 great-great-great grandchildren

making a total of 1,250.

Another inscription just below the listing given above is a scriptural citation, "Exodus I:7." Your first guess doubtlessly is correct. The passage reads: "Go ye forth and multiply and replenish the earth."

Near the grave of Lazarus is that of a younger brother, Eli, who came to Illinois with Lazarus and like him settled on the prairie. Eli also left many descendants—not so numerous, however, as those of Lazarus.

These two brothers and their wives with one other man met in September, 1818, and formed the Middle Fork Primitive Baptist Church. That was the first group of any organized society formed in Franklin County. The minute book of this old church with its "Articles of Faith and Rules of Decorum," written in a fine hand with a quill pen, tells of the selection of pastors, admission, dismission, and transfer of membership, but strangely omits any mention of money. The church formed then still carries on, and the Webb reunions still are held.

A second burial ground that suggests a story is the cemetery at Benton. The story here really began in an older cemetery in the heart of the town where John McMillan Wilson, an attorney from New York, first was buried. It was he, and three other students at Miami University, Oxford, Ohio, who formed the Greek letter fraternity Phi Delta

Theta, apparently the oldest of college social fraternities in America.

Another burying ground that suggests several stories is the one about three miles north of Mulkeytown. Here a shapeless sandstone is at the grave of Priscilla, the quadroon slave whom Brazilla Silkwood had bought from a Cherokee chief when that tribe was encamped west of Jonesboro during their Trail of Tears march from the Great Smokies to Oklahoma in the winter of 1838–1839. Priscilla's grave is beside that of Silkwood and his wife.

Another cemetery with the marked grave of a slave is at the site of early-day Douglas Camp Ground about six miles north from Eldorado. Here a rough sandstone marker near the northwestern corner of the cemetery is at the grave of a slave woman brought by the Douglas family when they came to settle there. When burial was made, this was outside the area of burials. For more than a century only the sturdy original marker and tradition combined to identify the grave. A few years ago, however, someone placed a low flat stone beside the first sandstone one. This newer stone bears only the name, Aunt Hannah.

Wandering in almost any old cemetery can be interesting to those curious.

🌸 ALL ROADS LED TO FRANKFORT

LONG AGO SOMEONE said, "All roads lead to Rome." Anyone looking at a map showing postal routes of southern Illinois about 1830 could say with equal justification, "All roads led to Frankfort."

Since the town is little known now, some may be curious about that once important traffic center. Where was it? Why and how did it begin? Which trails and roads converged there, and what has happened to the town?

First it should be located. Frankfort is situated on a prominent hill, long called Pasteboard Mountain—we don't know why—about two miles east of West Frankfort, where Frankfort Heights is now. It had its beginning when a palisaded fort was built on the crest of Pasteboard Mountain, where Logan School now stands. This defense post was one of a series of such stations spaced along the trail leading from Equality toward Kaskaskia.

The first one of these defense posts had been built in 1802 at Equality by the seven Jordan brothers (sometimes spelled Jourdan and pronounced Jur-din). The second defense established was Brown's blockhouse at Eldorado. The third and fourth ones were Karnes's and

Gasaway's stations in the Raleigh (Curran) and Galatia (Gallatia) vicinities. The one built by the Jordans at Frankfort thus was spaced fifth in the chain.

Francis Jordan apparently was the leader of the group of brothers, relatives, neighbors, and militia from Equality who built the fort that was to be called Francis Jordan's Fort, Frank Jordan's Fort, Frank's Fort, and lastly Frankfort to distinguish it from another and apparently older place called Jordan Brothers' Fort or Tom Jordan's Fort, two miles south and about a half mile east of Thompsonville. The Jordans evidently were fort builders.

One end of practically every main trail in southern Illinois was pointed toward Frankfort. First, there was the early and important road from Shawneetown, already mentioned. A second much traveled one came from Golconda. The road from Jonesboro by way of Bainbridge was a third one. Another came from Brownsville, thirty miles away. A fifth trail was from Kaskaskia by way of Little Muddy post office. A sixth, really two parallel roads until just before reaching the fort, came from the Moore's Prairie-Mt. Vernon regions. Another road led to Frankfort from McLeansboro, twenty-six miles away. None followed land lines; they just wandered across the country. Many forked out within a few miles of Frankfort and so made the map look much like a spider's web with its center at the village.

There is an interesting story about the location of the McLeansboro road. Since it was not easy to lay a direct course through the woodlands, a novel plan was employed. According to the tradition, a mare from McLeansboro was taken from her colt and brought to Frankfort. When released at the fort, it is said, she "took a beeline for home." Men followed her and blazed the trail on trees. However the road was laid out, it was a surprisingly direct one.

Frank Jordan's Fort and that of Tom Jordan remained important posts during the War of 1812. Some killings by the Indians in the vicinity of these forts are cited as reasons for the declaration of war with Great Britain. When the railroad came, about ninety years after Francis Jordan's Fort was built, it avoided Pasteboard Mountain and passed a point two miles or so to the west, and the new town on the railroad became West Frankfort.

A motorist approaching West Frankfort from the west can stop at Fairmount Church, near where the old Brownsville road passed, about two miles before reaching the city limits, and read a marker that tells of the final and decisive battle between the Shawnee and Kaskaskia Indians which began there in 1802. After passing through the city, he will see

Pasteboard Mountain on Highway 149 and the unmarked grounds of the fort. Continuing a short way to the east along the highway, he will find an inconspicuous roadside marker that shows the place where Moses Garrett kept an early-day tavern that also served for several years as the county seat of Franklin County.

❧ *LET'S GO FOR ANOTHER DRIVE*

ANOTHER INTERESTING drive in the northeastern part of "Egypt" is suggested here. Like the previous ones, this one may begin anywhere on the suggested route and go in either direction. Olney, home of the largest known population of white squirrel in America, is chosen as the point of departure.

Olney also has other claims to interest. It was here that the *Olney Times* on November 1, 1858, carried the following front-page banner line:

FOR PRESIDENT IN 1860, ABRAHAM LINCOLN OF ILLINOIS.

So far as has been discovered, this was the first newspaper in the United States to use that banner line. Lincoln's stock must have reached an early high in this region. It was in adjoining Wayne County that the first Republican county convention formally committed itself to Lincoln's candidacy.

From Olney one may drive north nine miles along Illinois Highway 130 to a marker beside the roadway that locates the center of population for the nation in 1950. That spot was literally the heart of the United States. This center of population is a constantly wandering one located each ten years. In 1960 it had moved to another location.

At Lawrenceville in Lawrence County, both named for James Lawrence, captain of the ill-fated *Chesapeake,* one passes through the earliest developed Illinois oil field. This county also has the unwanted distinction of having hanged the first and only woman in Illinois for the simple reason that she fed her husband "white arsenic."

It would hardly be fair if the journey were not continued from Lawrenceville to the Lincoln Trail State Monument on the west bank of the Wabash about ten miles away. This monument commemorates the fact that the Lincoln family entered the State of Illinois near there and continued northward alongside Route 33 toward Palestine.

At the monument, one may cross the Wabash to Vincennes in the "foreign country" of Indiana, where the George Rogers Clark Memorial is located. This memorial costing about $2,000,000 was erected long after the man it honors had died penniless. Murals, high on the encircling walls, depict episodes in his story. Upon its completion, President Franklin D. Roosevelt came to dedicate it.

There are additional places of interest in and about the town. Among these are the old cathedral and burying ground, the house where "Alice of Old Vincennes" lived, Greenwood Cemetery, the site of old Fort Knox, and other spots that pinpoint history. Returning to Lawrenceville and going south on Route 1 to Crawfish Creek about two miles north of Mt. Carmel, a historical marker beside the highway marks the site of vanished Palmyra, the first county seat of Edwards County when that county included the eastern part of Illinois from the extended south line of present-day Edwards County to mid-Illinois and north to "upper Canada." Anyone then living at the present sites of either Chicago or Milwaukee and wishing to transact business at the county seat would have journeyed to this spot. That was a long way to go for a marriage license, to try a case in court, or get a license to keep a tavern.

Mt. Carmel, with its biblical name, was considered in 1818 a "moral, temperate and industrious" village. There are a number of points of interest there. These include the ruins of the river dam and the locks that made the Wabash navigable. At that time a large water-powered mill stood a short way up the Wabash. A second dam stood a few miles above this one that controlled the water level at the Mt. Carmel locks. It was near Mt. Carmel that prospecting for oil in Illinois was first done at about the same time that oil was discovered near Titusville, Pennsylvania.

Albion, the site of early Wanborough then known as and presently referred to as the "English Settlement," was founded by English immigrants. It was among the most progressive settlements in the new state. In 1824 when an attempt was made to amend the Illinois constitution to permit slavery, opposition centered in the English Settlement under the leadership of Birkbeck, whose pen name was Jonathan Freeman.

Five miles north from Albion on State Illinois Highway 130 is a side road leading east to the aging village of Bone Gap, well worth visiting. Four miles farther north from the Bone Gap roadway is another highway leading to West Salem, location of the only known Moravian church in Illinois, one of the few in the nation west of Pennsylvania.

The observant and curious traveler making this suggested trip of 125 miles surely will find his time well spent.

❧ *TOURISM IS GROWING UP*

MANY PERSONS IN southern Illinois have toyed with an idea expressed in the word "tourism," now increasing in use. Heretofore, visiting places of interest had been prompted mostly by talk that included expressions like: "You should see ——." "Have you seen ——?" "Ever been to ——?" and ended in vagueness.

The tourist, and a native becomes a tourist when he goes sightseeing, found little to direct him to the place he sought and little to help him enjoy the place should he reach it. Maps were insufficient. Roads lacked guiding signs. Having reached his goal, after a few false turns and futile inquiries, the tourist found little there that helped. If he did not know the local story, and few places are impressive without their stories, the visitor frequently experienced a letdown.

It often was difficult to find a suitable parking place. Food, campsites for those who wished to pitch tent or park trailers for an overnight stay, along with other necessary conveniences, were crude and in short supply. Too often there was about it all an unkempt air.

Two recent visits to the Pounds Hollow recreation area in the Shawnee National Forest have aroused high hopes that a definite improvement program is underway. Pounds Hollow area is on the north side of the Karbers Ridge blacktop road that leads west from Illinois Highway 1 about twelve miles north of Cave-in-Rock. It is easy to find and it is easy to see, having tastefully designed but unobtrusive markers for the visitors' guidance.

The lake with its rocky wooded shores, picnic grounds, and bathing beach cannot be missed. Then there is the dock where rowboats may be had, with thankfulness that no roaring outboard motors are going to shatter the natural quiet.

Those who have known The Pounds for many years will find several late arrangements to please them. Among these is a campground with seventy-five sites for tents or trailers. Each site has its own cooking grill. Trash cans and clean comfort stations are near at hand. Plans to have ample water are underway. These graveled, uncrowded plots are in a delightful young forest, mostly pine. The writer has known the delights of camping in the pine forest of Maine and is readying camp gear for a few days among the young pines, about forty feet high, at Pounds Hollow.

Another pleasing feature at the Pounds is a cluster of eight double-sized tables, each with its individual grill mounted on a post so the user does not have to stoop. These picnic tables are at the beginning of the trails that lead past the fallen stone wall that the Indians left and along the brink of the cliff that borders the narrow valley. The trails have been laid out as smoothly as the surface will allow. Even those who have slowed down can leisurely wander along them, pausing at the frequently spaced, comfortable benches to sit and rest, always facing toward some pleasing view.

An interesting feature along the foot trails is an array of signs to tell the stroller about the area. Some of these help by giving the common names of flowers, shrubs, and trees. One such sign points to poison ivy and carries the advice, "If leaves be three, let it be." Another identifies the slippery elm, even giving its Indian name. Other markers identify the lowly persimmon, winged elm, tulip, oak, walnut, and white ash trees.

These labels also carry information for the curious. We are told that the fruit of the persimmon is relished by practically all woodland animals, even by boys. They tell of the use of slippery elm and that tea from sassafras roots was considered a great spring tonic. At one place there is a "sniff box" whose lid one may raise to enjoy the faint odor of the sassafras fastened in the box.

At the trail's beginning a prominent marker points the three millionth pine tree planted in the program sponsored by the Illinois Federated Woman's Club, under whose encouragement this significant reforestation project was carried forward.

There are maps along the trail to indicate points of interest and on each is a "you are here" marking that enables the visitor to know where he is.

A sign points the way to Fat Man's Misery and down a safe stairway in the crevices in the cliff to Ox Lot Shelter, where early lumbermen kept their cattle to haul logs to the narrow gauge railroad that then led to the sawmill on Saline River.

Where the stairway starts down there is a geological chart that helps to an understanding of the rock formation. At the bottom one finds the ox lot occupied by a picnic table and a cooking grill. There are ferns and beech trees with old, old initials carved on them. The oldest date found was '06.

Pounds Hollow has become more attractive since its improvement program has gotten well underway. Interest was added by visiting there and hearing two old gentlemen, Mr. Scott, past ninety, and Mr. Thacker, well in his eighties, tell of visits there a long lifetime ago. An old lady told of how her mother prepared food for the sawmill helpers and of how it was taken on a flatcar over the little railway to the men at noontime.

One is left with many questions. Why did the Indians carry rock from the creek bed to build walls on top of the bluff? Does the detached heap of stones on the bluff mark an Indian burial site? Where is the outcropping of rock from which pioneer boys got material for their slate pencils? Are the berry-bearing bushes on top of the bluff those of the "sarvis" berry? Where can one find a more restful spot than the upper length of Pounds Hollow?

GEOLOGY REVEALS EARTH HISTORY

FROM TIME TO TIME, stories are told about someone who comes into possession of a pair of magical glasses, spectacles that enable the wearer to see new and strange objects that others can't see. In a way, these stories are not so fanciful, especially in a figurative way. The glasses are really new interests, new purposes, and an increased curiosity, or a combination of the three. A number of people, about three hundred, tried the new glasses recently.

This group, many of whom were wearing magical spectacles for the first time, left the Golconda High School grounds about 9:00 A.M. in seventy cars and buses, bound on a geological field trip. The party was made up of pupils, teachers, and parents, along with some camp-followers like the writer, who wanted to see what it was all about and what they had been missing.

The group was equipped with maps and 24-page pamphlets of guide notes and diagrams. There also were some competent and patient guides from the Illinois Geological Survey under whose supervision the trip was being made. They pointed out features that many making the trip had frequently passed and had failed to observe.

The trip was about fifty miles in length. Not one of the miles was over territory new to this writer. Much of the way had been traveled several times. This time, however, new purposes made it a new trip and also showed that there always is more to see than one expects. It also taught that one sees what he is looking for. Although the official purpose of this trip was to make geological observations, the remnants of rail and picket fences, tumbled-down barns, and abandoned homesites where yard flowers and shrubs still grew intruded on the scene.

Unscheduled stops were made to look at bull tongue, diamond, new ground, an old Rose Clipper plow, and large wooden hogsheads. Strange to say, some of the party didn't see them at all. All this goes to show that there really are several kinds of magical spectacles and that people naturally will see through the spectacles they are wearing.

Since this was a geological field trip, perhaps remarks should be confined to things geological. Almost against the east side of the school ground, attention was called to the outcropping of stone named Hardinsburg sandstone. It also was pointed out that the rock layers dip to the west. That helps to give a better understanding of the old face of the earth and why it is often rough, wrinkled, folded, and cracked. Those of us less fully informed were not clear as to why Hardinsburg sandstone is so named and how it differs from another kind called Cypress that came a mile further along the way. It left some wondering just how such stones were formed and what niche each fills in the earth's long story. (When the writer went home he got himself a second-hand geology textbook.)

About a mile farther on was the smoldering city dump that some wished they'd hide and deodorize. The half-mile long string of cars then passed through the levee gateway into Golconda and turned south on Adams, the first street reached, to pass the Presbyterian Church. This church naturally is not geological in age but still is known as the second oldest church of that faith in Illinois. Another three-quarters of a mile to the south and we saw the Cypress sandstone outcroppings. About a quarter mile beyond this point, there was opportunity to learn that the basis of the soil here is very fine sand that was blown from the great sandbank of the Ohio River before that river carved out its present course.

About six miles on the way, the group reached the Ohio River; only the river isn't there now, having decided to take over the course once used by the Tennessee and Cumberland rivers. It is interesting to pause on the banks of that one-time Ohio and look across the valley toward the little station of Homberg and to think that the three-mile-wide valley once was filled with water from the melting Wisconsin glacier.

This old river channel, upon being deserted by the river, became filled with sand, gravel, and other glacial drift. It now is a potential source for a boundless water supply, available to a prospective industry. Don't be surprised if you come back a few years hence and see a sizable industry where the Ohio once flowed. The ridges that one sees wandering across the old valley are sandbars at the ancient Ohio. This valley is among the most impressive physiographic features of Illinois.

From Homberg, the tour returned to Route 146 and once more into Golconda. If interested in a more extensive tour, one can write to the Illinois State Geological Survey, Urbana, Illinois, and ask for the free Guide Leaflet 1962A. With it and a map one can spend a delightful and instructive day going over the fifty-odd miles of the whole tour. He will see that this small portion of southern Illinois has a great and varied appeal.

🌱 LOST AMONG THE KENTUCKY HILLS

BEING LOST CAN be a delightful experience if the time and place are somewhat carefully chosen. Such a coincidence occurred a few years ago when the writer attempted a short cut between towns in the Kentucky hills. After making one or two wrong guesses on turns, he became utterly confused.

The pleasing features of it all began when a rare fragrance was scented in the air. Rounding a turn in the road, he found the source of the odor—a vigorously steaming sorghum mill. A stop was made to observe and to chat, to enjoy the smell of the boiling sirup, and once again, using a short length of cane stalk, to taste the hot, fresh, and oft-time candied molasses as it was "stirred off." All this revived memories of many such mills that once were common in southern Illinois and brought to mind the fact that very few have been seen operating in recent years.

Alerted by this sorghum mill experience, the writer kept a sharp lookout for other features that once were familiar over the countryside but now have practically disappeared. Many fragments of the vanished and vanishing were found in the half day spent in being "lost."

There were many patches of tobacco stubs with healthy suckers that frost had not nipped. There were tall log tobacco barns that already had begun to smell heavily and pleasantly of the curing weed. Smoke rising through the roofs of barns here and there indicated that the firing process was underway to hasten drying and to influence flavor. All this brought to mind the time when southern Illinois had hundreds of tobacco patches and when Raleigh and Galatia were important markets, buying and processing a million pounds a year. Now it would be difficult to find even one small patch grown "for table use" in all the area. Aside from a few patches in the vicinity of Bone Gap in Edwards County no others are recalled.

Pale blue smoke rising lazily from kitchen chimney tops meant that wood-burning cook stoves were in use. A few fireplace chimneys showed that hearth fires had been kindled to drive away the autumn chill. Piles and ricks of wood indicated that some of the more provident were ready for cold weather. It undoubtedly would be a pleasure to go on a wintry evening to some of the places passed and sit before the log fire, popping corn and swapping stories.

A log lizard seen leaning against a rail fence started a lookout for older transportation devices. Before the period of search ended, a log wagon, some sleds, an arched-axle log cart, a road cart with a slat foot-rack, a top buggy, a fringed-top surrey, and a few regular farm wagons with spring seats came into view.

A spring house was found in use. The last one remembered in southern Illinois was seen near Vienna about forty years ago. They were handy before the coming of rural electrification and refrigeration. Several log houses were found, but none with the "dog trot," or open hallway between the main rooms.

Twelve shocks of corn were counted in southern Illinois last fall; in the aimless wandering while lost in Kentucky there must have been a thousand. Part of them had been "shucked out" and had piles of yellow corn lying beside them ready to be hauled to the crib. The fodder had been tied in bundles, reshocked, and ready for carrying or hauling to the feed lot. There were some pumpkins and crook-neck squash.

An elderly couple was met plodding toward a country store. Each was carrying a basket of eggs. The lady was wearing a bonnet, which evidently had been freshly starched and "done up." The man was wearing his "Sunday" hat and brightly colored galluses, the sole support of his trousers. Simply dressed, they were clean and genteel in appearance, typical country folk of a generation ago.

Before the wandering ended there had been pull-gates, plank fences, cattle guards, yards bordered with hedges of red and yellow coxcombs, long-necked gourds and sugar gourds, calico corn, tumble-down country churches, cemeteries abandoned by all except their permanent tenants, and fields purposely being returned to the wood.

The songs that one sings and the tunes he hums in unguarded moments often date him. Likewise, those understanding the uses of the things spoken of here are on the wrong side of seventy.

❧ *A FEW MILES ALONG MEMORY LANE*

THIS IS ABOUT a trip made on a Memorial Day to boyhood haunts. Knowing that men and "remorseless time" have left little beyond the solid earth as it then was, the schedule was arranged to permit loitering along the way. Thus, time could be had to pause and recall events that left pleasant memories. Thankfully, they are the ones that survive and remain most vivid.

The day was a success, almost literally a trip down memory's lane. The first stop was at the homesite where a favorite uncle and a champion custard-making aunt lived. The house is gone, likewise the old barn built around the log cabin of a first settler. No part of the rail fence maze that enclosed and crisscrossed the farm remains. The apple orchard with its rows of log bee gums is gone. One scraggly shade tree and a crumbling brick well curb are left on the edge of a field of wheat.

The highway that was gumbo then is gravel now. The last tree of the wood pasture where youngsters, both boys and girls, played and gathered nuts in season has been cleared away. Only those with long memories can see those same youngsters climbing trees or riding bridleless horses that were urged to plod aimlessly about, sometimes seeming deliberately to walk under low branches that forced the hitchhiker to tumble off.

Just across a narrow field was the place where the Allen cabin stood and where now only a bit from a milk crock rim could be found to show that people once lived there. It was here that the first memories of a three-year-old are centered. Among them are glimpses of the backwaters rising in Ash Pond and of some surprised wild turkeys that in turn surprised the boy. Others are of standing up and firmly grasping the sideboard of a farm wagon drawn by George and Weaver, and of tiptoeing to peer over the side at dead tree stumps, cornstalks, and tall weeds. It was fully as impressive as an airplane ride now.

The next stop was at a pile of rotting rubbish, all that remains of a boxed house, another boyhood home. The open well, now curbless, still is on location, a hazard to hopping rabbits and unwary prowlers. The watering trough made from a section of hollow log with planks nailed on the ends is gone, along with the two sections of white oak logs on which it rested.

Nothing remains of the barn and its attached buggy-wagon shed. The

log corncrib with its wooden hinged door and wooden latch that ceased
to baffle horse Charley is gone. The henhouse with its rising rows of
roosts around one end and darkened nests along the walls has been gone
for forty years.

Nothing is left of the chicken-tight paling fence or the pigpen with its
slopping trough, or the familiar ash hopper that served long and faithfully. The woodyard with piles of logs and poles, its sawhorses, much
hacked chopping block, both poled and double bitten axes, an iron
wedge or two, a crosscut saw, and a hickory log maul was missing.
Neither was there a tumbled pile of seasoning cookwood. The litter of
chips, barks, splinters, and sawdust, once a foot deep, has decayed.
Ranker than average grass and weeds indicate the woodyard's bounds.

A native white oak that stood by the road was cut when the roadway
was widened many years ago. The large elm that shaded the well died a
lifetime ago. A flourishing sour gum survives that a boy hacked severely
to see if it were true as old men said, "You can't deaden a blackgum." A
large walnut tree with broken limbs stands where an eight-year-old
planted a nut beside a front gatepost in 1895.

A long damson plum in the dooryard is gone but its progeny, growing
up through openings in the floor and fallen walls, has become a jungle
now spreading across the one-time garden plot.

This year's Memorial Day journey into the past ended at Pleasant
Grove Cemetery located on the farm where this boy once lived and
where he first watched people decorate graves in 1891.

If you are this side of seventy and grew up on a southern Illinois farm
or in one of its villages and want to see just how much all has changed,
take a day off, go back and slowly wander about looking for memories.
They are there.

Chapter 6

Business and Industry

🌸 *ANTIQUES TELL HOW PEOPLE LIVED*

MANY PERSONS ENJOY collecting antiques, meaning by that term the furniture and fixtures of earlier homes. Others, a much smaller number, are busily gathering old tools used by the craftsmen who made the antiques. Both alike show a tendency to become obsessed with their collecting.

A group known as the Early American Industries Association, primarily interested in old tools, recently gathered from several states at Williamsburg, Virginia. There, for three days, they visited in the shops where work still is carried on in the same way it was 250 years ago. They saw spinners, weavers, silversmiths, printers, wigmakers, bakers, blacksmiths, farriers, cabinetmakers, carpenters, pit sawyers, shoemakers, coopers, cooks, candlers, and millers carrying on their trades just as their predecessors did when the town was young. It was, as near as one can hope to find, an answer to the plea voiced in the old school reader, "Backward, turn backward, O Time in thy flight."

Only in Williamsburg has it been found that the past can be viewed so completely. A stop there makes vivid to the visitor much of a way of life that has all but vanished. It was this same way of life, perhaps practiced on a less pretentious scale than in aristocratic Williamsburg, that came west with immigrants to Illinois. Except for the silversmith, the writer has seen each of the craftsmen named practicing his trade in this region. The wigmaker, however, was only making switches, for wigs never were fashionable here. Today one doubtless could not find a spinner, weaver, silversmith, wigmaker, pit sawyer, cooper, or candler working in the area, unless it be someone pursuing the craft as a hobby. In two known counties there is not a licensed farrier. Even blacksmiths are extremely rare.

Among the exhibits at the convention was one of hand tools used by early craftsmen. This lot included more than 2,500 specimens used in the early shops of that region. To the one with an ear attuned to hear their stories, any number of these implements will tell its part of an interesting tale. They indicate the ingenuity of their designers, just as their products show the craftsmen's skill. Perhaps no better furniture has been made than that which such craftsmen helped to produce.

There is always some task being performed in the Williamsburg shops to enable visitors to understand the craft of the workmen of yesteryear. At the time of the visit a desk of cherry wood was being made in the cabinet shop by a master craftsman and his able assistant. No one need rush to buy the uncompleted desk for it already has been sold for a mere $2,500 with an offer of $3,000 for a duplicate. It truly exemplifies the statements of the poet who said,

> In the elder days of art, builders wrought with greatest care.
> Each unseen and hidden part, for the gods see everywhere.

In the opinion of this observer, the desk at Williamsburg is just as near perfect as the table in the Louvre at Paris which the guides there designate as "the finest piece of furniture in the world."

Many of the tools on display eloquently speak their parts, and articles of household equipment offer their contribution to the story of the past. There are huge four-poster beds with extra covers rolled on spindles at their feet, baby cradles, and trundle beds. Mortars and pestles of both wood and stone, rotary hand mills, an operating wind gristmill, dough trays, dutch and built-in ovens, and others of reflecting tin, dough boards, waffle irons with yard-long handles, rolling pins, cookie cutters of assorted shapes, bread boxes, meal and flour bins, and jars of yeast batter show pioneer breadmaking processes. Herb gardens indicate how food was seasoned. Gracefully sturdy tables, chairs, and benches bespeak a satisfying manner of life.

When one goes to Williamsburg, he sees hundreds of articles used by the pioneers in their ordered place. Taking a trip along the back roads of southern Illinois and pausing to peer into attics, basements, corncribs, barns, smokehouses, storage sheds, and other out-of-the-way places reveals a random wealth of similar things. After all, is not this phase of the pioneer's daily life as significant as the infrequent forays he made into politics and war?

❧ *THE KENTUCKY RIFLE*

As ONE WANDERS over the countryside, he encounters numerous objects which stand ready to tell their stories. A recent probe took me to an abandoned and rotting log cabin, where two forks of tree limbs were found fastened above some clinging bits of a fireplace mantle. On the same trip a carefully made powder horn and a powder charger shaped from the tip of a stag's antler were found. To those familiar with such objects, the tree forks and the horn and charger naturally suggest the hunting rifle.

This type of firearm was considered a necessary part of an early settler's equipment. No sensible homeseeking frontiersman passing through Cumberland Gap to settle in the forests beyond the Blue Ridge did so willingly without a trusty rifle.

It was the family's defense against wild beasts, Indians, and others who might seek to cause harm. It was a kind of wilderness symbol of law and order, one that tended to equalize men. It also was the newcomers' means of obtaining a meat supply from the bear, deer, elk, turkey, and other game found in the woodland.

To the settler, his rifle was an object of abiding affection, a pet on which he lavished much attention. After a rainy day, fine for some hunting, the hunter usually cared for his rifle first, even before drying himself by the open fire. The full length wooden rifle stock of curly maple or black walnut was carefully wiped and polished. The long octagon barrel was dried and greased, inside as well as out. In fact, no part was neglected. The reason for this is easily understood when it is realized that the daily wage of a man on the farm often was only fifty cents and the better rifles sold for up to eighty dollars.

Men often named their favorite guns. There were many an Old Betsy or Long Tom. Some old rifles had notches filed in one of the barrel's edges. One that is said to have belonged to Daniel Boone is in the museum at Frankfort, Kentucky. Along its barrel there are nineteen filed notches to indicate it had caused that many Indians to "bite the dust."

Frontier rifles generally were known as "Kentucky rifles" because of their wide use in the Kentucky region. The first of these fine rifles were made by German, Swiss, and some skilled French craftsmen in and about Lancaster, Pennsylvania—not in Kentucky. The place where the first ones were made is still pointed out to visitors at Lancaster.

Kentucky rifles were a development, not an outright invention. Many individual smiths who made them added improvements until a beautifully designed and thoroughly well-made gun resulted. Not many of these expertly crafted earlier rifles are left, and these are principally in the possession of collectors. Only rarely is one found, kept as an heirloom, and pointed to as "my great-great grandad's rifle." Almost never is such a gun in firing condition. These old-time rifles with their short stocks and octagonal barrels, sometimes over five feet in length, were very heavy by present standards and occasionally weighed fourteen pounds or more. Even the light ones weighed eight pounds. Because of their weight they usually were fired from rests and not "offhand."

Accurate almost beyond belief, the best of these rifles in the hands of an expert would drive a nail one out of three shots at forty yards. A turkey gun was about .30 caliber. One for deer was .45 or .50 caliber, while bear guns might be as large as .70 caliber. A round rifle ball of this caliber weighed a full ounce.

After boring, whatever the method employed, the barrel was rifled by using "saws" to cut spiral grooves on its inside from breech to muzzle. The lands or ridges between the rifles were then smoothed with "drags." Skill and exactness in this work determined the accuracy of the firearm. Rifling was to give the bullet a spinning motion and to prevent its veering to one side.

Even the gun's ramrod was most carefully made of straight-grained split hickory, whittled and scraped to almost perfect roundness. To prevent the bullet from being flattened as it was shoved into the barrel, one end of the rod was hollowed to conform to the roundness of the bullet.

Until the advent of fixed ammunition and repeating firearms, these rifles were the world's most accurate shooting irons. As the Colt revolver "civilized" the West, the muzzle-loading rifle did the same for the Midwest.

❦ THE OLD GENERAL STORE

A GOOD BUSINESSMAN regularly takes inventory. This generally is done about the New Year, just after the Christmas rush. From information gained he learns the value of stock on hand. This helps him to determine the profit or loss he has made. This article comes from boyhood observations made in a small-town general store where the process was employed.

The building, the nearby warehouse, the stock of goods, and the merchant are long since gone. An image of the store, its furniture and fixtures, its confused array of goods, and the groups of men sitting about the big stove, remain in memory.

Since this is principally about that long-vanished store, it might be well first to glance at the social life of the establishment which centered about the large wood-burning stove that Mr. McPherson, the man of all work, stoked with firewood that had been cut and hauled in to be "applied on the account" of some customers.

The stove stood in the midst of a four-by-eight-foot island of sawdust about two inches deep. This plot of sawdust was meant to receive the discarded quids of chewing tobacco and to protect the floor from poorly aimed streams of ambeer aimed at the spittoons parked on the sawdust patch. This patch also was littered with long thin shavings that the more expert whittlers removed from short boards and dry goods boxes. Even chairposts were not immune.

Men gathered about this island and stove. Some were customers; others were chronic visitors driven inside by cold weather from the benches beneath the nearby shade trees or on the store's front porch. Yarns were told and retold, along with tall tales and personal experiences. The latest local news was passed along. A wee bit of gossip or scandal might occasionally creep in. Current issues were discussed, opinions were expressed, and solutions proposed, often surprisingly logical ones.

Though these men frequently were untutored, they were intelligent, straight-thinking, and didn't depend upon radio or television for ready-made opinions. Items from newspapers sometimes were read aloud, for papers were scarce and many could not read. Altogether, they were a reasonably rugged bunch.

Many items that were inventoried then are curious now. A leather strap would hold a cluster of cowbells that now tinkle only in memory. Trace chains, horse collars, hames, and rope halters that hung on the racks then are rare now. There also were sets of leather harness, an occasional saddle, check lines, plowpoints, laprings, buggy whips, singletrees, laprobes, and backbands in a motley array. There were tin and wooden boxes of axle grease and of wool fat, the lanolin of today, then used to put a shine on horses' hoofs and cattle horns.

Not far from the stove, yet where visitors could not reach into it too easily, was the cracker barrel. Then there was the enormous cheese almost two feet in diameter and a foot thick with a slicing knife poised like a guillotine above it. Cheese and crackers were rated as delicacies. Scattered about the store were barrels of rolled hominy, much like bleached corn flakes. Other barrels held coffee berries, both green and roasted. The green berries, to be roasted by the housewife, were cheaper, sometimes selling for as little as fifteen cents a pound. In addition to the barreled roasted coffee those wishing to do so could buy packaged coffee, either Arbuckle's or McLaughlin's. These were among the first packaged named foods.

On the low rack, generally near the back of the store, there was a row of barrels that held sorghum, New Orleans molasses, vinegar, and coal oil. Beneath the spigots of these barrels there were more framed patches of sawdust to catch drippings.

There were barrels, bags, or boxes of bleached, sulphur-smoked dried fruits. Then there were barrels of flour, rice, black-eyed peas, oatmeal, navy beans, brown sugar, and other staples. These were weighed or measured to meet the customer's wishes.

Cornmeal was sold by the bushel. Then there were shorts and middlings that have worked themselves into today's cereals.

This store had gunpowder, bar lead, shot, musket caps, felt boots, steelyards, sneads, one-ounce bottles of quinine for malaria, and carpet warp. It had steel traps, window glass, horehound candy, stone fruit jars, churns and milk crocks, red striped candy in wide-mouthed jars with glass stoppers, licorice sticks, and fire shovels.

If only that small-town store, primitive even then, could have been locked that day sixty-five years ago and unlocked this year. What a collector's heaven it would make.

THE VILLAGE BARBERSHOP

WITHIN A LIFETIME village barbershops have changed radically. This was demonstrated recently when a friend displayed his stock of shaving mugs and other items salvaged from a long-discontinued "tonsorial parlor."

His collection made it easy, at least in fancy, to reconstruct the shop at Broughton where Tine Porter shaved men and cut hair two generations ago. The room he occupied was about fourteen by twenty feet. A door and window, neither boasting any expanse of plate glass, were at the front next to the two broad boards that made a sidewalk. The walls and ceiling of the room were of beaded planks. Once they had been painted white, but smoke, time, and dust had grayed them. The room was lighted by a kerosene lamp hanging above the barber's chair.

A wood-burning stove stood near the center of the room. At one time a space about four feet square was enclosed by a rail two inches by two inches nailed on the floor about the stove. The enclosed area was filled with sawdust, changed from time to time as its saturation with ambeer and a mixture of chewed-out tobacco might indicate. During one winter a rack where washed towels were placed to dry was suspended from the ceiling above the stove. During the months when the stove was used, a two-gallon copper tank was placed on it to provide a necessary supply of hot water. In summer the stove was removed to the back room, and a tank with its shiny valve at the bottom was placed over a kerosene burner atop a small table. It was thus that the heating and interior plumbing requirements of the shop were met.

Attached to a side wall of the shop where it would be most convenient to the barber and also visible to passersby, was a nice spindled rack with an assortment of individual shaving mugs for those who chose to have them. These mugs were reasonably decorative, each having its owner's name in neat gold lettering. Some bore insignia to indicate lodge memberships. Some carried mottoes, two of which are remembered. One said, "Forget Me Not" and the other, "Remember The Giver." After a lifetime the locations of several mugs remain firmly fixed in memory.

In each mug there was a cake of shaving soap and a brush. Owners who did not choose to be shaved with a razor in general use kept cased razors lying beside their mugs. One popularly named razor bore the sign of a tree and was known as the Tree brand. Another was the Wade and Butcher—ominous title. Owners of mugs were those who generally came for daily shaves. This was not so expensive, for shaves in Broughton then came at only ten cents, and haircuts were two bits.

Farther back along the same wall holding the mug rack was a marble-topped chest of shallow drawers with a tall mirror above it. In the drawers of this chest Tine kept a few towels and items of equipment not frequently used. On the carefully wiped marble top of the chest and on a shelf beside the mirror, there were some colored bottles of bay rum, witch hazel, and hair tonic that could be had at an extra charge. A lump of alum used for razor nicks was kept with the bottles. There also was a small bowl used when preparing hot towels.

Attached to the barber chair and to the wall beside the mirror were some reversible razor straps on which the barber from time to time touched up his razors with many a resounding thwack. It is now difficult to decide which was the more impressive, the explosive slap of the razor on the strap or the deft looping glides made over the oilstone as Tine honed a razor. Each alike was dextrous.

Those portions of wall space not required for equipment were lined with chairs and benches, with a number of spittoons strategically spaced. All combined to give the shop an interesting air. Nothing in the shop, however, was as interesting as the crowd that gathered there.

All day long the benches and chairs along the wall were occupied by customers, casual visitors, and chronic loafers. Here one heard the latest local news combined with rumor and gossip. Tall tales were told, and stories were passed along. Religious, social, economic, and political issues, both local and national, were discussed, often rather intelligently. The barbershop vied with the general store, blacksmith shop, the railway station, and the livery stable for recognition as the town's forum. Some vestiges of the forum feature still survive and much unprinted news is passed along. Debate and argument were animated.

The village barbershop definitely changed when sanitary standards were established by law. Barbers were required to pass examinations, and inspectors began to make their rounds. Soon electricity came, and electric clippers appeared.

Things certainly have changed since Tine's day. There are those who believe that the social significance of the village barbershop has decreased. All agree, however, that its sanitary standards have improved, almost in proportion to prices.

🌸 SOME UNIQUE ONE-MAN SHOPS

Many an early community boasted its local broommaker who operated his one-man shop in some shed or outbuilding. There literally were scores of these small factories. So far as has been learned, only three such broom shops are left in this part of Illinois. One of these is Mr. A. E. Seeley's shop at Newton. A second one is operated by Frank McDuffey in Wayne County and a third that of W. C. Cauble in Carbondale, the latter two being blind men.

There are other commercial broom factories in the state. One of these also is in Newton, only a few blocks from Mr. Seeley's shop. The Newton factory, working on an assembly-line basis, produces about as many brooms each hour as either of the individual craftsmen complete in a week.

When white men came to the New England states they found the Indians making and using brooms. These they made and bartered to the white settlers. The crude brooms of Indian manufacture were nothing more than an unworked handle of birch or ash to which some pliable splints of the same materials had been bound with rawhide. Slender twigs and shrubs like buckberry also were used.

When knives that enabled the Indians to whittle better came, brooms were made by binding many "splinters" to a limb handle. Old documents indicate that Indian squaws often went about peddling such brooms. Some householders used to make their own brooms. When settlers moved west, the art of making brooms was taken along with them.

The brooms of early southern Illinois were made of "splinters," husks, buckberry bushes, stems of bushes, and even of sedge grass. Some older persons will remember when it was not uncommon to see heavy brooms of buckbrush about barns, sheds, and henhouses. When it was a practice to sweep bare yards, such brooms were in common use. Brooms made from broomcorn slowly replaced the crude ones.

The growing of broomcorn received early encouragement from Benjamin Franklin and Thomas Jefferson. Records indicate that it first was systematically grown and used by Levi Dickerson, who planted a small plot in his garden at Hadley, Massachusetts, about 1795. This Dickerson's planting yielded enough to make twenty brooms, which his neighbors readily bought. The next year he grew enough to make two hundred brooms, and again, they found ready sale. With a full acre planted the third year, Dickerson definitely was in the broom business.

When others observed his success they, too, began to grow broomcorn and to set up broommaking shops in sheds or parts of their barns. Here during the winter they made brooms to be peddled the next spring, perhaps a hundred miles away. For many years the broommaking industry continued to be centered in the Connecticut River Valley; a region where Polish farmers now grow tobacco and onions.

When settlers reached the fertile lands of Ohio, Indiana, and Illinois, they found that it produced better broomcorn. Broommaking followed along. Many men contrived machines that, until a few years ago, could be found in deserted buildings over southern Illinois. Using helpers, some of these one-man shops became small factories. The New England "household industry to factory" story was repeated here.

The growing of broomcorn and the making and peddling of brooms was a year-round job. In summer the crop was grown. It was harvested in autumn. Brooms were made during winter and peddled in the spring. Then the cycle was repeated.

One wagon is personally remembered that came around each spring loaded with baskets and brooms—for the owner of this wagon made both. It also carried bundles of long white oak "splits" and supplies needed to bottom chairs for those in need of that service.

The center for broomcorn growing that once centered in Massachusetts moved across to Illinois and now is centered in Oklahoma and

Texas. A considerable amount now comes from Mexico where necessary hand labor is cheaper.

Today improved machines that greatly speed up the broommaker's work are used. Nevertheless, a great part of it still must be done by hand, just as it was more than 150 years ago. The broommaker remains a specialist. A visit to any one of the shops mentioned, and some peering into dark corners for discarded and obsolete equipment, is a delightful and often a rewarding experience.

The individual broommakers named still follow the early practice. They make up a stack of brooms. Mr. Seeley loads his on a pickup truck and calls on retail stores. The others sell theirs to householders, most of whom come for them. Sometimes Boy Scouts and other helpful youngsters act as salesmen for the blind and otherwise handicapped makers.

Broommaking still appears to be one industry where the skilled and industrious operator with his one-man shop is able to compete successfully with the factory.

🌿 SHOE REPAIRMEN BUT NO COBBLERS

NUMEROUS CRAFTSMEN whose arts once were common in southern Illinois have disappeared. Among those who have vanished are the local shoemakers, the men who could cobble a pair of shoes to completion. True, there still are repairmen who mend shoes, but none who make them. The tools, implements, and devices peculiar to this craft are occasionally found in out-of-the-way places, but rarely any more in this area.

Strange as it may seem, one of the remaining localities where the tools associated with the craft are frequently found is on the island of Saba in the Netherlands West Indies. On this picturesque, Dutch-clean island shoemakers were doing a thriving business more than 250 years ago. In fact the making of shoes was so important that it was proposed to change the name from Saba to St. Crispin for the patron saint of the cobblers. Today, no one makes shoes in Saba, but enough of their tools and working places remain to attract attention and to cause observers to realize that local shoemakers were important craftsmen in many parts of the world.

A few older people who grew up in southern Illinois will remember the small shops where the last of the local shoemakers plied their craft. There was little that could be called machinery in any of these shops, but each would have a practically uniform collection of hand tools. Every shop had its queerly shaped cobbler's bench with its sagging leather seat.

This bench invariably had a low rack along its back. On this rack, and often at places on the border of the seat, a looped leather strap was nailed.

In the loops of this bordering strap the cobbler kept his smaller and more frequently used hand tools, arranged in an order determined by the number of times he would reach for them. Tools were kept in ordered arrangement. The proficient cobbler apparently believed in "a place for everything and everything in its place." Efficiency experts making motion studies in industry might find it interesting to study the manner in which cobblers arranged tools to make them available with a minimum of motion.

Among the small tools and implements held by the loops of the strap were special knives, double-ended burnishers of wood and stone, and some —at a later date—made of metal. There was the ever-present lump of grime covered beeswax, through which the strong linen thread was drawn from hanks or spools until it was smooth and fully filled with the wax. There was a bundle or container of stiff hog bristles that were attached to the ends of the long thread used for sewing. The best sewing was done with two threads—or rather with both ends of the same long thread. It was passed in both directions through each hole and drawn tightly to complete a seam identical on either side.

There were awls to pierce the leather for sewing and for the wooden pegs used to fasten soles to uppers. The cobbler used toothed wheels that were rolled along to mark locations for even stitching or pegging. Rasps were near at hand to smooth the battered ends of pegs that had battered against the persimmon or dogwood lasts. Boxes or other containers held assorted sizes of the squared and pointed shoe pegs. Widths and lengths of shoes were measured by a device graduated in the lengths of barleycorn grains, that is, thirds of an inch. Tables of lengths in some old arithmetic texts included barleycorns, along with ells and other discarded units.

On shelves about the walls of the cobbler's shop would be found his assortment of lasts that ranged through many sizes and patterns. Some shaped for an individual's special needs might even have humps tacked on them to give space for the customer's corns or bunions. These could be removed and relocated to fit the individual's needs. It was not unusual for a cobbler to have two or three hundred lasts. At first, these lasts were made straight, and the same ones were used for either foot. Later models were made for the right or left shoe. Lasts often were made in two sections in order that they could more easily be removed from the finished shoe.

Clamps for holding the leather being tooled, boot brakes for stretching leather for the instep of high-topped leather boots, knee clamps, specially designed pliers, and shoe stretchers were in every shop. In some shops the cobbler also worked at harness making. Many were the check lines, cruppers, checkreins, bellybands, backbands, martingales, hamestrings, breechings, tugs, and polestraps they supplied to the farmers.

Once there were many such craftsmen here. We wonder if there is now even one man left in the state who is a genuine full-time cobbler, one who cobbles the complete shoe for a customer.

🌼 *A VETERAN HORSESHOER*

IF ONE LOOKS about carefully, he will occasionally find an old-time craftsman, still plying a trade that has well-nigh vanished.

Such an individual is "Hank," short for James Hinkly Beasley, who lives in Eldorado. Hank has spent a long lifetime there. As he expresses it, he was born "across the road" from the city hall on September 25, 1878. On November 8 he will cast his sixteenth ballot for a presidential candidate—in the same voting precinct where he has cast the other fifteen. Thus, you see, Hank has been pretty much a stay-at-home.

He has lived all of his eighty-two years in the same community, and has been shoeing horses and making horseshoes there since he was fourteen. When he was a younger man, he shod many work horses with "keg" shoes; that is, machine-made shoes that came in wooden kegs. Because these trade shoes were too heavy and clumsy for race horses, Hank and others began making the shoes they used, and Hank still does.

High-grade steel bars are cut to length, heated, and bent about a standard form or over the rounded horn of an anvil. He uses a basic form and a wooden hammer to do his bending so there will be no hammer marks on the edges of his product. The horse's hoof is trimmed to the desired shape. The frog and all underparts of the foot are carefully cleaned and trimmed with a queerly shaped farrier's knife that usually comes from Germany. The more capable and careful farriers use an adjustable guage to make sure that each hoof and shoe form the desired angle. When this has been done, the shoe is reheated and bent to conform to the particular hoof.

The shoeing of race and saddle horses is a complicated task. For instance, pinched heels are slightly spread each time, and a bar may be placed across the open end of the shoe to hold the spread. The toes of shoes may be weighted or thinned to alter the "reach" of the horse. Bottoms of the shoes often are grooved on a swage block that the smith generally calls a swedge. Hank has about a dozen such blocks for different patterns and width of bars. Sometimes the bottoms are rounded over their entire leg. At other times they are rounded only part way. Those with bottoms rounded on the outer side are used to prevent trotters from flinging their feet outward, causing lost motion. Those rounded inside are to keep pacers from "crossing over" with their hind feet.

The shoes are rather light in weight. They are made of bars one fourth of an inch thick and from one-half to three-eighths of an inch wide. In some cases, the shoes are made of aluminum bars and weigh less than three ounces each. Hank Beasley has a device of his own design that he uses to cold punch holes in the shoes for nailing them on. He also has a flatbed trailer that he built more than thirty-five years ago. On this he has mounted an anvil, a forge, a vise, and boxes to hold his home-charred coal or coke for the forge. Boxes also carry the assorted stock of half-ready shoes and tools, including a twitch kept handy to apply to the nose of a too restive horse.

When I first saw this mobile shop, it was very new. Just recently, seen on the roadside by his home, it seemed only a bit worse for wear. He regularly couples it on behind his 1935 Plymouth and makes the rounds of his regular customers. He also carries a supply of handmade shoes.

On the day of this visit Hank was "grounded." His driver's license had expired, and he was due to take the examination for renewal the next day. (Reports are that he passed.)

There must be something like a horseshoer virus in Hank's blood. His grandfather operated a stage from Shawneetown to Mt. Vernon and perforce often had to reset the shoes of his own horses. Hank's father was an owner and racer of horses which he regularly shod himself. Hank's son, H. E. Beasley, lives next door to Hank, and also shoes horses.

It is interesting to talk with Hank and hear him recount stories of past racing days, of the interesting horsemen he had known, one of whom was my employer in Santa Ana, California, in 1911, and of his own noted horse, Silas Patchen. He describes the old-time racing sulky with wheels as high as a tall man. He pictures the driver sitting close against the horse's hips with head just above the level of the horse's back and the horse's tail tucked securely under him on the seat.

He also tells of shoeing horses for "Pop" Geers and others whose names are prominent in the legends of racing. In fact, the first shoes that Hank ever made and attached himself were fashioned and placed on a horse under Geers' direction.

His first acquaintance with hobbled pacers came about 1890. They still seem to be his first love. When he becomes enthused, biting off a big piece of chewing tobacco (most likely "Horseshoe"), and starts talking horses and horseshoeing, it is hard to realize the spry 82-year-old is almost an old man.

If horseshoes bring good luck, Hank has added much to the world's good fortune. Those knowing him invariably refer to him as "Uncle Hank."

❧ *A VISIT TO A BLACKSMITH SHOP*

AN OCCASIONAL PERSON apparently comes into the world with an inborn urge to prowl and wander about. Such a one loves to go unhurriedly along the byways with a purpose that could be expressed in the refrain of an old song that says "the bear went over the mountain to see what he could see." With the same curiosity as that ascribed to the bear, there always is something to see along the sideroads of southern Illinois.

There are countless beasts and beasties, birds, harmless snakes and toads, vegetation in endless variety, rocks, houses, and barns. There is something new every foot of the way. The traveler need never be more lonely than he chooses to be, especially if he adds people and sounds.

It was a sound not often heard now coming from an old building at the end of a street in Waltonville, on Route 148 in Jefferson County, that caused the writer to turn aside for an enjoyable visit and an opportunity to muse over another bit of our vanishing landscape, the old-time blacksmith shop.

It was not difficult for one who as a boy frequented "Uncle" Silas Jones's shop to identify the sound. A sharp but pleasant ring told the listener that most of the "pings" were made by idling strokes on the bare anvil, that is, strokes to keep the hammer bouncing and make the working strokes easier and more accurate. Their rapidity also indicated the speed at which the smith was working.

The sounds came, as had been expected, from a blacksmith shop operated by Thomas Adkins who has been smithing sixty years. It is about as typical an old shop as is known in this section of the state. The open forge, with chimney well to one side, smokes furiously until it is well warmed up. The wooden cooling tub beside the forge is little different from those of a century ago into which the smith, closely watching its changing colors, plunged the heated metal to be tempered. Water from this tub once was a favorite folk remedy, just what for is not recalled. Aunt Jane Brown used it for something.

On a rack within easy reach there were about forty sizes of tongs, often shaped for a particular job.

There were taps, dies, and bolt-headers. Various patterned hammers lay about. There were ball peen, cross peen, and straight peen of different sizes. There were sledges weighing twelve or sixteen pounds each, used for forging and heavy welding. There were punches and chisels of many sizes. There were cold cuts and hot cuts, some with handles and others shaped for use in the hardy holes of the anvil.

There was a mounted try-wheel used to measure and match rims and tires for wagons and buggies. There were skeins and thimbles for wagon axles, and devices to shrink tires that were too large. There was a spoke shave and spokes to be fitted to hubs and felloes with pullers to spring them into the rim holes. There were patterns for hounds and frogs, and a hub cross of heavy timbers to support wheels while heated tires were being shrunk to fit.

There were reaches, shafts, poles, crosstrees, bows, and some spare fifth wheels for buggies. There was a rack holding strap and rod iron, with some bars of steel. There was an array of tool handles, boxes and bins of bolts, rivets, and screws. There was the rack with a few horseshoes, a clinching block, clippers, leather apron, oddly shaped knives, the foot stand and hand box of the horseshoer—with a few handfuls of the long tapering nails he used. There were piles of scrap iron and steel from which selected pieces sometimes were taken for use.

Mr. Adkins had two heavy anvils, about the 175-pound class. One was a clip anvil of solid steel. The other was cast iron with a steel faceplate. Both were hollowed in the base. With the bottom anvil inverted, it was into its hollow that gunpowder was placed when anvils were fired at Fourth of July celebrations. A second anvil, smooth face down, was placed over the base of the inverted bottom one.

Skilled blacksmiths were valuable men, one might say indispensable, in newly settled country. They fashioned and made tools and farm implements, even making and repairing rifles. They were versatile, working in both wood and metal. The demand for these men has practically vanished. Welding and cutting torches have superseded the forge, hammer, and anvil.

Why not, while opportunity still is here, visit a typical old-time blacksmith shop and know what they were like? There presently is the one in Waltonville, one in Mt. Vernon, another in Murphysboro, one near Golconda, and a little one-man hobby shop in Pomona. There doubtlessly are others not known.

❦ *FROM THE DAYBOOK OF A BLACKSMITH*

PEOPLE WHO ARE curious can find something of interest in nearly any collection of old records. This happened to me recently in pursuing the daybooks of Thomas Eaton, a blacksmith and the great-grandfather of Mrs. John Sill of Carbondale. The records covered a period of several years beginning with January, 1816. Though yellowed by time and somewhat water stained, most of the pages are easily legible.

They reveal the blacksmith as a versatile craftsman, one who did about every kind of job. But they also throw many a sidelight on the way earlier farm folk lived and worked. Too, they serve to remind those presently living that many of the tools, appliances, and methods of earlier days have vanished.

A large number of the terms used have been forgotten by most people, even by one chap past eighty who spent most of his spare time in boyhood visiting and observing at Uncle "Hidad" Jones's blacksmith shop. Among those terms appearing in Eaton's account was gudgeon; it was finally remembered that this was the long strap that was turned around the pin of a strap iron hinge. Eaton wrote that he "sharpit," meaning sharpened unnumbered "irons," really plowpoints. He also "drew out" harrow teeth, picks, mattocks, adzes, and axes.

It still is somewhat baffling to understand what is meant when he "upset" axes, wedges, mattocks, and a host of other tools; it leaves the writer a bit "upset" trying to determine just what it was that he did. There are literally hundreds of entries where he charges for "laying" axes, hand axes, broadaxes, heels, links, shoes, shares, (sometimes shairs), and hooks. Laying, more properly called layering, was the welding of a strip of steel to the working edge of a tool that had worn badly. The addition of this strip to the softer iron body of most tools made them about as good as new ones.

There are other puzzling terms. Just what is meant by "heel screw," and what did he do when he "bushed" a gun? Perhaps it was the same as breeching a gun, a common term. "A hoop on a tea kill" surely was a hoop on a tea kettle. Whatever it was, the charges were $.40. "A latch for a lume" also was $.40. "Sockets on a saw" were $2.00.

He made hoes for $2.00 and put an eye in a damaged one for $.60. His charge for ten wagon nails was $.60, but ten cart nails cost only $.30. These seem like rather steep prices, but it must be remembered that they were nails he produced by hand. He made linch pins to keep wheels on axles at $.20 each, king pins at $1.20, and wagon tires were from $3.00 to $10.00 each. He put a horn on a saddle for $1.40 and a "gulet" for $1.00. Whenever called for, he supplied open rings, a strap for a "valese," keys for ox "Steaples," or chocks for wagons.

He ironed hames, case hardened a frizzen for a gun, whatever a frizzen may be, for $4.00; he made a mill spindle, and "sharpit a fluke" (?). This smith made a bull "tung" plow, put an ear on a water bucket belt, and stocked a hoe with a pawpaw handle. Then he put rowels in a spur for $.40. He took a pair of steers at $38.00 to apply on account.

Fifteen harrow teeth from his shop, weighing thirty-three pounds, cost $8.20. A fire shovel was made for $.70 and one was repaired for $.40. A "tramel" for a fireplace cost $4.20 and a set of pothooks $1.00.

A man needed two iron wedges and got them, weighing nine and a half pounds, for $3.40. Eaton charged $.60 for "putting a heel to a shair." Some kind of a mill iron weighing sixteen pounds was supplied for $3.60, and two mill picks were $2.00. Mill picks were used when the millers "pecked" their millstones. He boarded a regular customer, Wm. Robinson, "for 5 days of illness" at a total charge of $3.20. On December 15, 1816, he charged William Daugham $3.00 for some stove pipe. A year and one day later Daugham met a charge of $1.40 for repairs to a stovepipe—that leaves one wondering if it was the same pipe. Bells for cows were sold at $1.40 each. An eighteen-pound chimney bar was made for $3.30.

On October 3 he mended a "chain for dogs" and on October 13 he supplied the same customer with "3 leg irons for Negroes, weight 21 pounds" for $7.70.

Another time "a leg iron for Tom" came at $1.70. Some time later, another leg iron weighing five pounds cost $4.00. Charges of the same amount were made for taking such irons off. A "gag" for another Negro cost $2.00 and repairs about a year later cost $.60. "Two yokes for Negroes" cost $8.00. These last cited entries give grim glimpses of another time.

One can read these old records and muse. They arouse as many questions as they answer.

❧ NEW-OLD INDUSTRIES

SOUTHERN ILLINOIS is attracting more and more visitors, both those who are "just passing through" and those who will remain for more extended stays. Among the latter are some who plan to stay permanently. Efforts by many agencies to attract people appear to be succeeding.

The region has much to interest the casual callers and those who plan to be here longer. Its offerings include places of historic and scenic appeal, unusual geological formations, hunting and fishing in season, pleasant campsites, bathing beaches, rivers and lakes for boating and water sports, and trails along which one may ride or plod in rocky woodlands. It even has extensive swamps for those who are inclined to wade them. Some places in the swamps, and also in the woodlands, appear so primeval that a visitor feels he is the first white man to penetrate that locality. In autumn the foliage colors are superb. In addition to all these attractions the region is just naturally a nice place to live.

Another attraction is being added slowly but surely: the trade in souvenirs and handcraft products, such as is found in all tourist areas, is beginning to appear. Whenever tourists congregate, they find souvenirs and gadgets galore. Many of these items are misfits; when one looks closely, he sees a label that says "made in Japan" or in some other faraway place.

The movement to supply tourists with the usual stock of souvenirs and useful merchandise has one slight but promising difference in southern Illinois. Those interested in tourism here are hoping for an increase in the heretofore meager offering of local handicrafts, the products of local artisans.

In many cases, these are the same products as those once made, perhaps a hundred or more years ago, and used in the region. They are made by the same processes that then were common but now are seldom employed. Some of those producing the artifacts now being offered learned their skills from an earlier generation and have worked at them through a lifetime; still others are those who appreciate and value the finer qualities in the earlier craftsman's product and set themselves to learn the required skills. This has been done in voluntary study groups, sometimes self-taught. On occasion these groups have had some skilled person come to instruct them. Some have worked in special night classes at Southern Illinois University. Others have gone their lone way.

A combination of these efforts has produced a number of individuals who are making attractive objects. Two or three groups have been interested in making pottery after the fashion employed by local plants that once operated here to supply the region's demands for stoneware. Now, instead of the pitchers, fruit and cookie jars, milk crocks, churns, churn lids, jugs, bean pots, and other similar products, these groups are making and decorating with colored glazes many kinds of trays, vases, cups, and bowls, individually fashioned. They have found that they can have something beautiful and useful and, above all, something that will be admired by those who appreciate these items and gifts.

The products of the present craftsmen are varied. There still is at least one blacksmith-gunsmith who can repair and recondition cap-and-ball rifles and can hammer out iron door hinges and other hardware—and even some of the early type iron fittings used at the kitchen fireplace. Having learned the skill in Spain, one smith can still make shoes for oxen. These men are the vanishing rear guard of old-time craftsmen.

At two or three centers, groups of women are making rugs. Some of these are woven; others are hooked or braided. One lady, with her husband's help, offers assurance that the nice home they own was paid for mostly with proceeds from floor rugs woven on the two hand looms in their basement. Not far from these weavers is an old lady who has contrived an automatic shuttle for use with her large cloth loom. She appears prosperous and happy, undoubtedly from her success in weaving carpeting that she cuts into rug lengths and sells readily.

A few women are making afghans and bedspreads. One such person has a good dozen specimens that informed people have valued at $200 or $300 each. She likes them too well to offer them for sale; however, she points out that she wouldn't make over $1.00 an hour for her work. We wonder if there is any individual in America who has a finer collection of this type.

A number of persons are interested in wood carvings and in fashioning attractive objects from bits of driftwood or from other gnarled and oddly shaped pieces of wood. Many pieces are particularly attractive when made from cedar that has been dead long enough for most of the white sapwood to be decayed, thus allowing the exposure of the richly red and fragrant heartwood. Many gnarled and twisted bits of wood almost cry to be made into lamps or nondescript ornamental pieces. Cypress knees are made into many things that range from pincushions to pepper boxes and parts of vases. Driftwood, combined with a good imagination, is being made into attractive objects that answer to no name. Two or three are doing wood carvings that often follow the contour and grain of the wood in an interesting manner. They have a weird attractiveness.

Leather workers, not using the stock stamped and marked pieces of leather so often offered craftsmen, are doing their own designs with good effect. One is rebuilding a saddle according to the best practices of that time when saddle making really was a trade. Some are doing clay modeling, then making molds, and casting duplicates in plaster. Sheet metal, silver, aluminum, brass, and copper are being made into useful and ornamental wares. Chairs are being bottomed with corn husks, cane, hickory and elm bark, and with whiteoak splits, all reminiscent of the time when such were common practices.

It appears that handicrafts are definitely coming into new life in southern Illinois. If statistics can be a reliable guide, this new trend may lead to an industry in the region with financial returns equal to several major factories. It can be developed without marked depletion of natural resources. And a handicraft seems always to bring happiness to the person practicing it.

BEGINNING OF THE ILLINOIS CENTRAL

RAILROADS PLAYED an important part in our Civil War. Perhaps none was so helpful to the Union cause as the Illinois Central.

White men coming to Illinois found only the rivers, plus poorly arranged animal and Indian trails, to serve as roadways. Therefore, most settlers located near rivers. Thus a north-south belt in the central portion of the state remained isolated and was settled slowly.

The settlements were agricultural. As farmers located farther inland, the task of moving products to river ports became greater. Much of the soil in this central belt was gumbo, certainly unsuited for roadways. Moreover, labor to build roads to the rivers was lacking.

In 1832 Lieutenant Governor Alexander M. Jenkins, long a resident of Jackson County, proposed that a north-south railway be built through the central and more isolated portion of the state. Three years later the proposition had become a state-wide issue. In 1836 the Illinois Legislature incorporated the Central Railroad Company to build the proposed road and authorized a capitalization of $2,500,000.

The company's first directors were Darius B. Holbrook of New York, Governor John Reynolds, A.M. Jenkins, Pierre Menard, Sidney Breese, and Albert Snyder, all from Illinois. The money needed for building was not forthcoming, however, and in 1845 the company surrendered its charter.

The next plan advanced was that the national government give public lands to a company which would build such a road. This aroused the opposition of senators and representatives from the eastern states. To meet their protest Stephen A. Douglas suggested adding a branch road to Lake Michigan at Chicago. He explained this would enable Illinois products to reach eastern markets, and that it would permit better shipment of goods to Illinois. The proposal was agreed upon. In 1850, largely through the influence of Stephen A. Douglas, Sidney Breese, and James Shields, the national government gave public lands to Illinois. The state in turn gave them to the Illinois Central Railroad.

The gift amounted to approximately 2,500,000 acres. Proceeds from land sales by the Illinois Central were to be used in building about 705 miles of road that would extend from the northern limits of the state to Cairo, with a branch from Centralia to Chicago.

The land was classified according to desirability and placed on sale. Fifty thousand acres, considered the best, were offered at $20.00 an acre. The next most desirable was 350,000 acres, priced at $15.00 an acre. Another 1,300,000 acres could be bought for $8.00 an acre, and the remainder, about 1,800,000 acres, was offered at $5.00 an acre. It was the policy to sell the land only to those who would occupy and cultivate it. If sold at stated prices it would net the railroad company approximately $25,000,000.

In return for this grant of land the company agreed to pay to the State of Illinois 7 per cent of the road's gross earnings. The first payment of $29,000 was made at the end of December, 1855. It also agreed to make the railway available, without charge, for military transportation. In return the road was exempted from state and local taxes. These provisions still are effective.

The road's construction engineer was Roswell B. Mason, who completed the job in less than the six years agreed upon. Mason drove the last spike at the town named for him, in Effingham County, on September 27, 1856, four days before the deadline. It was the best built and best equipped railroad in the west and opened a great area of desirable land for settlement. One of the greatest development projects of the United States, the Illinois Central still is called the Mainline of Mid-America.

Much of the additional capital needed to construct the road came from England where the project was widely advertised. Because of the interest aroused there, many English settlers came. Within a very few years, in 1861, they totaled 41,745. Numerous colonies of other nationalities likewise came to settle along the way.

When the Civil War broke out it found the Illinois Central and the lands lying along it prosperous. Without definitely planning it so, the railroad was ready to perform its great part in the war. But more of that later.

❀ *A CIRCUS COMES TO SHAWNEETOWN*

AT THE MENTION of the word circus, many memories come trooping back. For the writer, there was that very early morning trip to the corner west of his home where footprints showed an elephant had waded a slough rather than cross the flimsy bridge over it. There had been no opportunity to see the circus at either of the two towns between which it was passing. Discovering the tracks made by the beast, however, was the next best thing and left an abiding resolve to see such an animal in the flesh.

That opportunity came about ten years later when, armed with a cash reserve of ninety cents and stocked with a hearty breakfast, I walked the seven miles to Eldorado and arrived in time to see the elephants—seven of them—cross the railroad track in single file on their way to the circus lot in Mr. Elder's pasture. The rest of the morning was spent in watching the confusion of poles, ropes, wagons, canvas, planks, men, horses, cages, bars, boxes, and banners turn into an orderly arranged circus. Time until the parade was spent in carrying water to get a ticket to a sideshow.

Recently, I came upon a 112-year-old newspaper containing the announcement that a circus was coming to Shawneetown. It was in the May 4, 1855, issue of the *Southern Illinoisan,* a newspaper then published there, and told of a circus due to reach Shawneetown on May 11, just one week later. The combination circus and menagerie was "one of the best in America" and by its announcement, was on its "Southern Campaign." It surely came as near to justifying its use of the terms "stupendous, colossal, magnificent, and prodigious" as any of them did.

The notice opened with "LOOK OUT FOR THE ELEPHANTS." "The E. F. and J. Mabie's Grand Combined Menagerie of Living Beasts, Birds, Reptiles, etc. & & & will exhibit at Shawneetown, on May 11, 1855. S. B. DeSand, Manager and Director." It continued by stating that the proprietors took great pleasure in announcing that they had "recently enlarged their MENAGERIE" and that it was "now the largest of its kind in the United States." They had "succeeded in purchasing an enormous Polar or White Bear that landed at New York in August, 1854, at the enormous expense of $4,500 . . . the only living specimen of its kind in America."

Their collection of "Living wild animals" included "the most splendid specimens ever exhibited in America." They had "Six Beautiful Lions, two Asiatic Lions, Two Cape of Good Hope Lions, One African Lion and One California Lion; also three Young Lions, only six months old." They listed "a Monster White or Polar Bear of prodigious size and ferocity." They also had "The Great Male Elephant Romeo." (Romeo is among the great elephants of circus history. Though usually gentle, he killed at least two trainers.)

They listed "An Arabian or pack camel, a pair of Llamas or Alpacas; an African Deer, Rocky Mountain and Black Bears, Royal Bengal, Brazilian and Black Tigers, Leopards, Panthers, Cougars, Ocelots, Tiger Cats . . . Hyenas . . . Vultures . . . black and white Coons . . . Pelicans" and on and on.

They had "a great variety of Monkeys and such animals." They also offered "The two celebrated Ponies Dick Snowball and Little Fanny Fern . . . with monkey riders Peter Punch and Little Jenny Land for the amusement of the Juveniles." It was also announced that the great elephant Romeo would "go through . . . performances under the management of Herr Hoonsinger, the great elephant trainer." There was "a superb military band." The whole show was "under the superintendence of Mr. Beasley, the Great Lion Tamer who will enter the dens of the Wild Beasts . . . after which the Animals will be fed in the presence of the audience."

The closing of the notice said "Admission 30 cents. Children 10 years of age 15 cents. Doors open at 2 o'clock P.M."

According to a later issue of the paper, May 11, 1855, was a gala day in Old Shawneetown.

Circuses are still with us, but the old-time shows with their romping clowns and pungent animal odors are gone. Lucky are those that once knew them.

❧ THE GENTLE ART OF HORSE SWAPPING

JAMES FENIMORE COOPER's romantic novel, *The Last of the Mohicans,* was published in 1826. If there had been any such list as the present-day ten best sellers, Cooper's story would have surely been on it for a long time. In it he relates the pathetic passing of a once great Indian tribe. His novel also gave to American speech an enduring figure of speech. Since that time the phrase, "last of the Mohicans," has been used frequently to indicate in a somewhat poetical way interesting or admirable specimens of a disappearing type.

This phrase came to mind recently when two men were found dickering over a horse trade. Seeing and hearing them brought about the realization that the once numerous tribe of horse swappers has practically disappeared.

At an earlier time it was a rare community, indeed, that did not have one or more practitioners of the gentle art whose tactics ranged from harmless to vicious. Many of these were really sharp traders. Those among the roving Gypsy bands who swapped and moved on, thus not having to face possible subsequences, were particularly smooth.

In general, horse swapping was conducted on the basis of the thought expressed in the Latin phrase, *Caveat emptor*. To those unacquainted with Latin, its significance was "Let the buyer beware."

Naturally the horse trader didn't issue any warnings. He simply failed to announce any list of defects in the animal he was trying to trade. In later years when both horses and swappers began their steady decline in numbers, state laws were enacted to make horses sound and dealers honest, but the laws had no great effect.

The crafty swapper simply said something like, "No, I don't know all about horses, and haven't had this horse too long, but he appears practically sound." By that it was meant that the animal could get up, walk about, and eat. It was a kind of statement that gently warned the other party to back his own judgment.

The approach to a horse deal was always leisurely. After a few casual remarks and an exchange of opinions about weather and crops, they came around to the idea of trading horses. Present-day rulers of state do not open negotiations more cautiously when crucial affairs are to be discussed.

Among horses up for trade, major and minor defects were common. A horse might have the heaves, be spavined, or have thoroughpin. It could be moon-eyed, stringhalt, balky, cold-shouldered, subject to the studs, given to runaway, parrot mouthed, or even be a stumpsucker. Somehow, owners forgot to announce any such defects. They even took steps to hide them.

According to the lore of horse medicine, heaves could be temporarily suppressed by feeding sunflower seed to the horse or giving him a dose of indigo. (Neither remedy was guaranteed.) The horse that balked or took the studs seemed to be suffering from psychological quirk or mental block; the acute observer often could foresee this from the erratic movement of the animal's head and ears. The owner of such a horse, reading the signals, would call out a lusty whoa, dismount from the buggy or wagon, and pretend to fix the harness. He might even pick up the horse's front foot. Tricks like that seemed to ward off the onset, and the horse would go ahead. The best remedy the writer ever knew was to use a galvanic machine like those once used to treat arthritis. Its use is not advised, however, unless one fully believes he can control a runaway.

The stringhalt horse, if allowed to stand and become cool, was backed up a step or two before starting forward. Otherwise he might try to put his hind foot in the stirrup with the rider's. There was no way to hide the parrot mouth if the prospective buyer would part its lips and look at the teeth. This also enabled one to tell the age of a horse until it was about seven or eight years old, or of those who were very old. The how and why of a stumpsucker remains a startling mystery.

Again, horse swapping was an art with many a sly turn. Why doesn't some old, old man who was skilled at it come out of retirement and write a book? Perhaps such a book would be good required reading for those aspiring to be diplomats. Even better, why not look about for one-time swappers, brief them on the international situation, and give them free rein to settle world problems. They'd be sure to haggle as long as was safe to do so before saying, "Well, let's split the difference." Both sides then could go home firmly convinced they had gotten the best of the bargain.

If no living, functioning horse trader be found available it is suggested that the diplomatic delegation enlist the services of two second-hand car dealers.

❀ THE BOOM DAYS OF PATENT MEDICINES

RUMMAGING AMONG RELICS often starts a strange chain of memories. That happened recently when a small notebook filled with childish scribblings was found in an old trunk. It wasn't the scribbling that started the backward look but the trade name, Piso's Consumption Cure, on the book's cover. First came memories of a Mr. Travis from Peoria who gave the notebook a long lifetime ago. Then came recollections of Piso's and other "cures" proclaimed by painted signs and advertisements in the columns of the weekly papers.

Those old patent medicine ads were something different, but they never were modest. Before 1906 there was no national Pure Food and Drug Act to plague nostrum venders. Their offerings were not remedies; they were "cures" and were announced as such. Their advertisements apparently were written, with claims fully as sweeping, by the same people who wrote circus ads. There literally were hundreds of cures if the printed word were to be believed. In fact one nostrum was offered as a sure cure for twenty-six ills that ranged from headaches to painful feet, "if used according to directions." If the reader doubted the claims, he had only to read the accompanying testimonials that occasionally had survived the writer.

After the coming of the Pure Food and Drug Act and more rigid postal regulations, the patent medicine approach was changed. Consumption cures became remedies and finally retreated to cough sirups. Their great claims were toned down and their chloroform content lessened. Perhaps the old-time "consumption cures" were effective in lulling some victims to their end.

When some scattered copies of a weekly paper, issued between 1850 and 1910, were scanned, it was like having a host of half-forgotten faces parade past and having their names re-echoed. For example, there was that old remedy with the intriguing name of Cephalic Ease, which assured all that it was a specific for headache. The ad, however, did not state that "it dissolves instantly" and "affords immediate relief." Neither did it say that the relief afforded was "three-way," or is it "four-way" now?

Those were the days before hormones, the sulfas, antibiotics, tranquilizers, and assorted wonder drugs. The magic word then seems to have been "vegetable." Deemed especially potent were the "secret Indian remedies" especially those ascribed to the Kickapoo. This line was peddled over America and Europe and even in Australia by roving medicine shows with their Indian members. Kickapoo was a great name among nostrums for thirty years, and it made its promoters millions. A few older persons will recall seeing these shows in southern Illinois.

At one time there were literally hundreds of patent medicines sold over the counters of general stores. Some elderly persons will remember the distinctive cartons that held them and the labels they carried. A typical one of the old remedies was Hostetter's Celebrated Stomach Bitters with its picture of St. George slaying the dragon. (I am still wondering just why St. George should be there.) The alcoholic content of Hostetter's, once very high, finally was reduced to "25% by volume." Since medication did not render it offensive to the taste, its sales were tremendous. Its promoters became wealthy while some customers became inebriated.

Wine of Cardui for Women was another widely heralded remedy that many will remember in its yellow and black carton. They also will remember the kneeling Indian maiden, the standing white woman, and the streamer that said, "Take and Be Healed, The Great Spirit Planted

It." This medicine also was very popular with men until it was loaded with too much laxative. With Wine of Cardui went *Ladies Birthday Almanac* that extolled the virtues of the wine, and of Thedford's Black Draught.

While many of the patent medicines featured whiskered faces on their labels, one face of a woman stood out, the face of the lady who gave to the world Lydia E. Pinkham's Vegetable Compound, one of the all-time greats. There were Smith Bros. Cough Drops, Dr. Pierce's Golden Medical Discovery, and his *Common Sense Medical Adviser* that was printed in the millions. It was a rival of *Gunn's Family Physician,* another best seller.

These were followed by Paine's Celery Compound, Old Wahoo Bitters, Sarsaparilla, both Hood's and Ayers', Sirup of Figs that never knew a fig, Radway's Ready Relief (RRR), Plantation Chill Tonic, Kilmer's Swamp Root, SSS (can't remember what it stood for), Sloan's Liniment, Castoria (both Fletcher's and Pitcher's) that soothed the crying babies, Morse's Little Liver Pills, and Doan's Kidney Pills. A photograph made more than seventy years ago shows a great sign on the north wall of a building on the site of the First National Bank of Carbondale that proclaimed it the home of Doan's Kidney Pills. On the shelves of numerous older drugstores one still finds these and other legendary remedies still in stock.

Some people still diagnose their own ills, brew their remedies, or buy patent medicines and treat themselves, but the heyday of patent medicines has passed. True, they still appear on television where a colorless character appears with a mirror strapped to his forehead and begins his parrot-like chant with "doctors recommend . . ."

How some people would thrill to see the immaculate spieler of old, dressed in a fawn-colored double-breasted suit, spats, wing collar, signal tie, gloves, cane, and hightopper, mount the tailgate of a spring wagon, look calmly over the spring crowd, and launch into a real spiel. To those with memories of the Kickapoo Indian medicine show and the performance of the skilled pitch man of that day, the "doctors recommend" approach can only cause them to sadly shake their heads and mutter "How the mighty have fallen."

🌸 TRAVELING SHOWS

No ONE IS a juvenile who remembers seeing some lone showman plodding down a dusty roadway with a dejected and footsore bear or a performing dog on leash. Instead of a bear or dog, the animal companion could be a monkey or an educated pony. The musical part of the show—and no show could be considered complete without music—generally consisted of a violin, a flute, or a hand organ. Some showmen also sang, after a fashion.

These wandering showmen and their animal companions disappeared from southern Illinois long ago. Along with them went the Punch and Judy shows, medicine shows, and an occasional wagon show.

The one-man animal show followed closely on the frontier and came early. The man, part of the show troupe, is generally remembered as a foreigner. He and his supporting cast and props are recalled as dirty, neglected, and apparently much the worse for wear.

Appearing at any place where there was opportunity to gather a crowd, the showman would begin his chatter. Having attracted a small group, the show got under way. With proper tempo and some "hup's," and "ho's," his bear or dog, pony or monkey would go into its act. The bear, with the showman still holding the leash, would do a shuffling, spiritless dance. The dog would jump over a cane, through a hoop, roll over, stand on its hind feet, play dead, bark at command, and do other simple acts. The monkey would squeak, tip its hat, collect coins or listlessly perform other tricks. The pony would stomp, paw, kick, bare its teeth, gallop in a circle, prance, or toss its head.

When the act was completed, the hat was passed or the crowd was asked to pitch coins in a circle. Sometimes the monkey, when it was part of the show, would, with the typical appearance of sadness common to them, pass about the crowd holding a tin cup into which those attending were asked to place coins. Often the soliciting monkey had been trained to take each coin from the cup as it was received and place it in the pocket of the vest it wore. The bear, when it was not muzzled, was taught to sit on its haunches and catch any bits of food that might be tossed to it.

At one performance observed, the monkey's act took on a strange turn when a dog, apparently with the owner's approval, harassed the monkey until it took refuge on top of the hand organ. The dog's owner, apparently enjoying it all, paid no heed to the showman's request to curb the dog. The monkey's owner accordingly gave the monkey a stick about a foot long and as hefty as the monkey could well handle. At the next disrupting approach of the dog, the showman gave the monkey a push. It sprang upon the surprised dog's back and, holding on with its three free hands, began to belabor the startled dog. No one had to say, "Get for home Bruno!" With a string of sharp yelps, the dog made the first hundred yards in that direction in the proverbial "nothing flat."

Punch and Judy shows also were common. In these the performers were puppets fitted on the hands of the showmen. These puppets would appear above the stage or screen. Their manipulators remained hidden above or below the stage. Skillfully operated by the showman and accompanied by animated dialogue in a Donald Duck tone of voice, they invariably amused the audience. After each act they sold something.

Another type of show, one that lingered for a later time than those already mentioned, was the medicine show. This show usually had a larger troupe, often as many as a half-dozen members.

An occasional performer in one of these troupes might later attain fame. It is said that James Whitcomb Riley, the beloved Hoosier poet, toured with such a show. He wrote their skits and adapted their plays as well as picking the banjo and singing. This was after he had closed his career as a blind sign painter.

As in the Punch and Judy shows, a spellbinding pitch man would mount the rostrum after each number or act and sell some wonderful remedy, one that would cure about all human ills from dandruff and headache to corns and bunions, or "your dollar back after three days use." By then the show would be in the next town.

Another favorite product for sale at these shows was a pungent smelling liniment, that likewise was guaranteed "to cure toothache, headache, rheumatism, and aching joints." Once again there was the "your money back guarantee." The last medicine show seen in Carbondale was on Wall Street in 1940.

All those shows were amusing. They provided much of our out-of-the community entertainment. Does anyone know where one can get a hand organ and a trained bear? At latest reports there were only a dozen or so still going about.

❧ *HE TRUSTED A STRANGER*

WILEY GRISHAM was a part-time minister, a "hardshell" Baptist, who lived near the post office of Oak in northern Pope County in the 1880's. Those old enough to remember him recall that he wore long white whiskers and appeared always to be chewing tobacco. None remember any details regarding his sermons, but there are people still living who heard him preach and they remember the three-day meetings—actually short revivals—that he held in different places.

Tradition tells us that he was unassuming—a man of little property and simple tastes—but he had the kind of personality that one does not forget. He also is remembered as an ingenious individual, one who contrived and made useful devices, often after his own design. One of these, an automatic gate, survived him several years.

It was a boon to travelers at that time, when all cultivated fields and practically every homesite was fenced. Entrance to farmsteads was by gateways for those riding horseback or driving a wagon. Something was needed which the traveler could operate to open and close the gate without dismounting, and Grisham supplied it.

His gate was operated by long levers extending above and to the center of the roadway. A length of rope dangled from one lever. A hefty tug at the rope would open the closed gate. Beyond the gate another extended lever and bit of rope would close the gate.

Grisham made and sold these gates over a considerable territory. Some persons on this side of seventy may recall seeing such gates. Several are yet in use mostly for decorative purposes in the bluegrass region of Kentucky where lanes lead to old plantation homes, but none are known in southern Illinois.

Grisham also made and sold patented churns over the countryside. His master invention, however, was in no way connected with his rural surroundings. Its need was made apparent to him by the misfortunes of some men he knew who had become railway brakemen. Those were the days of link and pin couplings for railway cars, and lucky indeed was the man who worked for years as a brakeman and still had all his fingers and both hands. Grisham, knowing of this constant danger to brakemen, decided he would partially eliminate the danger by making an automatic coupler.

The models that Grisham fashioned were interesting. He used cigar boxes to simulate box cars. Their axles and drawbars were made of wood, split and whittled to proper shape and size. Car wheels were the end of spools that once had held Clark's O.N.T. sewing thread. The strangest parts of all were the automatic coupling devices whittled from yellow poplar wood with a pocket knife.

A collection of three or four of these miniature cars equipped with automatic couplings were carried by Grisham in a large basket to the home of Pleas Austin, then living between Oak and present-day Dixon Springs. They were demonstrated on Austin's walnut dining table before an interested group. Grisham coupled and uncoupled his model cars repeatedly. Then he reversed the cars, changed their order, and repeated the process until all present were thoroughly convinced. Dr. Edgar Austin, now in his eighty's and living in Florida, was an inquisitive small boy who looked on.

A short time later Grisham took his models to Washington, D.C., to seek a patent. While looking about and trying to master the patent-getting process, he met a man interested in the same objective. This man proved to be friendly, cooperative, and ingratiating. He proposed that Grisham, tired of waiting and not too well supplied with funds, just leave his models and go home. The stranger said he would attend to all details, bear expenses, and surmount other possible difficulties, all for a half interest. Grisham agreed and returned home.

After a considerable lapse of time without any cheering word from his newfound friend, Grisham returned to Washington. The "friend" was no longer helpful, nor was a half interest in a patent awaiting him. It is said that an attorney he consulted informed Grisham that he could not sell half an idea that could not be measured. So Grisham returned to Pope County, a sadder and wiser man. The coupling adopted by the Master Car Builders in 1887 carries many of his invention's features.

Other southern Illinois inventors have fared better. A man from Shawneetown made about two million dollars from the time lock. Successful pumps came from Eldorado and DuQuoin; Sparta and Ava helped along with development of the plow. Cobden men have patented basic machines for boxmaking. Legend has it that the Diamond plow was a McLeansboro creation. County records often carry information about patents because they once were applied for through county channels.

🏵 *THE PADDIES ARE GONE*

A SLIGHT BUT apparently durable old man with an uncropped grizzled beard and a strangely detached air was seen plodding along beside the highway a few days ago. This unusual foot traveler revived memories of a unique tribe of men that has practically disappeared from the southern Illinois scene along with log houses, rail fences, and well sweeps.

He carried rolled blankets, a couple of small tied-on bundles that may have been reserve rations, an extra overcoat, and a couple of blackened cooking containers, which readily identified him as a true "gentleman of the road." In the author's childhood, such men were frequently encountered; some estimated that their numbers once totaled a half-million.

The ones the author remembers were called paddies, and from that day to this all of them have suggested the adaption of the Irish name of Pat and they have been "paddies" to me. But many other names have come along to designate that wandering fraternity. They have been called hobos, tramps, bums, floaters, gentlemen of the open road, tin can Willies, bindle stiffs, and bundle stiffs, footpads, vagabonds, vagrants, boomers, homeless men, and a dozen other names.

Whatever they were called, there was one common trait among these strange strollers. All were moved by a powerful impulse to wander, an itching foot. People interested in the here-today-and-gone-tomorrow type of citizens have made attempts to classify them and have come up with three overlapping general classifications: hobos, tramps, and bums.

Members of the first group worked and wandered, somewhat as migratory workers do today. They either walked or hitched rides on trains. Now the counterpart of the old-time hobo moves in waves, often by truck or trailer to care for seasonal crops like ripening fruit. They then were, and still are, a partial solution to the need for seasonal labor. The word hobo came from hoe boy, meaning a farm hand. Without hobos, many of whom were skilled craftsmen, the lot of the pioneer would have been even more difficult.

A second group of homeless men were known as tramps, those who wandered and dreamed but worked only when it could not easily be avoided. They went about with strange political, social, economic, and religious views which they believed would provide a solution to all problems, particularly theirs, if only people would listen and pay heed. Some farmers distinguished between hobos and tramps by looking at their hands; if they were calloused and sturdy, the man got more consideration.

Third among the group were the bums. These were looked upon as beggars or moochers. They didn't work, wander, or dream as much as the others. They figuratively were the home guard—a remnant of which survives in the skid rows of many cities, where one writer says they were drawn by "soap, soup, sleep, and salvation," the bounties held out by welfare organizations. Most of the panhandlers of the cities came from these skid rows to work their chosen beats during the more productive hours of the day or night and return to the row for a bed and sleep.

With the passing of the hobo from the rural area, his gathering place or jungle also has vanished. These stopping places were located conveniently near railway yards, near the tanks where locomotives took on water or where tracks crossed and trains stopped regularly. This location enabled those who came riding the rods, the blinds, or the bumpers—as well as those coming by side door pullman or coal car—to debark when arriving or entrain when it came time to leave. Both arrivals and departures were unheralded.

Jungles were set up outside town and villages in order that they would attract less police notice. These campsites had rigid self-imposed regulations, a code of jungle laws. The areas were kept surprisingly clean. Those going away were not allowed to leave their litter scattered about. Any who engaged in behavior that caused law enforcement officers to call were made unwelcome. Drunkenness and fighting were banned. Loud noise was not allowed for there were those who would sleep.

They cooked and ate at all hours, depending upon when food was available. A man who ate food that he had not helped scrounge for was termed a jungle buzzard. Those who cooked or sat by the fires also helped to gather wood.

The jungle of my childhood memory was located on the bank of Brushy Creek near the village of Texas City in northeastern Saline County. It was convenient to the place where locomotives took water. The smoke and gleam of the little fires there lent a lonely cheer. It was at this camp where the author, as a small boy, looked hungrily on until he was given some mulligan in a tin can. By eating this he qualified as a jungle buzzard.

The bands of old-time hobos, tramps, and bums have disappeared from our landscape. Their pitiful remnants remain in the skid rows of the cities, but the hobo of romance, often an intelligent skilled man, is only a memory. The old man plodding along the road a few days ago was a straggling rear guard of a shadowy host that has passed.

❦ TO BROUGHTON ON A SATURDAY AFTERNOON

ON A RECENT SATURDAY afternoon two "boys," one well-fed and balding, the other gray and thinner, both tall, slightly stooped and unhurried, took the afternoon off to make a sentimental journey down memory's lane. They went back to Broughton, the place that was "town" to them when they were boys.

Broughton is not hard to find. It still is on the map. One would be almost correct to say it is still, period.

The once familiar town was found greatly changed. In fact, much of it survives only in ruins. In this, it is much like dozens of other southern Illinois villages that have seen better days, days when they were thriving and somewhat important trading centers. They are called trading centers here rather than shopping centers. The term describes them better, for it was in such villages that the trade and barter customs once typical of the pioneer era were retained and practiced longest.

In pioneer times there was very little money circulating in the recently settled areas. Thus people were, from necessity, forced to trade and barter. For "boughten" goods from the merchant's stock they traded venison, hams, hides, furs, eggs, poultry, home-cured meats, butter, dried fruits, sorghum, wild honey, ax handles, railroad crossties, in fact anything produced in surplus.

It was for this necessary trading that people living on surrounding farms and at cleared patches in the extensive woodlands made their regular trading trips to town. Most people chose Saturday afternoon as the time. They came laden with baskets of eggs, molds of butter, bags of dried fruits and other assorted produce. They came on foot, on horseback, and in farm wagons when the weather and road conditions permitted. Some arrived by sled, mudboat, or lizard. The ox-drawn wagons are recalled.

If the farmer brought more produce than was necessary to get goods sufficient to meet his immediate needs, some merchants would pay him cash for the balance due. This generally was at a market discount, often as much as 20 per cent. The practice more often used was for the merchant to give due bills. Sometimes these would be written out on slips of paper. At other times they were on printed tickets, somewhat like children's play money. A specimen recently coming to attention said "Good for Twenty-five Cents in Trade at Hamilton and Gaines." The owner had failed to trade it in before the store closed about forty years ago.

There once were two large general stores in town. Today a building occupied by one of them has been leveled. The other is a gaunt ruin occupied by a repair shop. Then there were two banks, two busy blacksmith shops, two doctors' offices, a drugstore, a milliner shop, a hotel, a large livery stable with a dozen or more rigs, a flour mill, carpenter shops, a cobbler's shop, a railway section house, and a railway station where the crowd gathered regularly "to let the train go through."

Those who knew any small town a lifetime ago will recall many other things that made it interesting. For instance, there were the barrels of green coffee berries that the frugal housewife took home to roast in her oven or in a skillet on the cookstove or fireplace hearth. This coffee was ground fresh for each making unless the grounds had been saved and were being boiled over, or was it "biled over"? From boyish memory no brewing coffee ever has had an aroma so delightful.

There were stock pens with high board walls in which livestock was gathered for shipping to market in railway stock cars. No one dreamed that trucks someday would come to take over.

Then there were the old men and idle men who sat on the wooden boxes, benches, ledges, porches, or about pot bellied stoves in stores, offices, or wherever facilities offered and weather indicated. Many among these were skilled whittlers, making interesting and curious objects. Among some cherished keepsakes is a short length of chain made from a broomstick. They also discussed many subjects, often with surprising insight and grasp.

The general stores offered barlead for casting bullets or making sinkers for fish lines. There was shot of assorted sizes, gunpowder in grain size for rifle or musket, fish hooks, and staging for fish lines. If no cane poles were offered the angler could cut a hickory or pawpaw pole.

No thinking person wants to go back to "those good old days." Likewise, no thinking person would dismiss their significance. To those of us who knew them, they provide delightful musings.

Chapter 7

Farm Life

❦ *ARTIFACTS TELL STORIES*

AN ARTIFACT IS some tool, implement, or device that man has fashioned for his use. Much of what we know concerning the manner in which earlier people lived has been learned from study of the artifacts they left. It is from a study of such objects found where ancient peoples lived that archeologists have learned much concerning the manner of life of men who lived before records were written. Southern Illinois is rich in archeological offerings.

Whenever archeology is mentioned many persons think of earlier or prehistoric peoples. In this field southern Illinois is particularly rich. It is also rich in a later mass of materials into which almost anyone may delve. These are the old tools, implements, devices, and products that our white ancestors used here. Interesting glimpses of the ways in which our ancestors lived is learned from a study designated by some as smokehouse-attic-closet-and-old-barn archeology.

It really is not necessary to turn back to prehistory to study archeology. An illustration of such an opportunity came recently when an old sickle or reaphook was found. Seeing this implement suggested some of the methods our grandfathers employed to harvest grain in southern Illinois.

This harvesting tool is a somewhat crude one. It has a wooden handle, a slender, curved, tapering, and sharp-pointed blade about an inch wide and twenty-four inches long. Hammer marks show that this blade was made by hand. This particular one was brought from Ireland to Randolph County a century and a half ago. It must have been, even then, a cherished heirloom to have been included in the family effects brought on such a long journey. It could just as well have come from ancient Egypt, for these tools have changed but little in thousands of years. No longer in common use to harvest grain, surviving reaphooks now are occasionally used to trim the grass beside flower beds and near shrubs.

When man first found that the seeds of certain grasses like wheat, oats, barley, rye, and rice were good foods, he doubtlessly gathered them, rubbed them out with his bare hands, then rudely prepared and ate them. It was only natural that a man would contrive some device like a reaphook to help gather grain.

The very earliest reaphooks found by archeologists on the sites where their users laid them aside or lost them centuries ago are long, sharp-edged stone knives. Traces indicate that those more primitive ones of wood have decayed.

That some kind of a wooden device first was used is indicated by practices still found in use among the American Indians. When white men came to the Great Lakes region, they found Indian squaws using short paddles or blades to beat, clip, and rake the grain heads from rice that grew along the margins of lakes and streams. They held the heads of the rice over the sides of canoes to beat or strip the grain, allowing it to fall into the bottom of their craft.

The metal reaphook used by the Egyptians and the manner of its use has changed very little for thousands of years. The sharp end of its narrow curved blade was passed among the stalks of standing grain to gather as much as the hand could conveniently grasp. These bunches then were clipped by the hook and laid in ordered piles to be bound into sheaves. Wisps of straw served as strings to tie these bundles that generally were carried to some sheltered place where they could be safeguarded and allowed to dry. Grain was too valuable and scarce to be left in unguarded fields.

This old Irish reaphook also brought back to memory an old custom that was a part of the early harvest. It was a custom, in some countries, that the poor be allowed to come and glean in the grain fields when the harvesters had finished. The biblical story of Ruth illustrates this ancient custom. These gleaners were permitted to collect the fallen heads and any remaining stalks of grain they could find, a custom in practice within memory.

About 1894 several neighbors gave a widowed Mrs. McFadden in Saline County permission to glean from their harvested wheat fields. The grain that she and her children gathered and rubbed out by hand was not fed to the chickens or pigs. Mrs. McFadden took it to the mill and received flour that provided her biscuit supply for several months.

Neighbors also allowed her to gather the ears of corn missed by huskers. All admired the industry and frugality of Mrs. McFadden and her children.

The very earliest threshing, that is the separation of grain from straw, doubtlessly was by rubbing the heads of grain in the palms. Next it seems to have been beaten out by flailing or by marching horses or oxen over the sheaves of grain laid in a circle on a threshing floor.

🌼 *GRAIN HARVESTING*

ONLY A FEW YEARS ago a flail was found in the feedway of a barn in the Webb's Prairie settlement of Franklin County. A middle-aged farmer assured me it had hung on that selfsame peg for fifty years. The rawhide thongs that linked the two sections of the flail were stiff and brittle.

Perhaps the flail would not have been so impressive if a modern grain combine had not stood in a shed beside the same barn. Taken together, the flail, hanging on its wooden peg, and the combine, standing beneath the shed, told their parts of an interesting story to anyone ready to listen.

The reaphook and flail were the principal tools of harvesting bread grains for many centuries, remaining so until the introduction of the grain cradle about 1750. It is this cradle with its strangely bent handle, long keen cutting blade, and rack of slender, curved wooden fingers, that one often sees among a collection of obsolete farm tools. Those who have seen the steady, swaying, rhythmical, and rather graceful advance of a string of cradlers as they followed across the grain field will not forget the image they presented.

Anyone who has heard the click and rasp of the scythe stones as cradlers pause to whet their blades will remember that distinctive sound. There also are memories of the swishing sounds made by the keen edge of the blades at their cutting stroke, the thud of flails, and many other sounds. Those old enough to have seen them also will remember the stooped, intent, and hurrying workmen who followed behind the cradlers to gather the bunched grain into bundles, and to tie it with thin strands of straw.

A primitive cylinder threshing machine soon was made to separate the grain and straw. The first of these was little more than a rapidly revolving sharp section of log, generally a hard-to-split sour gum, thickly set with nails for teeth. Nicknamed the Groundhog, it was powered by an ox or a horse walking in a treadmill; it might even be turned by hand cranks. Grain was threshed by holding the heads of the grain bundle against the whirling teeth until the grain had been beaten out and had fallen beneath and about the rude machine. With the improvement of these early threshers, flailing and threshing floors slowly disappeared. Today we know of only one threshing floor preserved in America. This one is in a rebuilt barn at the Saline County Museum in Harrisburg, Illinois.

Ingenious operators improved and increased the sizes of the primitive threshers. Concaves or fixed sections set with iron teeth next were arranged beneath the cylinder, and the straw was passed between the concaves and cylinder. An inclined table and belt of slats later were added to carry the straw away, while the grain fell between the slats. A belt-driven fan later was attached to blow away most of the chaff and trash. This grain often was recleaned with hand-operated centrifugal fans.

It was at about this stage in grain production that farmers came to settle on the Illinois prairie. Increased industrial development and an added population created a demand for more grain. The millions of acres of fertile land they found thus offered great opportunities. Improved transportation helped toward better distribution.

Cyrus McCormick, who had made his first reaper in a Virginia blacksmith shop, came to Illinois to develop and perfect his invention. Obed Hussey and others also made harvesting machines. The prairies of Illinois provided a ready-made proving ground for harvesting machines, a place to perfect their devices.

After some years, machines called headers came to gather only the heads of wheat for conveyance to the thresher. These machines were followed in turn by the modern combine. From the reaphook-flail stage to that of the combine was a long and significant step, suggested by the two objects found at the Franklin County barn.

After grain had been threshed by flailing, trampling, or with the early Groundhog, it still was necessary to separate it from the unwanted straw, chaff, and trash. In order to do this the flailed, beaten, or trampled bundles of grain were lifted with forks, and any loose grain was shaken from them. The straw was saved for feeding or for bedding farm animals. It also was used for stuffing straw ticks for beds and for hens' nests. The padding beneath household carpets was made of straw. It also was used to cover and protect apples, potatoes, cabbage, turnips, and other crops "holed up" for the winter. Seldom was it wasted.

After the straw had been removed, when the process was almost entirely one of hand, winnowing was begun. By this process the grain with its chaff generally was carried to a doorway of the barn driveway or to the corner of some building where a dependable breeze was most likely to be found. The mixture of grain and chaff left on the threshing floor was swept into piles, dipped up in shallow baskets or ladles, and taken to the selected breezy spot. The ladles were then held high and their contents poured in a thin stream over the ladle edges to fall through the breeze.

The heavier grain fell into a heap at the laborers' feet, while most of the chaff was blown away. When necessary, the process was repeated until the grain was sufficiently clean. If a natural breeze was not available, large fans, to be manually operated, were made of blankets on wooden frames. However it was done, winnowing was a tedious task.

It is not the reaphooks, flails, and combines, alone, that tell stories. Barns, basements, and smokehouses often yield other tools that talk to those who listen with properly attuned ears. There are mauls, wedges, and gluts that tell of rail making; frows, mallets, and board brakes that show the way clapboards were made. New ground plows, double shovels, crude grain drills, spinning wheels, hand cards, flax hackles, and many other tools are ready to tell us how early settlers did their work. Without these to see many a process remains extremely vague, often not being understandable to those who never saw the process in operation.

❧ THRESHING MACHINES RECALL OLDEN TIMES

A POWER PROGRESS SHOW of farm machinery is held at the Perry County fairgrounds in Pinckneyville each early autumn. At the same time and place the American Thresherman Association, an organization formed to memorialize olden methods of farming, particularly the harvesting and threshing of grain, holds its annual meeting. With these two appeals, no further reason was sought to justify spending a couple of hot but enjoyable days at the combined meetings.

Any inquisitive visitor soon learned that trucks, trailers, and lowboys had been arriving with strange cargoes for several days. Evidence of that fact was distributed widely over the fairgrounds. These carriers had come from many states and from long distances. Some were from as far away as Texas, Colorado, Minnesota, and Nebraska.

In addition to these arrivals from more distant places, there was a large area of the exhibit grounds covered with the most modern farm power tools, much like those seen on implement dealers' lots. Somehow, these were not so interesting to this old-timer as those tools that were "modern" a few generations ago.

After a preliminary look at random exhibits of the earlier planting and harvesting devices, the visitor came upon the very solid exhibit of threshing equipment. The most attention-compelling part of this was the score or so of steam traction engines. These engines had come from widely separated places. One, seventy years old, had come on a lowboy directly from Lincoln, Nebraska, where it had taken part in the centennial observance of steam traction engines moved by their own power on the roadways and over the fields of the United States.

Many of the men exhibiting engines at Pinckneyville were as interesting as their charges. Except for a few young men who apparently were determined to keep the romance of threshing days alive, none were youngsters. Their dress and mannerisms were those of the men following threshers fifty years ago. Come to think of it, one difference was noted: no tobacco chewer was observed. One and all appeared to be doing well at reliving the pleasantly remembered days. All in all it was an old men and boys' day. A listener often could overhear such remarks as: "Do you remember?" "As I recall." Many of these lookers once were the hand cutters, sack holders, or straw stackers, before the blower (cyclone) thresher came.

Some had driven bundle wagons. Others had pitched bundles or helped man the pump on the wooden box tank of the wagon that brought water to a constantly thirsty engine. This water most often was from a pond. Well water, generally hard, would cause scale in the boilers.

Some had been waterboys and had trudged barefoot to carry jugs of water to workmen in the field. A lucky one of these boys sometimes went afield on a gentle nag with his jug hung to the saddlehorn with a hamestring.

While the old men looked and reveled in memories, the present-day boys were doing as boys have always done about threshing outfits. They were clambering over the habitable parts of engines and separators, that is, so far as the men in charge permitted.

Old-time threshing methods were demonstrated and described by a narrator. An elderly man using a hickory flail, jointed with a rawhide thong and having a polish that only long use could give, deftly and rhythmically flailed a bundle of wheat, just as men were doing five thousand years ago. Good flailers were skilled men. Since no place had been prepared, the ancient threshing floor was described by a narrator using a portable loudspeaker—quite a contrast.

Then came the first thresher as we know it, a rapidly whirling cylinder set with iron teeth and turned madly by men at its cranks. The one used for demonstration was like the one used by George Washington on his Virginia plantation about two hundred years ago. It came from that period of time. Wheat stalks by handfuls were held against the whirring teeth until the grain was beaten out and the straw laid carefully aside. Grain and chaff were separated by being poured from elevated baskets at some breezy place. Large hand fans sometimes were used. This thresher was the Groundhog.

Other exhibits traced the evolution of the Groundhog through the bulky separator, which now has practically disappeared in favor of the self-propelled combine.

Threshing was a great time in any community. It had its social values. Men swapped work; women and children visited. Threshing dinners were tradition and women vied in their preparation. The names of threshing operators became household words. In the Broughton area the names of Charley Johnson, the Essareys, Thomas Allen, Ali Shriver, and Riley Bishop will bring memories to many older persons, just as other names will to those in other vicinities. Many will recall the names of engines and separators, like Advance, Case, Jumbo, Avery, Keck-Gonnerman, Aultman-Taylor, Russell, and others coming less readily to mind.

No one was heard expressing a wish to have the old days return. To a man, however, all wanted to remember those hot, dusty days of hard work and the great threshing dinners that went with them. Anyone interested in the way of farm life fifty years or more ago should note the next meeting of an American Thresherman Association and plan to attend.

🌼 FARMING THEN AND NOW

MUSTY OLD NEWSPAPERS are interesting whether they are found on an attic shelf, piled pell-mell in a box, or perchance used as wallpaper. Some have been thoughtless enough to paste them upside down. This may not have been entirely bad since it furnished inquisitive youngsters opportunity to learn to read upside-down print.

Recently, an 1848 file of *Prairie Farmer* came to hand. It was especially interesting since the publication is still going merrily along today. Established in 1841, the paper was generally regarded to be ahead of its time.

At that, the 1848 file made no mention of silos, tractors, photographs, color films, or cameras. Not a word was found concerning grain dryers, milk coolers, or hydraulic dump trucks. There was not a single Charolaise or Santa Gertrudis bull for sale. It spoke of hens and how to make them lay but said not a word about Specific Pathogenic Pigs.

There were no advertisements for materials to build farrowing pens, nor for infrared lamps to warm newly born pigs.

There was then, just as now, a protest that taxes were too high. The paper gave staunch support to education, which it insisted was neglected.

The paper carried no regular feature warning against sharpsters who went about tricking farmers. It declared, however, that a recommended paint was misrepresented. It told of grass plots where strips were given different treatment and results observed—an early evidence of experimental farming. McCormick reapers and John Deere plows were in vogue then, about the only name products still advertised in the paper.

One correspondent told of growing a thousand bushels of potatoes and placing them in his storage room at a total cost of three cents a bushel. However, the market price in Chicago was only twenty-five cents a bushel. General Semple was about ready to start his Prairie Car across country from Alton to Springfield.

Fence rails were scarce in many localities, and Professor Turner was extolling the virtues of the Osage orange hedges. At the same time he was declaring that budded or grafted trees never could be equal to seedlings. This, he said, was because a tree's vitality decreases in proportion to distance from the seed that produced it. That belief still was common sixty years later. Mention was made of a *Phrenological Almanac* to help one evaluate an individual by studying the shape of his head and the "bumps" on it.

One man bemoaned the fact that corn was planted with a hoe. He wondered why someone didn't make a device to lay off four properly spaced furrows at a time. There was speculation about wire fencing, just then coming into use.

Snakes must have been a problem, for there were numerous remedies suggested for their bites. One lauded the blended juice of horehound and plantain. Another said poultices made from the leaves and inner bark of white ash were wonderful. Another thought ambeer was a specific. A Union County man insisted that a sharp knife, fearlessly and judiciously applied, was the most potent remedy.

There was a protest against hogs running at large. One correspondent told how to train sheep dogs and accustom sheep to them. Another gave a recipe for making beer. The argument that wheat turned into chess or cheat raged on.

The Chicago market report showed that feathers were \$.32 a pound. Eggs were \$.10 a dozen, and chickens were \$.12½ each. Flour was \$4.00 a barrel. Wool was \$.25 a pound and oats \$.23 a bushel. Cornmeal was \$.75 a hundred pounds. Empty barrels were \$.75 each and salt was \$1.50

a barrel. The very best of lumber was $22.00 a thousand board feet and roofing shingles were $2.50 a thousand.

❦ DESERTED BUILDINGS TELL STORIES

ABANDONED FARMSTEADS with clusters of empty, tumble-down buildings are found beside little traveled country roads of southern Illinois. In some cases it would be better to say nearly empty for those moving away often left an assortment of objects no longer considered valuable. These discarded objects are ever ready to tell interesting stories to those who listen attentively.

Various tools, implements, and devices left at two deserted farms beside a dim roadway in a Pope County woodland are typical of such storytelling artifact collections. These two places provided an interesting rainy day afternoon of inside prowling. Numerous others may be found equally eloquent.

Two log buildings, with the assortment of farm bric-a-brac that one held, occupied the afternoon. One of these was a tumble-down corncrib of round poles with a roof so old it was moss covered. It was interesting for its carefully notched and fitted corners that showed skilled and accurate workmanship, particularly when lavished upon a building made of round poles. Comparison of these corners and those of an older building aroused an interest in log house corners; just how many patterns of notching were there anyway? Now we are photographing, sketching, and making models of corners for log houses we encounter in an effort to find out. Preliminary checking has shown a bewildering variety of corner patterns.

A larger carefully hewed two-story log dwelling had wide sheds added at each side, a fate common to many log houses when prosperity or an increasing family required more living space. Once this house had a large, twenty by twenty-four foot inside size, a combined living room, bedroom, and parlor. There were traces of a combined kitchen and dining rooms of boxed construction that had been added later but had since been removed from the north side of the main structure.

It must have been a nice house. Two lower-story windows and two half windows upstairs, all on the north side, provided light. Only a few small panes of wavy glass remained in broken frames. The wavy glass with its pale, purplish, fluorescent glow showed it to be very old.

Inside walls, carefully chinked and daubed, had never been painted, whitewashed, or papered. Little had been done to either the inside or outside woodwork. The only inside parts painted were the window and door trim. These were a flat blue. All other parts of both downstairs and upstairs rooms were left in natural wood finish. Square wrought iron nails, not too many, and wooden pegs held the house together.

Two wide sheds, one on either side, long ago made this old dwelling into a substantial barn and provided shelter for tools and implements. Wedged betweeen logs, lying on shelves and ledges, hanging from roof rafters, and scattered on a littered floor were many objects that told of the almost forgotten way in which people once lived and how they did their work.

Parts from an old grain cradle, a bull wheel from a binder, a moldy ball of binder twine, and some rolls of slatted binder canvas, hanging by wires from roof rafters to protect it from mice and rats, indicated harvesting methods in precombine days.

Parts of a new-ground plow, a broken double shovel, some hand hoes, a hand corn planter, a steel-beam walking plow with bits of brittle leather and rusted harness fittings, old horseshoes, trace chains, single-trees, and bridle bits showed how farmers raised their crops. A well windlass tied on a high ledge of one wall indicated how they dug wells and drew water.

A wooden harness sewing needle (rare indeed), homemade calf weaners, bailing wire muzzles for work animals, neck yokes for breechy stock, hollow black gum feeding troughs, and assorted other contrivances indicated an ingenuity that came from necessity. Two old badly rusted lanterns told of the before-daylight and after-dark hours of labor.

Archeologists seeking objects that help to tell how a vanished people lived dig at sites where old cities have stood. Anyone can follow their methods and prowl about deserted buildings and abandoned farmsteads to learn how his great grandfather lived and worked. Moreover, in practicing this surface archeology it is not necessary to dig—just look.

❦ THIS MAN HAS HIS OWN MUSEUM

A RECENT VISIT with a friend who collects and cherishes old implements and devices brought to mind the fact that many articles once in common use have about vanished from sight.

The first object that greets the visitor entering the garage where this man's strange collection is kept in easy disorder is a wooden cigar store Indian, about life-sized. With his war bonnet of carved feathers and a handful of wooden cigars, the figure is typical of numerous similar ones which formerly graced the fronts of many stores that sold tobacco.

After being greeted by the wooden Indian just within the doorway, the visitor views a collection of strange and ofttimes puzzling objects which fill many shelves and litter the garage floor. First there are the familiar candle molds that all recognize and few know how to use properly. There are grease lamps of pottery and metal with other devices designed to hold candles, pine knots, splinters, or perhaps tapers made from the pithy stems of weed stalks soaked in fats. Two candle lanterns, a kerosene lantern, and a coal oil lamp in my friend's unpretentious collection of lighting devices rather graphically tell the story of home lighting.

Beyond the shelf where these lighting devices were piled, there was no semblance of ordered storage. Thus, the next object encountered was a "floor dog." This dog was a low, staple-like device whose turned-down ends were driven into floor joists when laying floors. Wedges were driven against them to hold flooring tightly in place while boring holes for pegging or nailing planks down. When old buildings are dismantled, the floor joists often show scars where these devices were driven.

Next was an old dish containing an assortment of small objects. Among these were a couple of bullet molds, a powder charger, and four metal cherries of graduated sizes, which once were used to bore molds to the desired caliber. With these there were some file-like objects that gunsmiths used to cut rifling and smooth lands in the barrels of Kentucky rifles. A lead-smeared iron ladle and a wooden worm that had long baffled its present owner were found elsewhere in the collection to tell more of the early gunmaker's story. It should be remembered that the pioneer's rifle was more than a sporting device; it was an important means of providing food. Sitting against a rear wall was a wooden shaving horse, astride the higher end of which the workman would sit and, using his feet to operate the clamp, could securely hold the piece of wood being shaped with drawing knives, gouges, or other woodworking tools. No shop could be considered complete without a shaving horse. Wedging a piece of timber in the crack of a log building, as the workman without a shaving horse often did, was a poor substitute.

The next thing found was a heavy tailor's goose (If there were two, would it be tailor's gooses or geese?) along with an eight-pound sad-iron. (Again, why "sad"?) Farther along were found a corrugated wooden washboard, a wooden-stave tub, the half of a tight barrel, and a ten-gallon cast iron kettle suitable for heating water or boiling clothes. If to these could be added a gourd of soft brown homemade soap, they would tell the story of washday on an early farm.

A bootjack, pegging awl, cobbler's bench, some boot forms, a knee-operated sewing clamp, a tin box of wooden shoe pegs, a hunk of beeswax, a broadheaded shoemaker's hammer, a few hog bristles, some shoe lasts, and a measuring device marked in barleycorns went far toward telling the story of the local shoemaker who fashioned the footwear needed when it became too cold to go barefoot. A wooden apple peeler and a brass kettle meant apple butter. Cranes and trammels told of cooking at the family fireplace before cookstoves came into use. A pair of homemade wooden skates brought to memory the time when six bits could not be had for a pair of "store skates" and we made our own.

A farm dinner bell, a tin horn, a conch shell, and a wagon thimble served to recall the time when few carried watches and these means were used to call the workmen from the fields at noon. (One wise, tough-mouthed, old mule, a companion of our boyhood, learned to recognize these signals and would, despite our utmost efforts, start directly for the house when he heard them, even if it required going diagonally across rows.)

This could go on endlessly, for there were hundreds of other objects. All contribute their bits of history and reflect much about those who did not live in palaces.

🌿 *APPLE SEASON*

APPLE SEASON in southern Illinois comes each autumn. Loaded trucks move between packing, storage, and marketing sheds in the orchard counties. They continue to do so for several weeks. This lengthened shipping season comes from the addition of earlier varieties and the improvement of shipping and keeping qualities of later ones. Better methods of cold storage have helped. Through a combination of these, apples have become an in-season fruit available through practically all the year.

Because of its hardiness, productivity, and natural goodness, the apple quickly became and has remained America's king of fruits. Colonists coming to this country brought the apple along and planted orchards in the East.

Great sections of New York State and of Pennsylvania still are noted for their orchards. Even the Iroquois Indians planted them. One can hardly think of the Pennsylvania Dutch without thinking of their orchards, apple butter, and cider. It was from the New York–Pennsylvania region that seeds and scions used as nursery stock were carried to the Midwest. It was from there that the legendary character, Johnny Appleseed came.

Early settlers found many uses for apples. They went into the making of apple butter, pies, and dumplings. They were baked in the oven or roasted on sticks over the glowing coals of the fireplace on wintry evenings. Babies were given mellow apples to gnaw and toothless old people scraped and ate the solid ones. Even then an occasional boy or girl would polish an apple and give it to the teacher.

With the approach of autumn the apple crop would be gathered. A liberal amount of the very best ones were saved for winter use. These were arranged in a conical pile on a well drained spot in the garden. A thick layer of straw was then placed over them. Earth from a circular ditch at the base of the pile was heaped over all. Sometimes broad boards were placed on end and leaned against the mound to protect it from washing rains. This was the traditional apple hole, not to be opened until Christmas neared.

After storage of the select apples, the not-too-select ones remained. These were eaten out of hand, made into cider, or dried. Many farms, especially those with sizable orchards, had their cider presses where the culls and windfalls were ground and pressed. The resulting cider was stored in barrels, jugs, or stone jars. Since only a small proportion of it was needed for making vinegar, the balance was allowed to become hard cider. This hard cider was frozen or distilled to produce the "apple jack" of legend.

Then there was the major venture of apple drying, a busy time for the housewife. To those without apple peelers (parers to some) it was an onerous task. With a peeler that automatically kicked the peeled apple off the tines, a hustling youth, going all out, could peel fifty bushels a day. Since the mechanical peeler could not clean the bloom and stem ends of the apple, this had to be done by hand and required the help of three or more trimmers who also quartered and cored the apples.

In commerical plants and on farms where dried apples were a major money venture, some were smoked with sulphur fumes at this stage and then dried over heat. This produced a white dried apple that looked anemic and was, at least in imagination, not nearly so flavorful. Mostly, the quartered and cored apples were placed in slatted trays that were laid on low roofs or trestles to dry in the sun.

In some parts of the country where sunshine was more fitful the prepared apples were strung on twine or carpet warp and hung to dry in shaded and protected places. When golden brown and judged dry they were placed in muslin bags and stored in a protected place. Thus the winter's supply of apples was assured. Twenty-four pounds of dried apples made a bushel.

Perhaps it comes from a long memory tinged with a boyish appetite, but no sliced apple pie of today tastes nearly so good as those made from the withered, brown, sun-dried apples once used. The last one of this kind eaten was while visiting the aged parents of a boyhood friend at Harvell, Missouri. That was in 1948, forty-one years after the family had moved from our neighborhood.

Nothing is seen to show that people dry apples by the old process any longer. Is the art of making dried apple pies a lost one? Are there no more chilled stone jars of stewed dried apples with corresponding jars of sorghum gingerbread on shelves for perennially hungry boys to raid?

Some people have pleasant memories of dried apples.

❧ "EGYPT" STILL GROWS COTTON

It is cotton picking time once more in "Egypt"; that is, in a few of the counties of southern Illinois.* Wavering lines of workers made up of men, women, and youths are seen moving along the rows of its steadily lessening number of cotton fields. Each picker drags behind him, by a loop over his shoulder, a canvas or burlap bag eight or nine feet long. Sometimes these workers will be heard singing. Ahead of the zig-zag line of stooped and roughly clad harvesters, the fields look almost snowy white. Behind them it is drab.

The over-all picture is typical of a land where cotton is a main crop. It has a distinctly "down South" look. The scene also suggests bits of the story of cotton growing in southern Illinois, a story that began with the earlier settlers.

A large proportion of those who came to make their homes in the lower part of Illinois were from older settlements in southern states where cotton was a regular crop. These people brought along with them the beliefs, customs, cherished heirlooms, and even the crops common in the communities where they had formerly lived. The crops, naturally, were the seeds and plants they brought in bags, pokes, gourds, and bundles wrapped in bits of old cloth. Among these were cotton seeds.

In the early days, cotton growing was not too attractive commercially.

---

* See *Legends & Lore*, pp. 174–75.

A limited labor supply and the distance to established markets discouraged its extensive cultivation. Many settlers, however, grew patches large enough to supply the needs for household spinning and for use in the padding of quilts and comforts. Cotton did not become a major field crop until the Civil War came.

With the opening of hostilities and the North's inability to get needed cotton from its regular sources in the South, the country turned to southern Illinois for its cotton supply. Enough already had been grown here to show that it could be cultivated successfully. Governmental agencies found the seed needed and furnished it to those who wished to grow the crop. They also gave assurance that there would be a good market for all that could be produced.

Cotton growing boomed and soon thousands of acres were planted. Countless gins and presses were built. Carbondale alone had five busy ones. Others were located over the area from Chester to Shawneetown and south. Cotton became an important and profitable crop in a dozen or more counties. At one time it sold for a dollar or so a pound. There are records showing returns of as much as $800 an acre, a right tidy sum.

When the Civil War ended, the South's stored supply of cotton and its current crop became available. A sharp decline in prices naturally resulted, and cotton prices dropped to four cents a pound at the gins. Farmers accordingly could not afford to grow the crop and production fell off rapidly. In some localities, however, its cultivation was continued. In 1873 Carbondale had the largest market on record, ginning less than a million pounds in the year. Many other gins had ceased to operate.

Today there are only two gins left in Illinois. Both are in the Cairo vicinity. (Late reports are that one of these has ceased to operate.) Together they will produce perhaps less than a million pounds of ginned cotton. This is about half the amount grown in 1929.

A plant at Cairo once processed the seeds from Illinois gins for their oil and other by-products. Its tantalizing odors then assailed the nostrils of those who drove into Cairo over U.S. Route 51. This delightful experience ended with the closing of the plant. Seeds from the local gins now are sent to Tiptonville, Tennessee, or to Portageville, Missouri.

Each spring in early April, fields will be readied for another planting. If the weather is seasonable, seeds will be drilled and, in about ten days, the plants will appear. Chopping will begin almost immediately and rows of workmen, this time armed with hoes, will move slowly across the fields, cutting grass and thinning the stand of plants as necessary. Some enclosed fields may have geese feeding in them to eat the grass and cut down on hoeing. The geese do not seem to be too efficient, however. Some insist that they grow lazy—the blue geese more than the Chinese.

Passing these same fields on a July morning one will see thousands of snowy white blossoms that, for some unexplained reason, "fade" to a pleasant pink by nightfall. Hoeing and plowing go on. By October, the pods or bolls burst open and the fields are white again. Pickers come trailing their long bags and the first picking begins. Often they are the same ones who chopped and sang among the young plants in April.

Much of "Egypt's" cotton is grown by sharecroppers on a kind of half-and-half basis, just as it has been done for a hundred years. With the better fields producing about five hundred pounds to the acre and cotton selling for approximately 33 cents, the profit to a cropper is not great. One man said, "Cotton is a poor man's crop."

If you drive Cairo way, take a careful look at the dwindling cotton fields. Their total area now is about three thousand acres. A few more years and there may be no commercial production here. If this misfortune comes, another bit of the "down South" look will have gone from "Egypt."

🌑 *AS HUNGRY AS THE TOWN SOW*

ON A VISIT to a Seminole Indian reservation in Florida, a lean sow and two half-grown shoats were seen wandering among a cluster of Indian dwellings. The presence of this sow and her pigs partially explains why the Indians build their dwellings, called chickees, on posts about four feet high.

Seeing the mother hog and her offspring brought to mind an institution that sprang up, ran its course, and vanished a lifetime ago in southern Illinois. This vanished institution was known as the "town sow."

In earlier days when livestock was allowed to run at large, about every backwoods village had a typical specimen of her porcine majesty. This mother hog, when viewed in profile, was ample in length and height. When viewed from either fore or aft, however, she was disappointingly thin, distinctly the bacon type. With her arched back and long legs, she easily qualified as streamlined, and apparently was built for speed.

She was a wise and competent hog, if there be such. By some means, perhaps known only to the sow, she came to exercise a right somewhat like that of eminent domain over the village. Other hogs appeared to respect the town sow's homestead rights. She really did patrol her domain.

Appearing at rather regular intervals and generally from the same direction, she followed a planned course through the village in search of whatever a hog might devour, which sometimes included a hapless chicken that came near enough to be snatched.

The only way to keep this sow and her prowling pigs from entering the yard, the garden, the smokehouse, the henhouse, or even the dwelling itself was to fence them securely. Even fences provided no protection unless gates were so carefully locked that they could not be rooted open. To prevent this a section of crosscut saw was fastened, teeth-down, to the bottom of the gate. Some sows became rather skilled in working simple latches.

In addition to the consideration accorded her by other hogs, girls and small boys, and some not so small, feared and avoided her. Between the sow and the bands of small boys that played about the town and often annoyed her by throwing sticks and stones, there was a continuous tension somewhat like a present-day cold war! To grownups, particularly to men and properly trousered boys, she would yield the pathway. When doing this, however, she maintained a measure of dignity by appearing to wander aside casually, as if by accident.

With smaller boys—that is, those still playing about in long-tailed shirts—and with skirted females, it was a different matter. These she often would meet with ominous grunts, raised hackles, and even with bared teeth. Most dogs, so long as they left the sow and her pigs alone, were ignored. Dogs which had experienced the fury of the sow's swift, slashing charge, that easily bowled over the most powerful of them, left her alone.

Nearly all dogs, after a decisive encounter with such a sow, appeared stone deaf when someone cried "sic 'em" or they would emit a series of snarls and barks while charging about, apparently looking for a less formidable opponent. Any dog strong and skillful enough to catch the town sow by the ear and keep himself close against the sow's side while he hung on, and thus avoid her charges, immediately became a respected dog.

The ownership of a town sow was not difficult to determine. The underbits, overbits, crops, half-crops and swallow-forks in her ears told that. Should she become truly dangerous, she was destroyed or penned up, slightly fattened, and killed when hog killing time came round.

Presently, the town sow lives only in legend. A rare oldster may recall seeing one in some remote village before the open range vanished. Anyone who can remember when Quincy Brown would be sent to drive the roving hogs from beneath the Hardscrabble schoolhouse floor so that their squealing, bumping, and grunting would not disrupt the school is no longer a youth. In fifty years we have heard only two persons use the expression, "as hungry as the town sow."

❧ *KEROSENE LAMPS*

A VILLAGE IN the West Indies where I vacationed recently had no electric street-lighting system. Nevertheless, it has gone modern by distributing a couple dozen Coleman gasoline lanterns, United States made. These are filled, pumped to proper pressure, and hung at strategic points by a lamplighter who comes merrily whistling along the street at dusk each evening. He is much like the lamp tender that some of our villages once knew. Early the next morning he returns to collect the lamps, which generally have been burned out a few hours earlier. Residences are lighted, when they are lighted, by old-fashioned coal oil lamps.

The distinctive pale yellowish glow seen in windows where kerosene lamps are burning revives memories of times when such lamps were universally used to light rural homes in southern Illinois. Presently, one may drive many miles along our country roads without ever seeing a window reflecting the soft glow peculiar to the kerosene lamp. Many who once knew no other lights forget that there are millions in the world today who still use kerosene lamps and lanterns.

Thinking backward, it seems that a great proportion of all family life before 1900 was centered about the kerosene lamp—or around candles or grease lamps which were brought into use if the kerosene can or jug became emptied before the weekly or biweekly trip to town. Sometimes in anticipation of such an emergency, one of the children would be sent before nightfall to borrow a bottle of coal oil. Some used resinous splinters of pine, pine knots, or tallow-saturated pithy plant stems to supply a type of lighting which could hardly be considered bright.

Supper, never then known as dinner, was prepared in the light of a kerosene lamp resting upon the dining table or upon a conveniently located wall shelf. When the meal was ready, the lamp was placed in its accustomed position, which proclaimed about as effectively as though the words had been shouted that "supper's ready."

After the meal had been eaten and the dishes washed, members of the family arranged themselves around the same or another lamp to suit individual purposes. Some sat near it to read or perhaps to write a letter. Others, not requiring so much light, would sit farther away and play at checkers, at fox and geese, hullygull, or other forgotten games.

Then of course, there always was the rocker where the mother sat to make or mend the family clothing. Sometimes this was done after supper because it was the only spare time the mother had. Occasionally, it was because the children could then best spare the clothes for mending. At other times the mother and older girls would piece quilts or knit. Since a skilled knitter could do almost any part of the task except turning a heel or drawing in a toe without looking, little light was required. Activity within the lighted circle was common.

Whatever activities may have taken place in the lighted circle, there always was time and opportunity to talk. Incidents of the day were discussed, family history and traditions were re-recounted, and stories told. Songs sometimes were sung, riddles and puzzles offered, and assorted lore passed along. When neighbors, often carrying a lantern, came to "set until bedtime" the program of the evening was enlarged and bedtime was delayed. Whether bedtime came at the regular hour or belatedly, lamps were turned down and blown out. A light left burning through the night generally indicated sickness in the house.

Next morning came and the lamp was once more lighted for the preparation of the very substantial before-daybreak breakfast. After the breakfast dishes were washed, the lamp chimneys were carefully cleaned and polished. Oil was added to lamps as needed, and wicks were trimmed with care so as not to clog the air vent. They were ready for another night.

❧ HOMEMADE PLAYTHINGS

A VISIT WAS recently paid to a boyhood playmate, one with whom an enduring friendship began in preschool years. Just about every item of conversation would begin with "Do you remember?" and the talk frequently went in unplanned directions. At one time it turned to toys after a visiting grandson had dumped a box of assorted Woolworth-type playthings on the rug.

Children always have had toys but not of such endless variety as those manufactured today. Most earlier playthings were homemade, frequently the work of the children using them, helped occasionally by a parent. Many of the toys used then are seldom seen now, except in old smokehouses, attics, or barn sheds.

A common toy, once frequently found among the odds and ends in a boy's bulging pocket, was a spinning top made from the half of an empty sewing thread spool. These were not nearly so fancy as the machine-made ones with iron points that could be bought at the store, but those in the store cost a pretty nickel and nickels were scarce. A chap who felt a strong need for a top took his fifteen-cent Russel barlow and made one. Instead of the iron point a peg of hard wood was whittled to fit the hole through the spool. One end was carefully rounded and smoothed. The other was allowed to extend beyond the spool so it could be grasped between the thumb and a finger and given a sharp spin. One blue top we remember had wedges of yellow on its upper surface. When spun vigorously, this top appeared to turn green and thus created a mystery for young onlookers.

Normal boys love to contribute their full proportion of noise. An excellent device for this was the "bull roarer," used for centuries by boys over much of the world. North American Indian boys, believing that such wood had a magic that influenced weather, made their "roarers" of wood from a lightning splintered tree. Other boys, being more interested in noise than weather, made theirs of any firm bit of wood an eighth of an inch or so thick, about two inches wide, and eight or ten inches long. A small hole was made in the middle near one end. An end of a strong string was tied through the hole. The other end was then made fast to a staff about three or four feet long.

When whirled vigorously about the head, a queer pulsating roar resulted. A half-dozen boys with these devices could create quite a furor. By varying the length, width, and thickness of the whirling wooden part the pitch was changed.

Tinker toys, matched sticks, and building blocks were unknown to boys at that time. As a partial substitute for these a boy went to some spot where corn had been fed to hogs some months before. The cobs found there could be split into full length divisions when laid on a solid surface and tapped with a hammer or rock. Fences, houses, pens, barns, and other needed toy structures for a play farm could be made with the split sections.

A little wagon was joy to almost any youngster, but wagons cost money. A competent boy, sometimes with his father's help, built his own. Axles were made of sized timbers rounded at the ends to form spindles. Short sections of a small black gum log, which is almost impossible to split, with holes bored in their centers made wheels. Bolsters, tongues, hounds, beds, and other parts of the wagon were of scrap planks or clapboards. They were crude affairs but that bothered the boy little. The last one of these wagons seen was in an abandoned Pope County barn. (I wish I had "borrowed" it.)

May was the time of year for pawpaw and hickory bark whistles, which were effective noisemakers. Many a man who was a youngster sixty years ago will recall the shrill pipings of these whistles.

A boy without a sled felt cheated. It was not unusual to see a dozen or so of these sleds at school when snow was on the ground. Some came from a mile or more away. In fact, so many came to school one day that this former teacher took his pupils (winter of 1916–1917) to a nearby snow-covered hill and "fooled away" practically the entire afternoon coasting. Old men and women stop the teacher even today to talk about that afternoon. Not one mentions the arithmetic or geography classes of the day, but all readily recall the spills that sent them rolling into a ditch beside the roadway.

Many a boy fashioned his own slingshot and practiced until he could control the general direction of his shots. All grew to envy the accuracy of David when he went forth to slay Goliath. Bows and arrows were stock articles.

Throwing darts was great sport. Watermills were made of cornstalks and set to run in some small rivulet. Two small boys were found doing this in Bone Gap in the spring of 1962. Whittled windmills often were seen on the tops of posts or buildings.

Oldsters will recall other simple toys that youngsters of that day made and used—and enjoyed.

🌿 *LOG ROLLING HAS CHANGED*

TODAY THE WRITER arrived, leisurely and late, at the Thompson Street parking lot on Southern Illinois University's campus. Going west across the street toward the building which houses a cubbyhole office, his favorite hiding place, he came upon a scene of concentrated confusion. The place, orderly only yesterday, was literally torn up.

All that was left of a dozen big trees that had stood and watched us go home the day before were scattered about on the ground. They had become stumps, long logs, short logs, or cuts, large branches, and masses of broken brush. The ground around them had been deeply rutted and mixed with broken sidewalk scrap by bulldozers and tractors. Added to the furrows left by the tractors was a short and shallow trench left there by a groundbreaking crew two days earlier.

A tractor still was at work in its erratic, snorting, and determined way. It was using a grabhook to snake out saw logs for loading on a truck that served as a log wagon. Logs not suitable for sawing were dragged to one side where the tractor backed and twisted about to thrust the nose of its high lift under them and dump them on a mounting pile. It even pushed scattered brush into bunches and dumped it on the heap—a bit of work that pioneer logrollers performed while they "rested" from the backbreaking job of carrying logs.

Seeing a workman in a safety zone with hands in pocket, evidently a boss, we went to join him and to look and listen. In spite of the noises already suggested, there were also those of chainsaws that whined and put-putted. One lone axman was almost unheard; another pounded a wedge to relieve the pinch on a chainsaw. There was no swish of the crosscut. In spite of all the noises, we stood and thought—even foregoing the coffee-break.

To no one else present, for all were too young, could the situation have aroused more memories. It served to bring to mind the logrollings of boyhood days. Then, there were no tractors with high lifts, no chainsaws, and no trucks. The men—twelve in number at one of the rollings remembered—came with nothing more than handspikes, occasionally with an ax, and if they were fortunate, with a cant hook or peavey.

Handspikes were rounded pieces of strong wood about four and a half feet long, some three inches in diameter at the center, and tapered to a comfortable hand grip at each end. The cant hook or peavey was a swinging hook mounted near the end of a long handle that gave leverage when a log was to be turned.

Some of the larger logs were breasted by the men, rolled on chunks, cut about, and rolled into place, side by side. Smaller logs, and some not small, were carried by pairs of men with handspikes. It is recalled that there sometimes were four or five pairs of straining men carrying one short eight- or nine-foot log. These pairs of men often were so closely spaced that they could move only in lockstep. The pioneer knew no harder labor.

Some men developed better ways to roll their logs. Two of these were Ike Smith and Sug Pitman. But they had two horses who were able and willing helpers. Smith's helper was a strong-backed horse named Loge. Pitman's was Sealum, a dark red roan of medium but powerful build who was the best puller I ever saw. Both alike were expert helpers, fully as intelligent as any of those horses termed "educated."

It still is our belief that Ike and Loge made the best logrolling combination in America. The animal often worked the day through with his bridle hanging on a hame. He would follow at Ike's heels while the first log for a new heap was being placed. After that, Ike's voice boomed, "Let's go," "Whoa," "Gee," or "Haw." Once the heap was started, Loge knew where to take other logs. While Ike held the back end of a log with a handspike thrust into the ground to prevent it from slipping out of place, Loge would pull his end up a placed skid and hold it there until Ike elevated his part of the burden.

The Ike-Loge and Sug-Sealum combinations were rare indeed. All others we knew rolled more by manpower.

❀ *WINDMILLS*

THE LANDSCAPE OF southern Illinois constantly changes. Among the once familiar objects that have almost vanished are farm windmills. At one time there were hundreds of these that creaked, hammered, scraped, and rattled away as they spun merrily around to fill water troughs and tanks.

It is doubtful if a score of these mills remain working in all the area now. Here and there, a vine-covered slender iron tower with remnants of a steel-bladed wheel or vane drooping from its top shows where another mill is rusting away. Sometimes, the long lift-rod still dangles above all that remains of a useless pump. Towers and wheels of wood have long since rotted away.

Before the appearance of gasoline motors and before rural electrification, windmills served as sources of power for various purposes. They were used to saw lumber, to grind grain, and to operate machines as well as to pump water. The first mills were large ones with wheels forty to sixty feet across. These larger mills often were placed at the top of buildings mounted on a track and made to rotate about a large central mast. This allowed them to be turned by hand and remain pointed into the wind. A mill of this type, built on the site of an earlier one in restored Williamsburg, Virginia, still operates regularly, grinding grist.

The first of these large mills of record in the United States was built at Jamestown in 1620. Another one was at New Amsterdam (New York) about 1650. Southern Illinois knew at least two of these larger mills. One, at Waterloo, was built there at the time a town was founded. A second one, at Teutopolis near Effingham, was erected by the German group which settled there shortly after 1840. The Teutopolis mill stood about where St. Joseph's Seminary was built later.

These had large, sail-covered arms, fifty feet or more across. Each was built to saw lumber and grind grain. There may have been others of their kind in the region, but they never did become popular. Watermills were more efficient and easier to build. Moreover, obstructing forest and irregular winds handicapped those depending upon the wind.

The larger wheels were like those in Holland where they first were in use shortly after the year 1100. These were patterned after those used in Persia and China, perhaps two thousand years ago. For several centuries they were a main source of power. Even so, they were not always welcome. The ancient craft guilds of Holland opposed their use because they would have displaced workmen.

When the mills were found useful in pumping water from the coastal marshlands and shallow seas behind the dikes, they were readily accepted. They became so popular, in fact, that once there were eight thousand of these huge devices operating in Holland alone. In the hundred years beginning with 1600, by the use of these mills an average of more than forty acres a day was reclaimed from the sea and added to the farmlands of that country. Most of their windmills have been replaced with diesel motors, but many mills—some hundreds of years old—still pump water over the dikes. Without its windmills much of the romance of the country would be gone and Holland would hardly seem to be Holland.

The smaller mills that once dotted the landscape of the Midwest were our contribution to the use of windpower. The success of these unattended mills was made possible by an invention of Daniel Halladay in 1856. His arrangement automatically kept the mill pointed into the wind and "feathered" the wheel to control its speed. After the end of the Civil War, the windmill business in America prospered.

It was these smaller mills that pumped water for livestock on thousands of farms and ranches of the central United States. They were as common as cowboys on western ranches. During one fifty-year period, more than six and a half million of these mills were made and sold. Youthful memories of the Kansas landscape has it decorated with countless mills of this kind. Earlier Sears and Roebuck catalogs featured windmills.

By 1935 the industry had declined, and only ten thousand mills were made. The use of windmills increased for a brief time when radios needing six-volt A batteries came along; wind generators were used to charge them. Then a new crop of small mills appeared on poles and on short masts on the tops of houses. With rural electrification these disappeared. Only in isolated places and on lonely sea islands does one now catch a glimpse of such whirring generators.

Except for the arms-waving speaker that some term "windmills," an institution has virtually disappeared. Even the human windmill seems to be losing ground.

❧ THE LOST ART OF DRIVING OXEN

RUMMAGING AMONG THE odd materials, that nearly everyone somehow manages to collect through the years, can bring strange recollections. These paragraphs began in that way, or rather they began with three closely related findings that came within the hour on one afternoon.

The first was a February, 1913, entry in the writer's diary. There had been a deep, hard freeze followed by a rapid and complete thaw that left the all-dirt roads a quagmire. The entry for that particular day says, "When school was dismissed there was a yoke of oxen hitched to a log wagon waiting at the corner of the schoolground for the children living along the road toward the sawmill." The youngsters should have been grateful, for the mill was about a mile and a half away and the roads were terrible.

The second find was a photograph of a yoke of oxen hitched to a parade-type covered wagon, the one that was brought on a truck to Carbondale for a part in the centennial celebration of 1952. Some also may remember seeing this same wagon and its oxen beside the highway north of Carmi during watermelon season. Hundreds of persons attracted by the strange sight would stop to look and, incidentally, buy melons.

A bound volume of the *Prairie Farmer* for 1848 and one of the *Cultivator* (Genesee Farmer) for 1838–1839 made the third find. These farm magazines told the readers how to select, break to yoke, train, drive, and care for working oxen. The three combined could hardly fail to revive interest in the vanished art.

Even in 1913, more than fifty years ago, oxen were rarely seen in southern Illinois. There are, however, numerous childhood memories of ox teams. One of the very earliest is that of two yokes of oxen drawing a "portable" thresher along a country road from "set" to "set." There is also the memory of one lone covered wagon going west past Hardscrabble School on a long ago autumn day, a kind of straggling rear guard for the countless others that had gone before. Most numerous of such memories are those of the log carts with wheels about twice as high as the driver's head that regularly came out of the North Fork bottoms and passed along the rutty road during the logging season. These carts were moving entire tree trunks, often eighty or more feet long. With limbs trimmed away, the butt of each log would be suspended beneath the high axle of the wagon; the top portion of the log trailed. It was later learned that these long, long logs were to be used as masts for ships or as pilings for harbor piers.

The thousands of yokes of oxen that the country once knew have disappeared, leaving only a few of their yokes and scant trappings to remind people of their one-time importance. With their disappearance the skilled driver also has vanished. In America ox-driving can truly be listed as among the lost arts, and an art it was.

Those writing about oxen in the old farm papers mentioned gave sage advice on the selection of steers for training. One tells his readers that steers should have "large clear eyes and an intelligent countenance." They should be "placid and calm, not fools." It also was added that the one making selections should choose those that "walk in the same manner." They should be "two and a half or coming three years old," not mere calves that would be "stunted or taxed beyond their strength."

Having offered advice on the manner of selection these writers suggested the best methods of training. All agreed that the trainer should proceed slowly and gently, working first in a small lot or a large barn stall. He should talk calmly and distinctly and "in English," since many insisted that oxen understood that language best. He should also reward his trainees with an occasional pat or a nubbing, a supply of which should be carried in the trainer's pockets. In training, only a small switch should be used, for the best drivers used their lungs more and whips less. All insisted that oxen were ready and willing once they knew what was to be done. The present-day Society for the Prevention of Cruelty to Animals undoubtedly would approve the instructions given.

Oxen needed to understand and respond to only a few words. Among these was "get up" or some other starting command. "Whoa" stopped them. "Gee," which one writer spelled "jee," signaled a turn to the right and "haw" to the left. Then there was "back." With his scant half-dozen words it was marvelous to see what a competent driver could do with his yoke or yokes, for teams often were hitched in tandem.

There were select yokes of oxen in which the owners took pride. These were matched, mature, and well-fed. They were washed, brushed, and shod. Their hoofs and horns were dressed with wool fat and polished. Their shining horns often were tipped with glistening brass balls, sometimes as much as three inches in diameter. Their sturdy yokes and bows were carefully and exactly made. Their calm, slow, "as slow as an ox," movements gave a correct impression of power, even of dignity.

Oxen undoubtedly played their role, an important one, and have passed on. Only older persons can recall seeing them. There is no place in today's economy for them. Nevertheless, they deserve a grateful memory.

The echoes of the highly vocal drivers have grown faint.

❧ *BARBED WIRE*

MINOR INCIDENTS often suggest stories from Illinois history. One such incident occurred recently when a stop was made at a farm supply dealer's place in DeKalb, Illinois. Some spools of barbed wire were found on the dealer's yard. Finding the wire was not so unusual. It seemed strange, however, to find the labels on the spools saying "Made in West Germany."

This in itself was not so strange, for German-made wire is an increasing import. It did seem strange, however, to find it in the very town where barbed wire was invented and first manufactured. Seeing these few spools of wire brought to mind how it had its beginnings in Illinois, and the great part it has played in the industry of farming in America.

To better appreciate its significance, some note should be taken of the conditions existing in prewire days. The first settlers coming from Europe to the east coast of the United States found practically an unbroken forest that supplied ample timber for all building and fencing needs. These early settlers quickly devised the once familiar rail fence known as the Virginia or worm fence which for countless thousands of miles etched the landscape, even within the memories of some older persons. As the fringe of settlement advanced westward, so did the rail fence.

Except for the immense amount of hard labor required, fencing imposed no particular problem until the wide prairies of Illinois were encountered. Even here the first settlers located on the edge of the forests which bordered the grasslands or along the streams that crossed the prairies.

As settlers began to locate on the open lands away from timber, other methods of fencing were sought. Ditches with accompanying sod fences, skeleton fences of posts and rails, and assorted hedges were tried with varying degrees of success. Bits of the hedges are occasionally found now, but all that remains of the earthen construction is the expression, "as ugly as a mud fence." Strands of smooth wire were used, but livestock soon learned that this wire could be pressed against without injury and could be breached with ease.

At this stage of events a county fair was held about where Northern Illinois University now stands at DeKalb. Here a man named Rose exhibited a newly designed fence. It was a section of timber an inch square and sixteen feet long supported between posts by a smooth wire. Into this he had driven numerous brads whose sharp points were left protruding about an inch. The protruding points easily discouraged livestock from crowding against it.

Three men who later were to play significant parts in barbed wire development stopped together to view Rose's display. They were E. L. Elwood, J. F. Glidden, and Jacob Haish. Each one apparently left with the idea that if barbs could be attached directly to a wire, the fencing problem would be practically solved. These three men and others, perhaps equally intrigued by Rose's exhibit, began earnest efforts to design a better fence.

Haish was the first of the three to be granted a patent; that was on February 17, 1874. His patent was for barbs attached to a continuous iron strip. Wire of this type still was in use along the railroad right-of-way near Texas City in Saline County as late at 1893. Another patent was issued on November 24, 1874, to Glidden. In his design the barbs were attached to a two-wire twisted strand much like today's wire. On August 31, 1875, Haish was granted a second patent that differed from Glidden's in the manner of shaping and attaching the barbs. Others filed for patents. Glidden and Elwood formed a partnership. The situation quickly became complicated. One writer termed it a "barbed wire entanglement." Wire was off to a glorious beginning.

Ten thousand pounds of the new wire were made and sold in 1874. The next year 600,000 pounds were marketed. Five years later yearly sales had risen to almost 81,000,000 pounds, more than enough to build an eight-wire fence around the earth at the equator.

A glimpse of the few rolls of wire also revived memories of the pine tar smell of Cox's Barbed Wire Liniment, a staple remedy found in nearly every barn two generations ago. Also brought to mind were many badly scarred animals, principally horses that had run against or had become entangled in the fencing. Barbed wire was brutal but effective.

Now, a single strand of wire supported by insulation on frail metal posts does an effective job.

❀ FORGOTTEN GOODS

A STOP WAS MADE recently at an abandoned farmstead on a deserted lane in a lower southern Illinois county. A dilapidated section of paling fence with some inverted stone fruit jars on the tops of the old pickets brought about a realization that foods and food habits have changed radically within a lifetime.

First, the brown stone jars served to remind one of pre-tin can, pre-refrigeration days. The brown and gray glazed stone jars, half-gallon and gallon sized, with grooves in their tops to receive the crimped tin lids with their sealing wax, suggested the peaches, apples, pears, wild goose and damson plums, and berries that once were so highly relished. They also brought to memory the canned squash and pumpkin, along with the apparently vanished pumpkin butter.

Just what went into this old-time pumpkin butter is not known. Anyway the end product was smooth, sweet, and well-spiced, altogether a delightful spread. We can learn of no recipe. Perhaps it was made "by ear."

And pumpkin butter brings to mind the dried pumpkin that many housewives prepared. We do recall how this was made, for we watched. A medium or large-sized pumpkin was selected. As we remember, the more nearly red the rind the better the pumpkin. It was then sliced crosswise into rings about an inch thick. The seeds were scraped away and the rind removed with a sharp knife. The prepared rings then were strung on sticks—at our house they were tobacco sticks—and placed on a rack in the sun to dry.

The low flat roof beside the tumble-down smokehouse with some plaster lath racks beneath it suggested another method of preserving fruit—that is, drying it. Peaches and apples were the fruits most often dried, though some others were used to a limited extent.

Hickory withes with hooks still fastened to the crossbeams of the smokehouse told of the time when meat was home-killed. After being allowed to "take salt" for a proper length of time, it was placed on the hooks like those found and thoroughly smoked with hickory chips burned in an old kettle or fire pit. This smoldering fire was kept going for several days. Boards and old bits of carpeting often were laid above the racks of suspended meat to keep the smoke from escaping too readily.

Then along came the chemists with a synthetic product that was purportedly "just as good." Now, even the vaunted Virginia hams, grown almost anywhere but in that state, are quickly smoked with a paint brush or spray gun. It all doesn't add up, however, to the real hickory-smoked product.

Plaited strings of wispy onion tops hanging from pegs along the smokehouse ceiling beams indicated how onions were kept. There were other strings with remnants of pepper pods, stalks of sage that still smelled faintly, and some other herbs that we identified as mint, horehound, or catnip. One string held some badly frayed clusters of hops.

These bits of hops revived memories of Aunt Nan and of the hops that grew on tall poles in her garden. Then came thoughts of how she used these hops to make yeast for the light bread always found in her breadbox.

Here is how that yeast was made. First, she boiled hops in a kettle and drew off the resulting liquid. Into about a quart of this she placed three finely mashed potatoes. In this mixture, lukewarm, she dissolved two or three cakes of yeast from the previous batch. Cornmeal then was added to make a rich batter which was rolled out on a smooth board to a scant half-inch in thickness. It was then cut into squares of an inch or so, placed in a warm place, out of the direct sunlight, and allowed to dry.

Speaking of yeast brings to mind the popular brew known as California Seed Beer. To make this, some "seeds" were taken from a working stock and placed in water sweetened with sorghum, brown sugar, or honey. This mixture soon began to "work." In a few days the tangy drink resulted. Many seemed to like it and used it for a drink at mealtime.

Left to its own devices, California Seed Beer became vinegar and that suggests vinegar pie—another forgotten tidbit. People then, as now, liked pie but sometimes didn't have the makings. In such cases they occasionally used vinegar. Here is how they did it.

About a half cup of tart vinegar was placed in enough water to fill one pie. This was sweetened to taste with brown sugar, honey, or even sorghum. A lump of butter about as large as an egg was next added and the mixture was brought to a boil. Into this a heaping teaspoon of flour was stirred and boiling continued until the mixture thickened.

It was then poured into a pie pan lined with enriched pie dough. The top was crisscrossed with strips of dough and all was baked in a hot oven until like jelly. In memory such pies are still good, though one hasn't been eaten in more than fifty years.

❦ FODDER AND PUMPKINS

ONCE MORE IT IS the time of year "When the frost is on the pumpkin and the fodder's in the shock." However, the two elements in the picture that these words from James Whitcomb Riley suggest are missing, or nearly so. The once familiar field-long rows of ordered corn shocks and the acres dressed with stubble and dots that were golden pumpkins are not to be seen.

A few weeks ago men with tractor-drawn ensilage cutters trailed by high boxed wagons were following up and down the rows in many fields gathering and chopping corn for storage in farm silos. The bare fields they left were not dotted with pumpkins, for none were grown there. Pumpkins would have hindered the harvesters and in turn would have been crushed under the wheels of the implements used.

A couple of generations ago one would have seen another type of workman in the fields, dressed for the occasion and armed with a sword-like corn knife about two and a half feet long. Occasionally, one of these knives may yet be found stuck away in some abandoned farm building.

Cuttin' corn was rough work, and men dressed for it. A slouch hat was needed, one that hung low over the face and ears. Some men were known to have used a woman's borrowed bonnet. A heavy shirt with turned-up collar was worn. Often an extra cloth was wound about the neck and another around the wrist of the carrying arm. All this was necessary for protection against the day-long chafing of the stalks cradled in the arm and held firmly against the neck and shoulder.

Cuttin' corn was a seasonal job and was followed vigorously through long days. If cut before sufficiently ripened, the grain shriveled. Or, it might mold if the weather was warm and moist. If cutting was too much delayed, frost came, the leaves shattered, and the fodder was not as good.

A shock row regularly included sixteen rows of corn. Shocks were spaced about twenty paces apart. At the spot where the shock was to form, a "saddle" was tied. This was done by bending a number of stalks in the middle rows together and fastening their tops by twisting them. Several armfuls of corn were cut, placed on end about the saddle, and tied at the top with a bent cornstalk. After a few armloads were in place, this core of the stock was bound with a stalk. The skilled workman, cutting his corn with the least walking, planned to complete his armful as near the growing shock as possible. In the run of a day this saved a few miles of walking.

The worker sometimes carried a length of rope with an iron ring at its end. This he looped about the top of the completed shock and drew it as tightly as possible. He then tied it off with stalks of corn or, when it became available, with binder twine that perhaps had been saved by a band-cutter at threshing time and later tied together.

Pumpkins were gathered next and hauled on a sled to the pumpkin pile in a fence corner beside the feed lot. There they were chopped open with a corn knife and fed to cows and hogs; some horses learned to eat them. For cattle one was careful to remove the pumpkin stem lest the animal attempt to swallow it and choke.

"Shucking out" the fodder and hauling it in remained a fill-in job for winter days. This was best done in damp weather when fodder did not shatter so easily. Sometimes the shucked fodder was hauled to a spot near the feed lot and placed in long ricks. Fodder often was the farmer's only supply of roughage for his livestock during the winter. The neat piles of husked corn, shucked-out corn, were then hauled, generally on a sled, to the crib.

The shocks of corn, fields of pumpkins, and farm sleds have almost completely disappeared. In driving more than a thousand miles over southern Illinois roads in recent weeks, only twelve shocks of fodder have been seen, a pitiful rear guard of the army that stood in ordered ranks over the cornfields fifty years ago.

"When the frost is on the pumpkin and the fodder's in the shock" may be only a meaningless jingle to youngsters who have never seen fields of corn shocks and pumpkins, but to an old-timer it brings a vanished scene to memory.

❦ *CORN*

DURING A RECENT TOUR of the Illinois State Historical Society, a stop was made at the Pierre Menard Home in Kaskaskia State Park where tea and coffee were served along with something to nibble. The refreshments included cookies, light bread, or corn bread baked in the ancient stone oven. The square, muffin-like pones of golden brown corn bread drew our bid—for two helpings.

This rare treat revived thoughts about corn, the greatest of the food bequests of the American Indians. It also revived a realization that the present generation, served so efficiently by bakeries, little appreciates the past role of corn.

From that spring long ago when friendly Squanto taught the Pilgrims to plant corn and fertilize it by placing a fish in each hill, corn was the supreme food crop of the settlers and remained so within the memory of some oldsters still living. The method of its planting, cultivation, preparation, and storage followed closely that of the Indians.

Each spring "when white oak leaves were as large as squirrel ears" the first planting of corn was made. Others followed at intervals to assure a continuous supply of roasting ears. The Indians planted beans, squash, pumpkins, gourds (some to be eaten while young), and melons among their corn. The pioneers did likewise.

Corn was prepared in an almost endless number of ways. When sufficiently mature, the husks and silks were removed, and the ears were cooked in earthen pots or in rounded depressions in stones; heat was supplied by hot stones dropped into the water. The pots they used are long broken and gone, but the pot holes in stones are still found at a number of places in southern Illinois. Corn cooked in them, Indian fashion, still is good. We've tried it.

Ears of corn were roasted with husks on in the hot ashes and coals of a campfire, thus the title of roasting ears. We've tried this method with hobos in their jungle and didn't go away feeling sorry for them, especially when they could wangle some salt and butter for dressing. Corn cooked by either means was gnawed freehand from the cob; Emily Post was then unknown.

While corn was still in the milk stage, it often was cut and scraped from the cob and cooked with grease in pots and pot holes by use of hot rocks. When corn had become too hard to cook satisfactorily by either of the above methods, it sometimes was cut from the cob, cooked, salted, and dried for winter storage. We didn't particularly like it that way—too salty.

When beyond the roasting ear stage but not dry enough to crack readily, the grain was pounded in stump mortars with wooden pestles and cooked with meat and fats by the Indians and pioneers alike. At about this stage the pioneer began to grate (grit) his corn for the ever-welcome gritted corn bread.

Matured and thoroughly dried, corn came in for additional uses. It was soaked in a weak lye solution made from wood ashes until the skin of the grains was loosened. After the skins had been rubbed loose it was washed in clear water to remove the lingering lye, which it never thoroughly did. Cooked, this became the hominy of the "hog and hominy" combination. Those who have eaten such hominy will never forget the pleasant lye tang it had. It really tasted like hominy.

Thoroughly dried the corn was ground or pounded into meal for corn bread.* There were hoe cakes, johnny (journey) cakes, ash cakes, fritters, corn pones, fried corn bread, hush puppies, and perhaps others now forgotten. This corn bread in its various forms often was the only bread known by the pioneer. It was served at breakfast, dinner, and supper.

Corn also furnished meal for mush, was parched and carried as reserve ration by hunters, explorers, and woodland travelers. Many signs and

---

* See *Legends & Lore,* pp. 169–70.

It Happened in Southern Illinois

Southern Illinois has its eastern, southern, and western boundaries definitely fixed by the Wabash, Ohio, and Mississippi rivers. Its northern limits are less definite. The counties shown on the map are those generally accepted as being in the region.

From a collection of a few thousand pictures, the following forty-one have been chosen to represent something of the history, the previous customs, and the scenic features of southern Illinois.

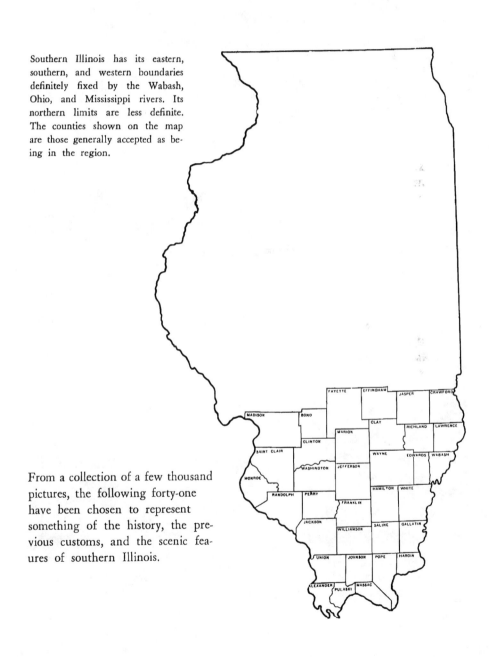

Left—Mother Jones remains an institution in American social history. *See pp. 18–19.* *Center*—Mother Bickerdyke was one of the most noted hospital workers of the Civil War. *See pp. 45–47. Right*—Robert E. Lee served for a time as a member of the Army Engineer Corps in Illinois. *See pp. 35–37.*

For a thousand years Indians made salt at the Equality salt spring. This is one of the kettles used by white men when they established a saltmaking industry there.

This stone wall at Pounds Hollow marks one of a dozen walled off enclosures in Illinois into which Indians are thought to have driven game. *See pp. 78–80.*

In the dead of winter, 1838, Cherokee Indians camped at this point west of Jonesboro as they moved along the Trail of Tears.

All that remain of Dutch John's Place are these ruins of a pretentious brick dwelling built by a Pennsylvania Dutchman north of Elizabethtown.

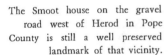

The Smoot house on the gravel road west of Herod in Pope County is still a well preserved landmark of that vicinity.

This sarcophagus in Woodlawn Cemetery at Carbondale indicates the determination of one southern woman not to be buried in northern soil.

A crude anvil used by Mr. Sanders, a blacksmith, during the War of 1812.

One of the last extensive blacksmith's shops in southern Illinois is this one at Jonesboro. *See pp. 152–53.*

Wes Richardson, who bottomed chairs, using his shaving horse at Broughton about 1947.

This is a stump mill like those used by early settlers. Although they were made in stumps outside the house, this one has been sawed off and moved inside.

A marker on the banks of the Big Muddy River indicates the location of the first commercial shipping coal mine in Illinois.

This is a traction threshing machine outfit. The bundles were hauled from the shocks in the field and threshed where the farmer wanted his straw stack. As the threshing floors and horsepower threshers vanished, this one came. It also has practically vanished. *See pp.* *178–80.*

Typical of the early privately supported academies of southern Illinois, Enfield Academy, where William Edgar Borah was a student, still stands.

This is the faculty of Southern Illinois College in 1868. With the coming of Southern Illinois Normal University, the school ceased to exist.

Broughton School, built in 1828, later served as a dwelling.

On the grounds surrounding this 130-foot high cross at Bald Knob, sunrise Easter services are regularly held. The cross was built through the efforts of Reverend Lyerla and a mail carrier named Wayman Presley, pictured on the right. *See* *pp. 261-63.*

A center for the training of candidates for priesthood was this monastery at Wetaug which has now disappeared.

This village jail stood in Pomona until recent years. Its six-inch walls were layers of oak heavily spiked.

An order for the execution of a slave for practicing witchcraft is shown below. No record of the actual execution has been found.

William Morrison owned numerous slaves whom he rented to those wishing laborers. This is the unique marker at his grave. *See pp. 287–88.*

McCormick's general store, with a post office attached, remained a widely known, modestly prosperous country store for a long lifetime, that is, until improved roadways doomed it.

General John Alexander McClernand
was a Shawneetown attorney who
early entered the service of the North.
He is listed as a political general and
one of the rivals of U.S. Grant for
command of the Cairo area.

Colonel B. H. Grierson began and led
one of the most noted cavalry raids
of the Civil War. His training headquarters was at the Eddy residence
which still stands south of New Shawneetown. *See pp. 317–19.*

This is marked as the earliest photograph of U.S. Grant in uniform. It shows him as a colonel when he took command of the Cairo forces.

No story of southern Illinois is complete without records of Fort de Chartres. This is the magazine of the old fort from which a hundred men went to help capture George Washington at Fort Necessity on July 4, 1754. *See p. 85.*

These are the mounds on which the log walls of the French Fort Kaskaskia once stood. Broken rocks in a depression reveal the site of the powder magazine. *See p. 84.*

Fishtrap Shoals south of Murphysboro marks the head of navigation
on the Big Muddy at low water
stages. First settlers set fish traps
here.

Much of the produce of
southern Illinois was shipped
downriver by flatboat or
barge. This is a group being pushed along by tow.

Early ferries were established at
important crossing points in the
rivers. Although this ferry is carrying automobiles and is powered by
gasoline, it still gives an idea of
an old-time ferry.

This tavern stood in Nashville and served travelers for a good hundred years. It was built before sawmills were available there as was shown by its short lengths of hand-driven weatherboarding and split framing timbers.

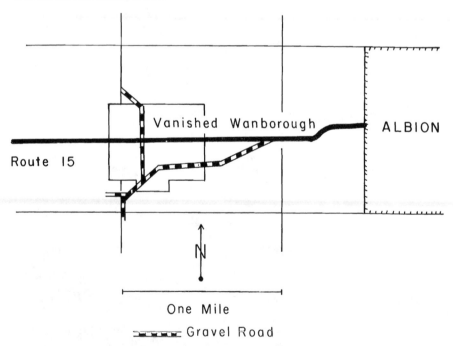

Route 15

Vanished Wanborough

ALBION

N

One Mile

Gravel Road

This map indicates the location of vanished Wanborough. Albion now occupies the site. *See p. 130.*

Five of America's most noted Doric columns are at the front of this bank
building in Shawneetown. *See pp. 123–24.*

Mrs. Graddy is shown in the tavern which she operated in New Haven.

A marker honoring Morris Birkbeck, who, with George Flower, founded the now vanished town of Wanborough.

This covered wagon was typical of the many like it that moved to the West.

Old Stoneface, one of the many scenic features in southern Illinois, is the rival of any such formation known.

superstitions grew up about it. Finally, it was the source of the popular and plentiful corn liquor of the pioneer.

❧ MUSINGS IN AN OLD KITCHEN

IF THE POET Gertrude Stein started to tell about a kitchen, she may have begun, "A kitchen is a kitchen, is a kitchen, is a kitchen," supposedly meaning that a kitchen really is a kitchen. The statement could not apply, however, to a pioneer kitchen. In those days, it would have been better to say, "A kitchen is more than a kitchen, more than a kitchen, more than a kitchen." This was made vivid by a recent pause in the kitchen of an old southern Illinois log house, crumbled beyond hopes of restoration.

Musing in this long-abandoned room suggested the great part that the kitchen played in the life of earlier days.

During that period of an almost self-sufficient economy kitchens also were shops where many activities were carried on and assorted handicrafts practiced. In addition to this, they were the social centers of homes.

Around their cheery fireplaces the families gathered on winter evenings to recount the incidents of the day and to plan those for the morrow. Bits of news that any member of the group had gathered during the day were passed along. Sometimes a member of the family who was about these firesides who could read, read to the others. Families gathered for family devotions, and stories were told and retold. Exploits were related and bits of lore were passed on; songs, particularly ballads, sometimes were sung. It was a great time when some fiddler joined the group and played the familiar tunes, never with a score to guide him. Children posed riddles and played such games as circumstances permitted, like fox and geese, hullygull, club fist, counting out games of several kinds, and guessing games that didn't take much space. All this might go on while men scraped and polished a tool handle, then oiled it, and toasted it in the flame, or while cotton was picked from seeds and burrs from wool. Women might card, spin, or knit without any interruption in the visiting. Many skills were taught and learned beside these kitchen fireplaces. Wastes from the household activities were swept into the coals with twig brooms or with a brush made from a turkey's wing. Wool, cotton, and flax often were spun into thread before these fireplaces.

This rising and falling whine of the great wool wheel, the gentler whir of the flax wheel, the click of knitting needles, the gentle ripping sound of hand cards as cotton and wool were formed into rolls or slivers for spinning, the plunk of the churn, and the thud of the cloth loom were among the familiar sounds heard. With the passing of the home crafts that produced them, these sounds also passed, to live only in the memory of a few older persons.

These fireplaces like the kitchens they adorned were no puny affairs. The backlog which might well be two feet in diameter and four feet long was dragged to the door with a horse and eased in on rollers. Oak and hickory were favorites for this. The forestick resting on andirons was a smaller affair, a foot or less in diameter. The space between was piled with smaller firewood sufficient for the weather needs.

As the evening lengthened apples from the apple hole were eaten, turnips were scraped, corn was popped or roasted. Popped corn often was made into candied balls, relished by youngsters. Parched corn was eaten or stored away in the pockets of boys as a kind of reserve ration. In the absence of anything better, acorns might be roasted like chestnuts. Walnuts, hickory nuts, hazel nuts, and pecans were cracked on the special stone with a depression worn by long use or often on one some youngster had found that had been used by the Indians for the same purpose. Hulls from which the kernels had been picked were thrown into the edge of the fire and their sputtering flames watched. The candied sap exuding from the end of a well-burned hickory log was scraped away and eaten by many a boy. It would be almost safe to say that there never was a dull moment beside a kitchen fireplace.

Hot or cold weather, kitchen fires were kept alive throughout the year. If perchance one did burn out, the problem of rekindling was not so simple. Sometimes it was done by borrowing a shovel of fire from a neighbor and bringing it home covered with soft dry ashes. Some homes had flint and steel with a box of tinder. This tinder could be a mass of tow from flax combings, a piece of punk, or specially dry rotted wood. A wad of cotton with a light mixture of gunpowder was sometimes used. The starting spark was gently blown to a blaze. As a last resort dry sticks might be rubbed together somewhat after the Boy Scout method of today.

All this held well into the 1800's before cookstoves became at all common. The first cookstoves of record came into "Little Egypt" shortly after 1800 but cooking at fireplaces continued for another long lifetime. Occasionally, you can find an old fireplace jamb where a crane once

hung. Naturally no one would want to revert to their use but they
should not be forgotten.

Did you ever eat long-cooked mush made in an iron pot swinging
from a crane above a hearth fire? If not, you've missed something.

❦ *SNIFFING AN ALBUM OF ODORS*

ONE NEVER KNOWS where a trivial thought may lead him. A few measures from the music of an old song or phrases from an almost forgotten
ballad often cause a train of memories to come trooping back. There also
are other strange and infrequently heard sounds that arouse their echoes.
Experiences like these are not unusual. In the present case it was not
sounds, but an odor that started the memory mill.

Instead of calling this particular appeal to the sense of smell an odor,
one is tempted to say fragrance, for that term could very well be applied
to the delightful smell that came from the crisp, buttered, oven-heated
slices of garlic bread recently served with thick juicy steaks broiled over
a charcoal fire beside a woodland log cabin.

Strangely, the memories aroused are not attached to some past feast
—far from that. Also, they are not about garlic alone, though garlic,
from its force of character, holds high place among remembered odors.
In location, however, these remembered scents are concentrated. They
are associated in memory with a one-room country school, the Hardscrabble of childhood.

The faint odor of garlic started it all, but there were several others
associated with it, one of which was distinctly a rival. That was the arch
stinker, asafoetida. With it came sulphur, coal oil (kerosene), turpentine, onion juice, weird concoctions containing goose grease, possum oil,
tallow, and beeswax, with occasional whiffs of camphor. These might be
termed aids to health and classified as medicinal smells.

Others, nonmedicinal, could be added. There was the smell of soiled
woolen clothing steaming beside the schoolroom stove, that of heavy felt
boots that needed airing, and of leather boots newly coated with a
dubbin made of tallow and beeswax. Most all the time there was no absence of odors.

Most impressive among the remembered smells of the well-warmed
winter schoolroom was the pervading and powerful smell of asafoetida.
This malodorous gum came from Afghanistan. It was considered powerful, somewhat in proportion to the fumes it gave off. It was an ancient

and highly esteemed remedy, being popular with Greek physicians over two thousand years ago. Its powerful and repellent scent was thought to ward off diseases. That belief still lingered.

Small tots, and some not so small, came to Hardscrabble School with lumps of the vile gum tied in small cloth bags and worn on strings about their necks. Some of the smaller ones of us, seeing these bags and smelling their contents, considered them somewhat as status symbols and thought that perhaps our unbelieving parents were neglecting us. Older children of unbelieving parents seemed pleased.

In addition to being considered a potent defense against diseases breathed in, asafoetida had other uses. A piece of gum "about the size of a thumbnail" placed in some whiskey was a ready remedy for the baby's colic when given, a few drops at a time, at proper intervals. The last folk use recalled for asafoetida was by an elderly gentlemen who, when fishing, placed a lump of the stuff in his can of fishworms. The reaction of the worms was not observed; anyway, he knew where to fish and caught fish.

There was one more use of asafoetida, and that was to test a speller's ability. According to the speller used, it had to have the "o" in it.

Garlic seems to have been next up on the list of disease repellents. A bag of crushed garlic was worn about the neck. It, too, kept people from unduly crowding the wearer. There is a bare possibility that repellents were slightly effective, since they helped to furnish a degree of isolation. Garlic has its other uses in addition to being worn about the neck. A bunch hung on the fireplace mantle brought good luck. A few bulbs kept in the pocket and nibbled occasionally assured good health. If disease entered the home, bunches of garlic hung about would drive it away.

Feeding a child garlic would cure bedwetting or worms. For these purposes it was finely ground. Eating garlic was thought to cure bronchitis. It also was a remedy for colds, rheumatism, and "lung trouble" when boiled in milk.

When high blood pressure came into prominence, garlic was a folk remedy. It also was used as a heart remedy. In many cases simply rubbing the soles of the feet would work wonders. Garlic bulbs and sulphur placed in the mouth of a mole's burrow would bring the inhabitant into the open. Onions and onion juice were considered as somewhat watered-down substitutes for garlic.

Sulphur came in for its place in the list of folk remedies and left its scented trail in the schoolroom. Mixed with lard or tallow it was an effective remedy for scabies or body vermin. A warm day or a heated room betrayed its user. Sulphur and molasses were about as regular as spring. They thinned the thick blood of winter.

It is strange how some trivial thought can start memories.

🌿 *LOST ODORS*

TODAY THE WIFE of a good friend sent a piping hot loaf of bread. When unwrapped, its fragrance brought to mind a chain of memories of other delightful odors.

Delving in our aromatic storehouse, the first one recalled was that of almost done apple butter being made in a large copper kettle over a steadily burning open fire in the back yard. The odor of the apple butter alone was delightful and, when finely grated cinnamon was added just before cooking was completed, the fragrance was delectable—we think of no better word.

To the memories of the fragrant apple butter should be added those afforded by wisps of smoke from the wood fire under the kettle and from piles of ripened apples, all scented by the natural tang of autumn air.

The smell of a boiling mixture of lye water and soap grease being made into soap in an iron kettle over a brisk fire near the ash hopper remains vivid to those who knew it. This odor, always pungent and changing as the soap neared the finishing stage, was termed a "clean" odor.

The mingled odors coming from a bakery may delight those presently passing along a city street. The present blend, however, is hardly so appetite-provoking as those that came from the old-time oven, indoor or out. The present-day bakery odor fades into insignificance when placed against the gingerbread highlight taken from an old-timer's smell album.

The smell of almost burned-out brush piles and log heaps at nightfall are not easily forgotten. Some will remember the distinctive fragrances of the different burning woods, like sassafras, gum, hickory, oak, and ash. Those who sawed logs or firewood will recall the distinguishing odors of a half-dozen different freshly cut woods. The lingering scents of assorted burning weeds and grasses also make a medley of smell memories.

Men who have plowed newly cleared ground will not forget the particular odor of the freshly turned earth, which was not at all like the old fields. In the same locality, this odor changes with the wetness of the soil and with the type of undergrowth.

The delightful aroma of warm wild honey will linger with those who cut bee trees. The sagey-peppery smell of homemade sausage, far different from the packing house variety, is not easily forgotten.

The faint smell of cured tobacco in a tobacco barn was different, and pleasing even to those not using the "weed." It was interesting to watch a prospective buyer pick up a handful of tobacco and sniff it. The freshness of corn meal could be rather accurately gauged by a sensitive nose.

There were the barnyard and horsey smells that have given way to those of gasoline and stinking oils. Along with the barn and horse smells have gone those of harness and shoe shops. Many will recall the sickening odor of a smoker's strong clay pipe, which was almost as bad as that of the asafoetida that some youngsters wore about their necks. Some men will recall the first time they smelled coal smoke. Some will recall the stale beer odor they encountered as boys when they passed an out-of-bounds saloon.

🏵 SHORT 'N' LONG SWEET'NIN'

THE MEANINGS OF verbal expressions may change through the years; they may even cease to be used at all when the practices they describe also pass. Two expressions, "short sweet'nin'" and "long sweet'nin'," are examples. To most persons now they are baffling, but to oldsters who in youth heard their elders use the terms, they are more meaningful.

Briefly stated, short sweet'nin' indicated refined sugar, cane or maple, which was carefully kept for special occasions in the sugar gourd on a kitchen shelf. Long sweet'nin' was honey, maple sirup, or sorghum, regularly called molasses.* This sorghum came by way of the local molasses mill, from cane grown on most farms from about the time of the Civil War and later. People preferred the term "molasses mill," apparently thinking it sounded better than sorghum mill. At times, long sweet'nin' might even include molasses made from pumpkins.

Sorghum molasses was the most commonly used long sweet'nin' of early southern Illinois after its production began here. In some localities favorable to its production maple sirup continued as a rival. Over all the region, honey, when it could be had, was rated best of all by nearly everyone. Some contended, however, that good new sorghum had no equal. (The writer joins them.)

In order to have a sufficient and dependable supply of honey, many

---

* See *Legends & Lore,* pp. 170–72.

farmers and village dwellers kept colonies of bees. Their hives, popularly called bee gums, frequently were arranged in a row along the garden fence or set at random in the shade of the orchard. Perhaps the hives were called gums because they often were made from sections of hollow gum logs. Their covers were broad boards nailed or held in place by a heavy stone. These log sections may not have been as efficient or convenient as those made of planks, but they were picturesque.

Many persons not able to afford short sweet'nin' and unwilling to settle for sorghum went into the woods and looked for colonies of bees that had escaped from the settlers and spread through the forest. Hunting bees became an important activity. Many men became highly skilled in tracing honey gatherers to their home. Most of this hunting was done in the late summer or early fall after swarming had ended and honey stocks for winter were highest.

A man going out to hunt bee trees generally would carry some kind of bait. Usually it was a piece of comb honey that the bees seemed to locate readily. Another favorite bait was corncobs moistened with brown or maple sugar sirup, both of which quickly attracted wandering bees. Unless he prepared one of these, the hunter looked for a place where bees went for water at the edge of some pond or pool.

The bee hunter would place his bait and wait. If a colony of bees was within reasonable distance, it would not be long before some of them would come to carry away loads of his offering. After taking on cargo, the bees would circle once or twice in an ascending spiral, then "make a beeline for home." This beeline was not such a straight one as the colloquialism would indicate. It regularly undulated or wavered from side to side, but steadily kept its direction.

The course of the heavily laden and thus slower flying bees was carefully observed and followed. Trees along its course were carefully inspected for high knotholes, and after a reasonable distance the hunter might again place his bait and repeat his observations. He often would move aside a hundred yards or so to check the directions from there and employ a crude but effective system of triangulation to help locate the colony's home. When the tree was found, the old barlow came into use to carve a deep X in its bark. No one but a sneak would molest a marked tree.

The writer will never forget his feeling of achievement as a fourteen-year-old when he found three trees in a day. Two were in Pemberton's woods, the third on Ike Smith's lower forty. One of these, an enormous oak, yielded a heaping washtub of fine comb honey. Loot from the three trees yielded enough honey for a winter's supply, even after giving

Bill one-third for providing the bee smoker, helping to fell the trees, and chopping out the hollows.

Now, even though barred by doctors from eating honey, he still has a strong urge to take some bait, go to the woodland, and try to find another bee tree and a supply of long sweet'nin'.

❦ *"SUGARING OFF" TIME*

THIS IS BEING WRITTEN during a cold snap in late winter. When the weather moderates, southern Illinoisans who wish to get an early start at making maple sirup and sugar should begin. The practice has all but vanished in the area, but a few still may be found making their scanty home supplies. It should be good sirup-making time until about the first of April, that is, as long as the nights are frosty and morning temperatures bring a thaw. Should the wind blow from the east or south, those versed in the lore of sugar making assure us that the flow of sap will be scanty. Wind direction really does have a marked effect, but why?

In earlier years sugaring off was a common practice in northern states. It marked the gathering of the first crop of the new year. The method was copied from the Iroquois Indians who were skilled sugar makers. According to an Indian legend they once did not have to boil the sap. Sirup flowed, ready made, from the tree. Their great Manitou, fearing that such a delicacy gotten so easily would demoralize a people, accordingly poured some water on the crown of the maple trees and thus diluted the sirup until it ever afterwards was necessary to gather and boil the diluted mixture.

There has been considerable discussion concerning the method by which the Iroquois made their sirup or sugar. Some say that they dumped heated stones into the wooden troughs and bowls or into earthen pots filled with sap. Others believe that they boiled the sap in birch bark containers placed over fires. The use of bark containers is not so farfetched as it may sound. It has been demonstrated that such can be done successfully if the portion of the bark vessel above the level of the liquid is properly protected against the flame. Whatever the method used, Indians quickly saw the advantages of the white man's pot and adopted it. Maple sirup and sugar, along with beans, squash, pumpkins, artichokes, corn, and tobacco, are among gifts from the red men.

The making of good maple sirup required skill. The pioneer had no thermometer to indicate a temperature of 219 degrees, proper for sirup, or 238–240 degrees, required to produce sugar. Neither did he have a hygrometer with its Baume scale to tell that the solids in the cooking sirup had reached 65 per cent, that proper for sirup, or 95 per cent required for sugar. Instead of using these, some of the boiling mixture was poured from the edge of a small vessel to see if it properly "sheeted." For sugar readiness the maker could see if it "haired," or he could splash some of it on a snow bank.

To rid the freshly made sirup of sediment, it was strained through thick woolen cloths. Instead of straining, one well-beaten egg for each gallon, or a small quantity of milk, could be stirred into the slightly cooled sirup. Sediment gathered on top with the coagulated milk or eggs and was skimmed off or strained out through a woolen cloth. The cloth also absorbed some of the coloring in the sirup and gave it a brighter color. These early sugar makers might not have known just why they did all the things they did, but they knew their processes were effective.

The 1860 report shows that more than forty million pounds of maple sugar were made in the United States. Many people in Illinois then made maple sugar, and local papers carried advertisements of dealers wanting to buy sirup and sugar. Recent reports indicate the present yearly production is little more than a quarter million pounds. Nearly all of this comes from New York, Vermont, New Hampshire, and Maine. The methods employed there have been standardized. Only in rare instances does one find sirup making carried on as a family project. Perhaps there are none of the old, half-faced camps, once so common, to be found with their kettles hung on poles over open wood fires. Few horse-drawn sleds with barrels on them go through maple groves to gather sap from buckets beneath spouts placed in selected maples. We wonder if some men still trudge about with buckets hanging from shoulder yokes. Genuine maple sirup is rare, and no one seems to have hit upon an artificial flavoring that can fool one competent to judge.

So far as we have learned, only two or three men in southern Illinois still make a bit of the sirup. One of these is Paul "Shiner" Norris in Effingham County, who does so purely out of sentiment. Shiner likes his product and stubbornly refuses to sell it. He did, however, invite the writer to have a breakfast of buckwheat cakes liberally moistened with his newly made sirup. I've loved Shiner since then.

❦ WHITTLING

ANY OLDER PERSON who goes prowling in out-of-the-way places can find many reminders of a way of life that has all but vanished. Some recent observances reminded the writer of a period of time that could be designated as B.C.C.—before cardboard cartons.

Until about the turn of the century, country storekeepers received most of their merchandise in slack barrels and wooden boxes. The boxes generally were sturdy ones made of straight-grained, soft pine boards that nailed easily and whittled readily. This method of packing has long since passed in southern Illinois but still is found elsewhere in the world.

A few days ago a sloop dropped anchor in the harbor of a small Caribbean island where the author was vacationing and began to unload goods packed much as they were before cartons made of corrugated cardboard came into use. Seeing the old type of packages brought to mind the times when such containers were common everywhere, and incidentally of an era when the whittling fraternity flourished.

The custom of men whittling as they talked must have been an almost universal one and was abandoned mostly because good whittlin' wood became scarce.

With those who whittled, it was more than a casual way to pass time. As they reduced the soft pine boards to symmetrical shavings and chips, they likewise whittled away at such problems as those times brought. With his razor-sharp barlow, the whittler removed bits of wood with machine-like accuracy and worked toward some general shape that gradually assumed definite proportions. At the same time, these men were figuratively whittling away at the problems of their day.

Not all the whittlers depended upon packing cases for timber. Some brought it with them. One man is remembered who "came to class" with a straight, even-grained, hard maple broomstick which he used as a walking staff. After a week or so of intermittent application of his keen knife the broomstick had become several links of wooden chain, a section of four bars containing nicely rounded wooden balls, an operating hinge, and a frog. All this was done without a break in the broomstick.

From time to time as he whittled, a man would pause to offer comments on such subjects as the protective tariff, morals, or how to make good shoestrings out of a groundhog's skin. All in all, the men who sat in the shade of the store porch and whittled joined voices to shape a logical working philosophy.

All this makes us believe that it would be helpful to have those who are striving to guide the course of the world's affairs take along a supply of whittlin' wood suitable for amateurs and start to whittle. Of course, among those at the top level, there always would be the moot question of who sits where. After all, the men who whittled usually compromised enough to reach reasonably logical conclusions.

In the shipment which we saw arriving at the island store, there were two slack barrels. Seeing these brought back memories of the varied uses made of them, from feed storage at the barn to hens' nests and hammocks.

Hammocks made of barrel staves were common. To make one, four strands of No. 9 wire about twenty-five feet long were used in weaving the staves together much as a section of picket fencing was made. The curve of the barrel staves gave a comfortable sag toward the middle of the hammock. After forming the hammock, it was contrived to hang between two shade trees. It thus became a comfortable form-adjusting bed, a place where one could go for a brief rest at noonday or after the evening meal. The free circulation of air it afforded made it about as much air-conditioned as anything the day offered. If the occupant wished, he could attach a small rope at right angles to the hammock, give it an occasional pull, and be gently swung to and fro.

After carefully thinking it over, it would be an excellent place to have the diplomats already alluded to relax at least thirty minutes each day. There they could doze, or just lie and look upward through leafy branches at the sky or at fleecy clouds floating lazily overhead. Perhaps after whittling for a time and then relaxing in a hammock, these hurried and harried people would find themselves calm enough to compromise on some of the perplexing questions of the day. Such a course might even calm the Russian representatives. All this might be improved by the addition of a few old-time horse traders.

One other calming appliance seen on the trip to and from the island boat landing was the rocking chair in much use on cottage porches. Should whittling and hammocks fail to produce results, this might be called into service. Since the time when someone coined the phrase "rocking chair money," this delightful old device has lost caste. Nevertheless the rocking chair was and remains a comforting appliance.

People may have been just as worried and "stewed up" in 1900 as they are now, but it isn't remembered that way. Why not revert, at least temporarily, to whittling, lying in hammocks, and gently rocking in chairs made for the purpose? People still doing so don't seem half so worried as we.

Chapter 8

Schools

❦ *SOME CALL IT NOSTALGIA*

SOMEONE SAID THAT a man becomes old when he turns to look backward, particularly if that backward glance is tinged with nostalgia. If that be true, the writer has been oldish today.

There are two good reasons, however, for this nostalgic backward look. First, it is an anniversary, another one on a somewhat long list. In addition, the day has been spent on Southern's campus where it all began on March 27, 1908.* That was our first day on the campus. This day, likewise, has been spent on the same campus, but it would not be correct to say amid familiar scenes, for little of the familiar remains. Among stray bits of the familiar no face known then has been found.

Most of the objects that a visitor would find upon returning after sixty years greet him as he approaches Old Main at the south end of University Avenue, beyond the familiar iron fence. Prominent surviving landmarks are Old Main with its broad front steps, the Science Building with the ageless little pump house snuggling among the trees and bushes behind it, and the stone-mounted cannon in front. Add to these the old Wheeler Library building, a marker or two, and some pine trees to complete the listing.

At the south end of University Avenue, just before the old campus is reached, the ancient visitor will see nothing but change on either side. At the west side of the avenue's southern end he will note the absence of Professor French's residence with its carefully planted yard where the rambling, dimly lit place known as Carter's came later to serve as a kind of student center (unofficial) for a generation.

---

* See *Legends & Lore*, pp. 195–97.

218

The visitor naturally misses a large cow pasture fenced with rails west of the French place, an area now occupied by University School and a portion of Woody Hall, a residence for 450 women. He naturally will not see faculty members come each morning with the family cow in tow, to carefully open the drawbars and turn Bossie to pasture for the day. Likewise, after school hours those same faculty members will not be coming to reclaim the source of the family's milk supply and lead her home. It was the best method then known to have something like "Grade A" milk. An imposing Home Economics Building, the Christian Foundation, some eating places, and shops are in the space between University Avenue and the Illinois Central railway, where there then were numerous residences.

At Old Main the same broad steps lead up both front and back, but the years seem to have made them higher and steeper. Anyway, the same fossils, the first ones remembered by a boy from Rector Bottoms, still are exposed in the stones of the south steps. One also notices the bricked-up arches on either side of the central portion of the third floor. That section then was the assembly and study hall where students were supposed to spend their time when not in class or when excused to study at the library. It also was the place where chapel was held daily.

This study-assembly hall had a scant four hundred (somehow we recall it as exactly 396) regular school desks, ample to seat all high school and college students even after all tardy arrivals had registered and the president had proudly announced, "Today we have 328 students enrolled," then adding in lowered tones, "including those in the high school." The actual number considered "college" was 238. Many of them had never attended high school at all but had qualified for entrance by presenting a second-grade teacher's certificate, occasionally given by a friendly and considerate county superintendent.

The amazing growth of Southern becomes apparent when the 238, rated college level then, is compared with the over twenty thousand full-time resident college students enrolled on the Carbondale campus this year, about eighty times the 1908 spring enrollment. The college campus then was twenty acres, now it is eight hundred acres in actual campus at Carbondale. A strange then-and-now comparison shows that in 1908 each acre of campus accommodated twelve college students. The Carbondale campus, now forty times as large, accommodates twenty-five students per acre. This would hardly indicate any justifiable criticism for enlarging the campus.

In passing, it should be remembered that the Carbondale campus acreage given above does not include farm and woodland tracts in use for experimental, demonstration, and study purposes, lands used to learn how to better use all lands. Neither does it include any enrollment or acreage for the Edwardsville Branch of the University.

But, back to 1908. The wildest visionary then strolling over the campus at Southern could not have dreamed that the quiet, conservative, perhaps slightly stodgy, little school he knew would within his lifetime become a major university, one of the fastest growing ones in America.

Those of us who knew Southern then would not want to turn the wheels of time backward. Nevertheless, we have no desire to forget that there then was much here that was fine, including many earnest, industrious, skilled, and consecrated teachers who perhaps were building better than they knew.

❧ STILL SITS THE SCHOOLHOUSE

A SCHOOLDAY POEM began with "Still sits the schoolhouse by the road a ragged beggar sunning." A scant few of them still do.

People may speak of the vanishing institution, but concerning the country school perhaps it would be better to say vanished, for two years ago only three were left in Illinois. Here and there one finds an occasional rural school building that has been converted to a farmer's storage space or into a residence. Some others, beyond all usefulness, remain with windows and doors gone, walls warped and roofs sagging, surrounded by weeds, briars, and bushes. They are almost ghostly. To younger persons they are simply little buildings well on their way toward disappearance. To oldsters who attended school in some of them, they arouse more than a casual interest. They call to mind a departed way of life.

Some will recall them as the ending place of mile-long morning plods over muddy or dusty roads. This was through fair or foul weather, winter and summer, but mostly winter, for school seldom "kept" in summer.

The trip to school began early enough to be there by eight o'clock. The start of the homeward trip began about twenty-five recitations later. It was a busy day.

Ages ranged from the five-year-olds, who somehow managed to get started, to those as much as twenty years old. It was a motley bunch. At one time Hardscrabble had an enrollment of eighty-one such pupils, enough boys to form two baseball teams that played in the corner of Mr. Pemberton's pasture beyond the roadway and rail fence.

The noonday recess was much like a picnic. Less hardy souls ate their lunch, called dinner, at their desks in the schoolroom. The more rugged ones went outside, eating in the coal house, on the leeward side of trees, atop fences, and against the ricks of firewood, before coal came. Others ate alongside the schoolhouse. Those living within a half mile often went loping home to lunch. Perhaps that accounts for the best miler I ever knew.

Schools served as social and cultural centers. They were used for church services, for the Farmers' Union, and for polling places at election time. Strolling entertainers with their magic lanterns, a new phonograph, and bits of magic came along. Singing schools and even writing schools offered night classes on a subscription basis.

School life was not always an unrelenting grind. Friday afternoons sometimes were given over to ciphering and spelling matches, to recitations, declamations, songs, and dialogues. In ciphering and spelling matches, pupils vied with each other to see who was best.

Friday nights often saw the meetings of a literary society. Adults of the community regularly came to these and occasionally took part. At these meetings "essays" were written and presented. There were readings and recitations that ranged from the definitely tear-jerking variety to those thunderously commanding.

One boy tried valiantly, in a squeaky adolescent voice, to literally shake the walls with Shakespeare's lines saying, "Friends, Romans, and countrymen, lend me your ears" (he might have said "years"). Ten years later this same boy heard one of the world's great actors say the same words. Only then did he understand.

Another feature of those Literary Society meetings was the presentation of a "paper" that carried a full stock of wisecracks and jokes aimed at the more prominent of the younger set.

A debate, with question stated and participants chosen well in advance, often closed the program. Two favorite subjects are remembered. One was "Resolved: That pursuit yields more pleasure than possession;" the other, "Resolved: That the American Indian has been mistreated." Having at different times advocated and opposed both subjects, confusion still reigns.

When a visiting school participated in a Friday night program, it naturally was more exciting. Then there was the always welcome last day of school with its round of speeches and inevitable leave-taking.

The country school has fallen into decay. Its blackboards are gone from the walls. The teacher's desk and richly carved pupils' desks are broken. Shelves for the dinner pails and rows of nails for coats and caps have disappeared. No switches or pointers are left on their racks. About all that remains is the steadily diminishing stock of oldsters' memories.

Were those days as pleasant as the stored memories, or is it that only pleasant memories are stored?

❧ PIE SUPPERS

WITH THE DISAPPEARANCE of rural schoolhouses, many of the practices and customs that clustered about them also are vanishing. An old poster evidently designed and lettered by a pupil was found by the writer in one of these deserted buildings. It announced that a Pie Supper ("S" reversed) would be held at the school on a Friday night in November, 1923.

Don't ask how it came to be preserved for thirty-five years on an almost inaccessible upper shelf of a corner closet. The reversed capital letter might have had some part in its first being laid there.

Pie suppers along with some similar affairs called box suppers were annual events. Some energetic teachers would hold one of each in the year. They definitely were fund-raising affairs.

Shortly after dark on the night named, people would begin to gather in the school that would be lighted for the occasion with kerosene lamps borrowed from neighboring housewives. Careful teachers saw to it that their schoolrooms looked as attractive as possible.

Girls from six to sixty brought pies or boxes. In each box or plate a number was placed. The corresponding number and the owner's name then were registered on a list. The identity of the pie owner was kept secret in this manner, except for those in the know. Along with the pies some woman who had been given the privilege brought a cake that would be sold to select the prettiest girl. There also would be a pair of ten-cent socks for the man with the dirtiest feet, a small mirror for the ugliest man, or a bar of soap for the dirtiest one.

A short entertainment program would be offered. The teacher of the school or a school director would then explain that the purpose of the sale was to raise money to buy library books, maps, or some other equipment for the school; it might even be an organ. Anyway, it was something that the directors evaded buying or for which their meager funds were not sufficient.

At this point the one crying the sale would take over. This "auctioneer" often was one of the school directors or some local man who secretly yearned to spiel. An occasional teacher would conduct his own sale. The writer once took over and finished one auction after the person duly selected, having abundantly "fortified" himself for the occasion, became somewhat unsteady.

People enjoyed these pie suppers. Two young men in our vicinity made a specialty of attending them for many miles around. They literally were pie supper specialists. It was their custom to be present at the very beginning of the sale and to make an opening bid on each pie, generally thirty-five cents. This was not so bad as it sounds, for pies could be bought at the bakery, if one went to the county seat, for ten cents each.

If some girl, knowing her pie, revealed that fact in some manner or some local swain instantly countered with a higher bid, the "specialist" stayed in to continue bidding and thus to harass the boy friend, but tried always to judge just when to quit. On one such occasion one of the "specialists" bought a pie for seventy-five cents, which topped the funds the boy friend had available. After the sale, this girl's admirer came and wanted to buy the lucky number for two dollars on credit. The sale was made, at cost, the privilege of paying later granted. Payment in full was made the next day. The wedding came a few months later. These two pie specialists sometimes misjudged the time to quit bidding and accordingly would find themselves with a surplus of pies. But they liked pies.

The prettiest girl sale was by votes of one cent each. This feature occasionally became very animated and added considerably to the proceeds. On one occasion the cake brought almost a hundred dollars. It also resulted in three fights and left a standing feud between boys of the two competing communities. (No regrets)

Do schools still have pie suppers? I'd like to attend another one.

🌾 LAST DAY IN A COUNTRY SCHOOL

A GENERATION AGO the countryside of southern Illinois, in fact that of the entire state, was dotted with one-room rural schools. There literally were thousands of them alongside the narrow wagon roads. Today, one may drive hundreds of miles over some of those same roadways and not see a single "little red schoolhouse" still in use. At last check there were only three of them left in the state. (Despite the prevalence of the term, the writer has seen only two schools painted red among a thousand or more he has encountered.)

The typical last day as observed in earlier schools is practically unknown. Youngsters, then as now, looked forward to the end of school terms with considerable impatience. As it drew near, they made a count-down on the remaining days, just as they tallied those until Christmas. Both days were anticipated with pleasure. There was this slight differ-ence, however: Christmas brought pleasure for itself, while the last day of school brought pleasure because it brought an end of book work and study.

The last day of school also brought partings that often carried a tinge of lingering sadness to many. Pupils of the same school might live miles apart, through woods, across fields, or along country roads that were dusty or muddy by turns. It was not easy to "go over to Susan's and play an hour." It might take the better part of that time to walk there.

The last day of school was a festive occasion. The teacher came earlier than usual, freshly shaved, and dressed in his Sunday suit with his shoes newly shined with soot from the lid of the cookstove. Pupils came freshly scrubbed, girls beribboned, and boys with a new spring, home-administered haircut. Larger boys who had dropped out to begin farm work early sometimes returned for this day; they were sometimes accused of coming back solely for the candy customarily given by teachers on this final day.

It was also a custom in many districts to have a last day basket dinner that honored the teacher, bade a farewell to the older pupils who were ending their school days, and served a social purpose as well. About the time of the first recess parents would be seen coming with baskets of food; some of them from the far corners of the district arrived in buggies or the farm wagon. Men and women alike would be dressed for Sunday.

If the weather was fair (and often it was not for the short terms then would end in early March), the dinner was spread on cloths laid on the grass or on planks. When weather was inclement, the meal was spread on planks placed across the school desks. In either case it was bountiful.

After eating, there would be a longer than usual lunch hour with games and visiting. The afternoon session was something different. There were recitations, which meant that pupils "said their pieces." There were ciphering and spelling matches, often participated in by pupils from an adjoining school. Once in a while some parents would enter such contests and sometimes vanquish both the visitors and the home guard.

As the program came to an end, the teacher would invite parents to talk, but was careful to call upon the directors first. Before the day ended, all would have an opportunity to "make a speech." Many, includ-ing some mothers, would say a few words, generally of praise. Older pupils also were invited to speak. The writer's first speech was a few shaky words said on the occasion of his last day of school at Hardscrabble. The next year he presided at a similar last day in his first teaching position.

With the program completed and the meeting dismissed, there were the usual leave-takings. The schoolhouse was locked until time for the fall term to begin. Pupils took their books and trudged away. Occasionally some boys who had grudges to settle went a short way down the road and "had it out." They felt safe in the knowledge that the teacher would not be there to punish them the next day.

Many older persons hold cherished memories of these last days in the now vanished country school.

❧ SCHOOLBOOKS OF ANOTHER YEAR

AN EXHIBIT OF elementary school textbooks is held at Southern Illinois University each summer. A good hundred publishers display their newer offerings, which are wonderful and beautiful.

An oldster who goes to these exhibits and wanders past the colorful texts almost wishes he could be a youngster again, if only to have opportunity to enjoy the new books more fully. Such a visit also reminds those acquainted with earlier schoolbooks of the great changes that have come since the days of the *New England Primer,* Webster's *Blue Backed Speller,* Ray's *Arithmetics,* and McGuffey's *Readers*—all memorable early-day texts that passed from use a good lifetime ago. The informed visitor cannot fail to see the sharp contrast between the books on display and those of earlier years.

The first of these was the *New England Primer* of which more than five million pocket-sized copies were printed and sold. Only a few dog-eared copies remain today. Remembering that schoolbooks were not plentiful then and often were passed to younger brothers and sisters, or even from parent to child, it can be safely estimated that ten million pupils learned to read from this primitive text.

Little that was cheerful could be found in a book that began with:

A—In Adam's fall
We sinned all,

and proceeded alphabetically through

H—There is a dreadful fiery Hell
Where wicked ones must always dwell.

Thus, it went on to Z and something about Zion. The uniform and ominous tone continued to the end. Nevertheless, it was the sole reading text for millions of learners.

Another schoolbook that became and remained a legend was the *Blue Backed Speller,* copies of which are occasionally found in attics and trunks at old places. This book was used to measure the spelling skill of millions at the once common spelling bees. It also contained assorted bits of information, somewhat like an encyclopedia. This book, perhaps more than any other, will remind some of the "blab" school where all pupils studied aloud.

In conning over his spelling lesson, the pupil would spell the first syllable and pronounce it. Likewise with the second, and then combine and pronounce both, repeating this process for each syllable to the end of the word. When a word as long as "incomprehensibility" was given, the feat of spelling and pronouncing became complicated. It was interesting to hear someone skilled in the practice skip nimbly through such long words.

Another among the legendary series of texts were the Ray's *Arithmetics.* From these texts other millions learned their basic mathematics. When it was said of someone, "He can solve every problem in Ray's *Third,*" he was being acknowledged as quite a mathematician. And he was, for the task was not an easy one.

Great as the foregoing were, however, they dwindle into comparative insignificance when compared with the fourth one named here, the series of readers edited by William Holmes McGuffey, one of the most unusual characters in American education. He was unusual in many ways, one being that his formal education was not begun until he was sixteen years old. He then worked and taught school during vacations to complete college in 1826 when he was twenty-six years old.

A few years after this he was asked to edit a series of school readers. This he agreed to do for $1,000, completion of the payment to depend upon the success of the publisher in selling the book. Before the series passed from use about 1900, they had sold approximately 130 million copies and had made some ten publishers a million dollars each.

McGuffey never received more than the $1,000 agreed upon, except for small fees paid for his help in revisions. Tradition does tell us, however, that the publishers on each Christmas would send him a barrel of hams. There is no record to indicate that McGuffey felt himself wronged. When he died in 1873, it is very doubtful if he realized even faintly the profound influence his readers had exerted on American education. McGuffey's *Readers* are most old-fashioned now. When they came from the press, they were radically new in concept. The author had departed from the concept of the *New England Primer* and had based his teaching plan upon the environment that lay about the pupil.

From the very outset, the readers were popular. At one time they were the standard text in thirty-seven states, all over the country, in fact, except in New England where they never came into general use. They were translated and used in Spanish language countries and in Japan.

Many of the stories and expressions that first occurred in these readers remain familiar to thousands. Nearly everyone knows of Meddlesome Mattie, the boy who cried wolf, the honest chimney sweep, the cruel boy who pulled the legs off a fly, the dog that led another injured one to the kindly man who had bound the injured foot of the first one, Ragged Davy and his flowers, and numerous other ones. Selections in his more advanced texts introduced many to the best of English literature.

The influence of McGuffey lingers. A museum in Ohio houses many of his personal effects. A log school where he taught in Kentucky is preserved. It is doubtful if any other series of books has exerted a greater moral influence over the country, and surely no other one has had a greater hold on the affections of people.

If you can find an old McGuffey *Reader,* stop and read it. It will be old-fashioned now, but it was much in the forefront a hundred or so years ago.

THE VANISHING COUNTRY SCHOOL

When one drives along the byroads of southern Illinois, he occasionally sees some lonely object apparently left to remind him that others, like it, once were common on the area's rural landscape. One also realizes that the disappearance of such objects has been so gradual and silent as to be hardly noticed.

One such institution now rapidly disappearing is the box-like country schoolhouse. This fact came to attention a few days ago when passing by Colbert School in the southeastern corner of Saline County, one of the last such schools left to mark the passing of an educational era.

The fourteen youngsters playing over its gullied and muddy playground brought to mind the time when there were thousands of such groups playing about and storing memories that often outlasted those of the classroom. Many still recall incidents that occurred about the fine old oak tree on a corner of some country school playground long after they have forgotten the countries and capitals of Europe.

At about the same time this visit was made a friend dropped by with a school director's minute book from another school begun in Washington County just over a hundred years ago. Assorted bits of information in it gave interesting glimpses of how such schools operated. It listed names of candidates for school directors and the votes each received eighty years ago. Some elections apparently were hotly contested. At one time an election was held to locate a new school building and authorize a bond issue of $500 to pay for it. There appears to have been no opposition.

Entries in the minute book reveal some interesting sidelights. In November, 1860, Doctor Scott was employed as teacher at $30 a month. The next year Mrs. Scott taught for $25 a month. Nineteen years later Miss Elle Scott, their daughter, received only $20 a month, the record low.

This book contains a list of all the school's teachers from the formation of Pleasant Hill School, District No. 4 (later changed to No. 34), Washington County, in 1860, until its close eighty-four years later. Those who taught summer terms of two months to favor those younger children less able to travel the muddy roads and endure the exposures of winter also were carefully noted. For many years their month was twenty-two school days. Attendance reports for 1868–1869 show that there were thirty-eight pupils enrolled, twenty-seven boys and eleven girls. One wonders if girls were that scarce or whether it was thought they needed less "learning."

The directors occasionally made official visits to the school and wrote reports of their observations. These some miscreant has clipped; that is, all except one.

Until the 1870's wood was used for heating Pleasant Hill School. In 1861 a winter's supply was bought by contract for $12.50 "to be paid as soon as money can be raised by taxes, and to draw interest at 6 per cent until paid." The next year the contract for wood was awarded to the lowest bidder at $2.74 a cord for eight cords. The following year the price rose to $2.75 a cord.

In 1895 the school bought a "flat and fixtures—$7.05." At another time it adopted *Barnes' Readers, Ellis' History, Raubs' Arithmetic, National Speller,* and *Ray's First* and *Third Arithmetics* for classroom study. In the spring of 1879 it paid $4.75 "for making fires" during the past winter. The next year the price rose to $6.40. A later entry gives the number of fires built and paid for during a past winter at $.05 each. In 1878 a coal bucket was purchased for $.70. Chalk and matches cost $.10, a broom was $.30. A tin cup, evidently the community drinking vessel, was bought every year or two as shown by the repeated entry "cup .05." When WPA days came, school directors furnished $98.20 worth of material for the building of two privies.

Typical entries each fall reveal what went on at the school during the summer vacation. One says "lights and putty $3.37." In October, 1885, coal delivery evidently was late. On October 23, records show that they bought "½ bushel coal .05" from a man living near the school. The next day they bought from another nearby farmer an additional "½ bushel of coal .05." In 1937 they began using "sweeping compounds" for which they paid $1.65. A blackboard bought in January, 1869, cost $10. Before that they used a section of smoothed plank wall painted black.

To those who have attended one-room country schools or have knowledge of them, a visit to one of the three yet to be found in Illinois or a casual reading of a directors' or trustees' record book arouses many a vivid recollection. Few indeed would wish them back. All, however, will acknowledge that they gave a basic education to America.

🏵 *FIRST ILLINOIS SCHOOL CLOSES*

OVER A PERIOD of several years the sale of abandoned rural schoolhouses in southern Illinois attracted little attention. It was different, however, at Portland School near Burkesville Station in Monroe County. Another abandoned school, but one carrying an interesting story in the state's history, was being sold.

The auctioneer announced the purpose of the meeting and asked for bids. After a few brisk bids the auctioneer said, "Are there other bids? Gentlemen, are you through? Sold to Mr. Sandefur," and the Portland schoolhouse became private property.

Its sale ended the last one-room rural school in Monroe County, also the oldest school in continuous operation in Illinois—some say in all the Northwest Territory.

As schools go, its story was a long one. It was in this settlement, then and still known as New Design, that John Seeley began the first English-speaking school in Illinois in 1783. Seeley's school began in a log cabin that some unnamed squatter had built, lived in for a time, and vacated.

Pupils from several miles around came here, often over trails blazed through untouched forest, perhaps infested with prowling Indians. The school was a rude affair with benches made of split logs that had been smoothed with the broadax. Equipment was meager indeed.

Like other efforts at education, the New Design School was a subscription affair. Parents paid a fee, based on the number of pupils sent and the length of time for which they were enrolled. Ages often varied from five to twenty-one. Texts were any books the student had available, from Bibles and ancient histories, to almanacs or the plays of Shakespeare. Teachers "set" the problems, and pupils made their own arithmetics. It was a stern school; in fact, the life of all who lived there was stern.

The first teacher, Mr. Seeley, was from all records and traditions respected, well-liked, and devoted to his work. It is reported that his successor Francis Clark, was "intemperate," not so well-liked, and, like others of those very early teachers, shortly moved on.

The third teacher was a man named Halfpenny, whose first name is not recalled. He taught in this and other schools of that region as they were established. Some say that as late as 1800 a good half of those who had attended school in Illinois had been Halfpenny's pupils. One historical writer called him "the Schoolmaster General" of early Illinois. In 1795 he left teaching to establish a much needed and widely known gristmill on Fountain Creek west of Bellefontaine.

John Clark, a Scotsman, followed Halfpenny. Clark was also a minister and is said to have been the first Protestant to preach in the Spanish territory west of the Mississippi. John Doyle, who had first come to the Illinois country as a soldier with George Rogers Clark in the Kaskaskia Campaign and had returned to live in the settlement, was the next teacher.

According to surveyor's records, this first school was in section eighteen near the southeast corner. When the first cabin was abandoned, a new house was built in the vicinity. Portland schoolhouse, just sold, was the fourth building in the district. Really, the first schools were community affairs rather than district schools because there was no law to provide schools until more than forty years had passed.

The Monroe County Historical Society initiated plans to have the site of this first school made into a park. Perhaps no better method could be found to memoralize the legendary one-room school than to place a suitable marker at the site where John Seeley taught his first subscription school.

🏵 *OCTAGONAL SCHOOLS*

THE CHARTER OAK schoolhouse in Randolph County, Illinois—doubtlessly the last school building of its kind in America to be used for classes—was abandoned a few years ago.* The school district joined with others in a consolidation, and the unique brick building was vacated.

Though Charter Oak was the last octagonal, or eight-sided, school used so far as is known in the United States, it was not the only one of its type built. There once were three similar schools in Pennsylvania and another in New Hamphire.

The last of these eastern buildings to see service, the Diamond Rock School near Valley Forge, closed in 1864. It was locally referred to as the "eight-cornered school." A Pennsylvania school was at Brandywine and a third near Newton Square, about six miles south of Paoli. The school at Valley Forge remained abandoned until the Diamond Rocks Scholars Association was formed to restore it.

Restoration efforts were successful, and on September 21, 1918—exactly one hundred years to the day from the time when the first term of school began there—the building was dedicated with appropriate cere-monies. Several pupils who had attended it and at least one of the former teachers met there after fifty-four years. No former pupil is now living. The last one, Mrs. Mary Rossiter, died in 1948 at the age of ninety-six.

The building is small but solidly built. Its stone walls are more than a foot thick. Each of the eight panels in the wall are eight feet long, inside measurement. The ceiling, almost nine feet high, is carried on joists sup-ported by two heavy crossbeams. Each panel of the wall, except the west one where the door is located, has a window with its dozen small panes of glass. The original recitation bench, the teacher's desk with the bell used by George Ralston in 1843, and the spectacles and spectacle case of Aaron Thompson, who taught the school in 1850, are there. A deer antler, properly mounted, makes the handle of a walking cane used by one of the teachers who was lame.

One of the cupboards or bookcases that stood beside the doorway has been returned, and some of the books actually stored there more than a hundred years ago are on the shelves again. Wooden pegs on leather thongs still pass through the sash to fasten the windows. Blue wooden shutters protect the glass from perennial stone-throwing boys. Also reminiscent of earlier days are the two hickory pointers.

These pointers, rather sturdy affairs, served a double purpose. They were used to point to figures, letters, words, or problems on the painted plank blackboards or on charts. They also were applied to the proper

---

* See *Legends & Lore,* pp. 206–8.

section of a careless youth's anatomy to point out the error of his ways.

Early pictures of the school building, pictures of former pupils, with drawings and newspaper clippings, all tastefully displayed, turn time backward. A visit to the "eight-cornered school" near Valley Forge will intrigue anyone interested in the pioneer school.

A group of women now keep the building open during the summer season, and thousands come to visit it. Apparently they are not afraid of being dispossessed soon. The lease given to the school by "George Beaver, Jr., of Tredyffrin Township" is for "the Term of Nine hundred and ninety-nine years."

Almost anywhere one goes now he finds an increasing interest in local landmarks, the places that tend to give reality to the always interesting story of the region. Southern Illinois has many such places, whose preservation would add interest and significance to the local story. One of these is southern Illinois' own eight-sided school in Randolph County. Each year a thousand people come to its green corn festival.

🌸 EWING COLLEGE

IF EACH VANISHED academy, seminary, or college of southern Illinois had left its ghost, the region could muster quite a phantom band. These "institutions of higher learning" represent both the persistent hope and continuous efforts made to provide youth with better educational opportunities.

Schools sprang up in many localities—among them Jonesboro, Equality, Eldorado, Benton, McLeansboro, Enfield, Sparta, DuQuoin, Carbondale, Fairfield, Albion, Cairo, Salem, Irvington, Bainbridge, Creal Springs, and Ewing. There were others, too.

Perhaps the greatest and most sustained effort to establish and maintain a college was in the village of Ewing on a byroad seven miles north of Benton in Franklin County. After more than fifty years of effort to keep it open, this school was formally closed in 1925.

It all began when Dr. John M. Washburn opened a four-month term of a high school in the Frizzell Prairie Baptist Church on April 15, 1867. Its first full academic year began on September 23 of that year. Step by step this high school became a college, moved to a campus in town, and graduated its first class in 1874. Judge Silas Bryan of Salem, the father of William Jennings Bryan, delivered the commencement address for a class of five.

The association of the Bryan family with the college continued. After the death of Judge Bryan, his wife came to serve as matron of Huddle-son Cottage, a girls' dormitory. One daughter, Frances, was a student; the other, Mamie, was a teacher. The son, William Jennings, came to the campus several times as a featured speaker.

If one may judge by prices published in annual catalogs, Ewing was a poor man's college. Rooms for boys in a dormitory that stood across the street on the south side of the campus rented for $.25 to $.50 a week per student, with two to a room. This gaunt old three-story building had in turn been a wool processing plant and part of a flour mill before being made into a rooming house for boys.

The boys were required to carry in their firewood and do the janitorial work. Rooms for girls in Huddleson Cottage were $.50 to $.75 per person per week, but girls were spared the chore of carrying firewood. In all cases, kerosene lamps were furnished. Meals in the dining hall cost $1.50 a week. The estimated annual total cost for a student at Ewing, as published in the school catalog, was $168. For some years the college also maintained a farm where those who wanted to could grow a part of their food.

The college had two literary societies, the Pythagorean and the Logossian. For a short time there was a third, the Euterpean. The first two named societies were chartered by the state in 1886. This, it was said, prevented the faculty from wielding too much influence on the organizations. Even at that time students did not particularly like supervision.

Football was furiously competitive. Eligibility rules were unknown; the school apparently operated on the principle that the stronger, swifter, and rougher the player, the more he was sought.

There were other diversions for the students too. That is suggested by the fact that the Ewing livery stable was one of the largest in southern Illinois, keeping more than fifty rigs.

None of the original campus buildings remain. The oldest of the buildings once used is the Carnegie Library of oversized concrete blocks. Shortly after this visit was made to Ewing the library building was sold for removal. A short time later the lettered cornerstone of Willard Hall that spelled out "Ewing College" was removed to become part of a memorial marker among the pines on the corner of the old campus.

When the library building was removed, only one building associated with the college remained. This was the dormitory for girls, finished just as the college was closing. It now is used for high school classes.

About the only familiar objects left to greet visitors returning after fifty years or so are the large pine trees. C. V. Clark, Class of 1897, doesn't think they have grown any in a half century.

One of the strange features of Ewing College is that its Alumni Association was formed in 1959, almost a generation after the school had closed. In 1960 the Association held its second meeting at which it was decided to publish a history of the college. This book, very much like a eulogy of the vanished school, was written by Dr. A. E. Prince, long associated with the institution and its last president. This history was printed by a former student, James C. Monroe of Collinsville. Both the writing and publishing were labors of love. The college is gone but an aging alumni deeply cherishes its memory. Many very old persons remember Ewing when it was a recognized cultural center of southern Illinois.

❦ *ILLINOIS' OLDEST COLLEGE*

BEFORE ILLINOIS was very old, several groups of interested citizens had been formed to establish and operate academies and colleges as "institutions of higher learning." In 1835 some of these groups were asking the legislature to grant them charters so that they could operate as corporate bodies, but the Illinois lawmakers were reluctant to issue such authority.

When the requests finally came up for consideration, a number of questions which now seem strange to us were asked. The first one inquired whether such institutions were needed. The second one asked if it really was necessary that such a group be incorporated. Finally it was questioned by some whether corporate powers could be granted to organizations of this kind without endangering the public welfare.

After considerable debate, the legislature decided to grant charters to four applicants. The first was given to a group of Baptists. It allowed them to found Alton College, "in or near Alton." This school previously had been known as Rock Spring Seminary, located between Lebanon and O'Fallon. It later became Shurtleff College. As a college, Shurtleff was discontinued in 1957 and its facilities are now used by Southern Illinois University.

A second listing shows a charter granted to a Presbyterian group for a school to be known as Illinois College. The third permit was given to a group of Methodists to establish McKendrean College in or near Lebanon. When this charter was amended later, the name became McKendree College. A fourth charter was given to Jonesborough College at Jonesborough. (Note how the spelling differs from today's Jonesboro.)

McKendree really had its beginning some years earlier when the

Methodist Conference met at Mt. Carmel in September, 1827. At this meeting, the establishment of a seminary was recommended and the sale of shares in the new venture was begun. Shares totaling 138½ were sold to 105 individuals at $10 a share. With $24 of the $1,385 total, a tract of eight acres was bought. (The same amount, incidentally, as the Dutch paid the Indians for Manhattan Island.)

Each share gave its holder the permanent privilege of sending a full-time student to the school. Building construction was begun in the summer of 1828, and the school opened on September 21. Its faculty consisted of two members, Edward R. Ames and Miss McMurphy, whose given name is undetermined. For his work during the first year, Ames was paid $115. The second year he received a slight increase and was paid $125, the rate of pay being $25 a month. Available sources do not show Miss McMurphy's salary.

In 1830 the physical properties of the school were "deeded to the Methodist Episcopal Church for safe keeping." Also in that year, Ames decided to leave the school and enter the ministry.

In order to have permission to preach, it was necessary that he pass an examination before a regularly constituted board presided over by the Reverend Peter Cartwright. A vote on his qualifications resulted in a tie which Cartwright refused to break. It happened, however, that a Negro man entitled to sit on such examining boards was seen passing along the road about this time with a load of firewood. He was called in, a new vote was taken, and Ames passed.

In 1833 Peter Akers became principal at a salary of $75 a term. (A lineal descendant of this Peter Akers now serves on its board of trustees.) During Aker's first year a request was made that two Indians be admitted as free students. Their limited finances would not allow them to pay, even though board and lodging was only $1.12½ a week. For those who could afford it, this was apparently a good bargain because it was stated that "the table shall at all times be well supplied with good wholesome food, well cooked, in sufficient quantity and suitable variety."

Even at that time there was a problem of discipline in "institutions of higher learning." This is shown in a letter from Akers asking the board to meet and sustain in a sterner disciplinary program. He felt that action was warranted because the entire student body, excepting two, had taken off one afternoon to visit the circus that had come to town.

Despite its problems, mostly financial, McKendree has carried on and has exerted an influence rare for a small college. Men from McKendree have played prominent parts in church, state, and school affairs.

The first president of Southern Illinois University, Dr. Robert Allyn, came from the presidency of McKendree to Southern to guide its course for twenty years from 1874 to 1894. Another McKendree man, Dr. Daniel B. Parkinson, served as president of Southern from 1897 to 1913. The early years of Southern were profoundly influenced by these men.

With its storied thousand-year-old bell, its picturesque early buildings, and substantial new ones built by students, Illinois' oldest operating college will interest those who visit its campus. Many who do so leave feeling that the colorful old school is saying, "Come whatever may, McKendree goes on."

❦ LAW SCHOOLS

IN 1828 JOHN MASON PECK, a member of "the Yale band" who had come to preach and teach in the West, began to hew timbers beside Rock Spring on the Lebanon-O'Fallon road in southern Illinois for "an institute of higher learning." The school he founded became Rock Spring Seminary, offering the first instruction beyond the elementary grades in the State of Illinois.*

Peck's school was followed through the years by a score or more of seminaries and colleges, almost always founded and helped by church and missionary groups in the East. Many of these had early years of reasonable prosperity and promise, only to languish and disappear, one by one. One of the early schools that survives is Southern Illinois University, established by the state in 1869 as Southern Illinois Normal University. Throughout its earlier years, the Normal School—a term by which it was known for some decades—differed little from the church and private schools that came and went. Its chief difference was that it was state-supported.

There were times, however, when the school at Carbondale showed a tendency to break through and to justify the use of the word "university" in its title. One of these departures came in 1875, the second year of the school's operation, when the board of control authorized the establishment of a law department with classes to begin in December of that year. The controllers based their right to do this on a clause in the law which established the school and set forth its purpose, and which authorized Southern to institute "such other studies as the board of education may, from time to time, prescribe." Judge A. D. Duff, a highly respected

---

* See *Legends & Lore*, pp. 189–91.

attorney who was later selected to conduct the law classes, advised them that their action was fully legal. The board accordingly set apart a room for classes. Though Duff was to enjoy full faculty status, there was a joker in the contract. His salary was to depend upon fees received from students enrolling for the course. Not enough enrolled to warrant a beginning, however, and the law department never materialized.

The idea of a law school in southern Illinois was not entirely a new one. Judge Duff had previously conducted successful "law institutes" at both Benton and Shawneetown. A photograph of the Benton class made in 1867 and a copy of the first lecture delivered before the Shawneetown class on November 27, 1871, are of interest.

All of the Benton group of fifteen matured and bearded students—many of whom had served in the Union army—passed the necessary tests and were admitted to the practice of law. All apparently were successful, some attaining a measure of distinction.

One member was C. H. Layman who moved to Jackson County where he served as county judge and member of the legislature. Later, he went to Idaho where he held the office of attorney general. A. P. Stover went to Jacksonville and from there to a responsible government position in Washington, D.C. Before enrolling in the law school, Stover had been a captain in the Union army. George W. Young practiced more than forty years in Marion and served as circuit judge. John Coker went to an office in the nation's capital. Alfred Duff became a well-known judge in Texas.

F. M. Youngblood practiced widely over southern Illinois and became noted as one of the most able trial lawyers in the region. Over a period of years his name appears in the records of many important cases; tradition represents him as charming, brilliant, persuasive, and relentless. A. E. Hensley went to practice in Mt. Vernon.

D. M. Browning became county judge of Franklin County and Grand Master of Illinois Masons. At one time he sought the position of Commissioner of the General Land Office and went to see President Cleveland about the job; unfortunately he arrived after the appointment had been made. Cleveland was much impressed with Browning, however, and asked him what he knew about Indians. Browning's laconic reply, "Practically nothing. Never saw a dozen," must have pleased the President because he offered Browning the office of Commissioner of Indian Affairs. Profoundly thanking the President, Browning declined this post.

In addition to the teacher, Judge A. D. Duff, seven others appeared in the group. They were A. R. Pugh, T. T. Fountain, a man named Morrison, Richard Verner, W. H. Williams, Samuel H. Dwight, and W. W. Barr. Those familiar with the history of the bar in southern Illinois will recall parts played by several of these. Though this first law class that met in a room near Benton courthouse was a small one, it could not be called unimportant.

No other record has been found of organized classes or "law institutes" in southern Illinois. Perhaps there have been no others. Perhaps, too, the history of the Normal would have been different if a few more students had enrolled for the law offerings in 1875.

Chapter 9

Special Days

🌺 *AN ECHO OF OLD CHRISTMAS*

THOSE WHO CAME from foreign lands and from other sections of our own country to make their homes in southern Illinois often brought with them their customs and their lore. One practice that came with the early French settlers was *La Guiannée,* a jolly greeting given at each New Year at Prairie du Rocher in Randolph County.* A second, from Germany this time, was Old Christmas with its "Three Kings" song. This is celebrated each January 6 in the Teutopolis region of Effingham County.

Each of these, really observed on the eve of the day honored, has its centuries-old history. And each is as firmly established in Illinois. Neither has been modernized, and thus both remain distinctly folk practices. *La Guiannée* came to the Kaskaskia-Cahokia region with the French in the early 1700's. Three Kings, already a feature of Old Christmas in Germany, began to be formally observed in Illinois shortly after the concentrated German-Catholic settlement was begun near Teutopolis.

Its present dramatized version was started here by Benjamin Voss, who came directly from Germany to Illinois considerably more than a hundred years ago. The door-to-door visit of Three Kings immediately became the most prominent feature of the Old Christmas observance among the German settlers. Both the German text and the English translation are credited to Voss.

The song is a narrative poem that tells of the journey of the Three Wise Men. One of these was Melchior, the smallish King of Nubia, who

---

* See *Legends & Lore,* pp. 213–16.

came bearing gifts of gold to represent wealth. With him came Balthasar, the middle-sized King of Chaldea, whose gift was frankincense, which is burned for its pleasing odor, and was considered emblematic of the common man. Gaspar, King of Tarsus, or Tarshia, largest and most impressive of the three in stature, brought myrrh, used in incense and in perfume. It was considered emblematic of man's humility.

During the enactment at Teutopolis a strong staff to represent divine support and strength is carried by Balthasar. Gaspar carries a broom to sweep away all trouble and misfortune. All are impressively robed and bedecked for the occasion. Their robes, made by local women, are carefully laundered after each use and made ready for the next appearance.

Though the Teutopolis area is about as concentratedly Catholic a community as one finds in America, calls made by the singers and their accordionist are not restricted to Catholic homes. The Lutheran minister invites and welcomes them, as do others.

As the place of call—a home, a hospital, the priest's house, the Sisters' home, the lodging of the infirm, or even a tavern—is approached, the accordion strikes up the air of the song. Someone opens the door and welcomes the troupe. One looking on at any place of call notes a respectful silence, even in a tavern, when the musicians enter. It is indeed a strange feeling one has in a tavern, where the walls are decorated with beer signs, pictures of pin-up girls, hunting scenes, arty calendars, pictures of sports events, and noted athletes. But somehow all of these seem to fade into the background and become insignificant. Each singer in turn announces the name of the king he represents. The seated musician starts playing, and the song is begun.

Where children are present the general expression of awe is evident. The middle-aged give relaxed attention. On older faces one sees a look of wistful remembering. Many an oldster will be seen making almost imperceptible lip movements in rhythm with the music, as if to form the words. Occasionally, a less restrained older person may audibly join in the song. In one case so many did this that it became a chorus.

The "Three Kings" song tells of the Wise Men's journey of thirteen days in which they traveled four hundred miles. It tells of the star that guided them until it had stopped over the crib of the infant Jesus. To represent this guiding star, a staff with a rotating star mounted on it is carried by one of the kings in the enactment. At the manger its rotation is stopped, and it rests just as the guiding star did above the place where the Christ child lay. Its stopping represents the end of their long journey.

The robed singers then kneel and extend their hands as if to present gifts they have brought. After a slight pause, the remaining portion of the song that extends greetings of the season and invokes blessings is sung, and a calm happiness seems to settle on the gathering.

The song is very old. The earliest record found indicates its use in Germany in 1072. Later records and references show increased observances. "Three Kings" is sung in German, just as *La Guiannée* is sung in French. This often baffles outsiders and the youngsters who are only casually acquainted with those languages.

🏵 *CHRISTMAS TREES*

FIVE THOUSAND YEARS ago the Egyptians placed ornaments on palm fronds and used them for decorations at the winter solstice. The Greeks, Romans, and peoples of those days used evergreens for the same purpose. The Germans and Scandinavians also observed the winter solstice by using trees. These were the ancients' "Christmas trees."

In the 1500's Martin Luther decorated and lighted a small evergreen in his home and thus made it a part of the world's Christmas legend.

The first decorated tree recorded for Illinois was one that the daughters of Gustave Koerner decorated at Belleville in 1833. They took "the top of a young sassafras which still had some leaves on it . . . dressed it with ribbon and bits of colored paper and the like" and "hung it with little red apples and nuts and all sorts of confections" made by "Aunt Caroline." "They put waxed candles on the branches." Koerner says, "Perhaps this is the first Christmas [tree] that was lighted on the banks of the Mississippi."

Much later, about 1900, trees became country-wide in use. Today eight out of ten houses in America have them.

Trees and trimmings can be bought now at countless places. When the custom began, both were homemade. This brief story of the first one in a rural district school will tell something of many others.

A farmer gave a small cedar tree, and the teacher sent larger boys to cut and bring it to the school a day or two prior to its use. To the boys, going a half mile for the tree, then carrying and dragging it back, was not a task but a privilege.

Its decoration on the day before its use was a grand occasion. White cloth and cotton batting were arranged under the tree to represent snow. A pupil-made cardboard fireplace, with mantle and knitted wool socks, was placed near the tree.

The tree was lighted by candles tied to its branches with string or attached with clothespins. Brilliantly colored crepe paper was cut into strips for drapes. Many yards of strung popcorn crisscrossed the tree. A bag of red cranberries made a long string that hung from the branches. Red haws made other strings, and clusters of the small red fruit of the buckberry with rusty rose pips were tied in place. Spiny fruits of the sweet gum tree were covered with tin foil saved from plug chewing tobacco. Surplus foil was cut into narrow strips to drape on branches or into small bits to make artificial snow. Glistening baubles hung from the branches, and a shiny foil-covered star was fastened at the very top of the tree. Bits of cotton looked like patches of snow. Expressed mildly, it made a first-class fireball.

Gifts were plainly wrapped, and names were written on them. They were tied on the tree, not stacked beneath.

A special program was arranged. It consisted of readings, recitations, songs, and a short dialogue. Among the numbers offered were: "Silent Night," "O Little Town of Bethlehem," "Jolly Saint Nicholas," "While Shepherds Watched Their Flocks at Night," " 'Twas the Night Before Christmas," "It Came Upon a Midnight Clear," and that ever-popular poem where each stanza ended with " 'Ceptin' jes' 'fore Christmas I'm as good as I can be." Others are forgotten.

Parents came to enjoy the program. Santa Claus with jingling bells and a tied-on cotton beard came dressed in the regular, oversized, pillow stuffed, red cotton suit to take the gifts from the tree and call names in a thinly disguised voice. He frightened the very young, thrilled the next age group, puzzled some beyond that, and dispelled the Santa myth with those sure of his identity.

The teacher also passed out the annual treat of oranges or apples and candy. This brought all pupils enrolled, even those who had dropped out.

The old-time, homemade, country Christmas tree has passed, but has left pleasant memories. It also left many a story of tragedy when trees caught fire and children were burned to death. Old files of the Christmas issues of newspapers carry many such stories.

Christmas still belongs to children, but memories of it belong to oldsters.

❦ GREAT DAY FOR IRISH

A GRANDSON'S REQUEST for relics of World War I led to the inspection of an old trunk in the garage where the remaining personal debris of that conflict has lain through the years—more than forty of them. At the very top was a package of about a hundred letters from a one-time U.S. Marine to his mother. With the letters there was a cluster of brittle shamrocks given the writer by Peggy (really Margaret), a waitress in the dining room of the Grafton Hotel on Tottenham Court Road in London at dinnertime on St. Patrick's Day in 1919.

Seeing the crumbly spray of shamrocks gotten on the special day of the revered Irish patron saint in 1919 turned thoughts to the early churchman. On March 17, those who can claim a drop of Irish blood, and countless ones who can't, honor the man who brought Christianity to the Emerald Isle nearly 1,500 years ago.

Through many centuries, the Catholic Church has given the day special attention. In addition to religious observances, church dinners long have been held and parades organized. The greatest and most colorful of all is the one that passes down Fifth Avenue in New York City. Other cities from London to Los Angeles and on to Melbourne, Australia, see marching groups with Irish flags, skirling bagpipes, and often spinning shillalahs. In countless places, men will quietly knot a tie of emerald hue, wear a simulated shamrock, or a bit of green ribbon to betray a feeling of nostalgia for a sad land he may never have seen nor plans to see.

Though Patrick became Ireland's patron saint, England, Scotland, Wales, and at least one country on the continent have claimed him. The year and day of his birth also are in dispute. It seems agreed by all, however, that death came to him on March 17, 493, but the place of his burial is doubtful. According to legend, he was buried near the spot where four undriven white oxen drawing the wagon that carried his body stopped on a slope beside the River Quoile in Downpatrick.

Of his earlier life it is known that he was of patrician birth and that he was seized and taken to Ireland when about sixteen years old. There he was sold as a slave and made a herdsman. Patrick was a devout youth and often stopped to pray. At twenty-one he escaped and went to prepare himself for the work of a missionary. After many years he began his work. Bumping over the land in a Roman chariot, he won converts and established churches—the first one being built amid the fields where he had served as a bondman.

Much that is magical has been ascribed to him. It is told that he banished the snakes from Ireland although there really never have been snakes there. The snake and toad story is doubtless of Norse origin. These people came and found no pauds (toads), but did find a prominent man named Paudrig, which meant toad-ridder or banisher in their language. They accordingly credited this man with ridding the land of toads—before the days of St. Patrick. The ancient writer, Pliny, says that snakes do not live where shamrocks grow.

Some of the relics connected with Saint Patrick are still in Ireland. Among these is the small hand bell he used in church services. It may be seen in a Dublin museum, and there still are some who believe it has magical powers.

Long before the Irish were scattered over the world, St. Patrick's Day was solemnly observed in the churches of Ireland. The practices of feasting, parading, and "drowning the shamrock" came later. The practice of drinking was explained by one man who said, "If the day is warm, men become thirsty; if it is a cold day, they naturally are chilled," hence the necessity for a drink.

The New York parade, arranged by the Ancient Order of Hibernians, seems to be the oldest in America. It was in full swing as early as 1766. In 1779 Lord Rawdon, commanding British troops, had five hundred "Irish Volunteers" parade behind a British military band. These "volunteers" promptly defected at the end of the parade and most of them went to join Washington's forces. Washington was made an honorary member of the Hibernians and was given a gold medal by them. President Truman likewise was made an honorary member in 1951 and stood with Cardinal Spellman in the reviewing stand on the steps of St. Patrick's Cathedral. The New York church is only one of more than 1,700 named for the saint. There is even a Protestant St. Patrick's Cathedral in Dublin, Ireland.

Bits of folklore also are attached to the day. Southern Illinoisans have long known that sweet peas planted on his day will bloom bountifully and that Irish potatoes likewise yield best when planted on March 17.

It truly is a great day for the Irish, and for those feeling an affection for that land.

❧ FLAG DAY

ANNIVERSARIES KEEP COMING around and people continue to observe them, seldom asking why. This is written shortly before one of these special and more recently set-aside days that will come on June 14. First suggested as a day for special observation by President Wilson in a 1916 proclamation, Flag Day now is widely observed.

There are numerous occasions on which the flag is flown, such as those in commemoration of individuals like Washington and Lincoln on their birth dates. At other times the flag is displayed in observance of a day set aside as a patriotic holiday. Two of these are Memorial Day on May 30, and Independence Day on July 4. A third day on which the flag is prominently displayed is Flag Day, a kind of birth date for the flag itself.

While the flag of our nation is among the older ones that have been changed the least, it is in no sense old. Flags and banners of a kind are about as old as man's record. In fact, they have been in use for thousands of years, as long as men have banded together to attack, defend, or to proclaim identity. Primitive people over the world have been found using crude banners around which they rallied, followed, and jealously defended.

Many of the emblems these flags bore are well known. The feathers that decorated the flags of the Egyptian pharaohs are remembered. The flag of Athens displayed an owl. Eagles belonged to the banners of the Roman legions. Seven hundred years ago the flag of the Danish country displayed a raven—it still does. During the Crusades the banners of the Crusaders displayed the cross; those of their enemies, the Saracens, had the crescent.

During the centuries there have been literally thousands of flags. In addition to its national flag, a country may have any number of special flags, banners, streamers, pennants, and assorted insignia. With the recent establishment of new nations with their added array of standards, the situation becomes truly bewildering.

Flags of many designs were used by the American colonists, both before and after their break with the mother country. The flag situation even then had become a bit confusing. Apparently it was this confusion that caused John Adams to propose "That the flag of the thirteen united states be thirteen stripes, alternate red and white; that the Union be thirteen stars, white on a blue field, representing a new constellation." This was passed by the Congress and signed on June 14, 1777, exactly two years after the act establishing an army had been passed. This June 14, 1777, is the one affording a date for Flag Day. It really was not the birth date of a new flag, but was more an effort to standardize a design.

Much is left untold about the new flag. Just who created the design for it? Was it George Washington, John Paul Jones, Francis Hopkinson, John Adams, Benjamin Franklin, or John Hulbert? All are mentioned. Or did Betsy Ross design it? The fact has never been determined, but Francis Hopkinson at about this time submitted a bill for designing a flag. Incidentally, the bill was not paid.

Several efforts have been made to include a flag of this type in George Rogers Clark's expedition to Kaskaskia and Vincennes in 1778–1779. No satisfying proof has been offered. If Clark's forces carried any flags or banners they doubtless were of their own contriving. The legend of flags being carried about a hill at Vincennes appears to be a fanciful one.

It is known that French and British flags were flown at Kaskaskia and Fort de Chartres during the time when those nations were in possession of the land. No account has been found telling when the national flag first came to Illinois. For a long time, however, southern Illinois did have an historic flag, the one carried by the colonial troops when they successfully stormed Stony Point. This flag was brought to Shawneetown by General Thomas Posey, who had led the storming. Until a few years ago it was on display in the Shawneetown bank.

The story of our flag is an interesting one for those who come to know more about it. There are earlier "Don't Tread on Me" and "Join or Die" flags of the colonies. There is the one of thirteen white stars on a blue field that flew at Valley Forge. There is the one of stars and stripes that drew the first salute of a foreign country at Ste. Eustatius in the Caribbean and the one flying over Fort McHenry that inspired Francis Scott Key to write "The Star Spangled Banner."

Always there is a thrill for those who turn a street corner in a foreign city and come face to face with the flag over the entrance to an American Embassy or Consulate. There seems to be a bit of America where one finds the flag.

🌼 *AROUND THE FOURTH OF JULY*

THE FIRST WEEK in July marks the anniversary of many events significant in American history. The most widely observed of these naturally is the Fourth of July. It is not alone, however. Others come to keep it company.

One of these that comes to mind is July 4, 1636, when Roger Williams founded Providence, Rhode Island. It is hailed as a day significant in man's progress toward religious freedom. Next is the day in early July when Washington surrendered Fort Necessity in Pennsylvania to the French during the French and Indian Wars. Then came the day twenty years later, when he assumed command of the Continental Army under an elm tree on the Boston Commons.

It was on July 2, 1776, that the Continental Congress adopted Richard Henry Lee's resolution that resulted, two days later, in the passage of the Declaration of Independence that fixed the birth date of a new nation. The declaration as approved was to a great extent the work of Thomas Jefferson, and had John Adams as its staunch and able advocate.

On July 4, 1826, exactly fifty years after its adoption, both author and advocate died, each apparently thinking back to that eventful day. Adams died, saying, "Thomas Jefferson still survives." Unknown to Adams, Jefferson had died a few hours earlier. He is reported to have died murmuring, "This is the fourth of July."

Within a few years after 1776, people began to celebrate the fourth as a patriotic holiday, a practice that has become practically universal. In the ensuing years other events came to be associated with the day. Work on the Erie Canal was begun on July 4, 1817. Stephen Collins Foster, composer of many cherished songs, was born this day, 1826. The cornerstone of the Bunker Hill monument was laid in 1848 and the Republican party came into being in 1854.

As one of purely personal significance, there was the fourth of July, 1919, when, having successfully "smuggled" himself into Paris, the writer saw three marshals of France ride in a parade down the Champs Élysées. Then he went to see a fellow marine, Gene Tunney, win the boxing championship of the A.E.F.

Perhaps the most significant of all later fourths came in 1863 in the midst of the Civil War and eighty-seven years after the establishing one. It was on this day that Robert E. Lee, acknowledging defeat of the Confederate army but still fighting in a desultory manner with an almost equally exhausted Union army, began his slow retreat to Richmond. The high tide of the Confederacy had passed.

On that same July 4, 1863, another great military defeat came to the South. General John C. Pemberton surrendered the key military post of Vicksburg to General Grant and ended the hopes of the Confederacy in the Mississippi valley. No longer could they have ready access to the food and other supplies that the territory beyond the Mississippi could furnish.

The significance of these two defeats, the one at Gettysburg and the other at Vicksburg, can hardly be stated better than by quoting portions from a diary kept by General Josiah Gorgas, an able southern leader.

One brief month ago we were apparently on the road to success . . . All looked bright . . . Now the picture is as somber as it was bright then. Lee failed at Gettysburg. Vicksburg and Port Hudson . . . surrendered 35,000 men and 45,000 arms . . . It seems incredible . . . Yesterday we rode on the pinnacle of success. Today . . . the Confederacy totters to its destruction.

Gorgas's appraisal was correct. Gettysburg and Vicksburg sealed the fate of the South.

It is natural that Illinois has a great interest in the siege and capture of Vicksburg. No state contributed more to the success of the campaign. Three men who played prominent parts had come from Illinois: Grant from Galena, Logan from Jackson County, and McClernand from Shawneetown. Many thousands of men—to be more exact, 36,312—went from Illinois to press the siege that almost literally starved the Confederates into submission.

An Illinois monument, the largest one of the battlefield, memorializes the soldiers from this state. It is modeled after the Roman Pantheon, and strange as it may seem, carries no carving or device to symbolize war. There are, however, many tablets and plaques, enough to carry the names of all Illinois men known to have fought there.

With each passing year these listings tend more and more to become only a great collection of names. To those old enough to remember when Civil War veterans were numerous, an occasional name found there will bring to mind some venerable man once known.

A visit to the battlefield at Vicksburg should make our country mean more to us. This is particularly true if thought is taken that the men who struggled so valiantly there did so from a conviction that theirs was a just cause. Right or wrong, it is only such basic convictions and the courage to fight for them that makes a nation great.

Right or wrong, Gettysburg, Vicksburg, and July 4, 1863, mark a high point of courage for both North and South.

🌿 COUNTY FAIRS

MEMORIES OF CHILDHOOD often are highlighted by those that came from an unusual or outstanding occasion, one that brought new and strange experiences. In this case the memories are of a day spent at the Saline County Fair when it was held at Eldorado in the late summer of 1892. Many things combined to make it a wonderful day. There was the early start and the long drive (only six miles) over dusty roads, seated on the hay-covered floor of a jolting farm wagon. Then there was the great assembly made up of two-wheeled carts, a few buggies (not one automobile), hundreds of horses, many farm wagons, and people, the largest group ever seen until then.

Numerous features of those early county fair days are revived at the larger ones today. There is the crowd with the holiday air, chattering and milling around. The barker still cries the sideshow and the spieler tries to sell his wares. The free attractions still are there to lead people on. They range from tumblers and tightrope performers to strong men and dancing girls. It seems that "Bosco, the snake eater, half-man half-ape, captured in the wilds of Borneo, eats them alive" has gone, however.

This brings to mind that eating places at that first fair are not recalled. For lunch there was only a basket of fried chicken, homemade light bread spread with butter and freshly made blackberry jelly. There also were the usual cake and pies, plus a cool watermelon that had been kept wrapped in a wet sack. Yes, there later was a poke of chewy candy from the stand of the taffy pullers, who made and pulled it before your eyes.

There was the usual array of sideshows with their barkers on platforms in front. There were streamers with large lettering above the stands. Not then reading, what they said remains unknown. Men wearing kady hats and shiny stars walked about carrying billies about the size of ball bats. They were the policemen. Down by the hitching racks there were groups of dickering horse traders. A careful observer could occasionally see a bottle with something red in it being passed about.

There were fretful, whining children, often barefooted. Mothers, obviously tired, went about in poke bonnets and often carried palm-leaf fans. Young ladies carried folding fans and parasols. Anyone becoming thirsty could drink from the pint tin cups tethered at barrels of water.

One feature of that faraway fair has long since disappeared. That was the horse-powered merry-go-round, or carrousel, that children called the swing. This contrivance was suspended beneath a great round tent by long iron rods that sloped down and outward from an iron collar at the top of a fifty-foot center pole that was held in place by guy ropes tied to trees or posts. This carrousel was spun by a horse that trotted around in the circle formed by the seating platform. As they now do, the swing of that time had seats and wooden ponies for the children to ride. Solicitous parents often rode with the children "to keep them from falling off."

The firing of anvils was a regular practice. That, with the resounding booms they produced, are gone. This firing was done beside the starter's stand just inside the field across from the grandstand. To fire anvils two were necessary. The first was set in the ordinary position, face up. On this one about a pint of gunpowder was spread with a trail leading to the edge of the anvil. The second anvil was placed face down on the first one, the charge of powder being between them. Here the helpers retreated to safety. The trigger man then took a wagon rod whose tip had been heated in a nearby (not too near) fire, poised himself to spring away, and touched the heated end of the rod to the trail of powder left for that purpose. With a great puff of smelly smoke and a heavy boom that could be heard a mile, the upper anvil bounced four or five feet into the air. People drew a long breath. The anvils were replaced and reloaded for the next boom. A man with a kady hat and a star wouldn't let a boy go across the track to help.

The booming of the anvils told that the races soon would be run. People were cleared from the track. It was soon cluttered with excited horses hitched to gaily painted sulkies with high wooden wheels. These horses lunged, reared, and dashed about in a most confused way. To this was added the shouts of the starter and other officials. The boom of a signal drum was heard. Suddenly all seemed to become ordered; there was a loud command of "Go" and the race was on. Practically every man there was at the rail. The drivers on their gaily painted sulkies and with colored jackets and caps went tearing around the track, shouting, talking pet talk, lashing their whips, trying to get the most effort from the horses. Only two of that starting group of horses are remembered, Logan and Warrine. These must have been the favorites.

The race was quickly over. Suddenly the mood of the crowd was changed. Groups headed for their wagons. In a short time roads from town were lined with walkers, horsebackers, and wagons. The day had been a great one and men were talking about it fifty years later. Considered as a local event, which it was, it was a great race.

If someone there had said that seventy years later another great trotting race, the greatest one in the world, would be held in southern Illinois, he would have drawn only a laugh. Nevertheless, it comes to pass several times when the Hambletonian, greatest of all trotting races, is held each autumn at the DuQuoin State Fairground. The writer plans to be present, sit high in the stand, have field glasses to watch the races, meanwhile recalling that first day at the Saline County Fair in 1892.

🏵 *MULE DAY AT ENFIELD*

In just about every region of America, old settlers' reunions and old soldiers' reunions were events looked forward to for months. With the passing of the soldiers' reunions, other special days have come to be observed in many localities.

Only a few weeks ago Ridgway had its Popcorn Day with thousands of bushels of popped and unpopped corn. Nearby, New Haven has its annual Pecan Day with loads of nuts. Likewise, Murphysboro has its

Apple Festival along with an attractive display of peaches of the human variety, and then Cobden has its annual days to parade its peaches from blooms to fruit. Enfield (in White County, sir!) has its special day, somewhat different from the others. It has a Mule Day, the first Saturday in October.

This year, at least early in the day, it appeared that the day might be observed without the product for which it is named. It was not long, however, until a lone chunky black mule, old enough to be very calm, was found behind the lumber yard harnessed to a high-wheeled road cart with a shiny red foot-track—the kind that was common before we had good roads.

Shortly afterwards, a span of toy-like mules whose combined weight was only 750 pounds was found hitched to a spring wagon. The combined weight of these pint-sized mules was about half that of a good farm mule when mules were the motive power used by many farmers. When the mile-long parade got underway in the afternoon, a span of husky mules appeared in the procession, pulling a high-wheeled, narrow-tired farm wagon with a hayrack and spring seat. The passengers looked like farmers who had come to town in much the same way on Saturday afternoons fifty and more years ago.

An earlier parade had been held in the forenoon. It was made up of pets, accompanied by children who walked or rode bicycles. The kittens were carried, and the pups mostly came along as reluctant and bewildered participants at the end of leashes.

The main parade of the afternoon was a varied spectacle. It had about a score of marching school bands, each preceded by a cluster of fancy stepping, baton twirling drum majorettes. There were many floats designed to show aspects of the community's past. Especially interesting were those that portrayed the fashions in women's clothing. They showed the dress worn by women since the days of Pilgrim garb through homespun, hoop skirts, hobble skirts, the sack, the flappers garb, shirtwaists with leg-of-mutton sleeves, and hats in strange array.

In its earlier years—this annual day has been observed in Enfield thirty-nine times—many awards were given for prize mules in various classifications. One old program listed a dozen awards. This year only one was offered, for the best sucking mule, but none was found. According to the present trend, the time may come when Enfield will have to hold Mule Day without a single mule. But mules live a long time. This is indicated by the old folk saying, "Who ever saw a dead mule?"

There were few in Enfield with whom I could "reunion," but it was enjoyable, nevertheless, to see the greetings of old friends who had returned for the special day. It was pleasing to hear people say, "Well, I ain't seen you in more'n twenty years," and then set out to bring the history of the past two decades up to date.

There was the display of old-time patchwork quilts with their assorted patterns and fine hand-stitching that seem to be returning as ornamental bedspreads for those lucky enough to find them.

A day spent at Enfield on Mule Day makes one wonder why many other places do not find some excuse to set aside a day for the "return of the natives."

🏵 *POPCORN DAY*

LOYAL CITIZENS of Ridgway, two miles east of Illinois Highway 1 in Gallatin County, refer to their town as the Popcorn Center of the World. On one particular day each year—a Saturday in early September—anyone visiting there would be inclined to agree, for on that day popcorn literally takes over.

The day comes with an explosion, in fact, with two explosions. First, there is the one resulting from millions of muffled pops made by the bursting kernels of *Zea mays everta,* better known as popcorn. Treats are being made ready for the popcorn hungry, which includes most everyone from the toothless babes to the toothless aged.

The second explosion, more visual than audible, is one of population. A sign beside the highway where it enters town indicates that eleven hundred people live there. On all but this special day the number given is correct. On the September Saturday set aside as National Popcorn Farmers' Day, however, it is far from accurate. On Ridgway's special day, according to estimates made by state highway patrolmen, its population is full ten times that given on the sign. Even so, it does not do so well as good corn, properly popped. Its bulk increases thirty times.

These annual observances begin early in the day. Really, they begin a week or two earlier with the arrangement of exhibits and d·splays. Farm implements, from antique to ultra-modern, are assembled. Curios are gathered. Streets for the over-two-mile-long parade are cleared to be roped off. Review and judging stands are built. Store windows are dressed. Parking lots are made ready.

On Popcorn Eve all make merry with a great square dance and crown the Popcorn Queen. Early Saturday morning about twenty state troopers start a busy day. Cars and people come by the hundreds. Buses come carrying gaily uniformed school bands that will take part in the parade.

There are fraternal, social, civic, and military groups. There is something different about Ridgway's special day. There are no barkers, no bunco games.

Naturally, the outstanding feature of the day is the many uses made of popped corn. First, each visitor is given a bag of crisp, fluffy, piping hot corn. There are two places about four blocks apart dispensing this corn. That makes it handy. A hungry visitor can get a bag at the first place, stroll past exhibits, chat a bit, meanwhile nibbling away, and restock at the second dispensary for the return trip.

Popped corn had been used in many ways—there was popcorn in variety: lollipops, pies, pictures, landscapes, models and buildings of varied kinds, all contrived with white and colored corn. It was folk art, some with artistic merit.

Seeing so much popcorn increased curiosity. Is popcorn really as important as Ridgwayites think? This led to some interesting bits of information. It soon became apparent that one of the early promoters who made a few million dollars out of popcorn was correct when he said, "Popcorn isn't peanuts."

It was learned that two out of five movie-goers buy a bag of corn and that these sales have enabled many movie houses to survive. It is so important that one national figure advised a convention of theater managers first to select a good location for a popcorn stand and build a theater around it.

Gallatin County alone grows more than twelve thousand acres of popcorn. It was learned that corn pops best when its moisture content is 13 per cent. Large plants process it accordingly and then seal it in cans or plastic bags that are important sales items in chain stores. It is being exported to many foreign countries. In addition to the millions of bags sold at movie houses, it is nibbled by television viewers around the forty million television sets in the country. It is becoming popular, garlic salted, for nibbling at cocktail parties. Popcorn definitely is big business.

The earliest records found tell of an Indian bringing a lot of popped corn to a Pilgrim Thanksgiving at Plymouth in 1630. Apparently the Pilgrims took over from there. Until the late 1800's it was used only around the open fireplace. Then came the popcorn wagon of memory with its tantalizing aroma that filled the frosty air on winter evenings.

The growing of popcorn has increased accordingly. Last year one county in the nation grew more than 14,000 acres. This year a half-dozen Illinois counties have grown 24,000 acres, 12,000 of these being in Gallatin County. Ridgway has some justification for its claim.

❧ *HALLOWEEN*

It is interesting to learn how special days of the year are set apart and celebrated. Halloween, one of the days regularly celebrated before the coming of Christianity, affords a good illustration. Two thousand years ago pagan people paid marked observances to the day. There are indications that the custom was old even then.

Several centuries before Christianity, the Druids of Britain, Ireland, and northern France set aside a day called Samhain, the summer's end, to be observed on the last day of each October. It was a festive occasion on which they did honor to their sun god. It marked the ending of an old year and the beginning of a new one.

In the observance of Samhain the Druids feasted upon the harvests of the past season, special attention being given to the recently ripened nuts and fruits. They also engaged in weird, mystical rituals designed to win favor with the sun god and to seek his blessing for another good crop season. Bonfires that would drive away evil spirits were lighted on the hills. Groups of masked, costumed individuals, carrying torches, were led by their priests through the fields.

When Christianity advanced into new countries, its missionaries discovered that people had regularly established festive days. Christian missionaries sought to displace these pagan observances by adapting them to the purposes of the Church. Through this plan of displacement, the pagan observance of the winter solstice was supplanted by the one that is our Christmas. The vernal equinox, in like manner, became Easter. Other special days are connected with other very old customs. In northwestern Europe the Druids annually observed a festival of the dead on November 1, when departed spirits were supposed to return to visit their kinsmen and to seek warmth and good cheer for the coming winter. The pagan day was given a new purpose more than 1,300 years ago when Pope Boniface IV designated it as a day to commemorate all saints and martyrs, known and unknown. At times it also had been called All Hallows.

On the evening before the festival of the dead, the pagans believed fairies, witches, and goblins returned to terrify the populace, to steal infants, to destroy crops, and to kill farm animals. Since these visitors came on the eve of All Hallows Day, the occasion came to be known as Halloween, sometimes spelled Hallowe'en. The sincerity of the early believers is shown by their custom of setting out bowls of food for the un-expected visitors.

The belief in the return of departed spirits persisted, but was evidently influenced somewhat by the coming of a new religion. The whole plan became more localized. The Cave of Cruachen in Connaught was said to be the place where the departed spirits dwelt. The opening to this cave was designated as the Gate of Hell. In this cave the spirits of the de-parted dwelt all the year until Halloween. Then the gates were opened and the impounded spirits rushed forth for their night of freedom. With escaping spirits there always went a number of copper-colored birds that took and exchanged babies, killed animals, and stole brides. Those who boiled egg shells could rest assured that they would not be harmed by these evil birds and spirits.

At one period in its existence All Hallows Day was observed on May 13. Pope Gregory III, who served from 730 to 741 A.D. moved the ob-servance to its present date of November 1, the same one on which the Druids had observed their festival of the dead. The Pope also caused a chapel to be built in St. Peter's at Rome, dedicating it to all martyrs and saints, known and unknown. In the year 834 A.D., Gregory IV made it a holy day for all Roman Catholic churches. From that time until now, All Saints Day has been observed by the Roman Catholic and Anglican churches and by some of the Lutheran faith.

The ancient customs in the observance of Halloween persisted in Great Britain and Ireland and came to the United States. Some of the same charms used in the British Isles to counteract the evils of the re-turning spirits were in use until comparatively recent years. People be-lieved that evil spirits shunned fire and light. Hence, great bonfires were kindled on hilltops on Halloween. There are indications that such fires are lighted even yet in remote parts of England and Scotland.

People presently have forsaken the belief that fairies, witches, and goblins come on Halloween to visit evil upon people. They have, how-ever, made the old beliefs into emblems. No observance of the occasion would be complete without witches mounted on brooms sailing through the skies. Likewise, black cats are not forgotten. Goblins are with us yet in hideous pumpkin faces. In addition to carved pumpkins, grotesque masks appear by thousands.

Halloween without jack-o-lanterns would not be nearly so interesting. The name of jack-o-lantern comes from a man so stingy and selfish that he was denied admission to heaven. Because he had played a practi-cal joke on the devil he was also refused admission to the devil's realm and sentenced to wander over the earth carrying his lantern until judgment day. Jack-o-lanterns are a part of the Halloween tradition. The children of Scotland fashion them from turnips and small candles; the American youngsters use pumpkins.

Some of the ancient practices of Halloween remain with us. Youngsters bob for apples. Apple seeds are popped on a hot stove lid to tell who loves whom. Nuts are burned on the hearth to see which lover would be congenial and faithful.

The "trick or treat" greeting of youngsters is not new. It has been used for a long time in America and in other lands. People have come to expect it and many make ready to give token treats. It would not be far wrong to say, "A good time is had by all."

Once it was an evening of destruction and vandalism. Wandering bands went about, often doing serious mischief. Gates were taken off their hinges and carried away. Roads were blocked by logs, by rail fences, and by bales of hay scattered across them. Some small buildings, especially outdoor privies, were pushed over. Windows were soaped and smeared. In one case a large farm wagon was placed atop the ridge of a hay barn. (We thought it was a great feat.)

Now parades are held in many towns, and prizes are given for different types of costumes. Some merchants invite the youngsters to decorate their windows with scenes typical of the season. Instead of an evening filled with fear, caused by a belief that the spirits of the dead would return to do evil, it now is an evening of wholesome jollity.

🏵 *A ONE-MAN REUNION*

IT NOW HAS BEEN fifty years since World War I hostilities ended abruptly and November 11 came to be known the world over as Armistice Day.

On that night in 1918, a company of U.S. Marines bivouacked on a Meuse River hillside near Beaumont, France. Since it no longer was necessary to observe the ban on campfires, a roaring one was kindled with timbers from a shell-wrecked barn, and eighty-four men gathered about the liberally stoked fire. The noise of fighting had ceased, and there was a strange, almost ominous, quiet over the countryside. Those men were convinced that "the war to end all wars" was over and that peace had come. The gathered men fondly hoped and believed it would be an enduring one.

Tonight, fifty years away in time and several thousand miles in space, another fire has been kindled and a phantom reunion is being held at the same place where a similar one was held three years ago. This reunion, like some earlier ones, is beside a small chunk fire between the same two low rocks on the crest of Bald Knob in Union County, southern Illinois.

Instead of the eighty-four men who sat about the fire on the night of November 11, 1918, the writer sits alone beside this feebler blaze. On that night men sat in compact groups on boards from the same wrecked building that furnished bonfire fuel. Tonight, the groups of men are only imagined as they appear and disappear in fancy, being vaguely imaged in the dim light. Tonight's fleeting glimpses, however, still bring clearly to mind some of the faces and figures of those who gathered about that first fire.

The men on the French hillside made up as motley a group as men in uniform well could. Clearly remembered are two old-line sergeants. One was Dan Daly, twice awarded the Congressional Medal of Honor, one of only six men who had until then achieved that distinction. Another was a rugged and stern-faced Turk, answering to the strange Polish name of Wladislaw Bednawski, who was fully as hard as he looked. Bednawski was an alumnus of Roberts College in Constantinople and spoke several languages.

Bednawski and Daly had served together in the Marine Corps for more than twenty years. Bednawski had seen Daly win each of his Congressional Medals of Honor. Both had survived the Boxer Rebellion in China, where Daly had won the first of his two medals; and Bednawski was with him in the West Indies when a second was earned. They were professional marines; the others of us were amateurs.

There also were other interesting individuals. There was Underwood, a poetry reading bartender from upstate New York. I still have his copy of Scottish Ballads. Cavanaugh, an accomplished tenor, amateur actor, and broker's clerk from Wall Street sat and silently peered into the fire. Judging from a newspaper account published some years later, Cavanaugh must have done well. The newspaper account told of his home's being robbed of $168,000 worth of jewels. Another sturdy chap was a mule skinner, who held the unusual distinction of having whipped his captain—because the captain had lashed him across the face with his riding whip. Later this mule skinner became an esteemed, prominent, widely known, and influential citizen who became mayor of one of America's great cities. The captain served to retire a colonel.

Among others about that fire some are readily recalled. One was a youthful teacher from Montana, who later drowned while swimming in the Rhine River. Another was a crap shooting boy from the hills of

Tennessee. As mail orderly of our company, I sent home several dollars to the bank in his Tennessee home town. A third was a bruising, cauliflower-eared boxer from the Bowery. (A battered, tottery old hitch-hiker picked up near Pinckneyville by the writer thirty-three years later proved to be the Kid's one-time sparring partner.) Another boxer was a student from the Colorado School of Mines, about as skilled in boxing with his elbows as any man could be.

Seated beside these men skilled in fisticuffs was a mere boy, a high school dropout, who had been through it all and said, "I am going back to finish high school." He did. There was Wilkinson who had mushed dog teams in Alaska and was going back there. Teamster Dawson vowed he would return to western Canada and again help electrify the railroads there.

Bennett, who seemed to know by memory all the poetry Robert Service had written, would go back to a butcher's shop in New Jersey. I still have his *Rhymes of a Rolling Stone*. Coates, advertising manager of a metropolitan newspaper in Texas, would return to publish his own magazine. Wilson, skilled pianist and accomplished artist, would go back to the music hall. Attorney Brewer would return to his Wall Street office and Papke to his harness shop in Kansas. Addison would barber in Minnesota while Porter would operate a linotype in Alabama. Award-winning Sanderson, the company medic, vowed he would go home to Michigan and enter medical school. Farm boys would return to the farm. Roussin would return to teach in Missouri. All these apparently held a common belief. They were content in the thought that they had helped to set the world to rights.

There was little hilarity. Almost to a man, the group appeared strangely aged beyond their years. Many sat, silently looking into the fire, absorbed in their own thoughts. Conversation was in muted voices. Scattered spaces between the seated groups were for others who had fallen by the way. No one was heard to express even a vague belief that another war, even more bitter than the one just ended, would, within a lifetime, be fought by their sons over the same fields they knew so well.

Many years have passed since the last meeting with one of that fireside group—Sheehy, the crap shooting boy from the Tennessee hills. That was in the railway station at Louisville, Kentucky, on August 15, 1919. It is natural to wonder how the fates have dealt with the men who gathered about that campfire on the hillside above the Meuse River on the night of November 11, 1918.

Churches

ONE DAY IN LATE December, 1811, two recorded incidents, out of the ordinary and disconnected, occurred at a place then called Fiddlers Green. This strange place name had been given to the spot on the Ohio River by an intinerant schoolmaster named Pittulo in 1800. The place must have appealed to the wandering teacher, at least enough that he paused to teach a subscription school for which he was paid mostly in pelts. These were shipped down-river to the New Orleans market. To add to his meager salary, Pittulo also grew vegetables for sale to passing flatboatsmen.

In time Fiddlers Green shed its first strange name and was alternately called Lusk's ferry or Lusk's tavern.* Before many years a village was laid out and called Sarahville, named for the wife of its promoter. A marker on the courthouse grounds tells something about the lady.

After another short interval, for some reason not explained, the young village was resurveyed and given the name of Corinth, "in the stead of Sarahville." This name, held by the village less than a week, was changed to the present one of Golconda "in the stead of Corinth." The town's present name, about the sixth one for the locality, is borrowed from a fabled gem market bearing the name in far away India. One may reasonably assume that Golconda will remain its permanent listing, at least it has held for more than 150 years. Thus Fiddlers Green of 1800 is Golconda of 1968.

The second event alluded to was the arrival of a steamboat, the first

---

* See *Legends & Lore,* pp. 303–4.

one to invade the Western Waters, and thereby usher in the glorious steamboat age. Another incident of significance was the arrival of a Presbyterian minister, the Reverend James MacGready, who had come from the region of the Cumberland Gap by way of the Wilderness Road. He said he was traveling for "observation and opportunity." The arrival of a minister in the community was of importance. A number of persons were pleased to have him and urged that he stay and preach for them. He did so.

After a short stay in the vicinity of the ferry, MacGready moved along to the locality of present-day Enfield where he found several Presbyterian families he had known before they came to Illinois. Among these were the families of two Rutledge brothers. In the family of one of these was a daughter, Ann, whose name was later to be associated in romance with that of Abraham Lincoln.

Reverend MacGready's work in the vicinity of Enfield resulted in the establishment there of a Presbyterian church, the first organized group of that faith in Illinois. A short time later, apparently the result of Mac-Gready's stay in the Golconda vicinity, a second Presbyterian church was formed there. When Old Sharon Church at Enfield ceased to function, the one at Golconda became, and remains, the oldest operating one of its faith in the state.

The church at Golconda was formed under the direction of Nathan V. Darrow, v.c.m., "Missionary from Connecticut." This was "on the Lord's day, the 24th of this month [October 1819] . . . This church was formed by 16 persons making Confession and Covenant." The building now in use by the Golconda congregation was built in 1869.

Records of these and other early churches indicate that church discipline and practices were somewhat rigid. The minute books of another Pope County church (Baptist) support this conclusion. In order to become a member of this church it was necessary that the prospective member subscribe to the following "Articles of Confession," the interpretation of which often aroused sharp arguments.

1. The New Testament is the only safe guide of conduct.
2. There is only one true God.
3. All people are fallen and depraved.
4. All salvation, regeneration, sanctification, resurrection, ascension and intercession come from the death, resurrection, ascension and intercession of Christ.
5. One who endures to the end is saved.
6. Punishment of the wicked is eternal.

7. Communion is only by those baptized by immersion.
8. The sanctity of Sunday, the first day of the week, is affirmed.
9. There is to be a resurrection of the body.
10. All should be tender and affectionate, one toward another.

Their "Rules of Decorum," adopted to regulate the conduction of this church's business sessions, were brief and rather pointed:

1. All meetings are to be opened and closed by prayer.
2. Only one person may speak at a time.
3. One must not interrupt the speaker.
4. The speaker must adhere to the subject.
5. No one may speak more than three times on any one subject.
6. There must be no whispering or laughing.
7. Members must be addressed as "brother" or "brethren." [Sister is not mentioned.]
8. No one may absent himself without permisson of the moderator.

❀ EASTER SERVICES ON BALD KNOB

PEOPLE GATHER about three wooden crosses on top of Bald Knob in Union County, southern Illinois, to hold a sunrise service each Easter Sunday morn. Each visit to the three wooden crosses on Bald Knob brings to mind an unshaped, weathered stone marker with its engraved cross that G. Don Coates and I found several miles within the German forest that borders the Rhine River on Christmas Day, 1918. Though they are widely separated in both time and space, each brings the other to mind. Both the grouped crosses on Bald Knob and the weathered stone in the forest were placed for one purpose: to serve as symbols of man's gratitude and devotion. Though fifty years of time and many miles of space now lie between that long ago visit to the lonely German shrine and the latest visit to Bald Knob, the memory of each revives that of the other. Bald Knob also brings memories of a solemn Easter service attended in St. Paul's Cathedral, London, in 1919. Each Easter also revives memories of that time when Joe Porter told the story of Easter to a group of six- or seven-year-olds at Gholson Grove Church and gave each of us a Sunday school card. That is my earliest recollection of Easter Sunday and the Easter story well over seventy years ago.

The forest stone stood, and we trust still stands, in a dense wood near the mouth of a very narrow valley where a free-flowing spring emerges to join another spring coming down from the high hills to flow through Hubertesburg Farm and join the Rhine River about two miles below the quaint village of Leutesdorf, Germany.

This stone beside an overgrown and barely visible trail in the German forest is similar to many other shrines, symbols, and memorials of religious intent found in that country.

Except for a rudely carved cross on a once smooth but somewhat weathered front, the Rhineland marker was shapeless. On the smoother side there was a sunken panel about twelve by sixteen inches. A cross in this protected panel remained in sharp relief. The sloping ledges at its bottom and the face of the stone beneath it carried weathered inscriptions that were practically illegible.

The date, 1697, just 221 years before our visit, was distinct. Enough other words were legible to tell that the stone had been placed there as an expression of man's thanks to God for being spared from a plague almost three hundred years ago and to voice a plea for its continuance. Two marines, with something akin to reverence, paused for a time beside the old marker and returned later to photograph it. A kindred feeling is aroused when a visit is made to the top of Bald Knob in southern Illinois, where we find three crude wooden crosses. Despite the fact that these crosses have been in their places for about a quarter of a century, they are new, newer by 240 years, than the stone marker in the Black Forest. Anything like the full story of that distant stone marker is, without doubt, lost forever. The story of the crosses on Bald Knob still is fresh.

These three crosses on the eastern brink of the mountain, for Bald Knob is more than a thousand feet high and may properly be called a mountain, were placed there through the efforts of Wayman Presley and the Reverend William Lirely. The decision to erect them resulted from a conversation between these two men as they walked home from services at a rural Union County church in the early spring of 1937.

Two or three Sundays later the first Easter sunrise services were held on the top of Bald Knob with about 250 present. They have been held regularly since that time. Depending somewhat upon weather and road conditions, attendance has varied. On some occasions as many as ten thousand have been present, and nationally known religious leaders have come to participate in the services. The first group of worshipers came from the nearby countryside. Many now come a hundred miles or more. A roadway that affords reasonable access to the rugged hilltop has now replaced the very rough one of earlier days.

Those attending now sit or stand on the sharp slope below the crosses and above the platform on which the choir gathers. In this natural setting the audience faces the east and, as the day dawns and the services progress, they see the sun rise over the distant hills. It is impressive, and those coming primarily out of curiosity soon cease to be mere sightseers and become worshipers. From the dream of two men many years ago, this unusual manner of Easter observance has arisen. There are definite indications that it may become a timeless event, as have some of the passion plays and religious pageants long observed at various places in Europe.

It was not until 1951 when the Bald Knob Christian Foundation was incorporated as a nonprofit organization that steps were taken to make the top of the mountain into a permanent memorial garden or shrine. A tract of land, including the eighty acres which Harrison Rendleman bought from the United States on August 31, 1870, was deeded to this foundation on March 18, 1953. Shortly thereafter plans were made for the erection of suitable structures, and the process of gathering funds was begun.

The one criticism heard comes in the form of a question. "How can they justify the expenditure of that much money to erect a memorial?" To this there is the reply, "The canvas on which the Alba Madonna (that once sold for $1,100,000) was painted is too small to make a rain cape. The paint and wear on the brushes used in making the painting would add only a few more dollars. The balance is an intangible asset that only those blind to the beauty and significance of the great painting fail to see." Also, the 261-year-old marker in the Black Forest of Germany would make a ton or two of crushed stone for a roadway.

🌿 *"EGYPT'S" STRANGE RELIGIOUS CULT*

FROM THE VERY first, southern Illinois has been an exporting area, and Wayne County has furnished its share of regional exports. These have ranged from the county's natural products to interesting individuals, eggs, grass seeds, political innovations, and at least one religious cult.

The natural products have varied from forest grown timber to the present outpouring of petroleum. As human exports, the county has sent out individuals as assorted as Bat Masterson, William Edgar Borah, and the Shelton Brothers. In the matter of eggs, it was reported several years ago that Wayne was the second largest producing county in America.

On the grass seed score, it once (and may even yet) grew and shipped more redtop seed than any other county in the nation. These seeds went to far places over the world, with carloads going to Russia. Though Russia's export of communism has not rooted well in Wayne County, Wayne's export of redtop has done well in Russia.

In the way of a political innovation, Wayne was the first county to make recorded endorsement of Abraham Lincoln as a candidate for the presidency.

It was also in Wayne County that John Battenfield formed and led a church group. This was not so long ago, and there are many still living who remember that dynamic leader and his followers.

Battenfield was born in Ohio about 1880 and grew up there. Very early in life he became interested in the scriptures and read them regularly; he carried his Bible to school and to his work. It is said that at fourteen he had memorized the book of Revelation, much of it as he sat on the plowbeam to rest his horses. His careful and constant reading of the scriptures continued, and there are those who state that in adult life he knew the entire Bible by memory.

In early manhood Battenfield went from Ohio to Wyoming, where he became a sheepherder—all the time reading and rereading the scriptures. Before the end of 1920 he returned east and settled in Wayne County. With deep religious convictions, a thorough knowledge of the scriptures, great fluency of speech, an aggressive personality, and a full measure of missionary zeal, he soon became noted as an exhorter in the Christian church. From this state he easily passed to the regular ministry.

At about this point Battenfield announced that he had received a revelation that the world would soon become embroiled in a great war that would destroy all people except a chosen few. These would constitute the "Incoming Kingdom," which he set about to form. With the help of his brother, who was a pleasing singer and an inspiring song leader, "Brother John" began to gather the group that he believed would be the ones to survive.

Within a short time they had about 250 followers, mostly from Wayne County. This group was no rabble. It had physicians, attorneys, teachers, craftsmen, businessmen, and successful farmers who disposed of their Wayne County interests and went to settle beside the Buffalo River at Gilbert, Arkansas, there to await the opening of Battenfield's predicted annihilating conflict.

Somehow, the war did not materialize at the predicted time, and a mild disappointment took root. Lacking a war or dire threats of an imminent one, an earthquake was prophesied, which also failed to come for those who took basket dinners to the top of a nearby hill, the better to see the holocaust—nor did a later foretold hurricane come. An attempt to raise a body from the dead likewise failed.

Somewhere in the interval Battenfield made a trip to New York State to proclaim the catastrophe he foresaw. This resulted in his temporary commitment to a mental institution there. With these adverse incidents and lack of incidents, interest waned and the settlement began to melt away. Today a few elderly persons who made the pilgrimage still live about the town of Gilbert or have returned to their Illinois homes. For many years the church and printing office they built of river boulders remained as Arkansas landmarks to commemorate a group that clung to a strange belief.

❦ SAINT JOSEPH'S SEMINARY

SINCE THE TIME when John Mason Peck established the first "institution of higher learning" in Illinois at Rock Spring, between Lebanon and O'Fallon, numerous southern Illinois colleges have come and gone. Among the early schools which have survived through the years is St. Joseph's Seminary in the German-Catholic community of Teutopolis. It now has finished more than a century of service to the community and the cause it serves.

Throughout its existence it has stood beside the old roadway that once was the Cumberland or National Road and is now U.S. Highway 40. It is within easy view of those who pass that way. Since its founding, the school appears to have received little publicity beyond restricted limits. Nevertheless, it has gone quietly, steadily, and effectively about its work and has wielded an influence far beyond its apparent proportions.

Though the early German settlers—typical of those of that nationality—gave more than the usual attention to the establishment of schools for their children, there is no record of a move to establish any means of offering training beyond the elementary schools until 1858. On October 19, 1860, a group of the community's leading citizens met with Father Hennewig of the Order of Friars Minor, the parish priest, and decided to found a college. Solicitation of funds was begun, with thirty-five men pledging $140. A site for the new college was selected on the lot where a great four-bladed windmill that ground grain and sawed lumber had stood. This projected school met the hearty approval of the local citizenry and of those in the council of the church under whose direction it would operate.

In the spring of 1861, shortly before the fall of Fort Sumter, ground was broken for the first building, and the cornerstone was laid with impressive ceremonies on July 2. This building, still standing, is now central to a greatly expanded plant. Stone was taken from a quarry a few miles away, timber came from the local woodlands, and bricks were burned on the grounds. The pit from which dirt for the bricks was taken became the school pond.

Though the building was incomplete and the basement occasionally flooded, it was decided to begin a school term in the fall of 1862. On September 15, a formal opening was held. The town was festooned with bunting, flags were hung, a band gathered to play, and high churchmen came to participate.

Classes started with fifty-one young men enrolled. Of these, forty-six were classified as collegians and six as seminarians, or candidates for the priesthood. At first the college accepted students of all faiths, but limited facilities later made it necessary to restrict enrollment to Catholics.

It is recorded that the purpose of the college was to give those attending "a thorough and scientific education that [would] fit them for higher professions or for business careers." In addition to these purposes it offered to those preparing to enter the services of the church courses in theology and philosophy.

In September, 1865, it was considered necessary to discontinue the seminary department, and the name was changed to St. Joseph's Diocesan College. Within a few years better times came and seminary training was restored. In 1875 conditions in Europe reacted to the benefit of the college when Germany exiled the Franciscan friars. A group of these exiles, among whom were a number of eminent scholars, came to America and Teutopolis bringing about twenty students with them.

Old buildings were repaired and enlarged. New ones were built. The college took on a new vitality. There was an increased enrollment, particularly in the seminary department. This trend increased until 1907 when it was decided to discontinue the collegiate division. In 1927 it was thought best to eliminate a preparatory department and transfer its functions to Westmont, Illinois.

Today St. Joseph's is a quiet little college with an atmosphere all its own. The casual visitor will not realize its substantial contributions to the community until he stops to talk with some elderly farmer and finds him capable of intelligently discussing Virgil and the old philosophies and philosophers.

🌼 *THE SHAKERS*

EARLY SOUTHERN Illinois had its "agues" and "shakes," otherwise known as malaria. For a brief time Lawrence County had a settlement or a "family" of the United Society of Believers in Christ's Second Appearance, regularly called Shakers. The association of "shakes" and Shakers is not too forced, since malaria contributed greatly to the failure of the group that settled on the Embarrass River in Petty Township.

These strange people came to this, the farthest west of their settlements, in 1808. Nineteen years later they were gone, leaving their watermill and other buildings to decay. They also left a cluster of unmarked graves in the local burying grounds. Added to these were many accounts, both oral and recorded, of consecrated effort, hardship, strife, and persecution. They knew the prowling Indians and raiding soldiery of 1812–1814. Much of this lore, in its turn, has vanished.

Their story really began in Europe in 1689 with a few dissenters from the established church. Being harassed on the continent, a small number fled to England in 1706. There the membership grew slowly, but their first church organization was not formed until 1742.

Among those joining the English group were two Quakers, James Wardley and his wife, Jane. With them came Ann Lee who was to become the leader of the sect, its "Mother Ann." Ann was born at Toad Lane, Manchester, in 1736. She was devout, intelligent, capable, honest, but unlearned, a factory worker with a magnetic personality that drew friends. From the combined efforts of these three the influence of the group grew.

Their increased activity brought sharp reactions from other church groups, from civil authorities, and from mobs that stoned them. They often were in prison. Out of jail, Ann and eight of her followers took passage on a sailing vessel, the Mariah, from Liverpool to New York, arriving on August 6, 1774. They stopped in the city and worked two years, Ann doing washing and ironing. In 1776 they settled at Watervliet, eight miles northwest from the center of Albany.

At Watervliet they began the first successful religious-communal venture in America. The men engaged in agriculture, horticulture, and the mechanical trades. Women worked at the domestic crafts and helped at such other tasks as they were able. All worked in cooperation, each at the task he could do best. None was servant to others. Their days of labor, beginning at 4:30 or 5:00 o'clock in the morning, were long and arduous. For relaxation they sang and engaged in ceremonial dances. It was from their practice of shaking themselves vigorously during dances that the name of Shakers was given them.

Their industry, application, and careful thought produced many of today's helpful practices, devices, and tools. They first packaged and wrapped garden and flower seeds for sale. They also propagated and sold the best of fruit trees, introducing the quince. They first dried sweet corn for market. They grew and packaged garden herbs and went to the woodland to gather others. They grew medicinal plants and gathered wild ones. Some of these they prepared as powders, oils, and ointments. From boiled cider and dried apples they made delightful applesauce. Some centers produced thousands of gallons of maple sirup.

The products of their looms were widely known. Their yard-square kerchiefs were unexcelled. At South Union, near Russellville, Kentucky, they grew, spun, and wove excellent silk. Their hats and bonnets were popular. Few have ever made more functional, but pleasing, furniture. A Shaker chest of drawers, a table, or even one of their chairs makes the heart of a collector happy.

A Shaker woman is credited with having invented the circle saw. They made machinery to plane, tongue, and groove, and to cut moldings on lumber. Babbitt metal, much used for machine bearings, was their development. They were the first to regularly grow broomcorn and make it into brooms. It is said that they made the first one-horse buggy in America. (If that be true, I thank them.) They made washing machines that sold widely. Clothespins are credited to them, likewise brimstone matches.

Their farmers gave close attention to the selection and development of better cattle, and even to the shipping of breeding stock to England. In 1847 they bought a Merino ram and two ewes, paying the unheard of price of $1,100 for them. They prospered financially. It is said that no Shaker feared economic insecurity or unemployment.

With all their accomplishments one may wonder why, in only a few over a hundred years in America, they ran their course and ceased to exist. Their decline and disappearance are explainable. One article of their doctrine banned marriage. Celibacy was required and strict rules to assure it were made and enforced. This left only those coming newly to the group, or children they adopted, to maintain or increase membership. Both combined did not accomplish the purpose. One by one their communities literally died away.

At no time did their membership in America approximate more than 5,200. Only twelve, all women, were living in 1962.

For a short nineteen years, Lawrence County was host to one of the twenty groups of these strange and almost forgotten people. No marker indicates the locality.

❦ HE DIDN'T KNOW THE ROOSTER WAS THERE

IT IS NOT UNUSUAL to see a church spire topped with a cross, a tapered timber, or a pointed steel rod. Even weather vanes with bars fixed beneath to indicate the points of the compass are not rare. It generally is easy to grasp the meaning that such fixtures convey.

There are other symbols less common, however, that arouse curiosity. One of these is a copper rooster about four feet tall, perched above the slender 125-foot spire of Saint Paul's Evangelical and Reformed Church in Waterloo, a block north from the Monroe County Courthouse. It is in easy view of passing motorists, especially those driving north through the town over Highway 3.

Being different from the ordinary, this rooster naturally attracts attention and occasionally causes curious persons to ask questions. Just how did roosters first come to be placed on church spires? When did this one come, figuratively, to roost on this spire? Who made it and placed it? What has happened to it since? Where are there others?

So far as has been learned, roosters first were used over Protestant churches during the Reformation. They were part of the "protest" and were used to replace the crosses universally used by Roman Catholic churches.

The purpose of the rooster emblem is to remind those seeing it that it was Peter who denied Christ on the eve of His crucifixion, and that those denials were marked by the crowing of the cock. By seeing the symbol the beholder is reminded that any denial of Christ surely will be noted. There also may be some remote connection with the belief held from pagan times that the rooster was helpful in making prophecies. Anyway, the rooster symbols are more used in Europe than here.

In all cases observed, both here and abroad, the rooster is mounted above a sphere, said to symbolize the world. The one at Waterloo is above two carefully spaced spheres. A pointed steel rod extends through these spheres to support the rooster and allow it to constantly point the wind.

The present church building, the second one on that site, was dedicated in September, 1856, more than a century ago. The first steeple of the building was replaced by the present one, and the rooster placed at its top in 1874. This hollow rooster was made of sheet copper by Louis Wall, a coppersmith who also made the spheres. Wall regularly made many copper kettles; some still are used by area housewives when apple butter season comes.

This copper rooster has been a durable fixture and apparently still is in an excellent state of repair. Through almost a century it has pointed the wind and stood to remind all that they should not, like Peter, deny their Lord. Through the years it has gathered a patina that delights all who admire the look of weathered copper.

The rooster is only one of about a hundred symbols seen in and about the church. The base of each side of the slender pyramidal spire has interesting symbols that evidently represent the Trinity. The most interesting features the writer observed, however, are in the tall stained glass windows of the sanctuary. Anyone can spend a calm hour by entering the side door, sitting in one of the church pews, and enjoying the soft glow of the fine windows.

Those who built this church must have built well. It now has that ageless look that enhances some buildings. The mortar joints still are solid, and no evidence of the masonry's having been tuckpointed is seen. To those unacquainted with the word, tuckpointing means to gouge out old mortar that has rotted and weathered until it is no longer serviceable and to replace it with new. The joints of this old church remain solid.

The church organization first was called the German Lutheran Church. For many of its earlier years all services were in German. By degrees English began to be used on certain occasions. During World War I a wave of something resembling hysteria caused the banning of German. Now one service, the early one on the third Sunday in each month, is in German. This service is well attended, and some think they discern a distinctive atmosphere in it.

The other southern Illinois church on which a rooster appears is the Zion Evangelical and Reformed Church at Burksville about eight miles south of Waterloo on the old Cahokia-Kaskaskia trail.

These churches were founded by the German-speaking immigrants that came to settle the region shortly after 1830. They brought with them the German practice of using roosters as symbols on church steeples.

One of the surprising things about the rooster atop the spire of St. Paul's Church was the frank admission made by a man who had lived eight years in Waterloo that he had never noticed the chanticleer.

He went to his office window immediately and looked at it.

❧ THE AMISH ARE UNUSUAL PEOPLE

A GROUP OF BEARDED Amish or Mennonite farmers came to look at farmlands in Union County. Because of their somewhat strange appearance, they attracted more than passing attention and aroused considerable curiosity. They were trying to find a locality that would be suitable for the establishment of a new settlement for their people. They found a suitable location and came.

Some observers asked for information about the Amish people. When it was explained that they were a religious group and lived on farms, questions were asked concerning their religious beliefs and practices. Others wanted to know about their farming methods.

Since there are not great numbers of them in the country, and they do not travel extensively, they are a strange people to many. But they are hardly a new people. As a religious group—and it is the influence of their religious beliefs and practices that set them apart—they are among the older Protestant sects. Apparently, they began with the formation of a group of dissenters headed by Conrad Grebel, a native of Switzerland, in 1525. About ten years later, Menno Simms, a Hollander, came to join this group. It was from his first name of Menno that the group came to be called Mennonites. A dissenting group of these Mennonites, led by Jacob Amman and named for him, became the Amish we know.

This Mennonite-Amish group, because they protested and disobeyed the religious edicts of the established church and state, was severely persecuted. According to one authority, five thousand were put to death during the first ten years of the group's existence. The book *Martyrs' Mirror* carries accounts of over four thousand burnings of individuals, many stonings, crucifixions, imprisonments, brandings, live burials, suffocations, severing of limbs, and other atrocities. The Nazis had precedents.

The group found a haven and an opportunity for the free practice of their religion in Quaker Pennsylvania beginning in 1683. From time to time after that, other groups settled in Pennsylvania and elsewhere in America. The Mennonite-Amish group in this country now numbers about 300,000 of which the branch known as Amish is about 45,000. They are distributed over seventeen states. Illinois has one settlement of approximately 150 families near Arthur, along the Douglas-Moultrie county line.

The largest of their settlements in the country is in east-central Ohio and the next largest is in the vicinity of Elkhart, Indiana. The oldest and most prosperous of their settlements is the one centered in Lancaster County, Pennsylvania, where the writer has spent several days driving about the countryside observing their fine farms and visiting with them. In fact, wherever one goes through any Amish settlement, he finds excellent farms.

There now are two general divisions of the Amish. They are known as the house Amish, who hold their biweekly worship services in the homes of their members, and the church Amish who have special houses of worship. The house Amish are the more conservative and cling most tenaciously to their earlier practices.

Male members of both groups, however, begin growing beards on the day of their marriage, and both groups shave their lips. The house Amish do not trim their beards while the church Amish do. The church Amish are somewhat less austere than the house Amish. The men of both branches wear flat-crowned, broad-brimmed hats and dark clothing. Their outer garments are fastened with hooks and eyes but buttons may be used on undergarments. Amish women wear black bonnets and dark dresses. Some may wear lace caps beneath their bonnets.

As one travels over the countryside, he notes the absence of electric service, radio and television antennas, lightning rods, telephones, and automobiles. He also will note that no valuable farm machinery is left standing outside to rust.

No other mixed farming countryside visited in America has appeared more generally prosperous. The writer would be glad to see a settlement like the Pennsylvania Dutch Amish come to the region.

Chapter 11

Law and Order

❡ *ORGANIZED CRIME AND SAMUEL MASON*

THE SOUTHERN Illinois region can claim several American firsts, some of which lend very dubious distinction. Two of these are organized crime and river piracy, with Samuel Mason acting as their architect. Mason remains an interesting character, and an example of an Horatio Alger, "rags to riches" story in reverse.

He was born about 1750 into a prominent and respected Virginia family. From youth he was a leader, captaining a company of militia on the frontier during the Revolution. He was a fighting captain and often exhibited unquestioned courage, sagacity, and daring in combat with the Indians. Many termed him a hero.

Before the end of the Revolution, however, Mason left the military service and in 1780 was keeping a tavern two miles east of Wheeling. Here his fair reputation began a sharp decline, and he was accused of stealing horses. The next year he left Wheeling and drifted into eastern Tennessee where he stopped in a cabin that belonged to General John Sevier. While staying there, he was accused of various crimes among which were the stealing of cattle and robbing the cabins of Negroes while they were attending Sunday services. He was asked to move on. Knowing that it would not be wise to ignore Sevier's request, Mason went to western Kentucky.

In 1794 he was at the new settlement of Red Banks, now Henderson, Kentucky, being listed as one of its original settlers. There his daughter, after a clandestine and unconventional courtship, married an infamous character named Kuykendall, much against Mason's wishes. Pretending reconciliation, Mason gave a dinner on July 9, 1794, at which Kuykendall was killed—some thought at Mason's instigation.

At Henderson he began to gather the nucleus of his band, one of the earliest members being a counterfeiter named Duff, reputed guide for George Rogers Clark from Fort Massac to Kaskaskia. As Mason's activities increased the settlers began the formation of a "Regulators" band to curb him. He accordingly moved to Diamond Island, seventeen miles down the Ohio.

After a short stay at Diamond Island, Mason found the situation untenable and moved farther down the Ohio to Cave-in-Rock. Here, assuming the name of Wilson, the first of several aliases, he arranged living quarters in the cave and placed a sign on the riverbank saying, "Wilson's Liquor Vault and House of Entertainment." He soon gathered an assorted band of criminals about him and launched an era of robbery, river piracy, horse stealing, kidnapping, and stealing of Negroes—in fact, almost any type of crime that offered profit.

Mason began his operations at a good time, for flatboating was increasing rapidly, and numerous boats were on the river. He pursued robbery methodically. Pilots were sent as far up-river as Shawneetown to safely guide boats, as was stated, "past the dangerous places." Some men along the way would put out in small boats and invite flatboats to land, while others waved them to shore near the cave. Sometimes armed bands sallied out from the cave rendezvous to forcibly seize boats that ignored invitations. Many boats were robbed, and robbery almost invariably meant murder, for Mason wanted no talkers left. Boats and boatmen continued to vanish along the Cave-in-Rock stretch of the river until the steamboat came.

A proportion of the boats were allowed to pass with no attempt at molestation. Concerning these Mason is quoted as saying, "They are taking that load down the river for me," for returning boatmen were methodically robbed. Mason was active, and business at Cave-in-Rock was brisk. Since it always has been a practice of outlaws to keep on the move, Mason left the cave in a year or so and went to operate on the historic Natchez Trace, the old route leading from Natchez to Nashville. There he plied his trade of robbery for many years.

Early in 1803, Mason, with John Setton and others, was brought to trial before a French court at New Madrid, Missouri. He appeared there as a cringing, pleading, whining prisoner, trying to blame others for all the crimes charged to him. Since none of these crimes charged to him had been committed on French soil, Mason, much to his surprise, was surrendered to the Americans at Natchez. On the way he and his gang overpowered their guards and escaped.

Mason was later murdered by two confederates, Setton and James May, who cut off his head, wrapped it in blue clay, and took it to the officials who had offered a reward of $1,000 for Mason "dead or alive." As they were about to receive the reward, they were recognized and placed in prison. Brought to trial for some of their numerous murders, they were convicted on February 4, 1804, at Greenville and hanged four days later.

❧ *ONLY ONE WOMAN HANGED IN THE STATE*

THERE ARE incidents in the story of any region that people would wish to forget. Among these are hangings. Since they actually happened and reveal something of the ways people lived, perhaps they should not be ignored. Anyway, the following grim story is given.

If it is the first, last, or only event of a particular kind, an incident naturally attracts attention, the more so when tragedy is added. All these combined in one incident that occurred on May 23, 1845. That was the day on which a woman was hanged in Illinois—only because she fed her husband "white arsenic."

This wife evidently had made previous attempts to hasten her man's demise along the arsenic route. She finally administered a lethal dose on August 15, 1844. Four days later her husband was dead. It seems to have been common knowledge that she had poisoned him.

In a short time she was arrested and placed in the county jail. A grand jury indicted her for murder. The prosecuting attorney wrote and filed an indictment somewhat sprinkled with pious phrases. Among other statements it said, "not having the fear of God before her eyes, but being moved by the Devil, . . ."

At the September term of Circuit Court she appeared and made plea for a change of venue. Her attorney contended that local prejudice was so great that a fair trial could not be had there. The case, accordingly, was transferred to an adjoining county.

Trial began on April 4 and ended the next day. The verdict was, "We the jury find the defendant guilty." Court then "adjourned to nine o'clock tomorrow."

When court convened the next day, April 6, sentence was passed. It was as follows: "the judgment of the law and the court pronounces it, is, that you, Elizabeth Reed, be taken from hence to the place of your confinement and that on the twenty-third of May next you be taken from thence to some convenient place within one mile of this courthouse and there hanged by the neck until you are dead and that the sheriff execute this sentence, and may the Lord have mercy on your soul." The change of venue had not helped.

Court records clearly tell the story to this point. From here it became a public spectacle, for hangings then were really public. There were no stockades, enclosures, or screens. All who chose could come to view, and many chose. It is from the account of one who viewed it that some glimpses of the actual hanging may be had. His story was related and recorded in 1932 when he was ninety-eight years old; this was more than eighty-seven years after he had attended the affair with his grandfather.

According to the account he related, people began to arrive two or three days before the day set for the execution. They came on foot, on horseback, and in wagons drawn by oxen. Many camped about the town. The crowd easily was the largest the town had known. Very old people recall hearing other very old persons say when wishing to describe a large crowd, "It was as large as the one at the hanging."

The execution took place from a scaffold built in a grove of large sugar maple trees "within a mile of this courthouse," as sentence required. The larger limbs of the trees were laden with men and boys who had clambered there to have the advantages of a grandstand seat. The ten-and-a-half year old boy whose story is mentioned sat on his husky grandfather's shoulders. From this favored position he could see the activities well.

He recalled that the woman, whom he remembered as a slight figure, came riding to the place of hanging on an oxcart that also carried her coffin. He said she walked and stood erectly.

Preliminary arrangements soon were completed and the trap was ready to be sprung. Just then, however, a limb loaded with men and boys broke and distracted the young observer's attention for an instant. In that interval the trap was sprung. When he looked again it was to see the writhing body of the dying woman spinning at the end of the rope.

According to old accounts the body was claimed by her relatives and carried back to the "bend of the Ambraw" where she had spent her girlhood. Entries in the records of the County Commissioners' Court about their meetings that followed the trial and the hanging show payments made to those who had parts in the affair. Among those mentioned are the jurors, those who guarded and fed the unfortunate woman, and the sheriff who received $50 for his services at the hanging.

🌸 *PEEKING INTO BOX A 1–40*

A SHORT BIT of time was spent recently loitering in a courthouse while awaiting the return of a county official. It was only natural to become curious about what was in a few hundred numbered file boxes arranged in ordered rows along the walls. This curiosity was satisfied by inspecting the handiest one that happened to be numbered A 1-40. It contained probate court records, as the others also did. This experience happened in Murphysboro, but could just as well have been in any other courthouse in Illinois.

Each one of the many packets of papers found in the boxes is a complete accounting of the property left by some individual. The property was listed with values estimated by appointed appraisers. Additional lists paralleling those shown recorded the amount for which each listed item was sold. These lists proved most interesting.

Two packets from Box A 1-40 were selected at random. One covered the estate of a prosperous farmer and livestock dealer, amounting to several thousand dollars. The other was for a poor blacksmith whose property yielded only $40.12½ when sold at a public sale. After deducting expenses that included a coffin at $3.00, a shirt at $1.00, and nine yards of "shroudery" for $1.75, a net balance of $13.92 remained for the widow, Anny, who had served as administratress and had signed the necessary documents by making her mark. Property sold, the amount received for it is indicated below.

1 Cow	$ 6.00
1 Heifer	3.31½
1 Lot of books	.37½
1 Plow, single tree & chain	4.52
1 Pair of gears and collar	.90
2 Hoes	.12½
The wood work of one two-horse wagon	10.87½
One set blacksmith tools	14.00
	$39.11

(they don't balance)

Though all this happened 120 years ago it still evokes sympathy.

The case of the prosperous farmer wasn't so pathetic. In this case there were long lists of the property for disposal with the estimated values given by appraisers appointed. Parallel lists also showed the amounts received at the sale, cried by a man who received $4 for doing so. The clerk of the sale received $2.80 for his services.

With the listings of the property and its sale value, there also were listings of the debts he owed. These lists yielded much that was interesting. Some random items taken from the lists are given here, with occasional strange words and spellings. We find two tin safes and "1 lot of palens," a skiff, a "spurr" and "1 lot of books." There was a "stilliard," a reel, a drovers whip, and some winding beams. He left two "rifle guns" and three "muskrat spears," which naturally leaves one wondering what such spears were like. A roll of carpet, several yards of linsey-woolsey, ticking, and cottonade were added. Coal oil was included, apparently valued at fifty cents a gallon.

Sets of wagon and plow gears, yokes, clevises, chains, and "3 boxes of tricks" were on one list. About every list inspected had its barrels, boxes, or baskets of "tricks" that today would be called "what's its."

A "sauceage grinder," three wooden washtubs, a dough roller and a coffee mill were set down. There were three washboards, some "Delf ware," a half-bushel "masure," and a wooden water bucket. A silver watch, a sewing machine and a clock were listed. Corner cupboards, wheat fans, mattocks, sheep shears, and shocked fodder were offered for sale. There were "trunnel" beds, feather beds, straw ticks, dinner bells, breakfast tables, kitchen tables, and "beaurows" in plenty.

On the appraisal list there was "one 40 gallon barrel of whiskey" valued at $.40 a gallon. The parallel list of sales says "part of a barrel of whiskey brought $11." (Just what had happened in the meantime?)

Livestock entries are interesting. A span of mules appraised at $275 sold for $302. A black and white cow brought $14 and a brindled one $12. A cow with "druped" horns and another with "crumpled" horns each went for $14 while two beef steers brought $75. A bell cow brought only $9.30; hogs were $2.50 a hundredweight. A calf yoke sold for $.30 while calves were selling for $4 each.

A listing of store accounts paid provides several interesting glimpses. Two pairs of ladies shoes cost $6. Four and a half dozen buttons came at $.90. Hair oil was $1.

It must have been a right well corseted family from the frequency with which "1 corsett—$1.25" occurs. Another entry coming fully as often says "30 corsett steels, 15 cents." Corsets bought must have been fairly satisfactory, only one of a dozen or so being returned for credit.

An occasional item among the clothing entries may leave one a bit puzzled. Why should "1 pair of fancy cloth garters" cost $3.50, while two pairs of garters cost only $.20? A "set of hoops" cost $1.85, two switches were $.60, but "Artificials" were $1.00 each. Two handkerchiefs cost $.80 and a lace collar was $.75. A "set of jewelry" was only $.40. Ten writing pens cost $.10 while clay pipes were selling for $.01 each. It is assumed that the buyer furnished his own pipe stems.

Selections from such listings could go on endlessly. Each tells something about how people lived and what they lived with, or without.

🌿 *A ROMAN HOLIDAY*

THE WAYNE COUNTY Historical Society is an active group. From time to time, its members pause to observe some significant event that occurred in that county. They select the event to be observed somewhat by random and do not wait for a centennial to arrive. Also their selections are varied.

It would be no great surprise next year if news should come that they were planning to re-enact the Ben Hur chariot race at the county fairgrounds. That would not be so farfetched as it might first appear. General Lew Wallace worked on the manuscript of *Ben Hur* while staying in Fairfield to attend to some land cases in the court there.

This year they have chosen to observe one of the tragedies of the county—a hanging. They really do not plan to re-enact the actual strangling, only parts of the trial and some of the events connected with a murder that occurred on the Fairfield-Carmi road on August 19, 1852. The actual killing took place in White County, and the case was brought from that county to Wayne on a change of venue.

The man killed was James Lawler, an Irishman. The man charged with murder was Henry Voltz, thought to have been a German with a very poor command of English. Lawler and Voltz were partners in the business of exchanging merchandise for furs and farm products. These they stored at Carmi and Shawneetown until a flatboat load had been gathered; then the cargo was taken down to New Orleans. At the time when the body was found, they had just completed the gathering of a cargo, and Voltz was on his way down-river with it. Word was sent along, and Voltz was arrested in New Orleans and brought back to Carmi. He was promptly indicted. The indictment described Lawler's wounds as "two gashes in his skull, four inches long and three inches deep." This skull is said to have been kept in a medical office in Fairfield until comparatively recent times.

Voltz was held at Carmi until time for his trial in Fairfield where he was brought firmly bound and under heavy guard. Even in Fairfield feelings ran high against the prisoner. There were no direct witnesses to the killing. All evidence was circumstantial. Yet the jury returned a simple verdict on a slip of paper—"We the jury find the defendant guilty as charged in the indictment."

All efforts to secure a new trial or any delay were refused. The judge's sentence was accordingly entered in the records. It was "That the Defendant, Henry Voltz, be removed from the court house to the county jail of Wayne County, there to be kept in confinement until the twenty-fourth day of May in the year of our Lord one thousand eight hundred and fifty three and on that day that the said defendant be taken from the jail by the sheriff of said county of Wayne and be hung by the neck until dead, dead, dead, etc." (The "etc." doubtless was meant to replace the phrase, "And may God have mercy on his soul," that usually occurs in records of that time.)

In February, 1926, an old, old man wrote a letter telling of the great crowd that gathered at the west edge of town where a gallows had been erected between two low hills so that all could see. He tells of the ride of the prisoner from the jail to the place of execution seated on his coffin, and of the tense excitement that ran through the crowd. It apparently was, as all hangings then were, a Roman holiday.

There has always been a lingering doubt about Voltz's guilt. He insisted in his farewell speech from the scaffold that there was a man in the crowd who could offer the word that would free him. There is also a story that another man admitted on his deathbed that he had killed Lawler.

None is proud that a man was hanged. The execution is looked upon as a tragic reality, an unpleasant part of recorded history.

❧ THE FEAR OF PRISON WALLS

Boys once thought that there was an open season on watermelons that extended from the time they began to ripen until killing frost. On that presumption two chunks of lads, after a sultry summer day in 1900, paid an unannounced nocturnal visit to the combination tobacco-watermelon patch of Frank Willis. Two larger melons that successfully passed the fingernail and thumping tests, and as thorough a "curl" inspection as the limited moonlight permitted, were detached by the boys and rolled into the adjoining sorghum. (Both melons were ripe.)

The crime committed, like most others, was far from a perfect one.

No F.B.I.-trained operative was needed to discover the culprits. Two fathers, ordinarily indulgent and kindly, turned grim and set about making proper adjustments. Among the actions they prescribed was a "manly" call upon Mr. Willis. They even volunteered to go as far as the house of a neighbor they wanted to see—in easy sight of the Willis place.

To the boys' amazement Mr. Willis was surprisingly courteous, calm, and dignified. He was even considerate enough to invite his callers to share a really nice melon from a number lying in the shade and covered with wetted burlap. (This melon was hardly as tasteful as either of the night before, but time has sweetened it.) It is just possible that the whole procedure had been prearranged by Mr. Willis and the two fathers.

After a considerable amount of hesitancy and stammering the boys managed to say enough words to add up to "We're sorry." The wronged melon grower surely was a criminologist far in advance of his time. Without railing, ranting, preaching, or threatening, he calmly assured his youthful visitors that he wasn't angry. He then explained that success in such a little crime could easily lead to offenses more grave, perhaps even to the penitentiary. He mentioned the case of a nearby neighbor who had that very week been taken to the prison at Chester (Menard) for raiding a neighbor's smokehouse. After a bit more of small talk and an invitation to "come and see me again, boys," two subdued youngsters departed with high regard for Mr. Willis and a stern resolve to avoid all penitentiaries, and even for the time being to forego watermelon patch raidings.

Now, the only survivor of this little drama has given in and has gone, luckily by invitation, to the same awesome prison envisaged in boyhood. This voluntary journey was made with members of the Southern Illinois Editorial Association. Having accepted the invitation, he thought it would be well to "case the joint" somewhat and thus know more of the host institution, and how it got that way.

It was learned that there was no central state-maintained prison for Illinois until 1827 when one was built at Alton. Funds for its building came principally from the sale of about eighty thousand acres of land belonging to the salines near Equality. This first prison, containing twenty-five cells, was on a ten-acre plot of ground that constituted the prison bounds. They were the walking limit of certain civil-case prisoners, such as debtors, who were sometimes allowed outside the locked jail. Those sentenced for criminal offenses had no such privileges.

In 1858 another penitentiary was built at Joliet and newly sentenced prisoners were sent there. The Alton prison was abandoned in 1860. With the coming of the Civil War, the Federal Government took over the Alton plant and used it as a place to hold Confederate prisoners of war.

By the mid-1870's prison facilities at Joliet became inadequate, and the Illinois legislature, on May 24, 1877, authorized the building of another penitentiary at Menard. In October of the same year work on a cell house was begun. On March 21, 1878, it was ready and about two hundred prisoners, brought from Joliet to Menard for work on the building, were quartered in the recently completed cell house.

Since that time many new buildings have been added, and appearances changed accordingly. One characteristic, however—that of grimness—has remained. The whole plant wears a look of brutal solidity, both from without and from within. Perhaps this should be expected for, after all, prisons are not built to invite guests but to confine reluctant tenants. A visitor to the penitentiary at Menard comes away feeling that he has visited a remote walled city.

At not many places, however, are efforts to rehabilitate, reform, and reclaim prisoners more evident or more consistently applied than they are at Menard. The life of a prisoner is still no plush assignment, but Menard definitely represents a far cry from the punitive and often vicious course prisons once pursued.

❀ BACK TO PRISONS

THE AUTHOR ONCE spent a day, voluntarily, behind Menard's high prison walls. That day, despite the air of human tragedy always to be seen about prisons, was not an unpleasant one. It did rekindle a long-time interest in prisons.

Come to think of it, my interest in prison dates from the time when another small boy and I slipped away from our families to make a quiet inspection of the calaboose where a young neighbor had languished overnight.

This village bastile was a very small affair, only about eight by ten feet. As I remember, it was built of two-by-fours and two-by-sixes. The floor was made of these timbers placed on edge, jammed tightly together, and generously spiked from the sides. The walls were made of the same timbers laid flat and nailed through each layer. The ceiling was like the floor. The building was roofed in the conventional manner with clapboards.

As I recall, there was only one window about a foot square, with no glass but with sizable iron bars so closely spaced that a hand would hardly pass through their openings. The door, built of timbers arranged diagonally and spiked heavily, was four inches thick. It was hung on great iron hinges that had been made by the local blacksmith. Low bunks in the corners had straw-filled ticks and a few drab covers. There was a slot in the door through which a plate of food could be passed.

A low shelf held a bucket for water, a tin washpan, and a cup. A towel, considerably the worse for wear, hung on a convenient nail. Plumbing facilities consisted of a stone jar with a wooden lid. The walls, once whitewashed, had scaled to a pale gray. We felt sorry for Albert who had spent a night there.

Perhaps the most secure jail in southern Illinois was the one on the lower level of the old Alexander County courthouse at Thebes. This one had stone walls three feet thick with a vaulted stone ceiling. Narrow windows were crisscrossed with heavy iron bars. With a floor of stone and double doors of heavy iron-like boilerplate, it was truly formidable. Even now, a century after it was abandoned, a few repairs would make it a good jail—good when measured in terms of preventing escape.

Perhaps the easiest jail in the region was the old one of brick at Elizabethtown in Hardin County. In photographs of old Hardin County jail, one can easily distinguish fourteen scars resulting from holes left by fleeing tenants who had dug out through the crumbling walls and had not paused to mend them.

Nothing cheerful has been found about old prisons, from the boyish inspection of the village calaboose to the recent Menard visit. However, there was more of an air of hope—an *esprit de corps,* if there can be such in a prison—at Menard than has been observed at any other prison previously visited.

Though it was easy to see that discipline was exact and rigid, there was no evidence of any cruel intent. Likewise, the faces of the prisoners, though unsmiling, did not reflect the belligerency that is usually displayed.

As we walked about the prison yards at Menard it was easy to recall stones in the Paris pavements that mark the location of the French Bastile, the place of countless tragedies of injustice. It also brought memories of the Tower of London with its water gate, prison cells, the beheading block, and the headsman's ax, of which Raleigh said, "It is a sharp remedy but a sure cure for all ills." Also there came to mind the slightly sunken stone, always wet with the spittle of passing boys, that marks the Heart of Midlothian in Edinburgh.

While at Menard, it was remembered that, in bygone eras, people could be hanged for a half-dozen or more crimes in Illinois, or imprisoned for debt and given a diet of bread and water. Also, there was a time when the whipping post, the "cat of nine tails," the stocks, the pillory, the branding iron, and the cropping knife awaited violators. That was the era when ten- to five-hundred lashes, "well laid on" were given those adjudged guilty of various crimes, and at a very early time slaves who attempted to run away could expect to have their heel tendons cut.

The story of prisons and prisoners is indeed a grim one.

Chapter 12

Slavery

"EGYPT" AND THE MASON-DIXON LINE

WHEN THE PENNS and Baltimores did not agree upon the boundary between their colonies, Charles Mason and Jeremiah Dixon, two British astronomers, were selected to resolve the issue. They accordingly surveyed a line beginning at the Delaware River and extending westward 234 miles. Their work was completed in 1767. Years later this line, named for the men who surveyed it, separated the free state of Pennsylvania from the slaveholding one of Maryland, and thus divided the North from the South.

As settlement of the country advanced westward, the line was likewise lengthened. It did not, however, continue a straight course. It followed down the Ohio when it reached that river, then up the Mississippi and along the northern boundary of Missouri. In this meandering it looped south to form the boundary of southern Illinois on three sides. The lengthened line legally divided free from slave territory, but it did not so sharply separate those friendly to slavery from those who opposed it.

At almost all points along the border between slave and free regions, the band where slavery and antislavery advocates lived and were in direct contact was a narrow one. A short way on either side it was distinctly the North or the South. This was not the case in southern Illinois where feelings ran high, and the merging band often was a hundred miles wide. Perhaps there was no section of the long line where sentiment was so mixed over so wide an extent and where it was more actively exhibited.

Several causes had helped to produce this situation. First was the bringing of five hundred slaves to the region by the French promoter Renault in the early 1700's. They were to work on farms and about the mines which the French hoped to establish. When the mining bubble burst, many of the slaves were sold to French farmers of the region. Though the Indians had held slaves before the coming of the French, it was Renault's action that fixed the practice among the whites in the region.

A second step advancing slavery was the coming of the English-speaking settlers from the slave states. Many of the immigrants brought slaves with them. It is true that some of these slaves they brought were freed. It is a matter of record, however, that others were bought, kept, sold, and bequeathed, regardless of laws.

A large proportion of the settlers moving in from the Southern states definitely came for economic betterment. A smaller proportion came for the announced purpose of escaping a slave environment. Whatever motive may have influenced them, they maintained the usual back-home and family ties that immigrants naturally seem to cherish. Those coming with announced antislavery feelings gave little evidence that they were in any wise anti-South.

Two later state elections, bitterly contested, show that any early sentiment favoring slavery continued in the southern part of Illinois. In the election of 1824 when a vigorous effort was made to legalize slavery by the adoption of a new state constitution, this region voted overwhelmingly for the proposition. A decisive majority here favored slavery. An added indication that slavery had strong support is found in the incidents surrounding the killing of Elijah P. Lovejoy, Alton editor, in 1837.

This friendly attitude toward slavery on the part of many did not wane, and it was again shown in the senatorial election of 1858. Though the contest was between two dominant figures, slavery was distinctly the issue. Voters in the southern counties gave Douglas, considered favorable to slavery, a large majority. Lincoln, opposing it, received only a meager vote.

Thus southern Illinois, a region that later proved to be one of great strategic importance, came to the eve of the Civil War with a marked proslavery bias. This could explain the delay or failure of some leading individuals to commit themselves to the national cause when the conflict broke. Also, it helps to explain the internal dissensions and strife that continued in the region throughout the war. It certainly created an atmosphere that encouraged groups of dissenters known as Copperheads or Knights of the Golden Circle. Altogether, southern Illinois experienced a rather warm "cold war."

🏵 MORRISON HAD LABORERS FOR RENT

KASKASKIA STATE PARK attracts thousands of visitors each year. Most of these hurriedly pass by Garrison Hill Cemetery on their way to the lookout pavilion.

William Morrison, whose marble canopied grave is found in the cemetery on the hill overlooking the site of vanished Kaskaskia, was an unusual man.* This early citizen of Randolph County was the merchant prince of the upper Mississippi Valley when Kaskaskia was its metropolis. His home, regularly referred to as the Morrison Mansion, was the most pretentious one in the town. Morrison was wealthy, and his business interests were many and far flung.

He was a great Indian trader and fur dealer who sent his tradesmen, trappers, and fur buyers far up the Missouri to the region of the Yellowstone. He was the first man to send an overland trading mission from this region to the Spanish town of Sante Fe. This expedition, going out from Kaskaskia, marked the opening of the legendary Sante Fe Trail, one of America's storied roads that takes an equally important place with the Cumberland or National Road that led from the East to Illinois.

It is evident that Morrison favored slavery. That he bought, sold, owned, and rented slaves to others is a matter of record. The buying, selling, and owning of slaves in Illinois was not unusual. Numerous others did the same, regardless of the fact that the law frowned upon the practice. Despite the fact that Morrison was friendly toward the institution of slavery, he sometimes appeared in court as "next of friend" for a slave or orphan.

There are instances on record where he stood as "next of friend" for a Negro who otherwise could not have brought suit in court against a white person. In one case it appears that Morrison also paid the court costs. The unusual feature relating to slavery in Morrison's case was his practice of renting his Negro servants and slaves to others.

Many persons in Missouri, Kentucky, and Tennessee rented their slaves to the men operating the saltworks near Equality and at Browns-

* See *Legends & Lore*, pp. 145–48.

ville. So far as has been found, Morrison is the only Illinoisan to rent his Negroes to those who would use their labor in or out of Illinois. He rented out both men and women.

Morrison continued this practice of renting or hiring his servants to others over a period of about two years.

The first entry selected states that "Col. Swartz this day hired Negro, Harry, by the month at $12.00 per month, came home on the 29th day of May, 24 days of service." The next entry is for a woman and indicates the difference in value placed upon the labor of men and women. It says, "Rachel hired to Judge Pope this 9th day of October, 1831, at $5.00 per month, returned home 28th December." Rachel did not remain at home long. On January 17, 1832, she was hired to Edward Robbins at the same wages paid by Judge Pope. The time she served there was not found. At another time "Mary, Negro woman" was hired to a Mr. Piatson. The next entry shows that "Martin commenced his month on this day 11th October, 1831." It does not state for whom he worked nor when he returned.

Morrison often rented boatmen to captains of steamboats and other river craft. The first entry selected covering this is as follows: "Dangerfield entered on board the 'Michigan,' Captain Hill, on the 13th of June, 1832." At about the same time Guthrie made a voyage to New Orleans and "returned home on 7 June, 1832." This entry is marked "Paid." Judge Pope was a somewhat regular customer as the following entry shows. On July 23, 1832, "this day Wash, the mulatto boy, was hired by Judge Pope at $10.00 per month, returned 23 December," just in time for Christmas. Perhaps Judge Pope also operated a sawmill for we find another entry that says, "Big Joe hired to Mr. Pope 24 March and went to the mill, ended services on the 9th of April." Again, "Big Joe hired to Mr. Pope on the 20th day of May, 1833, and went to the mill, ended on June 15, 1833." Still later, "Big Joe began service at Mr. Pope's on the 8th of November 1833."

Altogether Big Joe must have been a desirable workman since he often was hired by steamer captains for trips to New Orleans. We find him hired on January 20th to Captain Swain of the steamer *Missourian* along with Little Joe, who had previously served on the *Ben Franklin* under Captain Castelman for $18.00 a month. Both Big Joe and Little Joe served on the *Missourian* in January and February, 1833, along with Ruben, Walsh, Harry, and Isaac. At another time Charles was hired to the captain of the *Missourian*. Another entry shows that a group of Negroes Morrison rented were given $32.00 expense money while in New Orleans.

Morrison wielded great influence in the Illinois region. His story would make an interesting book.

❧ THE DRED SCOTT DECISION

As ANNIVERSARIES keep coming around, they afford opportunity for one to pause and review bits of history. An approaching one, on March 6, marks 110 years since the United States Supreme Court handed down a noted and far-reaching decision.

Justice W. O. Douglas, a member of the present Court, has spoken of that decision as probably the most unworthy, ill-advised opinion in the Court's long history. The verdict concerned a Missouri slave. Issues raised by this case were of national interest. Since a significant part of the whole incident occurred in Illinois, perhaps it is of more than average interest here.

Dred Scott, then called Sam, was born about 1800. He first was owned by a Virginia planter named Blow. In 1818, Blow left the farmed-out lands in Virginia and went to Alabama, taking Sam with him. Not particularly prosperous in Alabama, Blow moved to St. Louis in 1830, where he kept a boarding house until his death a year or so later.

In the settlement of Blow's estate, Sam became the property of an army surgeon named Emerson, who was stationed at Jefferson Barracks. In December, 1833, Emerson was transferred to the U.S. Army Post at Rock Island, in the free state of Illinois, and took Sam with him. In May, 1836, they were transferred to Fort Snelling, in present-day Minnesota, where General Winfield Scott was then serving.

At Fort Snelling Sam acquired a new name that he carried back to St. Louis and into history. This new name, Dred Scott, apparently came from one of the nicknames applied, out of his hearing, to General Scott. The General often was referred to as "Old Fuss and Feathers." Likewise, he was called "Great Scott." In the language of the slaves, "Great Scott" easily transformed itself into "Dred Scott." It is this latter nickname, borrowed by other servants and applied to Sam, that the simple, illiterate slave carried back to St. Louis. No other explanation for the change of name has been found.

From Fort Snelling, Dr. Emerson was returned to Jefferson Barracks post, and about 1841 was ordered to Louisiana where he died leaving Sam, now renamed Dred, to Mrs. Emerson. For a time Mrs. Emerson leased Dred Scott and his wife, Harriet, to a Dr. Bainridge. For the services of Dred, Mrs. Emerson received $5 a month and for those of

Harriet, $4. In 1843, Mrs. Emerson moved to Massachusetts, apparently leaving Dred and Harriet much to their own devices. In this dilemma, Dred sought and renewed friendship with Henry and Taylor Blow, sons of his first owner.

In 1846 the involved chain of events that made the name of Dred Scott prominent in the history of American slavery began. Dred Scott made petition, signed by his "mark," to a Missouri court asking permission to bring suit for his freedom. It was granted. This was not an unusual procedure and attracted no special attention. No one suspected that it was the opening step of what was to become the nation's most noted slave case.

As a main basis of his claim for freedom, Dred's attorneys contended that his residence in the free state of Illinois and later in Minnesota automatically made him free.

After trials, decisions, appeals, and reversals in the courts of Missouri, the case came to the United States Supreme Court where it was argued twice. On the same day that the Court rendered its decision, denying freedom to Dred, his current owner, a man in New England, transferred his title to Taylor Blow, youngest son of Dred's first master. Blow held Dred until May 26, 1857, when he was freed.

Dred did not live long to enjoy his freedom, dying of tuberculosis on September 17, 1858. He first was buried in the Wesleyan Cemetery at the corner of Grand and LaClede in St. Louis. Later the body was moved to Calvary Cemetery and buried in Lot 177, Section One, the Blow burying ground. This practice was then permissible in the case of a family's slaves.

In its decision, written by Chief Justice Roger B. Taney and concurred in by seven members of the Court, some sweeping statements were made. It declared that when the Constitution was adopted "slaves had no rights which the white man was bound to respect." It held that slaves were mere chattels and that owners could take them wherever they chose. It denied to them the recourse of the courts.

Many look upon the Dred Scott Case as the one incident doing most to make the Civil War inevitable.

🌾 EMANCIPATION CENTENNIAL

CENTENNIALS COME, slowly but surely. The one-hundred-years-ago-today days generally are not identified by an event that left a lasting impression on history. It was somewhat different with September 22, 1962, however. An even hundred years ago that day President Lincoln issued the Emancipation Proclamation, declaring all slaves held in areas of rebellion to be free.

This proclamation did not apply to Illinois where slavery had ended legally in 1843 after at least 170 years of recorded existence. The observance of the centennial, however, does serve to recall some aspects of slavery in Illinois that are of interest.

In those parts of the South that had not been occupied by Federal forces, slaves still were held as personal property. They were valuable and owners clung to their property. Freedom did not come in a day.

It is not necessary to go into the South to find this tendency illustrated. It happened in southern Illinois where slavery was perhaps older than in Virginia. It was definitely a general practice here among the Indians as early as 1673. On their trip down the Mississippi in that year, Joliet and Marquette stopped to visit with the Illinois tribes. At one of these stops the Indians gave the French explorers a slave boy, a "pani," so called because he, like most slaves held by Illinois tribes, had been seized during raids on the Pawnee living west of the Mississippi.

Records indicate that both the Indians and the French continued to hold slaves. Records of the missions, established and kept by the Jesuits, indicate that slavery was nothing unusual, the first slaves being Indians.

There were few or no Negro slaves in the Illinois Country before 1720. In that year Renault, a French promoter with dreams of great fortunes to be made in mining, came to the region. He brought along five hundred Negro slaves from the West Indies. Some of these were taken to work in the Missouri lead mines. Others were settled at the village of St. Phillippe in Monroe County to grow food for the miners. When mining did not prove so richly rewarding as had been hoped, some of the slaves were sold to the French settlers in Illinois. This apparently marks the beginning of Negro slavery in the state. When the British came to possess the country at the end of the French and Indian Wars they did not interfere with the French practice.

When, through the efforts of George Rogers Clark, Virginia gained control of the territory, nothing was done to interfere with slavery. Virginia yielded her claim to the national government and it was agreed that the "ancient privileges" of the French be respected. This left them with their slaves in Illinois.

When the new nation enacted the Ordinance of 1787 for governing the Northwest Territory the "ancient privileges" of the French again were assured and slavery continued. This ordinance also said, "there shall be no slavery nor involuntary servitude except as a punishment for crime, whereof the person shall have been duly convicted." Territorial governors decided that this provision did not apply to slavery already existing, only that additional ones could not be brought into the territory. But they were. Sometimes this was done openly and is fully recorded. By one means or another the practice, though somewhat restricted, was continued, even after Illinois became a state.

Before the end of the Revolutionary War, immigrants from the older states, principally from Virginia, Maryland, and the South, began to arrive. Many brought their slaves. Some were freed before being brought into Illinois and others after they arrived. Some were never freed. In fact, the freeing of slaves was little encouraged. Those doing so were required to give bond that the freed slave would not become a public charge.

An example of this is found in Pope County where William Beam, who, incidentally, signed by making his mark, freed twelve of his slaves in August, 1823, and at the same time gave a bond of $13,000 guaranteeing that they would be self-supporting.

The lot of the slave in Illinois, as elsewhere, was a bitter one. He could not travel about freely. His right to bring suit in court could be exercised only if some white man would appear as "next of friend." He could not testify against a white man. In some towns his appearance was a signal for the hurling of stones. The Black Laws continued to the end of the Civil War.

Numerous records show the sale of slaves in Illinois long after it became a state. Two slaves, Macklin and Frank, were sold together by the executor of an estate at Golconda for $325 in 1829. This is not a singular instance.

Altogether, the story of slavery in Illinois is an involved one. Much of it remains to be told. Enough is known to show that slavery, by one method or another, was more common in southern Illinois than is generally thought. Perhaps all this helps one to understand why the Emancipation was much opposed by many Illinoisans, also why there was much pro-Southern sympathy in this section.

Chapter 13

The Military

❧ HIGH SCHOOL BOYS RETRACE
CLARK'S TRAIL

As THIS IS being written in February, 1963, William Garrison, a history instructor at University School in Bloomington, Indiana, and a group of high school boys are moving briskly across the frozen countryside from the Pierre Menard home near where vanished Kaskaskia once stood on the Mississippi River toward the site of old Fort Sackville at Vincennes on the Indiana side of the Wabash River, 180 miles away. Garrison's party consists of fourteen American students and his ten-year-old son, Matt. As nearly as it may be determined, they are walking the route that was followed by George Rogers Clark and his 130 men on their march to capture the British fort in February, 1779, an even 184 years ago.

Like Clark's men those boys carry their own camping equipment. Also like the men on that early journey, they have two pack horses to carry extra equipment. This group is prepared to sleep in the open, though they may stop in barns or abandoned schoolhouses. Clark's men, following the dim, often flooded, and sometimes frozen trail, saw many "drisly" days. On this journey the weatherman seems to be cooperating. He is giving them a frozen land and "snow flurries."

Just as Clark chose men best fitted for their task, these boys have been carefully chosen for their undertaking. No one seeing them doubts that they will succeed. Anyone whose faith in youth may be faltering has only to look at this group to be cheered. Superbly conditioned, sturdy, utterly confident, and calm, they know they will come through. The one looking at them, likewise, has no doubts. Clark's men had an "antic drummer," a mere lad it seems, as their mascot. This group has ten-year-old Matt.

293

Most of the men in Clark's small army were youthful. Clark himself was less than twenty-seven years old. If, by some magic, the group beginning this 1963 march could meet the one Clark led, there would be no great age barrier. These boys are reliving one of the great episodes in American history. It could well be that they are even making educational history and helping to initiate an admirable practice, that of acting out historical episodes of our history.

Other groups of boys have done similar jobs. One such group was a troop of explorer scouts at Clarksdale, Mississippi. A year or so ago these boys spent many days studying old maps, army orders, and other written accounts, and checking the accuracy of tradition to discover just where and what happened during the efforts of the Yankees to travel Yazoo pass and take the Confederate's stronghold of Vicksburg. They tramped and canoed over the swampy lands where the Yankees had cut levees, dug channels, and had tried to get their gunboats and other assorted river craft past the Vicksburg barriers. These boys encountered much the same maze of bayous and swamps filled with brush and fallen trees. When this group's efforts ended, perhaps they had the best and most thorough stock of down-to-earth knowledge and information concerning the complicated and confused Yankee efforts at Vicksburg during the winter of 1862–1863.

Several years ago a troop of Boy Scouts—now middle-aged men—sought out and marked the grave of Dr. George Fisher beside the blacktop road south of Ruma in Randolph County. Another group of Randolph Scouts retraced several of the old trails and roadways in the county.

It seems as though southern Illinois could borrow ideas from these ventures into direct study of history and retrace other historic roadways, traces, and trails. They could re-enact the journey Clark began at the mouth of the creek a mile above Fort Massac in June, 1778, and "retake" Fort Gage at Kaskaskia on the night of July 3–4. In fact, the journey of the Indiana boys is a direct challenge to some other group to re-enact the first part of the campaign. This would be an easier task and only about half as long a journey, nevertheless an interesting one. These two combined should make history come alive.

Other choices of projects are available. It would be interesting to retrace on foot and camp along the Illinois portion of the Trail of Tears that the Cherokee Indians followed on their enforced removal from the Great Smokies to Oklahoma in the dead of winter in 1838–1839. The entire trek was a thousand miles long, too much for one group to attempt. The section from Golconda in Pope County to the Mississippi ferry point near Cape Girardeau would be an interesting section and a more convenient one.

Then there is the Ford's Ferry Road from Ford's Tavern in Kentucky to Pott's Tavern in Gallatin County—liberally besprinkled with blood-curdling stories. Historic Goshen Road from Shawneetown to the Goshen settlement in south Edwardsville awaits explorer scouts, likewise the Kaskaskia-Shawneetown Trail, Miles Trace, and others.

Projects of this kind naturally will not appeal to softies. They well could be a part of a much needed physical fitness program and at the same time add to an appreciation of history.

A BOY'S DIARY OF MEXICAN WAR

MANY MEN GO to war as buck privates and, occasionally, one of them keeps a diary. Some of these which would provide interesting sidelights on the Mexican and Civil Wars are lying about southern Illinois, often unnoticed. One which was recently brought to attention was kept by Thomas Douthard Tennery of Greenup.

It begins as follows: "1846–June 29. Left home and went to Shelbyville, Illinois." That was the day Tennery started out to join the forces being recruited at Alton for service in Mexico. His daily entries for the following year and three days range from the mildly humorous to the philosophical, tragic, and revolting. The "Nothing unusual happened today" entries are not so frequent as in most soldier diaries.

Mustered into service, Tennery arose "to the beat of the reveille" on the morning of July fourth to begin an interval of soldier life. On the fifth he was sent to Jefferson Barracks, twelve miles below St. Louis, and reached there at six o'clock in the evening.

On the next day his entries begin to sound typical of soldiers. Men were complaining about the bread issued, diarrhea was rampant, there was much strong talk, and there were some desertions. The next few days record a number of deaths and military funerals, several of them for men recently enlisted. Military funerals impressed the new recruit, especially the one of Captain Page. A full regiment assembled to honor the captain "who had had his jaw shot away in battle on May 5."

Tennery tells of a nearby place that had a "grog shop, ten-pin alley and everything necessary for disappasion [sic]."

His training at the barracks was vigorous but brief. On July 23 his regiment embarked on the steamer *Sultana,* fourth of a series of steamers to bear that ill-fated name. (The sixth and last of the *Sultanas* exploded near Vicksburg in 1865 with a loss of more than seventeen hundred lives, one of the great marine disasters of history.)

Entries about the down-river trip tell of Fountain Bluff, the Devil's Bake Oven, and Grand Tower Rock. Succeeding entries carry to "Orleans" and then to an ocean-going vessel going toward the mouth of the Rio Grande. On the gulf he was impressed with the schools or "flocks" of flying fishes, leaping dolphins, and sharks nine feet long; and he writes about seasickness.

He speaks of the friendly feelings among all troops, from both North and South. For August 12, he writes: "Let those who are vain or ignorant enough to talk of disunion in the United States be silent forever, when they consider the ties of kindred and the feelings existing from Maine to the Rio Grande and from Florida to Oregon."

He mentions strange vegetation, sudden showers, the use of the lasso, the prevalence of mumps, and of many deaths from measles. He tells of a riot among troops from Georgia, evidently a feud between two companies, in which an estimated twenty or more were killed. He tells of the time that he "gathered and cooked a mess of delicious crabs."

There were long marches without water. "A dead pony was floating in the pond." "Killed a peccary." "Went to the hospital and received a large dose of calomel." "A large mail, I received a letter." Then came a series of entries telling of wattle huts, mesquite, chaparral, prickly pears, sand storms, corn tasseling (January 26), sleeping in mattamores, and frequently, "——died in camp this morning."

Then, "shot through both legs at Cerro Gordo. General Scott visited the hospital and talked with each patient." A few days later General Taylor came, a "heavy set, corpulent and old looking man." "There are not enough mattresses for the sick, consequently a great many have to lay on the brick floor." "The care is according to the nurse's disposition. . . . litter bearer kills self."

"Five soldiers tied up and whipped . . . in public market. . . . It still chills one's blood to see free Americans . . . whipped like dogs in a market yard in a foreign land . . . Two burials today among the chapparall and prickly pears."

"Of all places a camp is the greatest place for news. Every man feels at liberty to tell all he hears and sometimes what he thinks, for truth."

On June 15, 1847, he left for home. "How the heart rejoiced at leaving this country, where we have endured hardships, been exposed in battle, been in hospitals, and seen death and suffering in every shape and form, suffered from tyranny practiced, had the rights of American soldiers trampled by their own officers. A soldier becomes the football of passion, his life regarded as public property, as nothing. He is prepared to meet death or danger at any time in any form."

"No language can describe our feelings on this occasion. The black smoke from the funnels drifting back, points like a finger of scorn at Vera Cruz in the rear, that city of woe and misery . . ."

Subsequent entries reported: "Awoke in New Orleans . . . passed Baton Rouge . . . passed Vicksburg . . . passed Memphis . . . arrived at Cairo . . . landed at St. Louis . . . got to Salem."

🌿 ON THE EVE OF THE CIVIL WAR

PEOPLE OFTEN FIND things they are not looking for. This happened to the writer recently while he was scanning century-old files of the Chicago *Tribune*.

That was on the eve of the Civil War and the papers were filled with slavery, secession, nullification, states rights, and politics unlimited. Also there were the figures of impressive men stalking across the pages.

A region designated as "Egypt" was mentioned frequently. In this case "Egypt" meant southern Illinois. It was only natural for me to then follow along the "Egyptian" trail to learn more about the section indicated. Reading the old papers soon made the tensions and turmoil of that time more real and emphasized the unique situation of "Egypt" in the North-South struggle. It also made it easier to understand why there was violent clashing of opinions here, particularly in the southernmost counties.

Most "Egyptian" settlers had come from slave states to which they were bound by memories, family ties, beliefs, practices, and traditions. It is true that some had left their earlier homes for the avowed purpose of escaping a slave environment. Almost all, however, came hoping for economic betterment and were indifferent or even favorable toward slavery. It often was their desire to escape being "poor whites." Other immigrants came from northern countries of Europe to become part of a strange admixture.

There was much sentiment favoring secession. That this divided loyalty existed is shown by the region's newspapers, by election returns when slavery was a distinct issue, and by court records and other documents.

The attitude of the region's newspapers is indicated by Chicago *Tribune* reprints like the following. The Golconda *Herald* for April 17, 1861, said, "Should you of the North attempt to pass over the border of our state, to subjugate a Southern state, you will be met this side of the Ohio River. . . . You shall not shed the blood of our brothers until you have passed over the dead bodies of the gallant sons of Egypt." The *Herald* also advised that preparations be made for war; the intimation was that it would be local.

An earlier issue of the *Herald* told of a mob that went on the night of January 5, 1861, to the home of the Reverend John M. West, who had preached against slavery and secession. They halted near the West home and sent two men to his door. When asked to identify themselves, they gave the names of Clodhead and Grasshopper. Fearful, West refused admission and barred his door. The mob then began to hurl stones, about fifty of which came through the broken window. At the time of the incident the Wests were being visited by a Mr. Davis and his family. Without any means of defense, these families, about a dozen persons in all, could only huddle against the walls. Luckily, they escaped injury. The mob left, but before a messenger sent from the West cabin could return with help, the mob came back and hurled more stones.

Early in February a mass meeting was held in Brooklyn, now Brookport, a few miles down-river in Massac County, and sweeping resolutions favorable to the South were unanimously adopted.

The Jonesboro *Gazette,* in its issue immediately after the fall of Sumter, said, "News of the surrender of Fort Sumter was received with becoming features and expressions of joy by almost everyone in Jonesboro." In the same issue it also said, "We learned that the news of the surrender of Sumter was received with great rejoicing by the people of Vienna in our neighboring county of Johnson. The cannon was brought out and fifteen shots were fired in honor of the United South." Sentiments favorable toward slavery and secession also were published in other papers of the region.

There were stories of mass meetings, both those favoring and those opposing slavery and secession. The *Southern Illinoisan,* a paper then being published in Shawneetown, told of a rousing Union meeting at present Brookport. Its account ended with the classic blooper: "The ladies, God bless them, are for the Union to a man."

In Johnson County, a free Negro was trailed by bloodhounds, seized, and placed in the unheated county jail where he was badly frostbitten. He then was sold for a term of months to a farmer in the county. Men came during his first night at his new master's place, took him away, and sold him south into slavery.

Other accounts tell of the kidnapping of free Negroes, sometimes of entire families, and of their sale down-river. In some cases armed men from Illinois followed the trail of those kidnapped and forcibly rescued them. Some prominent men of southern Illinois were openly charged with taking part in these kidnappings.

Southern Illinois was a seething mass of conflicting convictions. Few sections of the country showed a more mixed pattern of thinking. The story of the area in the war is an interesting one.

🏵 THE RACE FOR CAIRO

IN THE CIVIL WAR the southern Illinois town of Cairo played a role that was as important as that of any city, next to Washington, D.C.

When Beauregard's batteries began to bombard Fort Sumter in Charleston harbor, it became evident to the most trusting that a clash of arms was inevitable. Both North and South realized that war had actually begun, and that there was little hope of ending it without a full test of power. Each government acted accordingly and formed the military plans that it thought best for its purposes.

In the eastern section of the nation, Washington naturally was the strategic center for the North, just as Richmond became the same for the South. Each of these cities, from time to time, operated as a defense center, or as one from which to launch offensives.

In the western field of action, Cairo was immediately recognized by both sides as a point of military value. The first troops that could seize, fortify, and retain control would command the confluence of the Ohio and Mississippi Rivers, and thus have a decisive military advantage. Since it was almost a hundred miles farther south than Richmond, and near the heart of the Confederacy, Cairo naturally became a convenient point from which to launch military campaigns.

While it is possible that the South may have thought of Cairo as an advance defense station, the North very obviously wanted it as a base from which to launch offensives. It was needed as a funnel through which men, munitions of war, and needed supplies could be passed southward.

Military operations in both North and South began immediately after Sumter. Southern troops quickly began an advance northward alongside the Mississippi with the confluence of the rivers as their objective. On April 15, President Lincoln issued his proclamation calling for 75,000 troops to suppress insurrection and to enforce national laws and edicts. On the same day Simon Cameron, Secretary of War, called upon Governor Richard Yates of Illinois to assemble six regiments of armed men, and to have them ready for immediate service. He also directed that four of these regiments be sent to Cairo at once.

Governor Yates relayed the message he had received to General Swift in Chicago on the nineteenth. Forty-eight hours later, that is, at 11:00 on the morning of April 21, the first section of this indifferently armed force of 595 men with four six-pounders left Chicago by special train bound for Cairo. A second train left the next day. These trains reached Cairo on April 22–23, after the first one had stopped at the Big Muddy railroad bridge north of Carbondale and had left an armed guard there. A military post, sometimes consisting of several hundred men, was maintained there throughout the war.

The troops from upstate did not reach Cairo one bit too soon. Confederate forces already had reached Columbus, Kentucky, only twenty miles away. It is said that some advance units of Confederates were only eleven miles across the river from the Illinois town. The early arrival of Federal troops also enabled the North to stop the shipment of ammunition and supplies, much needed by the Confederates. Steamers from St. Louis carrying these supplies were intercepted near the mouth of the Ohio and forced to land at Cairo where the contraband goods were seized.

Those directing the military affairs of the nation had immediately seen the obvious advantage of possessing the point at the confluence of the river. Nothing has been found to indicate that the urgency of measures to establish control of the point originated with the people of southern Illinois or first occurred to Governor Yates.

Until operations actually began, southern Illinois was distinctly pro-South. The southern tip of the state at the very best could be termed no more than a lukewarm region, with strong Southern inclinations.

After occupation of the area by Union forces, the attitude of the people gradually and greatly changed from one of indifference or disloyalty to one of loyalty. In part, this change resulted from the measure of increased prosperity that came with the troops. In addition to the military forces that regularly passed through or were stationed at Cairo, there also were hundreds of workmen and skilled craftsmen who came to work in Cairo and Mound City.

Prices rose and a period of unexpected prosperity resulted. The foundations of several respectable fortunes were laid. Many who had never hoped to accumulate more than a competence became reasonably well off. The population of Cairo increased from 2,188 to 6,267. Mound City likewise prospered and grew.

❦ *DANIEL BRUSH AND HIS VOLUNTEERS*

THE OUTBREAK of the Civil War found southern Illinois a land of sharply divided loyalties. Early in 1861 the views held by the people in the lower end of the state became evident in action. Those in sympathy with the South at first were the more active; oral traditions, newspaper accounts, and other documentary materials tell of numerous mass meetings held by the pro-Southern faction.

Groups of men held meetings in various localities. Evidently they were part of an organized group, for the same names appear in the accounts of meetings at several places. The resolutions they adopted were much alike; in fact, the wording is often identical.

There are few mentions of the meetings of those loyal to the North before Lincoln's call for volunteers to suppress the insurrection. However, one of these early meetings to advance the cause of the Federal government was held in Carbondale in April, 1861.

An account of this meeting, a typical gathering of this period, is recorded in the papers left by Daniel Harmon Brush, a prominent citizen of Jackson County. Brush operated a bank in his building, which stood at the southwest corner of Illinois Avenue and Main Street in Carbondale where the Hub Cafe now is. In the rear of his bank building was a telegraph office.

On April 20, a representative of the government called on Brush to ascertain that the secrecy of telegraphic messages passing through the office was assured. Told that all due precautions would be taken to maintain secrecy, the representative went on his way. Thereafter, Brush refused all malcontents—he personally knew and named them—and access to the telegraph office except on business, and then only through his personal office. This turned much wrath upon him. He patiently listened to mutterings, threats, and maledictions against the "abolitionist government" and its friends, as well as against him personally.

The malcontents were determined to verify a rumor that troops were coming down from Chicago on the Illinois Central en route to an appointed rendezvous at Cairo. Though they did not learn anything through the telegraph office, they did not have long to wait. About midday on April 22, a trainload of soldiers with military equipment passed through town without incident, except that they heard the cheers of loyalists and the mutterings of Southern sympathizers. Before reaching Carbondale, however, the train had stopped at Big Muddy bridge north of town and had left a company of soldiers to guard the bridge. This guard was maintained throughout the war.

The passage of this train brought the definite realization that a war was on. Brush decided that it was time for action. He and some others posted notices that a meeting of Union supporters would be held on April 23. He also announced that they would carry the "Stars and Stripes," his designation for the flag, along the street to the appointed meeting place. Rebel sympathizers vowed that he should not. They would "tear it down and trample it into the dust."

Some of the more timid wished to abandon the meeting, but Brush and others stood firm. When the time came, Joseph B. Thorpe, named elsewhere in Brush's records as an active Southern sympathizer, was the first to join Brush as he marched with the flag along the planned route and joined the parade while the "rebel yell" and cries of "Down with the flag" came from across the square. The meeting, a tense one, proceeded according to plan, and strong resolutions were passed pledging loyalty to the national government. Though this meeting did not silence Southern sympathizers, it did quiet them somewhat.

Two days later, Brush's forty-eighth birthday, he climbed the roof of his store building to raise the Union flag and make a speech that declared his convictions. He tells us that the large crowd which gathered was about equally divided in sympathies and that the yells and shouts of both factions were mingled. Brush kept the flag flying above his store, however, until he had raised a company of men and had gone with them to Camp Douglas at Anna where the company was mustered into the service of the United States by none other than U. S. Grant. Brush became the captain of this company. He was promoted through the ranks to become a colonel and for a brief time was breveted a brigadier general.

On a recent visit to the Illinois memorial on the Vicksburg battlefield, the writer paused in front of the bronze tablet that carries the names of Brush and of others from Carbondale who were still with the company at the siege of Vicksburg.

🏵 SHELTER FOR AN ARMY

THE CENTENNIAL of our Civil War has been observed, and its observance has renewed interest in the conflict. Many new books, some intensely interesting and others hopelessly dull, have appeared. Others are on their way to prove that the 2,000-year-old saying, "Of the making of books there is no end," still is true.

Some of the recently published volumes are written from a new viewpoint. Instead of the high strategy, lofty ideals, noble principles, mistakes, and master strokes that Civil War books usually describe, the recent grist of books gives more attention to the lowly, laden soldier always trudging toward another battle.

Now, a hundred years after the war began and after the last of the two million combatants have answered the final roll call, the hardy, hungry, homesick, muddy, and vermin-infested man, the somewhat happy-go-lucky chap who bore the brunt of the conflict, is receiving more of the attention he has always deserved.

From pictures, drawings, letters, diaries, as well as from legends, the man with the musket is becoming more real. This assorted material, much neglected heretofore and called trivia by some, is being used to tell more of the soldier's daily way of life.

They help us to know more about how he was clothed, fed, rewarded, punished, disciplined, drilled, doctored, and sheltered.

A look at the soldiers' "tended field," for example, is interesting. Naturally an army cannot be kept always in the open. When troops were to stay in a locality for an extended length of time, somewhat permanent shelters—much like the barracks of World Wars I and II—were erected. The great problem of shelter lay with the field army, the one on the move. A very small proportion of such a force could find protection in existing buildings or other shelters, hence it became necessary to provide tents.

The most highly rated tent that came into early use was a round one called the Sibley, sometimes the Bell. It was cone shaped, eighteen feet in diameter and twelve feet high. Its support was a center pole, and its edges were pegged to the ground. A Sibley would house about a dozen men. If the soldiers planned to stay in a certain place for some weeks or perhaps months, a round pen, or palisade of posts, with the same diameter as the tent's base and about four feet high was built; the center pole was lengthened accordingly, and the tent stretched on top of the palisade. It then would shelter about twenty men.

Heat for a Sibley tent was provided by a conical stove, with a pipe extending through an opening at the top of the tent. Sometimes an oven for cooking would be built, and the stove would be set upon it. These tents got their name from a man who had gone with Frémont through the Indian country and had observed Indian tepees. The problem of transporting these tents discouraged their continued use, however.

Another type in general use was the tent with walls, which is about as old as armies. These continued in use for officers' quarters and as hospitals and kitchens until the end of the conflict. Then there were the small A tents, so called because they resembled the first letter of the alphabet. When they were pitched on top of rectangular pens or stockades, they made an excellent shelter for two men. If the pens were lengthened and two tents stretched end to end, four or five men could crowd in. At other times these tents were stretched over pits that World War veterans knew as fox holes.

Then there were those objects of vivid memory to many, the pup tents. They were made, then as now, of shelter halves buttoned together to cover a space about sufficient to shelter a pup. When rain came, woe to the one who touched the inside of the shelter, for that was where the leak began.

After trying the foregoing shelters with varying success, the fighting men on both sides settled for a simpler arrangement. When they had to carry their equipment on their backs, they learned to get along with a minimum, so they settled for a rubber-coated cotton blanket or poncho about six by seven feet, with a short slit in the center with overlapping edges. This was worn as raincoat by day when required. The remaining camping equipment consisted of one blanket, rolled up and carried on the back. At night two men bunked together. One poncho would be spread on the ground, and their blankets were used for cover. In addition to its use as a protection against rain, the poncho often was used by men to mix breadstuffs when they did their own baking.

At its very best, the life of a field soldier was a trying one. It required considerable ingenuity just to contrive a fair shelter.

❧ COOTIES

As a member of the Marine Corps during World War I, the author dutifully and regularly wrote from Europe to his mother. When there was an opportunity, he enclosed mementos. Among such remembrances were sprays of shamrock from Ireland, daisies and heather from Scotland, primroses from England, poppies from Flanders, a silk handkerchief from France, and two lusty specimens of *Pediculus vestimenti* from Germany.

The two little "critters," readily available from a densely populated corporal, were placed on the letterhead beside the "Hubertsburg Farm,

Leutesdorf, Germany" heading. Before they could scamper away, molten candle was dropped on each unsuspecting victim. The hot wax instantly ended their career and left them firmly attached to the paper. There they have remained, still viciously life-like and hungry looking, through fifty years.

A Civil War letter found recently speaks fully as eloquently about the "varmints" which pastured off Union and Confederate soldiers alike.

The two letters mentioned, written fifty-five years apart, are supplemented by personal memories of the aggravating part played by the little pests with the big name that have played a part in all recorded wars. They went along to war with Egyptian soldiers six thousand years ago. They have regularly accompanied the military since then. In World War II they were greatly hindered by DDT though not utterly defeated. The *Pediculus* tribesmen in Korea are said to have acquired a measure of immunity and to have ignored DDT, even to have prospered on it.

While the insect has long borne his proper and full name of *Pediculus vestimenti,* he has answered to many another one. Among them are "active citizen," "arithmetic bug," "Arkansas lizard," "walking dandruff," "bosom chum," "shifting freckle," "mechanized mole," "seam squirrel," "pants rabbit," and "grayback." In World War I he generally answered to the name of "cootie."

The cooties paid no heed to rank, race, or nationality. They ignored all rank, as readily biting a major general as a private soldier. Though every man started out with a resolve to be cootie-free, the field and trench soldier generally "got 'em" no matter how carefully he tried to avoid them. It was always amusing to see one of these careful boys find his first inhabitant and shyly dispatch it. Seemingly he thought it was only lost and not the scout of an advancing horde of permanent settlers. Yet a cootie's residence in the clothing of an individual was "for three years or the duration of the war."

With no opportunity to boil clothing and with no hot flat iron to roast them, the soldier used other processes. He removed his undershirt, turned it to "read the seams" or "skirmish." Sometimes he carefully folded the garment to better expose hiding places and moved it quickly through a flame. The least one could do was to turn his undershirt just before going to bed in the hopes that he could go to sleep before his "livestock" found the way around to the grazing ground. Fleas, crab lice, head lice, and bed bugs were in pest proportions, but it was the plain old body louse that was the enduring evil. In addition to the annoyance of its bite, it sometimes was a carrier of typhus, trench fever, and relapsing fever.

This major pest could be a source of amusement. It was not unusual in either the Civil War or World War I to see men grouped in a crowded circle about a sheet of paper. This meant either of two things: a cootie race or a cootie duel. If a race, the selected contenders were dropped inside a centrally located small circle. The first one to reach the line of a larger circle or to tumble off the edge of the paper was declared the winner. Invariably wagers were made, and money changed hands.

Instead of a race, cooties often were matched in mortal combat. In this game, two husky "leatherheads" were placed on a smooth surface and gently maneuvered to meet head on. They gave no quarter nor asked any. Sometimes both became casualties, but there was never a shortage of heavyweight gladiators, and bets were numerous.

Men have done noble deeds in war. It adds to their glory when we consider that the soldiers who fought valiantly at Shiloh, Gettysburg, Vicksburg, or Lookout Mountain, and those who swept across Georgia with Sherman's Bummers, often were cold, hungry, homesick, ill, and almost without exception, heavily infested with *Pediculus vestimenti*.

❧ FROM AMPLE TO SCANTY RATIONS

AUTHORITIES HAVE long recognized the soldier's healthy appetite and have tried to satisfy it with plain foods.

As early as 1861, our regular army was the best fed in the world, with a daily ration of meat for each man of twelve ounces of pork or bacon, or twenty ounces of beef. He received twenty-two ounces of soft bread or an equal weight of flour. When neither bread nor flour was available, he was given twenty ounces of corn meal.

With each hundred rations, the men drew fifteen pounds of beans or peas and ten pounds of rice or hominy. They also received ten pounds of greens or eight pounds of roasted and ground coffee, with fifteen pounds of sugar. A half-bushel of potatoes, or some compressed, kiln-dried vegetable that baffled identification, was sometimes added. To season this food, there was an allotment of four quarts of vinegar, two quarts of salt, a quart of molasses, and four ounces of pepper.

If any of these items were not used, they could be sold back to the subsistence department, and the money was placed in a "company fund" to buy other eatables that would lend to the soldiers' diet variety. This fund showed a strong tendency to disappear without very visible results and was a subject for conjecture and griping.

The foregoing ration was for soldiers at army posts. With field armies, the collection and distribution of food to the man at the front was a colossal problem. Unlike the well-fed troops in quarters, those in the field—numbering hundreds of thousands—often were pitifully hungry.

When battle neared, men were issued rations for three days at a time. For each day, they were given one pound of hard bread, three-fourths of a pound of bacon or pork, or twenty ounces of fresh meat, with portions of sugar, coffee, and salt. These they carried in haversacks to which they occasionally added a "stray" pig, a wandering barnyard fowl, wild game, or perhaps fish caught with pole and line or by chunking. Berry patches, pawpaw and persimmon trees, as well as convenient gardens and orchards, spiced their rations.

The hard bread issued to the field soldier quickly became known as hardtack, a term that described it well. It was a plain bread, made of water and flour, and baked to a stonelike hardness. The crackers varied in size but were generally a little less than three inches wide, a bit longer, and about a half-inch thick. Nine or ten were considered a daily ration.

Men equipped with sound teeth and strong jaws could bite and chew hardtack. Others not so fortunate soaked it in coffee, fried it in grease, or cooked it with meat. Even when soaked in liquid, hardtack never really became soft, like dunked toast, but was a rather solid mass that needed chewing.

In established camps, food was cooked in a regular kitchen. When troops went afield, kitchens naturally were left behind. The company would be divided into groups of three to six men, called a mess. They cooked, ate, and contrived shelter together. A strong companionship grew between members of these groups; a few older people who knew Civil War veterans may recall the tone of affection present in the voice of Uncle Boyce Mayberry when he said, "Frank Wilson, Zachariah Allen, and I were messmates for three years."

Food was cooked in pots, tin pans, halves of canteens, or a faithful skillet. Meat was boiled, fried in the skillet, or broiled on a musket ramrod over a small campfire. Dough for bread sometimes was cooked in like manner. Bacon occasionally was eaten raw.

The prudent soldier mixed his sugar and coffee when he received them so he would not run out of the one before the other. Coffee was highly prized. The supply generally was adequate and "coffee breaks" were frequent. A tin can with a wire bail was the universal coffee pot that was hung above a small fire to boil.

So long as these veterans lived, memories were cherished by those who brewed coffee and sipped it with hardtack around their little fires. A vivid boyhood memory of the writer is that of having seen forty or more old soldiers at the Broughton Reunion when they gathered about the fire to drink coffee, to nibble at hardtack, and to recount incidents of war days.

Animosities were so forgotten that they invited a "rebel" to join them.

❧ *LIVING OFF THE COUNTRY*

SINCE THAT TIME when men first began to wage armed conflict in a manner that some have been kind enough to call civilized warfare, there have been a few practices that belligerents have accepted and observed. One of these has permitted an invading army to live, in part at least, off the enemy country. This often has been done at great inconvenience and hardship to the civilian population.

Invading armies were not supposed to leave a country so destitute that the lives of the people were endangered from starvation. This thought often has received only lip service, and few military men professed to see much wrong with the practice. The above indicates very well the international viewpoint at the outset of our Civil War.

In our war, a few considerations made the situation somewhat different. One of these was that the South was not at first looked upon as an enemy country. It was only a bit of our own country, out of line. In the second place, many in authority thought that foraging, once begun, would arouse greater antagonism to the national government and cause the wavering loyalty of border states to turn toward the Confederacy. Perhaps a third reason for the slow start of foraging was the fact that our armies were made up of civilians without the more hardened attitudes of professional military men. Moreover, the Ten Commandments also bothered many.

From the very first, men in training camps bought food not available in army issue from farmers or others who had it for sale. They also went raiding at night and collected fat hens, geese, or turkeys. Sometimes pigs running at large—"wild pigs"—fell victims to these hungry troopers. Accounts concerning the training camps near Springfield, Illinois, make prominent mention of such cases. It is not strange that these practices moved south into Kentucky and Tennessee with the invading troops.

Before long the army began to take needed supplies from the countryside. At first, it was accepted practice to give receipts for supplies taken from civilians. Then it became customary to give receipts only to those who were "loyal." Many persons naturally became "loyal" when yielding their property, to either side as it might appear best. As Union forces moved deeper into the South, practically no protest of loyalty received consideration. Foraging off the land became an almost universal custom.

Gathering supplies along the path of the invaders was pursued in a somewhat haphazard manner in the beginning. Soon, however, the practice was organized and placed under the direction of army officers. Early morning would see the foraging detail—often only a collection of foot soldiers—start out on their daily routine. As they advanced through the countryside they would accumulate wagons, horses, harness, saddles, oxen, beef cattle, grain, flour, fodder, hogs, molasses, honey, fruits—in fact, about anything eatable or usable. An occasional forager might slyly take some article for personal use. (One of my grandfathers brought home a silver spoon from Georgia.)

Foraging was not without its hazards, especially when carried out in the vicinity of the armed enemy. There are numerous records of foragers being captured and shot or hanged for their activities.

As foraging became more refined, the food gathering activities of soldiers not detailed for that particular job were discouraged. Nevertheless, much of it occurred, sometimes in an amusing manner. One Missouri soldier tells of a comrade spying a nice fat goose. Wanting it desperately, the soldier took a stout fishline and hook which he duly baited and tossed before the hungry fowl.

When the goose had taken the hook, the soldier "set" it firmly and started walking away, the goose naturally following. Seeing his goose leaving, the startled farmer shouted at the soldier, who quickened both his pace and that of the goose. The soldier, apparently afraid of the angry honker as much as his owner, cried out, "Mister, call your goose back! He's trying to bite me!" With all due speed, leader and led reached camp. It is recorded that "The lieutenant had a nice roast goose."

Many explanations were offered for taking food. All pigs were "wild," calves were "deer," hens cackled "disrespectfully" at the flag, and so on.

Perhaps the most noted of all foragers were those with Sherman's army. They left Atlanta with five thousand head of cattle and reached Savannah with ten thousand. Their campaign-weakened horses were replaced with the best steeds remaining in the South. All in all, much of Sherman's march over a route sixty miles wide "from Atlanta to the sea" was much like a great picnic.

Not only did Sherman's men forage. A rabble of troops "lost" from their units, along with deserters from the Confederacy and an assorted band of camp followers, attached themselves to the army and made up a band that wantonly raided and plundered. They are memorialized in history as "Sherman's Bummers."

❦ PRIVATE GEORGE GRIFFITH'S CIVIL WAR DIARY

A GROWING INTEREST in the Civil War surely has helped in the rediscovery of old letters and diaries kept by boys who went to war. One such diary, now in the possession of Mrs. Willard Ingram of Eldorado, was kept by George Griffith who served in the Ambulance Corps, Third Division, Fifteenth Army Corps.

Many such diaries sound like embellished weather reports. Weather, of course, was of great importance to boys who lived out of doors. And, along with the ever-present weather, there was always the emphasis on food. Some entries point up the task of feeding armies.

Railways of that day would now be termed "dinky." Few highways could make even mild claims to being improved. Refrigeration and other presently used methods of food care lay far ahead. Hardtack, salt pork, and beans were staples. Most of the food for the army in the field was hauled long distances over the countryside in lumbering, slow-moving trains of covered wagons. One mired or broken wagon might block a road and delay urgently needed food supplies for hours. Roving bands of enemy cavalry often appeared to seize or destroy poorly protected trains, both railway and wagon.

The practice of foraging increased as the armies of the North moved deeper into the South. By the time Sherman's forces were closing in on Atlanta, foraging had reached great proportions. In fact, it extended beyond real necessity and became a means used to punish and break the spirit of the civilian South as well as to destroy supplies needed by Confederate forces.

There were certain rules, rather flexible it is true, to regulate the practice. An example of a rule to protect property is illustrated by an order credited to General Sherman. Plantation owners had protested vigorously against the use of fence rails as fuel for mess and camp fires. Sherman is said to have issued an order stating specifically that only the top rail could be taken from a fence.

Griffith's diary during 1864 makes frequent mention of the practice of foraging and of other means of supplying the army with food. Thus, on Tuesday, March 2, "Today we was up to the mouth of Flint River after foraging but did not git any so we camped near the river to knight." Fortune dealt more kindly the next day when he said, "This morning we started about daylight and went 8 miles down the river and got loads and to knight we returned."

His unit reached Chattanooga, Tennessee, on the afternoon of July 2, 1864, "and camped just below town and the boys are after grub." A new look came in the food situation on July 19 when "there was about 15 hundred head of cattle passed here today." This was fresh beef, transporting itself to the soldiers at the front.

Griffith's diary indicates hardtack as their regular bread ration. On July 20 he tells us that "Sage and Colter made some bread and Jo and me went and got some." The next day a detail went out "and got two loads of corn for the horses." On August 11, "we was out after corn." The next day, "we was agin today for corn and some of the boys are Spreeing today." (Probably they had found the liquid form.)

He mentions visits to orchards and tells us that "B. Knopp and me made some peech pies." On the same day "the rebs captured some cattle going to the front." Two days later "the cattle was recaptured." On August 24, "we was out after corn again today and the sick was out at the peech orchard with the pickers." On each of the next ten days "we was out after corn and fodder."

Griffith was moving toward Atlanta. On September 15, "we hierd a cook." Foraging kept a brisk pace, however. On October 20, "we drawed rations this morning we got only half rations [because] the rebs had the road cut yet."

On November 2, "the foragers have got back after three days with corn, potatoes, pork, molasses and everything they could git." The next day "some cattle passed going to Atlanta, the gards are all conscrips and some of them are sick of it."

Combining the effects of foraging by the soldiers, by the ever-present mass of bummers or camp followers of endless variety, by freed slaves, and even by deserters from both sides, great sections of the South were left destitute.

Private Griffith's diary shows that foraging in the Union Army was not his sole interest. While many entries tell of gathering food and supplies, others have to do with amusements, paydays, clothing, church, shelter, wounded men, and bits of musings.

Thus, on Saturday, February 13, 1864, he watched horse races in which "the adjutant of the 80th Ohio run a little gray and an orderly of the 2nd Brigade a sorrell." The outcome was not recorded.

On the Sabbath following the race, the church was "crowded."

Griffith appears to have been a regular and attentive churchgoer. He often records the minister's text. He tells of his first attendance at a Catholic service and of the impression it made upon him.

On Tuesday, May 17, he records that "there has bin some fighting goin on at Madison station today and we are expecting a fight here they are getting ready."

On Wednesday, June 22, his unit began to move and marched ten miles before noon. The next day, "we marched 16 miles to Paint Rock and the boys are in the creek swimming . . . the old general was out looking at them." June 24, "Today has bin very warm . . . we marched 17 miles to Scottsborogh." The next day, "we left Scottsborogh this morning about 4 and marched 20 miles against 4 this evening up to Mud Creek." The following day, Sunday, "We have bin laying up at Mud Creek today resting." Two days later, "the ordnance train went to town and left the ammunition."

A day or so later his unit began to move. Day by day it was five miles, ten miles, fourteen miles, fourteen miles, four miles, sixteen miles, then fifteen miles "past Tunnel Hill and Buzzard Roost." On July 8 they were "up at 4 and marched 18 miles out of Dalton." For the next day, "Got marching orders last night and marched to Cartersville 12 miles." Mixed with all these entries are two recurring ones—"Some of the boys went out after forage" and "It rained." One day while they were "laying by" the "7 Illinois passed going to the front." Likewise, another "1500 head of cattle passed," more beef on the hoof taking itself to the front.

Another day when his unit was halted "the 18 Wis 4 Minn and 80 Ohio" passed. The same day "we went to Allatoona and the 59, 48, and 65 Ill and the 26 Mo is here." Two days later, "I got a letter today the first in three months . . . 16 trains passed here. This morning [July 22] we got word our men was in Atlanta."

On Saturday, July 23, "Gen. McPhersons body passed here and Geneaarl Grearson [sic] passed here wounded and 400 prisoners. It is said that Gen Hood is killed." (This was only a rumor since Hood lived until 1879.) The McPherson-Grierson mentions are of more than passing interest to the writer since one of his grandfathers was a Grierson cavalryman and the other was McPherson's orderly and present when the General was killed.

A day later, "Today I was out and got some rostenears. This eavening we went out and got some planks to make some houses."

A few days later two hundred horses (seemingly remounts) passed to the front and more beef on the hoof—three thousand this time. Next day they were making pies. For September 3: "Well we have news to knight that Atlanta is taken." The next day, "The boys are having a good time there at the bridge . . . no mail today the rebs has been tearing up the railroads."

"There was 500 prisoners passed going north for safekeeping." Two days later, another 500. Entries like these occur frequently.

Under the date of Monday, October 9, Griffith records: "This day 3 years ago I went to camp but was not ordered up at 4 o'clock to be reddy to move as we was this A.M."

On Saturday, October 22: "Well it has been cool and cloudy today the regt is taking a vote today for president. I was over and give one for old abe."

Payday came occasionally. Griffith tells of being paid for three months and says "I started $6000 home today." He must have omitted the decimal point. Soldiers then were given a clothing allowance and were charged with the clothes issued to them. On blank pages preceding the diary, he records "Clothing drawn this year." Pants were $2.50, socks $.32, shoes $1.48, shirts $1.53, and drawers came at $1. A rubber-filled canvas sheet having a slit in the center through which one could thrust his head and use as a raincoat cost $3.10.

As the diaries and letters of those bitter years are read, one wonders if the world has ever had a more individualistic and carefree army. The pictures their writings present range from those of deadly combat to others somewhat like hazardous picnics.

🏵 PRIVATE GRIFFITH AT WAR'S END

DECEMBER, 1864, saw Pvt. George F. Griffith, Civil War Ambulance Corps, blithely marching, occasionally skirmishing, but constantly foraging, across Georgia and "from Atlanta to the sea." He welcomes 1865 at Savannah. Entries in his diary for the next four months, leading up to his discharge, present an intimate glimpse of an enlisted man's life in the waning days of the conflict.

Six days after the New Year, he reports, "General Logan come back today." Four days after that he casually informs us that "many of the boys were tight and had gone to the theater," and, in the same breath, "some of the corps has the smallpox and one of our mess was sent off."

On January 19, "we left camp at 6 A.M. and marched across the river and camped in the road for we couldn't get any other place for mud and water . . . it rained all day and very cold . . . mud was so much bad that the teams mired all along and was left until morning . . . a detail was made to pull the wagons out of the mud and just as they got ready to go they was ordered to pull the wagons back instead of forward . . . the rebs cut the levy and let the water in."

The army was shortly back in form. "We got orders to march at 6 A.M. and marched out to the warf and laid there all day . . . and went back to town." Each of the next three days they did this and then they "loaded mules and ambulances on board boats . . . I guess we will get off some of these times."

After a few additional trys they were "put on the Lanberry with the brig persia P in toe and left for beuford [Beaufort], some of the boys got seasick." The next day they were "off the boat and marched 18 miles." The next day it was eight miles. The same day the rumor factory reported, "They are making out our papers."

Then it was "15 miles to hickery Post office" with "some fighting in front." After two days of skirmishing and advancing, "The 63 Ill charged the rebs and drove . . . I saw Sam again today."

On February 8, "the troops are tearing the railroads today." On the 11th they "crossed the Edisto River on a pontoon and took Orangeburg depot . . . captured a pontoon train." February 15, "a man died in an ambulance . . . boys buried him while the troops was skirmishing." Columbia, South Carolina, was reached a day later. "Nice town . . . a good portion of the town was burning to knight. . . . So this is the place where secession commenced and it ought to end here."

On March 19, "Some shells exploded this eavening and killed 5 men and wounded 16 . . . we will have to hall them when we leave here. The boys are throwing rockets tonight."

The moving again. "Marched 21 miles, 20 miles, 20 miles, 14 miles, 18 miles, 13 miles, and were within 16 miles of Camden." On March 25, "Some of the foragers were captured and killed and some of the rebs captured and killed and one man killed them [evidently in reprisal] . . . had goose for supper." The next day, "Foragers a little shy today and propose staying close to the troops." But, on the morrow, "the foragers was out again and got some of the nicest hams I ever saw . . . we have had ham and cornbread, molasses and coffee for supper and we are boiling one to take with us if we march tomorrow."

Payday came on March 28 and he says, "I have 8 months paydiew me." In the margin beside this entry, thirteen is multiplied by eight, $13 a month evidently being the monthly pay of a private. "Poor John McClure was killed today and Andy Campbell taken prisoner . . . some four or five others with him . . . Colonel of 63 Ill taken with him . . ."

"Fifteen miles to Pedee River . . . captured 17 pieces of artillery and some prisoners without much fighting. . . . Foraging not so easy . . ."

Three more days and they were in Fayetteville. "The darkeys are plenty . . . plenty of grub . . . good supper . . . lost some of darkey followers . . . nice honey and ham . . . most of the boys on mules and old horses . . ." (Apparently gathered from farms passed.)

Then he records, "Was on ground today where first victory of the Revolution was gained at Moors Creek in 1776."

"Quartered in negro huts . . . boys are raising thunder and awhile are shooting their guns . . . some of the boys in town looking for grub . . ." He then described some released Union soldiers, "some paroled prisoners . . . some of the hardest men I ever saw any place . . . lousy and naked and poor and bony . . . some with Itch . . ."

The next entry: "Nothing going on today only the boys are all gone to town and some are refusing to go on duty. 50 Ill left for Springfield to be mustered out . . . got some stuff from the Sanitary Commission—3 lbs. potatoes, 3 lbs. onions, 3 lbs. Boston Crackers, and some clothing . . . I got one shirt."

The next day was April 1, and "They are making out our papers." This was still going the next day and the next. On April 4, "Well we was mustered out of the service of the United States today . . . went to town and laid on the warf to knight." Then came the notations, "On board the Nevada to Fortress Monroe . . . on Louisiana to Baltimore . . . on train started home . . . Harpers Ferry . . . Cumberland . . . Martinsburg . . ."

His last entry about his service career was dated April 11. Succeeding pages of this diary are torn from the book. Griffith was discharged at Wilmington, North Carolina, and lived until May, 1924.

The only entry of note not connected directly with the war is a recipe for making beer.

❦ CIVIL WAR HAD HORSE MARINES

AN ASSORTED PACKET of Civil War letters, most of them addressed to Miss Martha E. Patten, Ottawa, Illinois, have recently come to attention. Some of these were written by a man who indicated that he was serving in the United States Marine Corps with the gunboat flotilla on the Ohio and Mississippi Rivers.

The letters tell of marine combat in a region near home, instead of in faraway places of the earth. They also correct a long held misbelief that there never have been any horse marines. There's an expression you often hear in the Marine Corps, directed at the teller of tall tales: "Go tell that to the horse marines." Now it appears that, in the Civil War at least, there were horse marines.

The Marine Corps had its beginning on November 10, 1775, when the Continental Congress authorized the enlistment of a small force to supplement ship crews. The first men for the newly created military organization were recruited at the Tunn Tavern, a haven for sturdy souls on Front Street in Philadelphia. This first company was gathered by Robert Mullan, keeper of the tavern, who became their captain.

To attract the kind of men he wanted, Mullan's recruiting poster made great promises. Each man would have one pound of beef or pork each day, as well as a pound of bread. He would have ample flour, raisins, oatmeal, cheese, butter, sugar, and molasses. Moreover, he would be given a daily half-pint of rum or a pint of wine. He was also promised lemonade. According to the recruiting poster, a man was allowed to assign half his pay to a wife, if he had one. This would "keep her from want" while the man was at sea. The poster was rounded out with the assuring statement that each one accepted could, upon his return to port, "cut a Dash on Shore with his girl and his Glass." A century and a quarter later, recruiting posters had become more subdued and simply said, "Join the Marines and See the World." (That's the one that got the writer.)

From the day when Mullan recruited the first company until now, the marines have gone a hectic course over the world. They have fought in all the nation's wars, large and small, recognized and unrecognized. Intervention and marines were long thought of together. "The marines have landed and have the situation well in hand" once was almost a stock expression.

When the Civil War came along, a sprinkling of marines came to the naval yards at Cairo and Mound City in southern Illinois. It was with a group of these that the marine who wrote some of the letters I recently read saw duty. Then, as now, marines were assigned to all kinds of duty. This author of the letters had slodged over horrible roads on foot, but he was also for a time with a unit of mounted marines. He helped to build fortifications and to man them when they were attacked. He fared forth with others to capture men charged with military murder and saw them "hanged by the neck until dead! dead! dead!!!" He served on gunboats, helped to gather rations over the countryside, and joined in raids on the enemy's ammunition depots to return with needed gunpowder.

He vividly describes the horrors of the battlefield with its dead and maimed, and its cries of distress. Never once, however, does he intimate that he wanted to quit before the issue was properly settled.

Since the Civil War, the marines have continued their habit of finding troubled spots. We are glad we knew some of the old breed of Leathernecks and *Teufel Hunden,* typical of that branch of our armed forces who held a kind of roving commission.

Martha E. Patten, who saved these letters must have been an unusual young lady. Her collection of letters came from about fifteen servicemen, several of whom were relatives. They ranged in rank from privates to lieutenants. All expressed admiration and high regard. Some letters carried a more than veiled proposal of marriage. The last letter in the collection she left was addressed to Mrs. Martha E. Linfor, her name after she married the marine in question.

⚜ A MUSIC MASTER GOES FOR A RIDE

ONE WOULD NOT think it logical to select a music teacher to lead one of the most daring cavalry raids of a great war. Nevertheless, this was done by General Grant in 1863 when, busy in his efforts to capture Vicksburg, Mississippi, he decided to make a master stroke.

He would send a cavalry force on a deep raid into the South to tear up railway tracks, destroy military installations and army stores, and to lay waste whatever else was of obvious military value to the Confederacy. In addition to all this, such a raid would divert the attention of the enemy and disrupt his plans.

As commander of this force of raiding horsemen, numbering about 1,700 men from the Sixth Illinois Cavalry, Grant named Brigadier General Benjamin Henry Grierson, a bearded, come-lately cavalryman, but a seasoned music master.

Grierson was born at Pittsburgh, Pennsylvania, on July 8, 1826. At an early age he showed marked aptitude in music, and his parents sent him to an academy in Youngstown, Ohio. After graduation he became a music teacher and band leader there. A short time later, Grierson moved to Jacksonville, Illinois, where he continued to teach music and direct a band. A few years before the Civil War began, he became interested in a mercantile business at Meredosia, near Jacksonville in Morgan County, but maintained an active interest in music. This was the situation when he enlisted as a private in the military service.

Promotion came rapidly. In a short time he became a major and, a bit later as a colonel, he was commander of the Sixth Illinois Cavalry that trained at Shawneetown. The training camp was located on the Henry Eddy farm just south of New Shawneetown. The attractive Eddy residence, still standing west of the railroad and south of Shawneetown High School, was headquarters for the camp. Barracks for the troops and stables for their mounts were nearby, and surrounding fields were drill grounds. It is not so easy now to visualize the fine old house as the headquarters of a military training camp and the center of a bustling army post.

After completing their period of training at the Shawneetown camp, Grierson's regiment marched from there through Eldorado on the Goshen Road and bore westward to entrain on the Illinois Central for action in Kentucky and Tennessee.

It was the privilege of the writer to serve as one of the color bearers in the Memorial Day parade of 1921. As the marchers went over the section of the old roadway from Eldorado to Wolf Creek Cemetery, "Uncle Mun" told of the march his unit had made sixty years earlier over the same section of roadway. He told of the gay spirit the men felt in their excellent, individually owned mounts and equipment, and of the song they sang when they marched past what is now Mahoney Park in the northwest part of town.

It also was the writer's privilege, a few years later, to talk with "Uncle Mun" on the day when he and another veteran named Karnes, who had served with him in the Sixth Cavalry, held their farewell visit at the Karnes house near Galatia. They were the last two known survivors of their regiment.

The force that Grierson had on the storied raid traveled fast, far, and light. They left LaGrange, Tennessee, forty-three miles east of Memphis, on the morning of April 17, 1863. In sixteen days of elapsed time—after series of forced marches and foraging for food and horses needed to replace their jaded mounts—they reached Baton Rouge, Louisiana, on May 2.

They had spread havoc as they went, skirmishing and laying waste a wide strip of country six hundred miles long. All this was over a strange land and over unfamiliar roads. They had destroyed many railway tracks and burned bridges of the Vicksburg and Meridian, and of the New Orleans and Jacksonville railways; thus, they definitely upset the enemy and disrupted his plans.

Altogether it must have been an exciting ride on which the music master took his horsemen. An excellent, recent movie based on the raid —"The Horse Soldiers" with John Wayne—also indicates the excitement. About this significant raid Grant said, "General Grierson was the first officer to set the example of what might be done in the interior of the enemy's country without a base from which to draw supplies." The general plan used by this military amateur was that used later by Sherman when he marched "from Atlanta to the sea."

"For gallant and distinguished service" on this raid Grierson was made a major general of volunteers. After the war he was commissioned as brigadier general in the regular army and retired in 1890. Not at all a bad record for a bandmaster.

Grierson must have been well liked by his men. One survivor, Boyce Mayberry, living in Hamilton County, told of an evening when the men were sitting by a campfire. Mayberry, then eighteen, was strumming a jew's-harp. Grierson passed by and stopped to listen. He soon took the crude instrument, played a few tunes, evidently his favorites, and passed on.

Of the nine known to the writer who served with Grierson, all expressed a savage pride in their old outfit. One of these men, Reverend Frank Wilson at McLeansboro, who served as chaplain and continued a life in the ministry for over fifty years, remarked in his old age, "I shall always be proud to have ridden with Grierson."

❁ *A CONFEDERATE PRISON CAMP*

The centennial of the Civil War is past and southern Illinois is pausing to take note of the role that this section had in the conflict. For those with this interest there are two cemeteries in Alton worth visiting.

One occupies a small portion of the old city cemetery, the one having the Lovejoy monument. Union soldiers, members of the Alton garrison who died at that post during the war, rest in the plot. Watched over by the national flag flown each day and a cannon like those they knew then, their graves are in ordered rows, marked by familiar appearing stones. Lettering on the stonework above the entrance says "U.S. NATIONAL CEMETERY."

The second cemetery is in North Alton. A thin black arrow on a white marker at the intersection of State and Rozier streets at the 2300 block on State points west to the field where 1,354 known war dead are buried. They are a part, but only a part, of the prisoners who died and were buried there. Two words above the pointing arrow tell us that it is a "CONFEDERATE CEMETERY."

A visitor to this burying ground is impressed with its simplicity. The usual array of monuments and gravestones is absent. In fact, only one marker is evident on the five-acre plot enclosed by a sturdy iron fence. Nor is the well-kept, hilly ground crowded with shrubbery or trees.

The lone marker, a square stone shaft about sixty feet tall, stands a short distance within the north entrance gate. On the east side of the shaft, at its bottom, there is an inscription telling visitors that the marker was

> ERECTED BY THE UNITED STATES TO MARK THE BURIAL PLACE
> OF 1,354 CONFEDERATE SOLDIERS WHO DIED HERE AND AT
> THE SMALLPOX HOSPITAL ON THE ADJACENT ISLAND WHILE
> PRISONERS OF WAR AND WHOSE GRAVES CANNOT NOW BE
> IDENTIFIED.

Four large bronze tablets, one on each side of the base beneath the shaft, carry the names of the 1,354 known dead. These names are arranged alphabetically and there are no indications of military rank. After all, why should it matter now?

There is convincing evidence that this listing does not nearly include all who died in the prison or on the adjacent island, the same one toward which Abraham Lincoln and James Shields are said to have journeyed to fight a duel that happily did not take place. Skeletons unearthed in 1936 indicate that many, some say thousands, were buried on the island during the smallpox epidemic that raged at the prison in late 1863 and early 1864, reaching its peak in March of the latter year.

It might be of interest to know something of the Alton penitentiary before it became prominent as a military prison. Completed and occupied in 1833, it was the first prison built by the state. It began with twenty-four cells. By 1857 this number had grown to 286. In 1847 Dorothy Dix, one of America's able advocates of prison reform, cited it as about all that was bad in prison management. By 1860 her efforts, joined by others, had influenced the building of a new penitentiary at Joliet. The one at Alton accordingly was abandoned. For some years the Alton prison had been leased to individuals who operated it. The lease still had several years to run. This was the prison's status when war came.

The army took over the abandoned penitentiary for a military prison and garrisoned it in February, 1862. The first consignment of prisoners arrived on February 9. By April 1, the number had reached 791. At its peak the number totaled five thousand; four thousand of whom were prisoners of war, the balance federal prisoners. Among the recorded admissions are the names of three women. One of these was paroled. The other two died in prison.

Late in 1863 smallpox appeared among the prisoners. For a time its presence was kept secret. When it became known, something like panic resulted. Frantic attempts to escape were made, but few succeeded.

An isolation camp was established on the adjacent island. Records indicate that many hundreds were sent to the island, with no record of their return. Guards, prisoners, and surgeons being sent to the island looked upon the assignment much like one of death. When one knows that mass burials of sixty guards and prisoners together were made in a common grave, they could hardly be blamed. The peak of the scourge was reached in March, 1864. After that, conditions improved somewhat, but still remained grim.

Shortly after the war's end, the prison became only a cluster of buildings wrapped in horrid memories, along with many rows of crudely marked graves. For many years it was not unusual to see some man wandering pensively about, evidently engrossed in thoughts of the time when he was a prisoner of war there.

Why doesn't someone write the full story of the Confederate prison at Alton?

❧ CIVIL WAR REUNIONS

NOT MANY PEOPLE can remember back to the reunions held by Civil War veterans around 1900, but those who do will recall some interesting small details. For example, there were the bronze lapel buttons that had been given to each honorably discharged veteran and were worn proudly. This small button might be called the ancestor of the Victory, the Good Conduct, and the many other medals and campaign bars issued to those serving in later wars.

There also will be memories of old men proudly wearing tattered and moth-eaten remnants of the uniforms brought home at the end of the conflict. One man might have a peculiar cap with a front-slanting top and wide, shiny visor. Another perhaps would wear a cavalryman's hat. A third would have on an old blue jacket with its row of freshly shined brass buttons, any missing gaps being filled with dissimilar ones. Whatever the bit of dress might be, it was worn in simple pride.

A boy with no money to spend at the stands and shows—which did their best to spoil the spirit of the day—would come to stand beside a group of veterans and listen in awe while the men recounted the incidents of their service days. In that way he heard stories of Grierson's Cavalry raid and of Hood's fierce charges at Atlanta. Lookout Mountain was stormed again and the siege lines moved in to strangle and capture Vicksburg.

Their stories were filled with the cold, snows, rains, and mud of winter, and the dust and heat of summer. They told of comrades, often their boyhood friends, who perished. They seemed to derive a sad pleasure from relating their unrecorded stories. Any boy who stood respectfully by and listened came away with an enduring interest in Civil War history and a sober respect for the men who bore the brunt of it. Such an attentive listener also seemed to encourage a bearded veteran to talk.

At many of these reunions, campfires like those of service evenings were rekindled. In cooking pots and smoke-blackened tins, men cooked beans and brewed their black coffee just as they had done forty years before. This they drank from tin cups, as near the boiling point as they could. One old man is recalled who brought a tin preserve can with a wire bail and said it was the one he brought home at the end of the war.

On one occasion army hardtack was served. Those with teeth strong enough nibbled at it. Others dunked it in their hot coffee to soften the almost rock-hard biscuits. This was a re-enactment of an almost universal field practice. Some have said that "Coffee won the war."

A second old man brought along an army musket with its steel ramrod. While others made coffee, he casually took his ramrod, impaled a hunk of meat he had, and broiled it over the fire. Some bits of this he doled out to complete a typical evening meal, like millions eaten by soldiers in the field.

At another time some men who had "messed" together a lifetime earlier borrowed a skillet and made flapjacks. It was interesting to observe these men as they went about their task. A mixed batter was poured into the greased skillet and placed above a bed of glowing coals.

When it was thought that the bottom had been cooked sufficiently, the flapjack was turned. It was here that the cook's skill was tested. He had no long-handled pancake turner and perforce must use the skillet. With a quick, deft movement that combined a twist and jerk, he satisfied himself that the flapjack was not sticking. It was then adroitly tossed into the air in a manner that caused it to turn over, and carefully caught so that it would land flat in the skillet. Many men took just pride in this skill.

These simple practices, re-enacted at many an old soldiers' reunion, were like those carried out countless millions of times by campaigning soldiers. They revealed a part of a Civil War veteran's life that seldom occurs in texts.

Chapter 14

Rivers

🏵 *THE DARK BEND OF THE AMBRAW*

The french spelled the name of the river Embarrass, and pronounced it Em-ber-rah. The spelling remains the same but things have happened to the pronunciation. The English came and called it Em-braw. Now it is am-braw. This strange name for a river is explained by the fact that its sluggishness, and countless bends filled with driftwood and snags, made navigation difficult enough to embarrass the best of boatmen.

Whatever the pronunciation, it still is a small, dull, and muddy river that meanders hither and yon in an aimless and indecisive way across Jasper County, Illinois, and on through Lawrence County to join the Wabash. Before the coming of railroads, it was declared a navigable stream and numerous flatboats, to carry products down-river, were built on its banks at Blakman's Mill, just south of Charleston.

In early days the dense swampy woodlands along the stream were difficult to penetrate, and building of roadways was practically impossible. Settlers did not look upon the region with favor. The densely wooded and swampy region southeast of Newton and beyond the Embarrass soon became known as the Dark Bend, now shortened to The Bend. It continued to be a neglected region and government surveyors did not come to run section lines there until after Illinois became a state. In fact, their surveys were not completed until 1839. None of this land was sold until the forties and very little of it until the mid-forties. Nevertheless, it did not remain entirely unpeopled.

It attracted a curious lot of settlers, more properly called squatters, who often came to avoid the long arm of the law. Among these were robbers, horse thieves, counterfeiters, and sundry other lawbreakers. This lawless element soon developed a kind of mutual defense fraternity that thwarted the arrest and conviction of its members. It was almost impossible to convict a Dark Bender. These bands continued to be an annoyance for many years; one group about Chauncey remained active until after 1856.

This swampland into which men came to squat proved to be an excellent feeding ground for livestock. Horses and cattle thrived on the lush grass, and hogs fattened on the mast of pecan, hickory, and oak. These squatters in hiding could thus easily manage for plenty of meat. They simply went into the woods, selected the hog they wanted, and shot it, regardless of its ownership. To remove all evidence, they would cut off the head of the pig and toss it away. Tradition has it that Greasy Creek and Hog Jaw Pond came by their names in this manner. One man apprehended scalding a headless hog—a distinct violation of law—pleaded that "Yuh jes caint scald a hog good with its haid on." His expression became a colloquialism.

Cattle, horses, and hogs that strayed or were "enticed" into Dark Bend were generally considered lost. Few dared to go there searching for them; they apparently believed that they also might be "lost."

Counterfeiters moved in early. One of these, a "Doctor" Sulver, came with his son-in-law in the very early 1820's. It was this man, according to legend, who set up the forge which was found many years later on the bank of a branch that has since then been known as Mint Creek. Other counterfeiters followed.

The beginning of the end of the reign of the lawless in the Dark Bend country came when Joseph Picquet from Alsace in France prospected for a colony location and selected the region about present-day Ste. Marie. Here he bought thousands of acres of land to which his relatives and friends came from Europe to form a *Colonie de Freres,* or Colony of Brothers. This group started arriving in the late forties.

About 1850 German immigrants began to settle around the fringes of Dark Bend. Despite the fact that some of their barns and houses burned mysteriously, they stayed and others came until, finally, the dark days of the Dark Bend were ended.

Today the land is cleared of its dense forests and drained. Mailboxes beside the gravel roadways bear many German names, those of the people who came to settle and "civilize" the locality that once knew a very different way of life.

❧ *LOCKS AND DAMS ON THE OHIO*

LOCKS AND DAMS across the Ohio River appear rather drab to many who stop to look. However, as more is known about them, they become more interesting, and their importance in river traffic takes on more meaning.

At normal stages of the river, the water surface at the first Ohio dam at Pittsburgh is 710 feet above sea level. At Cairo at low water stage the river level is just less than 271 feet above the sea. Thus, it is seen that the river drop between Point Bridge at Pittsburgh to Cairo Point where it joins the Mississippi is 439 feet, enough to make it, normally, a rapidly flowing stream. This drop, of course, is not at a uniform rate.

At many places there are rocky ledges across the stream. At one time these caused rapids and, at lower stages, many rocks were exposed while others were only slightly submerged. The river sometimes was so shallow that a man could wade across it at a point above Cave-in-Rock, about where Dam No. 50 now is. There were numerous other such places between there and Pittsburgh. These shallow and rocky stretches seriously restricted the use of the river at some seasons. At lower stages passing them was risky, even for skilled rivermen with boats of shallower draft.

The U.S. Army Corps of Engineers undertook to remove some of the danger to navigation by building dams across the stream, situated in such a manner as to deepen the water over rocky ledges. For this purpose more than fifty dams have been built between Pittsburgh and Cairo. These have turned the river into a kind of canal or meandering water stairway with high and unevenly spaced treads, the kind that might have appealed to Paul Bunyan had he chosen to come wading down the Ohio.

Four of the more than fifty dams are along the Illinois section of the river. The first one that boats approach coming downstream on the Illinois border is Dam No. 50 near Cave-in-Rock. It is easily seen from the hilltop above the storied cave. Dam No. 51 is at Golconda; No. 52 is at Brookport; and No. 53 is at Olmsted.

The dam at Cave-in-Rock is on the left, or on the Kentucky side, of the river and hence is not so easily observed from the Illinois shore. The others named have their locks on the right or Illinois shore, and one can get close enough to see them operated without leaving the car.

The largest tows on the river appear cumbersome and unwieldy as they are pushed along, and they are. Many of them carrying the largest size or "jumbo" barges are 105 feet wide and as much as 1,000 feet long. If the total length of the tow is more than 600 feet, it is passed through the 110 feet by 600 feet locks in sections. It is interesting to see, and often hear, a pilot and mate maneuver the front section of such a tow into and through such a lock without touching either walls or gates. Once the front section is properly placed, the rear portion is detached and backed out to allow the closing of the gates. After this the lock is flooded to elevate barges going upstream or partially drained to lower those going downstream. The remainder of a long tow then passes through the lock in like manner and is coupled to the detached part and proceeds to the next lock.

The operation of the locks appears to be effortless. In fact, it is practically so, since it requires no more than the opening and closing of a few valves. The flowing water does the work of swinging the enormous gates.

If the visitor is statistically inclined, he can find much of interest in the study of a particular dam and lock. The one at Brookport is used as an example. In 1959, the latest year for which figures were available, more than twenty million tons of assorted freight, enough to fill approximately a half-million railway freight cars, passed through these locks.

The types of cargoes were varied. About 600,000 tons were stone, sand, or gravel. Over 6,000,000 tons were coal and coke. Some 7,500,000 tons were oil and gasoline. There were 1,400,000 tons of assorted chemicals and 2,800,000 tons of steel and steel products. The balance was unclassified.

The total of freight carried on the Ohio in 1959 was more than eighty million tons. Converted into ton-miles, this amounts to more than eighteen billion, or equivalent to carrying one ton eighteen billion miles or a hundred round-trips to the sun.

The Ohio is indeed a busy river and will surely remain so. After all, transportation is one of America's and the world's major problems, and its future is being scientifically studied and planned. Cairo may yet become the great transportation center of which its planners dreamed.

A study program of enlarging locks, deepening channels, and improving a system of signals is kept in operation.

🌸 BARGING COAL THEN AND NOW

THE MINING and shipping of coal has gone merrily along in southern Illinois for more than 150 years. In that time it has changed much. This became apparent a few days ago on a halting trip between Carbondale and Chester.

The first stop along the way was made at the east end of the highway bridge across the Big Muddy where old Highway 13 enters Murphysboro. Just south of this stopping place is the spot, now covered by the railroad dump, where the mouth of the first shipping coal mine in Illinois began. Dirt and debris that have fallen down the bluff, along with grading for the railroad that runs alongside the river, have left no visible traces of the old entry. Access at other places, however, reveal the old workings under the higher land east of the river.

The coal mined here was hauled in small cars over a wooden railroad to barges for shipment down the river. These barges, then generally called flatboats or broadhorns, were small by present-day standards. Information left us indicates that the larger of them would carry about 150 tons of coal. Smaller barges in use now carry about 900 tons; larger ones carry up to 3,600 tons. At that time the very small tonnage of the earlier barges represented many long days of labor for the miner with only a pick and shovel. Entries in the records of the Port of New Orleans tell of coal barges from the Big Muddy arriving there as early as 1810. It is interesting to stop at the site of the first shipping mine in Illinois and picture the primitive scene.

A second stop on the trip was made at the large coal loading dock beside the Mississippi about a mile south from the place where Highway 3 crosses Mary's River below Chester. Here, on a level below that of the highway, the Missouri Pacific Railroad built its present structures about 1950. Since the docks are on a lower level than the highway and are screened by young trees, they can be seen only poorly by the passing motorist. A better view may be had by parking on a drive-out beside the pavement and going to the west guardrail.

The loading dock really is a row of fourteen immense, steel-clad piers about sixteen feet in diameter and are anchored on the bedrock at the river bottom. These piers extend about seventy feet above the river, even at flood stage. They support the buildings and equipment necessary to convey coal to waiting barges. They also carry an arrangement of cables necessary for moving barges into proper positions for loading.

Coal to load the waiting barges reaches them from the railroad over an endless belt more than six hundred feet long. This belt, turned up slightly at the edges to prevent the coal from falling off, conveys a rapidly moving stream of coal its full width and more than eight inches deep. It carries 1,250 tons, two and a half million pounds, of coal to barges each day. This is more than the Big Muddy mine already mentioned has produced in its lifetime.

If one stops to look early in the morning, he will see hundreds of hopper-bottomed cars on the gently sloping tracks north of the shed where the coal is dumped at the rate of more than a large car each two minutes. The brakes on waiting cars are released and the car rolls into position. Its hoppers are opened while a heavy vibrating shaker is lowered on its rim and started. In a minute a large carload of coal is completely emptied into the immense pit below.

Though the pit is covered by a grating through which one could not fall, the visitor still has an unpleasant, eerie feeling as he looks from the walkway into the yawning space. From the bottom of this pit, coal is conveyed along the rapidly moving belt to the end of the long boom where it falls into waiting barges.

The contribution of southern Illinois to the nation's coal supply is partially realized as one watches the operations at this loading dock.

It is only when one stops to look at this major operation and compares it with the dinky barges to which Valentine Taylor and his one mule hauled coal from the first shipping mine in Illinois, that the progress of coal mining in the state and its shipment by water becomes most impressive. More freight is carried on the rivers today than was carried in the boom days of steamboating. It is not nearly as spectacular, however.

Coal shipping from southern Illinois becomes even more impressive when one stops to recall that only a small proportion of the coal from the region goes through the shipping docks described.

If only the strip mines would carefully level off their diggings and plant them in trees!

🌊 THE WORLD'S MOST UNUSUAL NAVY

IF SOMEONE should remark about our navy on the "Western Waters," most persons would think immediately about our war craft on the Pacific. In Civil War days "Western Waters" would have had a definite meaning. The term then was applied to the Ohio, the Mississippi, and their tributaries, all definitely without a navy now. At one time it had a real navy, one made up of a few hundred craft. Some of these were among the more heavily armored ones afloat.

This unusual navy that quickly grew up remains unique. History offers little to parallel it. Its story should hold more than passing interest for southern Illinois, for it was on the six-mile stretch of the Ohio from Mound City to Cairo that this strange flotilla had its rendezvous. Here much of it was assembled, built, and outfitted. Here it also returned for repairs after battle. Numerous steamers were made into gunboats. After the war many surviving boats were turned back from gunboats to steamers.

This assorted flotilla came into being early in the war, served its purpose, quietly vanished, and was almost forgotten. It began within a week after the fall of Sumter when James B. Eads of St. Louis was called to Washington and asked to design and build war craft for use on the rivers. Captain John Rodgers was loaned from the navy to assist Eads. In July three gunboats, the Lexington, the Tyler, and the Conestoga were completed at Cincinnati. These were wooden vessels built at the insistence of Rodgers. Low river stages delayed their arrival at Cairo for six weeks.

In the month of July bids were asked and accepted for seven others, all to be armored. Delivery was promised by October 10. Work began promptly. A force of four thousand men worked day and night to build the hulls. Subcontractors worked to have boilers, engines, equipment, and armor ready.

The first of these seven boats, the *St. Louis,* was launched on October 12. These seven boats, known as the Cairo class, were built on standard river hulls. They were about 175 feet long, 75 feet wide, and had a draft of six feet. This allowed them to operate on principal streams. Each carried thirteen guns and had a casement or belt of armor sloping up from the water line.

Before the seven boats of the Cairo class were completed, two other powerful boats, the *Benton* and the *Essex,* former snag boats, were converted into gunboats. They had the usual casements of sloping armor plus three inches of plate on their hulls. They were three hundred feet long, formidable craft in any navy of that time. These nine boats, seven of the Cairo class plus the two last mentioned, made up the hard core of the navy on the Western Waters. Much credit for victories at Fort Henry, Fort Donelson, and Memphis was due them for the services they rendered.

About the same time a new series of river craft appeared. They were steamers converted into rams. Each had a below-waterline extension, a beak, built on its front. This made the entire boat into a kind of projectile that could be aimed at the opposing craft. They were used successfully by both the Union and Confederate forces. Boats of the Ram Fleet came from designs and plans made by Colonel Charles Ellett, Jr., who commanded the first group. A book, the *History of the Ram Fleet and Marine Brigade,* tells their full story.

The next two boats added to the Cairo flotilla were the Choctaw and the Lafayette, side-wheel steamers. These were 280 feet long and were armored with one inch of steel having an inch of India rubber beneath to "make the shot bounce off." That didn't work so well.

One of the storied boats added to the river fleet was the *Eastland,* a fine boat 280 feet long. This boat, partially completed, was captured by the Lexington, Tyler, and Conestoga on a daring raid up the Tennessee in early February of 1862. It was taken to Cairo, completed, and commissioned in August. Its record was an enviable one until March, 1864, when it ran aground in the Red River and was blown up to prevent its capture by the Confederates.

In the fall and winter of 1862 about twenty "tinclads" were added to the flotilla. These were small river steamers with a half or three-quarters inch of armor plate. None of the tinclads drew more than three feet of water, some less than eighteen inches. They could go up many creeks and were most useful against guerrillas.

After the clash of the *Monitor* and *Virginia Merrimac* in April, 1862, the demand for boats of the Monitor type increased. Eads accordingly built two such boats with turrets. They were followed by four others, larger and screw-driven. These were double turreted craft. Much improved over previous models, many of their best features still are used in warships. These four boats were the *Winnebago,* the *Kickapoo,* the *Milwaukee,* and the *Chickasaw.* To all these boats should be added the many barges built to carry mortars.

The Western Waters indeed saw an unconventional naval war. It can hardly be compared with any other, before or since.

❦ GUNBOATS OF THE RIVERS

INFORMED PERSONS agree that Cairo, at the very southern tip of Illinois, was an important military center during the Civil War. The farthest south point in free-state territory, Cairo was a point toward which hastily gathered forces of both the North and the South were rushed, the North winning the race by a few miles. In the earlier years of the conflict it easily was the most important western military center, the one where the national forces were assembled and organized into armies that were sent afield to subdue the rebellious South.

The names of many men who became famous for their part in the war first came into prominence here. Among the Illinois men were Grant and Grierson, Lawler and Logan, McClernand and Turchin, and perhaps a full dozen others who attained general officer rank. Army activities there were great. Its often repeated designation as a military rendezvous is justified.

In addition to the army activities centering in and about Cairo, a unique development that did much to change military history grew there. Cairo was the gathering place of armored naval craft for use on the Western Waters. These craft did much to radically alter earlier naval practices.

It is true that some armored craft had been built earlier and had shown their usefulness. France had one such vessel, the *Cloire,* in 1859. Britain had the *Warrior* in 1860. Floating batteries on armored barges had been used effectively in the Crimean War. The way already had been pointed. The United States, however, did not have a single armored naval vessel at the outbreak of the conflict.

When Union forces abandoned the naval yard at Norfolk, Virginia, early in the conflict, they scuttled an uncompleted wooden ship that was being built there. The Confederates promptly raised the hull and began to make it into an armored vessel. When the North knew of this they sought means of defending themselves against such a craft.

John Ericsson, a Swedish born engineer, the inventor of the screw propeller that still is universally used, proposed a solution. He offered plans for an armored craft, even less vulnerable than the *Virginia,* nee *Merrimac,* that the Confederates were hastening to completion.

Events moved rapidly. An act to authorize the building of an armored craft was passed August 3. On August 7 Ericsson submitted his plans. They were accepted by the naval board September 16. The contract for building the ship was awarded October 4. The armored ship was launched January 3 and hastily fitted for service. At eleven o'clock on the morning of March 6, the tugboat *Seth Low* started for Hampton Roads with the newly commissioned *Monitor,* for that was the name of the vessel in tow. They arrived after nightfall on the eighth.

The small *Monitor* took position behind one of the federal boats to screen itself from the view of the Confederates. The *Virginia* returned the next morning to complete its planned destruction of the remaining wooden vessels of the U.S. Navy, begun on the afternoon before. The vessels had been little better than sitting ducks.

At the approach of the *Virginia* the queer-looking *Monitor* steamed out to meet it. The historic first battle of ironclads was on. The *Virginia* retired to its base with neither scoring a decisive victory. One thing, however, was demonstrated: the long age of wooden ships and iron men was ended.

Even before the clash of these two armored vessels, the leaders of both sides had foreseen that armored ships were coming. Three days after the fall of Sumter, James B. Eads, a retired St. Louis man with engineering abilities, was told to expect an important call from Washington. It came, asking that Eads come to Washington for a conference. Arriving there, he was asked to undertake the building of a flotilla of armed river boats for use on the Ohio, Mississippi, and their tributaries. Eads accepted.

In a short time the work of converting steamboats into armored fighting craft and the building of new vessels began. This work centered at the Mound City shipyard that had begun operations in 1856. The national government took the yards over. The Ohio from Mound City to Cairo quickly became a great naval yard with four thousand men working around the clock.

Large barges held blacksmith and machine shops. Likewise other barges served as warehouses where supplies were stored. Some barges became woodworking shops where timbers were shaped for vessels being built or for damaged ones being repaired. There also were barracks for workmen and military guards. An old cut shows great lumberyards on shore with oxen dragging timbers about.

Prominent in all this were the sloping shipways, remnants of which still may be seen. Up these ways the largest river craft were drawn on wheeled carriages, pulled by great chains wound on a steel shaft hundreds of feet long. Old drawings, bits of description, and treasured mental images of the "ways" as they once were impress their great importance.

❦ *IT IS A GREAT RIVER*

THIS IS WRITTEN after twelve days and more than seventeen hundred miles as a nonpaying passenger aboard the Mississippi Valley Barge Line Company's giant towboat, *Valley Transporter*. The journey was from Cincinnati, Ohio, to the port of New Orleans by way of St. Louis.

The *Valley Transporter* did not make the journey alone. At times it was nudging along as much as five acres of barges loaded with a full twenty thousand tons of assorted freight. This would be equivalent to about five hundred railway carloads, or approximately five full-sized trains.

This journey made more impressive the fact that the river still is a great freight carrier. It also left a conviction that the river continues to cast its spell over the men who follow it and that the romance of the river life has not vanished. It also served as a reminder that the rivers within Illinois and along its borders have from the first coming of white men played a major role in the region's development. Without doubt they will continue to do so.

At first the rivers were the ready-made roadways over which settlers came to locate homes and develop the country. It was to the Ohio-Mississippi and their tributaries that these same settlers turned to ship their surplus products to distant markets. They still are doing this, and in an ever-increasing volume. Shipping history is continually being made.

It was principally over the rivers that the region first exported its products before other means of transportation were developed. Numerous meat packing and curing plants, such as those at Chester and New Haven, sent their output to market in this manner. Pig iron left the furnaces in Hardin County, as well as from those at Grand Tower, by water. Great loads of steel products from scrap iron to massive machinery still are promiment in today's river cargoes.

Joe Shetler shipped many flatboat loads of potatoes from the Pope County village that was named for him. Mixed cargoes went out from a hundred places. William Boon loaded such a cargo at the mouth of Big Kinkaid Creek west of present-day Murphysboro near the end of December, 1811, and was on the Mississippi with it when the New Madrid earthquake occurred. There are records of numerous other boats being loaded and sent out from the old town of Brownsville and from Murphysboro. Others left Equality; some went from Mitchellville on the south fork of the Saline River. More were loaded at the site of the old watermill about two miles southeast of Broughton. In fact, about every stream large enough to afford passage of a medium-sized barge—say twenty by forty feet—has a flatboat tradition.

In some cases history is repeating itself. As early as 1810 coal was being mined at a slope shaft just below the bridge on old Route 13 at the east side of Murphysboro and carried on barges to New Orleans. Now, more than 150 years after the first shipment from the Big Muddy Mine, great barges are continually leaving the coal loading dock beside the Mississippi on the road to Chester. In two cases history is reversing itself. At an early date much salt was being shipped downstream from Shawneetown. Now great barges of salt are coming upstream from the Louisiana mines. Alcoholic beverages are another reverse. In 1834 Cincinnati made and shipped down-river 5,500 barrels of whiskey. A single tank barge recently carried more than 375,000 gallons of wine, reloaded from a French tank ship at New Orleans, upstream to Chicago in one trip.

Anything like complete information concerning the amount and kind of freight being sent along the rivers in earlier days is difficult to find. Some spot selections, however, may be interesting for comparison today. In 1820, a total of 2,400 flatboats passed the falls of the Ohio at Louisville. In 1830 this had increased to 4,000 with a cargo total of 160,000 tons. (The average cargo then was forty tons. Now it is above six hundred tons.)

One hundred fifty-two boats are recorded as having passed Vincennes on the Wabash in 1826. In November, 1834, there was an average of twenty-five boats passing Shawneetown during the daylight hours of each day. In the same year sixty were counted passing Memphis on one day and seventy-seven on another.

Despite the fact that the greatest amount of freight in history is being moved along the rivers today, it still is a lonely river. This is especially true along the Mississippi from Cairo to New Orleans. Most of its banks down to the very channel are covered with a tangled growth of young forest. Except for short distances where they are not required, there are high levees on either side. The trees and levees seldom permit a glimpse of the countryside. About all one sees are a few smoke stacks, the roofs of higher buildings, and intriguing church spires. At higher river stages the boatman has the queer experience of riding along on a water level that would submerge many lower buildings if there were no levees. Because of these and other factors, the river remains almost a world apart. Perhaps it will ever be so. Drive down to the Mississippi or Ohio some day, watch a big tow go by, and try to realize that more than eighty million tons of freight move in like manner along these inland waterways in a year.

Chapter 15

Towns—New and Old

❧ SHILOH HILL IS WORTH VISITING

MANY SOUTHERN Illinois villages have been planned, laid out, and begun with promise. A number have grown into towns of importance, while others have slowly vanished. A few, only a few, have lasted on through the years with little or no growth, yet they have stubbornly refused to die. Typical of such villages is Shiloh Hill in southern Randolph County, a few miles west of Campbell Hill on the way to another cluster of houses known as Wine Hill.

Long before the village of Steuben, for that was Shiloh Hill's first name, was platted in 1856, the community had achieved some importance. It was the location of Shiloh Hill College and had a widely known blacksmith and machine shop. Some reminders of the college survive and the charter, granted it by the Illinois Legislature well over a century ago, still is in existence. The sturdy building that housed the college remains with some antiquated school desks, long discarded textbooks, and odd fixtures like sections of plastered walls painted to serve as blackboards. Each year finds a decreasing number of those who attended the school, a good lifetime ago, returning to stroll over the school grounds and to muse in the deserted rooms.

Shiloh College ceased to operate about a hundred years ago, and the building was rented to the local public school district. That plan was continued until 1954 when school consolidation sent the Shiloh Hill pupils to other schools. Now an occasional farm or community meeting is held in the old building. Otherwise it stands unused. The college still exists legally and remains as a kind of memorial to a group of pioneers who established the region's first school and later converted it into a college. The story of the school provides an illustration of the early efforts to provide the means of a better education. A reading of the minutes of the meeting at which the school was created in 1832 is interesting for the earnestness and progressiveness shown. Free textbooks were provided to the pupils there 125 years ago.

The first plat of a village shows College Square in the northeast corner of the town and Public Square in the southwest corner. Both remain well-kept and attractive grounds. The school lawn is mowed by adjoining property owners in order "to have it look well." The Public Square has been made into a picnic ground with ample shade and tables and with a large concrete floored area where youngsters play at basketball and where dances are sometimes held. This also is the place where the annual homecoming is held on the third Saturday in August. Old-timers come to these meetings to renew acquaintances, others to reaffirm their loyalty.

Another enduring institution is the village's fine old blacksmith shop that has stood at the southeast corner of the village since its founding. To those who would peer into the past, the smithy offers some fine glimpses. Here one can see some of the ancient ironworking craft still practiced, as well as many ghosts from earlier shops. The ring of the anvil as the smith bounces his hammer on it will arouse many echoes for those who knew such shops before acetylene and arc welding did so much to supplant the earlier smithing. By the practiced ear of some listeners, the size of the object being worked upon as well as the type of work being done can be determined.

The present shop has gone modern to a degree. There is an electric motor with shafts, pulleys, belts, and gears to supply power that once came from a kerosene motor, and before that, from horsepower or manpower by way of a crank. The motor operates a drill press, hacksaw, bandsaw, planer, grinder, and bench saw. Smaller motors with blowers attached take the place of the leather bellows that the smith would occasionally allow an eager boy to pull. Many of the old-time tasks still must be done by hand.

Every corner of the old shop has something of interest. The east end, shortened by twenty-two feet when the two-story section that once was used for wagonmaking was removed, has much left to indicate the way in which wagons were made. There are patterns for axles, bolsters, standards, frogs, tongues, hounds, and felloes for different-sized wheels. An adjustable roller arrangement shows how heavy strap iron was rolled into tires of proper size. Some of the once plentiful stock of skeins and thimbles, or housings, are still there. Two tire shrinkers remain, one to shrink hot tires and the other to shrink cold ones.

Then there are spoke shaves, a cone for forming hub bands, the stample in the floor where wheels being worked upon were fastened on top of a barrel stand for convenience. Drawing knives, tenon cutters, spoke pulls, coping saws, and numerous other tools peculiar to the wagonmaking trade are all about. There is even a paint grinder that was used to grind and mix the lead and oil that painted Shiloh Hill wagons seventy-five years ago. The shop here is much like the one where the Studebaker brothers began the manufacture of their noted line of horse-drawn vehicles that became so famous over America.

About the rim of the forges are the headers, swages, cold-cuts, hot-cuts, chisels, hammers, and tongs in endless varieties. A rack on the wall holds a few horsehoes of various design.

To those interested in local history, an afternoon visit to Shiloh Hill and a picnic in its pleasant little park should be enjoyable.

❦ THE AMERICAN BOTTOM

SECTIONS OF southern Illinois answer to various names. One of these distinctive regions, termed the American Bottom, lies between the Mississippi River and the bluffs, from one to seven miles to the east. From south to north it extends from the mouth of the Kaskaskia River to the city of Alton, occupying about four hundred square miles of area, approximately 288,000 acres. Portions of it are in Randolph, Monroe, St. Clair, and Madison counties. It is perhaps as fertile as any equal area of farmland in the world.

The American Bottom is really the silt-filled, rocky channel of an ancient river that carried water from the melting ice sheets to the north a few million years ago. As the ice sheet melted away and its flow lessened, the once wide and rocky channel filled with silt, in some places to a depth of more than a hundred feet. Only a small channel, just large enough to carry the present Mississippi River, remained to wander across the alluvial plain.

When white men came to the vicinity after the visit of Joliet and Marquette, they found it a region abounding in plant and animal life, a land that had at an earlier time supported a relatively dense Indian population. The crops the American settlers planted flourished beyond expectations. It was a fruitful region in which they established their settlements.

It must have been a delightful country, especially when viewed as a place for farming. One writer describes it as "beyond all belief, the only spot that travelers have not exaggerated."

Just at the time the French seemed to have become well and solidly established, the French and Indian Wars came. In 1763 the French admitted defeat and ceded the land to the British who came to occupy it in 1765. After another thirteen years, George Rogers Clark conquered the region for Virginia. The men coming with Clark liked the country they found. When they returned to their homes in the east they carried glowing accounts of the country.

Some of Clark's men returned to settle in the new land. Neighbors listened to their glowing descriptions and came with them. One of these groups, led by Shadrach Bond, Sr., settled on the rich bottom land. Because settlers from eastern colonies were principal settlers in the new region, it became known as the American Bottom, a name it still bears.

The story of the American Bottom would fill volumes. The countryside is replete with places and individuals of interest and significance. The names of many who shaped the early history of the state are closely associated with the region.

Among the places with stories of interest are Cahokia, Fort de Chartres, Prairie du Rocher, Kaskaskia, Bellefontaine, Whiteside Station, Piggot's Fort, and the Pierre Menard home. It was at Cahokia that the first church mission was established in 1699 and it was here that the great Indian, Pontiac, came to his end.

Fort de Chartres was the last of three French forts built on or near the site and was the greatest military fortification on the continent at that time. This last fort, begun in 1753 and completed in 1756, cost a million dollars, for that time a great sum. In 1763 it was surrendered to the British. It is said of this great fort that it never fired one shot in anger.

Fort de Chartres has at least one other distinction. It was from here that soldiers were sent to help capture George Washington at Fort Necessity on July 3, 1754. Its surrender to the British at the close of the French and Indian Wars definitely ended the hope of French empire in the Illinois country.

The village of Prairie du Rocher, four miles east of Fort de Chartres has existed since 1722. In this village and in the vicinity about it, some of the customs, practices, lore and beliefs of the early French survived the longest. The careful searcher still can find lingering bits of lore peculiar to the early French. A visit to the Prairie du Rocher on New Year's Eve, when the ancient *La Guiannée* is observed, is a treat to students interested in the folklore of the people who settled there.

This could go on at great length. The American Bottom has many a story to tell to a listening ear.

❧ FROM FLORENCE TO GRAYVILLE

A MEMBER of the Southern Illinois Editorial Association invited the writer to the organization's picnic at Grayville. Feeling friendly toward editors in general, the invitation was accepted. The inviter almost spoiled it, however, by adding, "You'll find nothing unusual about Grayville." Naturally, we didn't agree.

The writer went home to prowl through notes in his garage-library, search his memory, stop to talk with people in Carmi, and look at some county records. Soon he was convinced that Grayville really has been different.

First, it got off to a somewhat confusing start "At a Stone which is placed 22 poles and five feet South of Said NE quarter Corner of Section twenty township No three South Range 14 West." With this point of departure definitely fixed, the town site is carefully described in eight closely written ledger pages. With much freewheeling spelling, the "cize," "dimentions," and "dementions" along with the names of streets that "sepparate" the "Lotts innumeratted" are given. Whatever may be said about the spelling, one can't easily mistake the words.

The survey and plat was made by "John Storms, County Surveyor of White County, State of Illinois" for "Thomas Bishop, Proprietor of the Town Florence," for that was the first name of a town at the site of Grayville. Notes and plat were filed at Carmi on July 12, 1836.

Surveyor Storms evidently planned to have little sneaking in alleys, for only three were included in the plat. To these three he gave the names of Little Ally, Dark Ally, and High Ally. Incidentally, each alley was a blind one.

In 1849, thirteen years after Florence had been platted, a second town was surveyed by the same John Storms. It likewise began at "The large Stone which is placed 22 poles and five feet south . . ." Like the first town, this second one is described over several pages. It lay east of earlier Florence and was named Grayville for the four Grays listed, along with two Griffings as proprietors.

Storms' spelling seems to have improved somewhat during the thirteen years, but he still used few alleys and thus added to the problems of present-day utility companies.

The combined towns prospered. A plank road leading to Albion was begun in 1850. The toll gate for this road was located about a mile north of town. At the same time another plank road was being built toward New Harmony, Indiana. This road was opened November, 1851, with a celebration at New Harmony where, the Grayville *Advertiser* revealed, "many fair ladies danced in bloomers," then a new article of women's apparel. The *Advertiser* stoutly defended their privilege to do so.

Great sawmills came early to Grayville. There were several stave mills, one producing four million staves a year. The Empire Mills were the greatest producers of flour in that section of Illinois. Ten thousand hogs were slaughtered and packed at Grayville each year. It definitely was a prosperous and progressive community.

Grayville was not backward in cultural progress either. William Dobell, writing to his sister in England on January 7, 1842, told of the rising interest in schools in the English settlement. He expressed satisfaction at the friendly attitude toward schools in the town and expressed hope that all there would soon learn to read and write.

That this interest did not die out soon is shown by the formation of educational and cultural facilities. A literary society came in 1872, a normal college in 1879, and a military band in 1879 when only two members already could play instruments. This band became the Ninth Regiment Band, well known for several years. A philharmonic society was formed in 1880. The Odd Fellows and Masons came about 1850. Earlier than these, however, was the coming of churches about 1837 and the Sons of Temperance in 1849. This first temperance group was followed by several others.

On a military basis, Grayville has some claims to distinction. Revolutionary War veterans came to live in this region. It has furnished the military with its quota of men from lowly privates to admirals. At one time, however, it was a locality of divided loyalties. This was during the Civil War, when according to a letter from Sydney Spring to Governor Yates, written on May 2, 1864, seventy or eighty members of the Knights of the Golden Circle paraded openly on the streets of the town under command of an ex-senator named Sam Martin. The letter stated that Martin had declared that if he fought at all it would be for the South.

After all, perhaps there are some interesting stories about Grayville. I believe the one extending the invitation was wrong when he said, "You'll find nothing unusual about Grayville."

❧ *SHAWNEETOWN*

IN 1949 THE Catholic Church at Cahokia observed the ending of its first 250 years of continuous existence. The settlement of Prairie du Rocher began much more than two hundred years ago. Shiloh Methodist Church near Belleville recently observed its one hundred and fiftieth anniversary. In the past decade many places in southern Illinois have marked their centennials. Perhaps it can be said that the region is growing up.

Shawneetown recently came to observe its susquicentennial. It had completed 150 years of corporate existence. The settlement really is older than that, for it dates back to the time when Michael Sprinkle came to locate his shop there several years earlier.

Sprinkle, an artisan who combined the trades of blacksmith and gunsmith in the shop he established at Shawneetown as early as 1800, was the first settler of record at the place where the old Gallatin County village now stands. Even before the coming of Sprinkle there was a village of the Shawnee Indians there where traders and trappers stopped. It also was the point on the river nearest to the place where the Indians had made salt at the saline springs for many centuries.

By 1800 a mighty migration of peoples was getting underway. Shawneetown found itself one of the logical gateways to an inviting territory. Roadways soon were extended from this central point and a stream of immigrants began to cross the Ohio by the Shawneetown ferry and to move inland. For many years it remained the most important port of entry into the Illinois Country.

The volume of production at the saline springs steadily increased, and they became a principal source of salt for the Midwest. Hardly realizing it, Shawneetown increased in importance. It became a shipping point for salt and a port for river craft. Its importance became such that a town was platted there before the region was surveyed by the national government. This brought it a measure of distinction as one of two towns laid out by government surveyors and sold as town lots before any of the surrounding lands were measured. Only one other city in the United States —Washington, D.C.—shares this distinction.

Lots at Shawneetown were the first lands sold from the public domain in the state. A government land office was established there, and sales to the public began in 1814. This office closed on May 2, 1856, after it had sold more than three million acres of government land.

Despite the fact that it was beset with many disadvantages like floods and roistering rivermen, the town prospered. In 1816 the first bank in Illinois Territory was established by John Marshall in a room of his residence that still stands hard against the levee a short way below the place where the paved highway reaches the river in the old town. Two years later—that is, in 1818—Henry Eddy and Peter Kimmel came down the Ohio on a flatboat with some type and a crude press to establish the Illinois *Emigrant,* the second newspaper to be published in the state. Some of the original type still was in the town 125 years later. Shawneetown became the financial capital of the state and the trading center for a great area.

Before Illinois became a state, General Thomas Posey came to visit his daughter and her husband who lived there and brought with him the American flag that the troops he led had carried in the storming of Stony Point. The flag still is in existence. Posey died in Shawneetown and is buried in the cemetery north of town.

Shawneetown had become a significant river port from the outset, but with the coming of steamers, it became one of the more important ones along the river. Much of the marketable produce of the region was shipped from the town, and most of the goods sold by early-day merchants of southern Illinois were brought here and hauled to local stores in ox wagons.

Famous rivermen stopped here. It was at Shawneetown's Riverside Hotel that Mark Twain became acquainted with an interesting youngster named Thomas Sawyer Spivey. There is a story, apparently with a basis of fact, that from this acquaintance Twain gathered the name and much of the material for his immortal classic, *Tom Sawyer.* It also was here that he found a leading character, Mulberry Sellers, for another volume, *The Gilded Age.*

Lawyers of note came to plead in the court at Shawneetown. Among them were John A. Logan, Robert G. Ingersoll, John A. McClerland.

Shawneetown is easily one of the better starting points to begin study of the Illinois story.

🌼 IN AND ABOUT SALEM

As ONE GOES about in southern Illinois, or in any other section of the state, and passes through different towns, it is interesting to pause and try to determine why a village was first located there. Such inquiry invariably uncovers an interesting story or two as well as some historical sidelights.

Some places seem to have been natural sites for villages. Apparently a town just had to be there. Salem in Marion County, at the northern limits of the section of Illinois called Egypt, was such a place.

For one thing it was a region of reasonably fertile soil. Too, it was divided between woodland and prairie and offered the advantages of both. Another point in its favor was its locality, where a half-dozen trails or traces converged. One of these important trails used by the French and Indians came up from Kaskaskia to join their Cahokia-Vincennes route. It was along this trail from Kaskaskia to the Salem vicinity and eastward to Vincennes that George Rogers Clark led his band through flooded grounds and icy waters to retake Fort Sackville at Vincennes in February, 1779. It was an expedition of great significance in our history.

Another often traveled trail came north from Frank Jordan's Fort, now West Frankfort, and led on to the north. The Goshen Road from Shawneetown to the Land of Goshen or Goshen Settlement joined with the road from Frank Jordan's Fort northwest to Mount Vernon and offered an easy means of reaching Marion County. Still another road came from the Carmi region and passed on toward Edwardsville. Even before a village was formed, this was an important travel center.

The first settler to locate in the Salem vicinity—in fact the first of record to settle in the county—was Captain Samuel Young. Though he is regularly referred to as Captain Young, no record has been found to indicate how he acquired the title. Young came to Illinois from Virginia by way of Tennessee. He was a skilled hunter and found more pleasure in the chase than in farming. He accordingly turned over the farm he had started to his son and gave his own energies to hunting and fishing.

The manner in which the village of Salem was established seems to have been somewhat informal. Nine men who thought that a village should have some form of legal existence met on July 1, 1817, and unanimously passed resolutions to set up a government. With nothing more than this resolution to sustain it, the village seems to have drifted along until 1854 when, records indicate, the village was platted. It was made a city in 1865.

Salem and its vicinity can claim several points of interest. Not far to the east of town are the crumbling ruins of one of the noted early stopping places of the state, Halfway Tavern, built in 1819. Once it extended along a front of seventy feet. Necessary stables and other out-buildings combined to make it a rather impressive appearing place. The ruins of

It Happened in Southern Illinois

one remaining building serve to remind visitors of the interesting procession that once moved by.

The birthplace of William Jennings Bryan is beside the Public Library a few blocks south of the courthouse square. The front rooms contain mementos of the "Great Commoner," Salem's most noted son. Bryan moved from this home when he was six to a rather pretentious one that his father built about a mile northwest of town. Bryan's father, Silas, was a man of considerable influence; he was in turn a teacher, state senator, circuit judge, and delegate to numerous conventions.

Salem has been noted for other things. It was once one of the greatest seed cleaning centers in the nation. It is claimed that more redtop grass seed was bought and sold here than at any other place in the nation. A principal market for the seeds was in Europe, where some say that most of them were used in dyeing cloth.

For almost a century Salem has been noted for its annual Soldiers' and Sailors' Reunion. This began shortly after the end of the Civil War and recently was still attracting thousands of visitors. With the passing of the veterans of the war between the states, its direction passed to the organized veterans of later wars.

The enumeration of things for which the town can claim distinction could go on endlessly. One of the state meetings that exerted great influence in railroad and internal improvements for the state was here in 1854. A branch of the American Colonization Society, designed to settle American Negroes in some foreign land, was formed here as early as 1833. In 1942 Salem was the eastern terminus of the great pipeline bringing petroleum products from the beginning point of the line at Longview, Texas.

This only suggests a few of the stories that await those who wish to rummage in Salem's story.

🏵 GRAND TOWER

MANY PEOPLE go to Grand Tower to see a captive snapping turtle that is larger than most men or to eat a family-style Sunday dinner in a local eating place. The town also has many historic spots to visit, and endless stories—some older than the town.*

When Joliet and Father Marquette passed down the Mississippi in 1673, they recorded and described the large rock that is now called

---

* See *Legends & Lore*, pp. 313-14.

Tower Rock. It has had other names. At one time the French called it *Le Tour.* It was also *Le Cap de Croix,* meaning "Rock of the Cross" in English. This name was given to it after three Catholic missionaries stopped with the Frenchman Tonti, LaSalle's lieutenant, to erect a large wooden cross on the rock's crest in 1678.

Numerous persons have met death in the rapids that sometimes rage about the base of the rock. Canoes avoid the hazard, as boats still do. Indians believed that evil spirits dwelt in the Grand Tower region, and white men acknowledged these beliefs by coining suitable names for landmarks. There is the Devil's Backbone, a rocky ridge about a half-mile long that begins at the north edge of town. This Backbone has one spot missing, perhaps a missing vertebra, where a railway spur once extended to the ironworks between the Backbone and the river.

At the north end of the Backbone, there is another gap, then the Devil's Bake Oven, about a hundred feet high, on the brink of the river.

A visitor interested in plant life will find rare ferns on the river side. He also will find yard plants from the time when people lived on the Oven. The Oven, Tower Rock, and the Backbone have been noted landmarks for almost three hundred years.

A band of immigrants who had come down the Ohio and were ascending the Mississippi to Kaskaskia were attacked and killed by Indians at the south end of the Devil's Backbone. They had gone ashore at the rapids between the Devil's Backbone and Tower Rock and were pulling their boat upstream with a long rope. Indians surprised and killed all of them except one, a boy named John Moredock, who hid among the rocks until the Indians had gone. He then made his way to Kaskaskia for help to bury the slain. Moredock, who had lost both parents and numerous brothers and sisters, vowed vengeance and continued his efforts to gain it until the last one of the Indian band was slain.

On the west side of the Devil's Backbone, between it and the river, is the site of two vanished iron furnaces that operated until after 1870. Some partially uncovered coke ovens show where there once were scores of them. Another furnace was south of town. Iron ore was brought to these furnaces from Missouri and coal from Murphysboro. It is said that Andrew Carnegie once considered making Grand Tower a Pittsburgh of the West. Once there were lime kilns at Grand Tower, also a large box factory that many remember.

A shipyard north of Grand Tower, near the site where the generating plant now is, built river barges and at least one steamer, the *Mab.* Coal brought on the railway was loaded on river barges at a tipple downtown.

Walker Hill, east of town, once had a noted amusement park where the Silver Cornet Band was widely known. A study of dates carved on the grave markers in the nearby cemetery east from the site of the amusement park will indicate the years when cholera raged in Jackson County.

First known as Jenkins Landing, the town was a busy river port where goods were received and from which the products of the region were shipped. The northern section was called Red Town because the houses were painted red. Storms and time have removed all except three or four of these houses, but markers still name many abandoned streets.

Grand Tower, whose one-time population was about four thousand, has dwindled to less than a thousand. Even so, it remains a quaint town, one well worth visiting.

🌿 *VINCENNES*

AN ATTRACTIVELY designed concrete bridge with seven spandrel arches crosses the Wabash to join the Vincennes, Indiana, country with southern Illinois. Long before the bridge was built, however, the two states already were closely connected.

A difficult ford across the river at the bridge site was used by great herds of buffalo passing between pasture lands and salt licks. Roving bands of Indians and early whites also used the ford and trail. Later there were ferries and, before the Civil War, a wooden bridge. This bridge was built with a drawspan that allowed steamboats to pass.

In addition to the back and forth crossing at the bridge site, the river was a convenient north-south route of travel long used by Indians in canoes and dugouts. It also was used by the French who came to explore, to establish missions, and to trade with the natives. The river was a ready-made route for licensed French traders known as *voyageurs* and for the *coureur de bois,* or bootleg traders. The locality of the bridge thus was an early-day crossroads where much legend has gathered.

It is not known just when white men first settled in the vicinity. It is known, though, that François de Vincennes was in command of some French soldiers and Indian allies there before 1736, when the place first appears with his name.

It was from this post that Vincennes lead a band of French and Indians down the Wabash to join similar forces from Fort de Chartres in Randolph County, Illinois, at the mouth of the Ohio. This was the ill-fated expedition of the French against the Chickasaw Indians living farther down the Mississippi. It ended in disaster, and its leaders were captured. A number of the captives, Vincennes among them, were slowly roasted at the stake on Palm Sunday, 1736, when the ransom demanded by their captors was not forthcoming.

For a good seventy-five years after the death of Vincennes the post on the Wabash remained an important military, trade, and church center. Men, both Indian and white, whose names are prominent in the history of the Northwest Territory came here. Pontiac, the Indian chief, knew the place both before and after it became British Territory in 1763. At a later date Tecumseh and his brother, The Prophet, passed back and forth as they sought to unite the Indians in their efforts to drive out the whites. Still later Tecumseh came here to confer with Harrison, but to no avail.

Colonel Hamilton, with several hundred soldiers and Indian allies, came from Canada in the autumn of 1778 to rebuild and strengthen the British fort and to name it Fort Sackville. Before winter settled down Hamilton had completed his work and had sent most of his helpers and Indian allies back to Detroit. On February 5, 1779, George Rogers Clark with 170 men began his memorable march from Kaskaskia to capture the fort and give the American Colonies their claim to the Northwest Territory. Many look upon Clark's exploit as a near military miracle.

Some years afterwards, William Henry Harrison, later to become our ninth president, came to build his home, Grouseland, that still stands and is visited by thousands. The little old capitol building, about twenty by thirty feet and two stories high, from which the government of about half of the United States once was administered, has been faithfully restored, as has the printing plant of the first newspaper in the region.

Vincennes was the point at which the Lincoln family entered Illinois on their move from Indiana. A memorial on the western side of the river commemorated the entry. It was on this migration that Lincoln is reported to have visited the printing plant of Elihu Stout in Vincennes and to have first observed the printing process.

Few places in the midwest offer a greater number of points of historical significance than Vincennes. Perhaps no three names associated with one locality suggest more of disappointment, neglect, and ingratitude on the part of a nation than do those of George Rogers Clark, Father Gibault, and Francis Vigo, men who gave much to the nation and received little in return.

Those interested in history will find a visit to Vincennes most rewarding.

🌿 *LA BELLE FONTAINE*

IF ONE LEAVES Illinois Highway 3 a half mile south of Waterloo and goes west toward a farmhouse at the road's end, he shortly crosses one of the most historic trails in southern Illinois. More than two hundred years ago it was the much traveled trail between the French settlements of Cahokia and Kaskaskia. Now it is only a worn, bush-grown gully.

Less than a half mile north of the place where the gravel road crosses the old trail, there is a gushing spring. The early French called it *La Belle Fontaine*—in English, "The Beautiful Fountain." This spring still provides a bountiful water supply. Near the midway point between the two principal French settlements, it was much used by those traveling between.

When George Rogers Clark came to win this region from the British in 1778, his soldiers who passed along the trail saw the country and liked it. During the next few years some of them returned to settle here. In the first group was Shadrach Bond, the elder. With him was his nephew bearing the same name. It was this younger Shadrach who later became the first governor of the state.

Other men whose names are prominent in the story of early Illinois came along the old trail. Among these were James Moore, Henry and Nicholas Smith, Robert Watts, and Larken Rutherford. Soon they were followed by the Lemens, Ogles, Pulliams, and Whitesides. These men settled over an area extending some miles from the spring, but Bellefontaine remained the settlement's landmark.

Some of the settlers selected locations in the bottoms toward the Mississippi and thus caused the region to be called the American Bottom. Another group led by James Lemen settled a short way south from the spring and called the place New Design. The Whitesides settled north of the spring and called their place Whiteside's Station. By 1800 there were 960 settlers in the area. Two hundred eighty-six of these lived in the vicinity of the spring.

It was to this settlement that John Seely, Francis Clark, and John Doyle came, in order named, to teach the first English language schools in the Illinois country. At about the same time an Irishman named Halfpenny came to teach in various localities over the area. Halfpenny attained some note and is popularly recalled as the "schoolmaster general" of early Illinois. He later established a much needed and widely patronized gristmill on Fountain Creek, a short way west of the spring.

The first Protestant churches, Baptist and Methodist, were established at New Design in the southern part of the settlement.

La Belle Fontaine settlement evidently was one with above-average educational and intellectual standards. One indication of this is offered by the will of James Moore, dated May 21, 1787. In this will Moore listed the titles of his books. This is said to be the first such listing of a private library in Illinois.

That Moore treasured his books is shown by his naming and bequeathing certain volumes to his children. Thus, to his son, John Milton Moore, he gave *"Paradise Lost* of Milton." He also gave to his son Enoch, spelled Henoch, "the seventh volume of *The Spectator."* One may wonder just what influence Moore's books may have exerted on the intellectual life of the area since tradition relates that others borrowed and read them.

To reach the spring without struggling through the overgrown trail, a person may go south out of Waterloo past the Lutheran school on Church Street west of the state highway. Approach is easier in this way. But, if the visitor goes to the spring from the point of crossing on the gravel road mentioned earlier he will pass the Moore cemetery, one of the state's oldest marked burying grounds. Struggling through the bush and briars here and carefully avoiding the burrows inhabited by groundhogs and skunks, one sees many old gravestones. The names still legible are reminiscent of early Illinois.

Whichever way one may go to the spring, he will find two interesting buildings there. One is the sturdy brick farmhouse. The other is a log building now used as a granary and storeroom. Both are said to date from the time when James Moore lived there. The lower story of the brick dwelling and the attached kitchen are the older portions.

The log building, according to tradition, is the first building that Moore erected and is the one in which his son, John Milton Moore, the first recorded white child of English parentage, was born in the Illinois country.

🏵 *HIGHLAND*

NUMEROUS SOUTHERN Illinois towns have individualities which make them intriguing. Such a town is Highland, in Madison County. An observant traveler who stops there somehow senses that the town is different in an interesting way. At least that was the experience of the writer several years ago when he spent a day in its Lindendale Park and attended a gathering of his wife's clan. That interest has increased as more of the town's story has been learned.

Highland really began in Switzerland about 1830 when Dr. Casper Koepfli read a book written by a Mr. Duden. Duden's book extolled the virtues of Missouri so convincingly that the doctor resolved to head a group to form a settlement there.

Arriving in Missouri in September, 1831, Koepfli's band did not like the rough and heavily forested region nor the institution of slavery. Deciding to look elsewhere, they went to Vandalia, then the capital of Illinois. On the way back toward St. Louis they came to gently rolling Looking Glass Prairie in Madison County. They quickly agreed that its wooded border was an ideal settlement site.

Returning to their temporary stopping place in Missouri, those of the group who wished to move to Illinois drew up a contract to form a kind of communal settlement and pooled their resources for that purpose. From their common fund of $6,195.23, they bought equipment and supplies along the way back to their chosen site. Among their purchases were a horse named Fritz, some cows and calves, and twenty-six chickens for which they paid $2.25. A like amount was invested in "a large jug of whiskey," which was promptly broken and replaced by "a small barrel" of the same—less likely to break—for which they paid $3.37.

Thus equipped, they proceeded to their selected site, bought a thousand acres of land, and built a large double log house. Here they passed the winter. Most of their time was spent in hunting—for game was abundant—and in writing letters inviting persons they knew in Switzerland to come to America. In a year or so many of those invited arrived to settle and develop nearby farms, but the communal arrangement, like so many other similar ventures in Illinois, did not last.

No village was formed until General Semple, founder of Elsah, and a man named Bagsby came in 1837 seeking a suitable location for a town along the projected Alton–Mt. Carmel railroad. Semple and Bagsby, with the cooperation of local men, laid out the town of Highland, later named Helvetia and then renamed Highland. A few dwellings, a large steam gristmill and sawmill, and a store were built.

At about this time plans were made to extend the National Road from Vandalia to East St. Louis. Highland, in true Chamber of Commerce style, sought to have the road built through it and pledged donations of money and labor. Its efforts were successful. The presence of the Swiss workmen on the road-building job attracted many others who were curious to observe these unusual people, to hear them talk, and to mingle and work with them.

Highland continued to grow steadily until 1849 when an epidemic of cholera killed scores. This misfortune was repeated in 1852 with equally disastrous results. Despite these misfortunes Highland grew and prospered. Breweries, a wool mill, a carriage factory, and a distillery were started there. A powder maker, coopers, and other highly skilled and well educated men came to ply their trades. Musical and literary organizations were formed. It came to be known as a town far above the average culturally with excellent churches and schools.

The equal of any pipe organs in the world are made at Highland, and the Swiss national anthem is said to have been composed there.

No story of Highland, however, can be told without mention of the Helvetia Sharpshooters and the Helvetia Milk Condensing Company. The sharpshooters organization, prominent over the nation, was more than a shooting club. It owned and developed Lindendale Park and encouraged the better types of social activities.

The Helvetia Milk Condensing Company launched one of America's major industries when it began operations on June 14, 1885, by condensing 150 gallons of milk. So successful was the venture that before the industry ceased to operate at Highland in September, 1923, numerous branches had been established over America, and the original five hundred shares with a par value of $100 had increased to a value of $20,000 for each share; in the meantime they had paid millions in dividends.

Highland still is a clean and interesting town, and it is well worth stopping there for a leisurely visit.

❧ TEUTOPOLIS, TOWN OF
THE TEUTONS

WE HAVE COME to believe that almost any town beside an Illinois highway will furnish an interesting story to the curious. This conclusion was strengthened during a recent visit to Teutopolis, on the old and storied National Road about four miles east of Effingham. It was found that this strangely named town had not one but several interesting stories.

Unlike many other towns, this one did not come about by accident. It was planned and really had its beginning in Cincinnati as the result of some wide-awake thinking by a group of German Catholics who were living in the Ohio city and its vicinity. It also was there that, after lengthy discussions, the name meaning "City of Teutons" was selected.

Among the Ohio group was a carpenter named Clemens Uptmor who conceived a plan whereby those able and willing to do so could contribute ten dollars each month to a fund for the purchase of government land in some state west of Ohio on which to form a settlement. Three men made up the original group. The next month there were six additional members and a few months later the total had reached 141, with funds increasing accordingly.

In early 1838 this group decided that it was time to take action. They selected a committee of three and sent them out to seek a suitable location for a colony.

After fifteen weeks of prospecting they returned to Cincinnati to make their report. They requested, however, that they not be required to reveal publicly the exact location of the tract chosen because they feared that "land sharks" would buy it up and profiteer on them. They also wished to take other selected representatives to see and evaluate the lands.

Two additional members were added to the original three-man committee, and all prepared to depart immediately. In late June, 1838, this group set out on foot for Illinois, but they took along one saddled horse that was ridden in turn. The main purpose in taking the horse was to carry along $16,000 cash in the saddlebags. Throughout the long journey two "heavily armed men walked along either side of the horse."

They reached the Teutopolis region without mishap, looked the region over once more, approved it, and proceeded to the U.S. Land Office at Vandalia where they completed the purchase of ten thousand acres of the public domain at a cost of $1.25 an acre. This deal was closed on July 6, 1838.

Upon their return to Cincinnati a plan for the allocation of the land was adopted. It typified the thoroughness ascribed to the Germans. It was divided into town lots, outlots, and farm tracts of forty and eighty acres. Each member received one town lot, one outlot, and forty acres of farmland. Some who had made sufficient payments were granted an additional eighty acres. Before drawings were made, a plat of the entire tract was prepared, and each division was numbered. Allocation was made by drawing these numbers from a hat. There is no record to indicate dissatisfaction with the method.

Each participant was required to make a minimum contribution of ten dollars toward the erection of a church, and all unallocated lands became church lands.

Though each stockholder had been given a town lot, few built upon them, preferring to build on the farm tracts they had received. The village thus grew slowly. One of the handicaps of the new settlement was the absence of a gristmill. Since there was no desirable mill site on a nearby stream the need was met by the erection of a large windmill. This mill, forty feet high and with wings fifty-three feet long, began operation July 4, 1845. It remained one of the region's noted landmarks for years. The tower of the church now stands about where the mill stood.

Perhaps no community in Illinois has been and has remained so solidly German Catholic as Teutopolis. Few have retained as much of a distinctive German culture. Now, 120 years after its settlement, much of the folklore and many of the customs, beliefs, traditions, and practices of Germany are observable in the area. The influence of the church in the community is impressive. The community itself is a distinctive one, and those who pause at Teutopolis enjoy the experience. Friendly visitors to Teutopolis meet a friendly community.

✷ THE KASKASKIA OF THE CARRIBEAN

ON ST. EUSTATIUS ISLAND, "The Golden Rock" of the Caribbean, I've found another "vanished village" that in some ways can be compared to our own long-gone Kaskaskia.

It is a great distance between the roadstead where fleets of merchantmen once dropped anchor beside St. Eustatius and the site where Kaskaskia stood in Randolph County. Nevertheless, both have interesting associations with our Revolutionary War. Now, the historic strand beside "The Golden Rock" and the one-time metropolis of the Mississippi are both deserted and peopled with the ghosts and memories of their past.

In 1778 Kaskaskia was the most important town in the Mississippi Valley. At the same time, the anchorage at Fort Orange on St. Eustatius, where many hundreds of vessels dropped anchor in one year, was perhaps the most important port in the West Indies. In that year both fell. St. Eustatius was seized by the British and Kaskaskia by the militia of Virginia.

Fort Orange really came to attention in the Revolution before Kaskaskia. The first small but significant event occurred on November 16, 1776, when the U.S. Brig of War *Andrew Doria* came to the anchorage beneath the Dutch fort. It was flying the recently adopted "Congress Colors," a new flag on the high seas and one that had not previously been recognized by another nation.

The arrival of the new flag posed a problem for Governor Johannes de Graaff. Should it be saluted as that of a sovereign nation? The governor decided to do so and ordered a twenty-one gun salute fired. Knowledge of his action aroused the sharp anger of Britain. Governor de Graaff soon returned to his homeland and was asked to explain his action. In defense he stated that he had "latterly suffered smallpox, was growing old, and had already had too much of colony life" after twenty-six years. At any rate, de Graaff had given the first official salute to the American flag.

For some years afterwards St. Eustatius remained a great Netherlands West Indies port which supplied the American colonies with some of their sinews of war. This much displeased the British and helped bring about war between Holland and Britain. Before the Dutch had learned of the declaration of this war, Admiral Rodney of Britain appeared off the roadstead and demanded the immediate surrender of Fort Orange. The governor, with nearly all his vessels away on convoy duty and trusting to the "honor and humanity" of the British commanders, felt forced to submit.

Rodney's forces promptly began to pillage, wreck, and burn the more than a mile of wharves and warehouses. They took such treasure as they could carry away and put the torch to other goods; in this manner $200,000 worth of dyewood and rosewood from Brazil were destroyed. Total damages amounted to $20,000,000. St. Eustatius paid an enormous price, at least in part because she had paid salute to a new flag.

After the demolition wrought by Admiral Rodney's men, St. Eustatius declined rapidly. Ten or more forts about the island were abandoned and dismantled. Today, remnants of their crumbling walls, outlines of the barracks buildings, powder magazines, and cisterns remain to tell bits of "Statias's" story and of the days when twenty thousand people lived there. (Now there are only nine hundred on the entire island.)

At the same time that the British were laying waste to "The Golden Rock," George Rogers Clark was gaining possession of Kaskaskia. The loss of St. Eustatius cut off one of the American colonies' sources of supplies, but Clark's success in Illinois gave the West to the new nations.

The action of de Graaff was finally given recognition by our nation in March, 1939, at the close of naval maneuvers in the Caribbean. Three U.S. battleships paid a surprise call on the island and anchored at the old roadstead. Aboard one of them was President Franklin D. Roosevelt. He had come to pay a deserved sentimental call on behalf of the nation. It was also appropriate that the island's highest pinnacle—with its ruined walls, cisterns, and abandoned cannon—has long been known as Roosevelt Land, named, it is said, for a relative who settled there before the family came to America.

Eight months after the first three naval vessels had stopped, the battleship *Wyoming* came on a second call. It brought a bronze tablet with the following inscription:

In Commemoration
of the
Salute to the flag of the United States
Fired in this fort on November 16, 1776
by order of
JOHANNES DE GRAAFF
Governor of Eustatius
In reply to a national gun salute
fired by the
United States Brig of War Andrew Doria
Under Captain Isaiah Robinson
of the Continental Navy

Here the sovereignty of the
United States of America
was first acknowledged to a
National vessel by a foreign official

Presented by Franklin Delano Roosevelt
President of the United States of America

This bronze tablet, mounted on the base of a small tapering shaft within the walls of Fort Orange, reminds the visitor of an interesting episode of American history.

Chapter 16

Speech

🌼 *LANGUAGE OF HORSE AND BUGGY DAYS*

OUR LOCAL speech, in fact speech everywhere, continuously changes. Words serve their purposes and pass from common usage along with the objects and activities to which they refer. A recent visit to the Horse and Buggy Museum at the north side of Gettysburg, Pennsylvania, made this plain.

The exhibits there brought to mind many once common but now seldom used words, words now without meaning except to a few. Very naturally, words suggested by the visit apply to horses, buggies, and wagons. As an example of this, everyone knows that buggies and wagons have four wheels. Many, however, do not know that each buggy had a fifth wheel and fewer still would know just where to look for the fifth member. Likewise, they would not know where to look for the reaches of a buggy or the hounds of a wagon.

Most people would not know where to find the thimbles and skeins. Not many would know that a discarded skein sometimes was used as a dinner horn. Both buggies and wagons had felloes that might require soaking during dry spells. These felloes might even have tires wired on them. At other times their tires were shrunk on them and then they were boiled in linseed oil.

Bolsters held the bed of a wagon and were not placed upon it as in a bedroom. Sideboards were on the wagon bed and not in the dining room. A sideboard load was a big load. Bumper boards were added to sideboards at cornhusking, then corn shucking, time. Wagons had coupling poles that were extended when hay frames were to be used, or longer poles were to be hauled on the running gear.

356

Brake blocks were held in shoes. In the absence of brake blocks, wheels could be snubbed for unusually steep hills. Wagons had bands on their hubs and bands rode on wagons. Some people still like to climb on the band wagon. Buggy washers were not laundrymen. They were leather rings that were placed around the spindles in the ends of the hubs. A buggy's dashboard always held a whip socket, but the proud owner of a six-bit buggy whip seldom left his prized possession there at night gatherings. Boys no more hesitated to steal buggy whips than they did watermelons. The dashboard of the buggy became the instrument panel of the automobile. Buggy and carriage poles were not for fishing.

A twenty-four inch buggy meant that the bed was twenty-four inches wide. A runabout was a topless buggy and often was undercut. Now sports model automobiles have replaced the runabouts, and buggy lanterns are headlights. The sprung axles of the old-time buggy often caused wheels to roll at a queer pitch. Men made bows that were fastened by brackets on the sides of the wagon box. Buggy bows were the frames of buggy tops. A factory at Metropolis in Massac County once made untold thousands of these bows. Wagon standards held the wagon box. Spring seats or wagon boards accommodated passengers.

Fly nets, check reins, and blind bridles were standard equipment. In winter or on special occasions a horse blanket, often form-fitting, replaced the net of summer. When plow harness was used with a wagon, rings and links might be dropped from the traces. Lap links (laprings) fastened swingle trees (single trees) to the double tree. A boy out looking for trouble sometimes slipped a lapring in his pocket to use in lieu of illegal brass knuckles. He could always explain that he had it for its intended use in farm work.

Linch pins, king pins, wagon wrenches, stay chains, back bands, belly bands, cruppers, breeching (called britching), hame strings, axle grease, wagon jacks, neck yokes, check lines, now have only vague meanings for many.

Farm jargon surely has changed.

🌺 DO YOU UNDERSTAND WHAT I MEAN?

OCCASIONALLY A person explaining something or telling another about an incident will ask, "Do you understand?" or "Do you know what I mean?" Perhaps both questions are in order with the following hodge-podge of phrases and sayings brought to mind by an overheard remark.

A part of the remark declared that someone was "as mad as flugence." This phrase left me wondering just what degree of anger was represented by "flugence." Is it greater or less than that of old scratch, a wet hen, or a hornet? Or does it mean "as mad as all get out"? Is one mad to the extent of flugence sufficiently angry to warrant his planting his pepper crop? Is he so angry that counting to ten would not calm him? Would the degree represented by flugence cure the hiccoughs? Would it cause the irked one to express anger on New Year's Day and therefore cause him to be angry all the year?

On the other hand, flugence may represent a mild degree, such as that which one who had merely gotten up on the wrong side of the bed would experience. Would he be on a high horse, have his hump up, or only be mildly at loggerheads with the world? Perhaps it would be only that of the ordinary redhead born in August. Could it possibly be the small degree of anger that could be overcome by visiting a neighbor's house and eating some applesauce?

Whatever the degree represented by flugence, according to the account I overheard, the wrathy one did not pull in his horns, get off his high horse, keep his shirt on, keep his tongue in his teeth, or pussyfoot about.

According to the story, it all started because someone got liquored up and spilled the beans; that is, he let the cat out of the bag. As a result, the fat was in the fire. The victim, not being mealy-mouthed, chicken-hearted, or prone to beat about the bush, promptly took foot in hand and set out to correct the situation. He would do it in three shakes of a sheep's tail.

He was going to see to it that people would learn to tend to their own knittin', to shinny on their own side, and to mind their p's and q's. He admitted it was a fine howdy-do but insisted that, at its worst, all would come out in the wash. Meanwhile, he would not stand stock still for a coon's age. Apparently he was as tough as whitleather, had cut his eye teeth, and knew which side of his bread was buttered.

The party starting the bit of offending gossip was small potatoes and his cake soon would be dough. He would see who was chief cook and bottle washer (that is, some punkins). The offended one certainly would not pull up stakes or fly the coop.

The thread of such a long story could be continued to its end in the same general phrasing and in much the same manner as it would have been related orally once upon a time. Conversations then were filled with many of these strange figures of speech that sound somewhat odd to us now.

How many now know what it means to hit the nail on the head, or just how dead is a door nail? There really is no nail in either case. How long has it been since Heck was a pup, and what are kivers? When is one's eyes bigger than his belly and when should Sunday-go-to-meeting clothes be worn? Who is a sawbones?

What has happened to people who are stumped? When is one too big for his britches? When do people talk turkey? How poor is a church-mouse? What does it mean to split the wind or douse the glim? If one has a stiff upper lip, plain hoss sense, is as tough as grissle, doesn't blow his horn too much, and knows when it is proper to polish an apple, just what would be his chances for success?

What does it mean to squall like a painter? What did people convey when they said "lots of," "down sick," "settle up," "great deal," "break the ice," or "Shoot, Luke, or give up the gun." Old phrases often are very expressive when properly placed.

Now, all this has ended without knowing the point, where "flugence" fits on the anger scale.

❧ *VANISHING WORDS*

A RECENT request for the loan of a barlow brought only bewildered looks from a group of university students. No one knew that the term "bar-low" was used to designate a single-bladed jacknife, once the prized possession of almost every boy. Naturally, no one knew it was named for a Mr. Barlow who first mass-produced it, or that the case knife, occasionally seen even now, was named for Mr. Case, another maker of quality knives.

The barlow served a boy in many ways. It was used to cut fishing poles, fashion bows and arrows, and to make willow and hickory bark whistles. The proud possessor could pick "goodies" from cracked nuts, play mumbledy-peg, disfigure school desks, carve initials on the bark of trees or other smooth surfaces, and skin rabbits. He also could peel apples or turnips, remove briars and splinters from fingers and feet, trim fingernails, bore holes, and do countless other tasks. It might even serve to bolster a quaking boy's courage while passing a graveyard in the dark. Barlows were indeed good and useful. Most of all, the single-bladed variety then cost only fifteen cents. A two-bladed, brass-lined one cost more.

If one should walk into a general store now, that is, if he can find one, and ask for a blacksnake, he doubtless would draw only puzzled glances. There was a time, however, when he would have been taken directly to the harness department and shown the merchant's stock of one-piece, short-stocked leather whips, braided or sewn over a very pliable core and with a loop at the end of the stock for the carrier's wrist. Sometimes the butt was loaded with lead which made it into an effective blackjack. In the hands of a skilled skinner either end of a blacksnake was much to be dreaded. Artists and horror writers placed such whips in the hands of slave drivers.

Before golf became common a caddy was not a boy, only slightly accurate in addition, who carried a player's clubs around the golf course and helped keep score. Once it was a tin box holding tea, coffee, or condiments. The same type of box also might be called a canister. Cedarware was buckets, tubs, and churns, often made of alternate red and white cedar staves that came respectively from the heart and sapwood of cedar trees. These sometimes were held together with brass hoops to make an attractive container. This cedarware was beautiful to look at, but when new, sure to flavor its contents for many weeks. A new cedar water bucket, with a freshly made and unboiled drinking gourd added, produced a startling flavor.

Clapboards were split from bolts of board timber by use of a frow, mallet, and brake. They were used for practically all roofing of buildings, to cover chicken coops, to make ash hoppers, to shield potato holes and other outdoor vegetable storage bins, and even to side or weatherboard houses. Coonskins were caps of the Davy Crockett variety. Linsey was short for linsey-woolsey, a cloth of linen warp and woolen woof or weft. Madder certainly was not used to indicate increased anger; it was to name a plant whose roots were used to prepare a red dye.

A firkin was a small tub-like wooden container designed to hold fifty-six pounds of butter or lard. Nubbins were dwarfed ears of corn, and noggins were small wooden cups. Noggin also was an uncomplimentary reference to one's head. A runlet or rundlet was a small barrel with a capacity of eighteen gallons. When someone said, "Use this jack," he didn't hand you some money or a device for lifting heavy weights, but a small waxed leather bucket coated inside with tar or pitch.

Johnnycakes, first called journey cakes, were small cakes made of corn meal and baked on a hot stone or board faced to the fire. Corn pone was produced in a similar manner but was large enough to be broken into smaller portions. Pattens were sandal-like footwear with soles of wooden blocks, sometimes being reinforced with bent iron straps beneath them.

A bit was a money measure, that is, twelve and a half cents: thus, two bits was twenty-five cents; four bits made a half dollar; and six bits was seventy-five cents, once a rather liberal day's wage for common labor. A picayune was a half bit or six and a fourth cents. One who haggled over trivialities was picayunish. A present-day workman would be puzzled if told to chink and daub a house. Then the cracks between the logs in a log house were chinked by filling them with stones or short sections of split timbers. They then were daubed by filling the smaller spaces between the chinks with clay or a mixture of clay, sand, and lime.

A potato hole was a mound of potatoes covered with straw, grass, or leaves, and then with a thick layer of earth. An additional covering of short planks or clapboards often was added to protect the earthen mound from beating rains. There also were holes for turnips, beets, cabbage, and best of all, apple holes that boys occasionally raided. A sander was not a device for smoothing boards. It was somewhat like a pepper box and was used to sprinkle fine sand over fresh writing to absorb the surplus ink. Sillabub was sweetened cream, flavored with ample wine and beaten into a froth.

A sleeper was not a dozing person, but heavy timbers near the ground to support the floor of a building. A spider was not necessarily of the genus *arachnidan*. It sometimes was a frying pan with long legs and a long handle which was used for cooking over glowing coals at the fireplace hearth. A spit was not an expectoration but a slender pointed steel rod on which meat was placed to be roasted as it was turned. A fence worm was the zig-zag foundation of the worm or Virginia rail fence. Trivets supported cooking vessels over a bed of hot coals. Sometimes they protected a surface from hot cooking vessels or sadirons. A tallow dip was made by repeated dipping and cooling of a candlewick. Pewter was kitchenware made of mixed lead and tin. Gum wax came from the sweet gum tree and was used as chewing gum. Girdles were not only worn by people; they also were the rings chopped around trees to deaden them. Poke yokes were worn by breachy livestock. Conchs were large spiral sea shells, sometimes with their ends ground off so they could be used as dinner horns.

Vanishing words also suggest vanishing objects and practices.

Chapter 17

What They Said About Us

❦ *HISTORY OF THE ENGLISH SETTLEMENT IN EDWARDS COUNTY*

THERE ARE many significant, though half-forgotten and unfamiliar, books that tell about earlier southern Illinois. Among these is the accurate, well-written, and somewhat rare *History of the English Settlement in Edwards County, Illinois,* by George Flower.

Flower was one of the leaders in the establishment of that important Illinois settlement whose influence upon the course of the new state continued for many years. In fact that influence still is evident. Having been actively connected with the settlement through the first forty years of its history, Flower was well qualified to record its story.

The book has varied appeal. First, the story of the writer, as incidentally revealed in the book itself and more fully by other easily available sources, arouses a sympathy, admiration, and curiosity that naturally add to the book's interest.

Too, Flower's manuscript covered a checkered course before it was published. It was completed and given to the Chicago Historical Society in September, 1860, and remained there with its accompanying papers until a few days before the Chicago fire in 1871. Then the manuscript and other material were very fortunately borrowed for inspection by someone who returned them after the fire. Had this not happened, the manuscript would have been among many irreplaceable papers burned. In 1882, some twenty-two years after Flower had given his papers to the

Society, the book was published through the generosity of Levi Z. Leiter.

To the interest one has in the author and in the story of the accidental saving of the manuscripts, there is added the kernel of it all—Flower's candid and fair story. All combine to make the book appealing to almost any reader.

Throughout the story there is constant evidence of the author's devotion, loyalty, and abiding faith in the English Settlement. Also, Flower writes with cherished memory and high regard for the estranged Morris Birkbeck who had worked so closely and diligently with Flower in the planning and direction of the colony during its earlier years.

The ruptured friendship between Birkbeck and Flower, never clearly explained, obviously left a deep hurt with each. Until their death, neither is known to have voiced criticism or censure of the other, which seems to be a somewhat strange omission, seldom observed in similar circumstances. Reading the book convinces one that until Birkbeck's death both really wanted and hoped for a reconciliation and the restoration of their earlier cordial relationship.

Flower's story opens with the formation of the friendship between the youthful Flower and Birkbeck, twenty-five years his senior. It briefly mentions their extensive trip together on muleback over the byroads of rural France. It tells how each came to meet and became attached to Edward Coles. General Lafayette, Thomas Jefferson, Andrew Jackson, James Monroe, John Adams, Robert Owen, William H. Harrison, Thomas Sloo, and a host of other great and near-great persons casually pass in review. The Shaker colony near Vincennes, the colony headed by Edward Rapp at Harmonie, and the work of Robert Owen on the Wabash are viewed, evaluated, and commented upon.

When one turns to Illinois history, hardly a significant character or movement of the period is omitted. Conditions existing in the early settlement are thoroughly treated. Flower tells of an unperturbed naked man sitting beside his cabin door to cool off. He writes about fleas, horseflies, drunkenness, hunger, crude cabins, and about dissatisfied Indians. Slavery, the beginning of towns, the importation of blooded livestock, and the opening of a public market place receive attention. The founding of an agricultural association and a county fair, the beginning of one of the first Illinois libraries, and the development of schools and churches are described. His observations are balanced and penetrating.

Any Illinoisan interested in the significant period of his state's history covered by the *History of the English Settlement in Edwards County, Illinois* will find it interesting reading. It may be difficult to find a copy.

Nevertheless, it should be on the reading list of those interested in local history.

☙ *ILLINOIS IN 1837 & 8*

WHEN THE French first came into Illinois country, they were accompanied by Catholic priests who, while administering to the spiritual needs of the soldiery, sought to convert the Indians to a belief in Christianity. Some of the early history of Illinois is contained in the official records of explorers, but much is contained in extensive accounts kept by the accompanying churchmen. A part of their early writings, known as the *Jesuit Relations,* fill about seventy interesting volumes. They are the best records we have of the earliest white men in Illinois and of the natives they encountered here.

Since that time many books have been written about Illinois. Some of them are well-known while others are far less familiar. Among the latter is a slim publication entitled,

> *Illinois in 1837 & 8*
> *With a Map*
> *Containing Also*
> *The Emigrants' Guide*
> *To*
> *The West*

The volume was published in 1837 by Grigg and Elliott at No. 9 North Fourth Street, Philadelphia. All in all it is an interesting book, well stocked with reliable information concerning the youthful state. It was quite obviously written from first-hand knowledge.

One of the features attracting the reader's attention is an unusual folding map on sheer, blue-tinted manuscript paper, pasted inside the front cover. It is fascinating both from the standpoint of what is missing, as well as what is shown. Numerous towns and roads that are now only legend are shown in bold type. The Goshen Road, one of the stage routes of early Illinois, wanders across the country from Shawneetown towards the Goshen Settlement at the south side of Edwardsville, seeming to ignore all land lines.

Another such road leads from Shawneetown by way of Vienna, Mount Pleasant, and Jonesboro to Hamburg on the Mississippi. It does not pass through Anna, for no such town then existed. Since that time

Mount Pleasant and Hamburg have joined a long list of vanished villages.

Several present-day towns are not shown in the Illinois of 1837 & 8. Among them are Carbondale, Marion, Harrisburg, West Frankfort, Benton, DuQuoin, Cairo, Metropolis, Centralia, Murphysboro, Herrin, Effingham, and numerous smaller ones. Town after town has vanished. Some of these are America, Caledonia, Trinity, Napoleon, Kaskaskia, Ewington, and Brownsville. Liberty is now Rockwood; Columbus is Sparta; Caledonia is Olmsted; Frankfort is West Frankfort; Tamaraw has become Tamaroa; and Illinois Town is now East St. Louis.

Chicago, even then, was the largest town in Illinois, though United States surveyors had completed platting only a tier of townships along the southern side of Cook County. Ten other counties at the north end of Illinois had not been surveyed at all.

The map shows a canal from Lake Michigan to Utica, Illinois. Projected railroad lines that were to become part of a great internal improvement scheme are neatly drawn in red ink that retains its brightness to this day. One such dreamed-of railroad led directly south from Vandalia to America on the Ohio. Another would have connected Edwardsville and Shawneetown, and still another led from Edwardsville to Mt. Carmel by way of Salem. Hundreds of miles of future rail lines are inked in by the meticulous penman.

The text tells us that the most prevalent disease in Illinois of that time was "intermiteant fever with biliousness" (malaria). It explains that "bad air" was to blame, as it was for milksick. But to prove that the entire region should be considered healthful, it cites the combined population of Illinois, Ohio, Indiana, Kentucky, Tennessee, Michigan, and Missouri—four million.

Among the state's seventy counties then, some had fewer than one inhabitant per square mile. These were Livingston, Jasper, Henry, and McHenry. Champaign County had 1,250 residents.

It was not too expensive for the Illinois emigrants of that day. One could travel as "deck passenger" from Pittsburgh, Pennsylvania, to the "Mouth of the Ohio" (now Cairo) for an $8.00 fare. Deck passengers rode in a sheltered space amidships, just forward of the engines. They furnished their own bedding and cooked their own food. Travelers going from New York to St. Louis could do so in twelve to fifteen days at a cost of $40 to $45, cabins and meals included. "Strict order is observed," the book admonishes.

The Emigrants' Guide section tells how to select land and build a cabin. It also gives the following cost estimates for opening a prairie farm:

320 acres at $1.25 an acre	$400.00
Breaking 160 acres at $2.00 an acre	320.00
Fencing 160 acres into 80 acre fields	175.00
Cabin, cribs, barn	250.00
Total	$1145.00

Readers were assured that the first crop of wheat, if a normally good one, would pay the entire cost.

Illinois in 1837 & 8 is blessed with a candidness that adds to its interest, such as its warning to "beware of extravagant statements you may hear." Many of its predictions have been fulfilled.

❧ FROM TIMBER TO TOWN

A NUMBER of interesting but often unfamiliar books about southern Illinois have been written, some of them by southern Illinoisans. One of these, *From Timber to Town—Down in Egypt,* was published in 1891 by the A. C. Clurg Company of Chicago. Copies of it now are somewhat hard to find.

On the title page the author is listed as "An Early Settler." The Library of Congress records show the name of the writer to be Mrs. T. Perley, and the University of Illinois Library lists the name as Mrs. T. E. Perley. Mrs. Perley, however, casts herself in the role of a man in the narrative.

From beginning to end the book is written in the dialect of early southern Illinois. Words are consistently misspelled in a way to more clearly indicate the pronunciation then in vogue. The manner in which it is all done justifies the statement that "A dialect is not a degraded literary language; a literary language is an elevated dialect."

The circumstances that prompted the writing of the book are related. According to author Perley's narrative, it grew out of the deluge of county histories that appeared in the early 1880's. These county histories, often interesting, invariably included highly complimentary sketches of "prominent citizens." In one such case, the tribute paid the author was so glowing that he was extremely embarrassed, so much that "the more I red, the redder I felt musself a gittin' in the face ontell . . . all of a suddent . . . I . . . flung it wi' full stren'th agin the furdes' wall." It was not so with "a passel of others who offered their congratoolations."

"Somethin' had to be did. The upshot was . . . I bought me a quire o' paper . . . and started out ter . . . tell all I knowed and turn the 'counts over ter Jeems to toch up."

It was planned to complete the writing in a few weeks, "But I was monst'rous begges' part o' my spar' time fur I dunno how menny ye'r, and jis reached the end. Jeems helped by takin' holt . . . and stickin' t' me thru thick an' thin, slingin' ink."

The author states that "havin' bin druv inter takin' up the pen as a weepin o' self defense," he "lays it down again wi' the satisfactshun thet et las' the truth hes ben tole an' jestis did."

In like manner the book of 287 pages continues to the end. The spelling, which at first may appear "over-did," right well indicates the pronunciation used.

The author was a Methodist during the Cartwright days. Perley calls Peter Cartwright by the thinly veiled name of Paul Wheelwright. The spelling and pronunciation of many names of places and persons are interesting. Elias becomes Lishy. Kentucky, very properly, is Kaintuk. Rebecca becomes Becky, Wesley is shortened to Wes, Tobias is Tobe, and James is Jeems. Eliza is Liza and Malinda is Murlindy.

Scattered references to places occur from time to time, but are not used in a way that definitely localizes the narrative. Incidents related seem to have occurred somewhere between the mouth of Little Muddy River, east of DeSoto, and the forks of the Goshen Road west of Eldorado. He speaks of the "Tomsons" and of Jordan's water mill. References and extended descriptions of camp meetings fit very well into the story of old Bethel Church, southeast of Thompsonville. One naturally guesses that the author must have lived somewhere in that vicinity.

For those old enough to remember the speech that older rural persons used a lifetime ago, the reading of the book is reasonably easy. Those unfamiliar with the dialect of those days will find the reading a bit difficult at first.

Nevertheless, anyone wishing to know more about the beliefs, practices, and social customs, including the manner of speech in early southern Illinois, will find much information in *From Timber to Town*. It is especially interesting for the vivid glimpses it gives of earlier days in the region, and no other book found has a better, sustained treatment of the dialect then common in the region. It is very evident to readers that the book was written by one with a first-hand knowledge and a direct contact with the time and locality.

❧ *THE OUTLAW YEARS*

READERS FREQUENTLY make inquiry concerning books available about earlier southern Illinois. Mention of some has been made. This is another that tells about the "land pirates" who operated along the state's southern border and farther south.

Most of the incidents related occurred outside of Illinois, but many of the personalities and practices involved are directly associated with this region. The narrative helps to make this region's pioneer days more real. After all, southern Illinois has a kind of vested interest, since it is credited with giving birth to organized crime in the country. This book *The Outlaw Years,* by Robert M. Coates, tells of the widespread lawlessness that raged in the area for fifty years or so immediately after the Revolution, before an organized administration of justice had been established. During that time this territory was The West and lawlessness was rampant, just as it was later on the plains and in the mountains as the frontier moved farther west. This first West did not have the blazing six-shooters and racing horses of the later one, but it did have men just as daring, as relentless, and as active. Also, these men were fully as cruel and unmerciful as any connected with the later flaming West of legend.

The bad men of this first West and the men who sought to control them went about their work in a less spectacular way. Instead of nosily racing on horseback across the open plains and through mountain defiles with guns ablaze, they moved quietly, sometimes stealthily, along the lonely streams and over dim forest trails. Wherever the scattered and sometimes fragmentary records of the forest West have been assembled and presented in a related manner, they make interesting reading.

The Outlaw Years, published in 1930, is one of the better results coming from materials gathered and organized about this area. Much of the information it contains apparently comes from the same sources that furnished materials for Otto Rothert's *The Outlaws of Cave-in-Rock,* which appeared in 1923. Both books are factual and are realistically done.

Coates' book has four main divisions, each named for a principal character. First came the Harpes, Micajah and Wiley, otherwise known as "Big" and "Little" Harpe. A second part tells about Joseph Thompson Hare, a Pennsylvania farm boy. Then comes Samuel Mason and his outlaw rendezvous at Cave-in-Rock. It ends with about a hundred pages given to John A. Murrell, skilled robber and grand planner.

The author relates how the Harpes, sadistic, cruel, and heartless killers, began their careers of recorded murders in December, 1798. By September, 1799, their known victims numbered about thirty, and there were several unsolved murders similar to those they were known to have committed.

Arrested and lodged in prison several times, they always escaped. In September of 1799 a posse surprised them, and "Big" Harpe was shot and paralyzed. When his captor drew a large knife to use in severing the captive's head, Harpe grimly told him to proceed. The severed head was placed in the crotch of a tree not far from the Kentucky shore, where it remained until the flesh had rotted away and the skull was bleached. "Little" Harpe escaped the posse and continued his mad way until February, 1804, when he was brought to trial in Mississippi. Convicted on a murder charge, he was hanged near the present town of Greenville, Mississippi. His head, too, was severed and placed atop a pole beside the trail he had helped to make fearful.

🏵 THE OUTLAWS OF CAVE-IN-ROCK

SOUTHERN ILLINOIS has served as host to many widely known persons who have stopped at various times and places in "Egypt." Perhaps the outstanding reception center associated with the earlier of these visitors, particularly the infamous ones, is the widely known cave on the Ohio River bank at Cave-in-Rock. Many characters of dubious distinction came to the cave and to Hurricane Island, downstream a short way from the cave. So much crime was committed in the cave-island area that several volumes would be required to tell the story.

A book about the criminals and crimes of the area, *The Outlaws of Cave-in-Rock,* was written by Otto Rothert, secretary of the Filson Club of Louisville, Kentucky, and published in 1923.

Rothert's narrative covers the period from the first mention of the cave by explorers and travelers until the last active member of the bands that practiced crime there rode on his coffin aboard an ox cart to his own hanging on a sycamore limb beside Lusk Creek at Golconda. During the past fifty years and more the cave had been a point around which legend had grown, and to which even yet additional bits are being added.

In at least one respect, *The Outlaws of Cave-in-Rock* differs greatly from most books recounting legends of crime. A large proportion of such books are based principally on hearsay and are liberally enriched by the writer's imagination. The basis of Rothert's cave stories are made upon writings and official records. Having sought out available evidences, Rothert found no need for dealing in fiction or giving away to imagination.

After all, it would have been difficult to imagine situations and incidents stranger than those that actually occurred. When the reader has finished, he is ready to agree with the statement that "truth is stranger than fiction."

An author could hardly devise a more horrible thing than the slitting of a baby's throat to still its crying, or the swinging of another by its heels to bash its brains out against a tree. It also would be difficult to create a more effective and dramatic way to dispose of a captured criminal than to sever his head with a hunting knife while the victim still was looking into the executioner's eyes and talking to him. Another criminal's head that had a price upon it was severed, encased in wet clay, and carried in a sack across the saddle with a counterbalance of provisions in the other end.

The imaginative writer might have tied stones about a body to sink it in a deep pool, but more imaginative murderers at the cave preferred to slit a belly and stuff the cavity with rocks that eventually fell out and allowed the body to float to the surface. While most authors drawing on imagination would think it unrealistic to write about a half-dozen murders in succession, Rothert charges the bloody Harpe brothers with a score or more of validated murder charges, along with numerous other unsolved killings that conformed to their style.

It was not murderers alone that came to ply their trade about the cave. Rothert vividly describes the operations of counterfeiters and of those engaged in river piracy. We learn that a flatboat trip down-river past the cave was extremely hazardous. Efforts were regularly made to entice boats to land at the cave. If the pirates at the cave failed to gain possession of the boat and its cargo in this manner, those at Hurricane Island within sight down-river vigorously tried to correct the omission. The record of many a flatboat ended in the cave's vicinity.

❦ DILUVIUM OR THE END
OF THE WORLD

FROM TIME to time religious sects have arisen to proclaim an early ending of the world, and particularly of those people not supporting the beliefs and practices of that sect. Generally, the ending was to be by fire. One such group had its beginnings in Wayne County, southern Illinois.

Before it ran its course this band drew much attention, and its story was told briefly in an earlier chapter.

In addition to that group, which drew most of its believers from two or three adjoining counties, there were other organizations formed outside Illinois which attracted believers in this region. Perhaps the most noted of these were the early Millerites. In general this group believed that a stern God would punish a sinful world.

Aside from the religious groups which believed that a dreadful fate was imminent because of man's erring ways, there was an occasional individual who thought he foresaw an approaching world catastrophe, one that would result from natural causes and not from an avenging God. One of these was George S. Pidgeon of Cairo. According to Pidgeon's *Diluvium or the End of the World,* published in 1885, the end would come sometime during the years 1889–1892 and would result from what now would be considered a small accomplishment of man.

Pidgeon begins his book by saying that much of the Sahara Desert once was an ocean bottom. Lacking rainfall and having its connections with the Atlantic Ocean and the Mediterranean Sea closed by upheavals, its waters evaporated and left the area one of drifting sands with much of the surface below sea level.

Men talked of cutting channels from the Mediterrean Sea, one between Tunis and Tripoli and another one from the Atlantic Ocean through the continental rim opposite the Canary Isles. These channels would cause much of the Sahara to be flooded and create an inland sea of about 220,000 square miles, approximately four times the area of Illinois. According to the figure Pidgeon gave, the waters of this inland sea would weigh 176 trillion tons, one thirty-fourth of the 5,852 trillion tons that he gave as the earth's total weight. This relocation of so much weight naturally would shift the center of the earth's total mass enough to radically affect its balance and cause it to wobble.

In his opinion, this change would be sufficient to radically shift the earth's axis and the climatic belts of the world. It would bring the great ice caps of Greenland and Antarctica into zones where they would rapidly melt. This melting of the great ice masses in turn would cause additional shifting of the earth's center of weight and further dislocation of its established axis.

Because of the shiftings of the earth's mass and its center of gravity, the whole earth would have a tendency to wobble and might even reshape itself. Pidgeon believed that water from the melting ice would raise the ocean level enough to flood millions of square miles of lower lands. This movement of the earth's center, the heightened water level, and the shifting of the earth's axis combined would cause tremendous movements of the ocean waters and even some breaking of the earth's crust.

Altogether the violent movements of land and water masses would destroy most life, particularly that of the higher animals, and certainly that of man. He states that it would make no difference whether this transformation occurred suddenly or took a relatively long period of time; the results would be the same. As proof that such things have happened before in the world's history, he cites the belief that Greenland once had a tropical climate, and that in remote ages ice sheets covered large sections of the earth's present land surface. Pidgeon's book, published by the Commercial Printing Company at St. Louis in 1885, still is interesting, despite occasionally confused tenses or mixed singulars and plurals. It surely is a rare bit of southern Illinois curiosa.

As we see, the earth definitely did not meet the fate Pidgeon foresaw. Perhaps it is because the canals through the continental rim of Africa were never cut. The great French engineer, De Lesseps, who was suggested for the task, then was interested in an early effort to dig the Panama Canal. Even if it didn't happen, it was a great dream.

🎖 THE OTHER ILLINOIS

THERE ARE THOSE who resent having someone say, "There is a book you should read." Nevertheless, there definitely is a book you should read. It is *The Other Illinois,* written by Baker Brownell, formerly of Northwestern University and of Southern Illinois University.

My first copy of this book was awaiting my return from a day out of town. As I was somewhat tired, bedtime came early. *The Other Illinois* was chosen as the book from which a few pages would be read as a mild sedative. One hundred pages soon were read and it was time to get sleepy. Instead of doing so, reading continued until the book was completed.

The Other Illinois concerns the southern section of our state, that portion from about the latitude of Vandalia to the southern tip. It is not a history, an economics or sociology text, an encyclopedia, a philosophical discourse, a guide book, or one of stories. It is all of these and more without the handicaps of any, the kind of book one wants to keep and re-read and talk about.

The book really is about people, the everyday garden variety of folk, those that live next door, on either hand, or across the street. It also is about those that live in the tar paper shacks on the far side of the railroad, and in the tumble-down huts on seldom traveled back roads over the countryside. It does not leave out those in nice houses on the right side of the tracks. In fact, people of all ages and kinds are never out of sight.

A motley throng parades across the 261 pages of the book. There are old-age pensioners, recipients of public relief, part-time miners, sub-subsistence farmers, consecrated mothers, as well as other mothers busily propagating dependent children, coal barons and business tycoons, trailer dwelling workmen, gangsters, representatives of organized crime, wholesome youth, river pirates, highwaymen, murderers, consecrated churchmen, militant missionaries, heroes and rascals, and earnest educators, along with an array of competent and incompetent public officials, some of dubious honesty. All these and others parade in close formation across the pages. There is not a picture in the book, for none are needed.

Lengthy mention of the folklore, traditions, and sometimes strange beliefs of a distinctive people are found with something of their record. I have always sensed, and even shared, the fierce, perhaps defensive, pride of natives. I know something of the beatings its people have taken, beatings that produced what Baker Brownell so aptly terms "a burned over people." Frankly, I am conceited enough to believe that I know right well this section of Illinois and the distinctive people that inhabit it.

Assuming all this as part of the background for judgment, I would evaluate *The Other Illinois*. It is a factual presentation, generally tempered with kindness. There is none of the "holier than thou" attitude or messianic complex sometimes evident in the efforts of those who would analyze a region and point to remedial measures. It is well and forcibly written, but always it is easy reading. The author must have worked very hard to make it so. Some passages of it are almost poetry.

With the varied and numberless individuals, incidents, and scenes that are passed in review, it is marvelous that confusion does not result. From its very beginning to its end the account moves easily forward.

The book begins with "Off to the south of the big-time Illinois and considerably older is another Illinois not well known even to Illinoisans. . . . This southern Illinois sits on the back doorstep as poor as Job's turkey, as beautiful as red bud trees in spring." This is followed by many pages of balanced and piercing scrutiny of the region's past and a thorough inventory of its present potentialities.

Brownell closes his book with the following sentences:

I have lived and worked in southern Illinois and have seen the cycle of seasons roll round again and again. I have traveled across these thirty-one counties back and forth too many times to remember. I, too, like the newspaper men hereabouts feel that I own the country. That is a little extreme, to be sure, for no one can own this stubborn beautiful land; but if belonging to it can be the privilege of a damn-Yankee from the north end of the state, then I claim that privilege.

Nothing heretofore written so well depicts the entire background of southern Illinois. Other writings will come to supplement it, but none are likely ever to supplant it. Anyone wishing to add to his understanding of this section of the state should read and ponder Baker Brownell's *The Other Illinois*.

As a native southern Illinoisan who has spent a lifetime here, I believe I see more of virtue and hope than *The Other Illinois* expresses. It possibly could be that I am prejudiced and that the wish is father of the thought.

Chapter 18

Random Stories

❧ *WANDERING IN A WONDERLAND*

I LIKE TO prowl. Once, engaged in that activity, an opportunity came to wander leisurely through a collection of old objects stored in two houses and a large garage in Benton, Illinois. Though somewhat confused, much was learned, and many memories revived.

Before the visit, only banks—real banks—were associated closely with money. After looking over a hundred or more toy banks in the collection, toy ones also became associated with money—real money. On one the appraisers had placed a valuation. Their appraiser's tag on the bottom said $400. At an auction a few days later it sold for $1700, first bid, to a collector who came from Pennsylvania.

There were many other toy banks. Some of the bankers tipped hats, ran around in circles, played tunes, rang bells, and made other queer responses when a deposit was received. It would be a real pleasure to do business with some of them. While looking at this collection of toys, we observed that reports of bank robberies are frequent, but one doesn't often hear of a bank's being stolen. If a would-be robber knew about a collection like this one, perhaps it would be fully as profitable and less hazardous for him to steal the entire bank.

In the drawer of a chest there were a hundred or more ladies' hand fans, large and small. They were made of wood, ivory, silk, paper, palms, and feathers. Fans once provided about the only air conditioning available. They were also useful in the one-time widely practiced fan flirtation that enabled any daring damsel to signal messages to an observing and understanding gentleman.

Coffee roasters and coffee mills told of the time when the housewife

375

bought green coffee at the grocery store, took it home, roasted the berries, and then ground them as needed in the family coffee mill. It then was boiled, really boiled, in a coffee pot to make the breakfast brew. In olden days boiling coffee was settled by adding some cold water or by pouring it back and forth, using a cup. There were tables and shelves laden with grease lamps, candle molds, and candle holders, along with hundreds of kerosene wall and table lamps. There also were carriage lamps that once adorned that "surrey with the fringe on top." There were many old-time family albums that once were used to regale visitors somewhat as color slides now are. One album had many ambrotypes and daguerreotypes, some of which would rate high in present-day photographic displays. A few of the albums had music boxes that played some old, old melodies when opened. Even though the portraits might be dowdy, the music was good.

One room had many, many china dolls along with boxes of spare parts—such as arms and legs and special materials for dresses. There were some old-type hand-cranked sewing machines that once were used to make doll clothes. It would not be safe to say how many thousand buttons, large and small, were tastefully arranged on cards. There were figure buttons, picture buttons, and many ornamental self-buttons. Many a single button was worth more than the entire coat, suit, or dress it once adorned.

An amusing item was a lady's boot jack with a frame across its front and a curtain arranged in such a way that no modest maiden need expose a shapely ankle. Wooden churns, milk crocks, ladles, butter molds, and milk strainers reflected home dairy practices when milk was neither Grade A nor homogenized, and no Vitamin D had been added. Brass and iron kettles, pendants, spiders, trivets, portable ovens, and other kitchen equipment seldom seen told of the days when cooking was done at the kitchen hearth.

An array of large, strange-looking combs indicated the hair fashions in vogue when there were no beauticians, hair dressers, or beauty parlors where lilies were gilded. A rack of walking canes were from a time when no man was thought well-dressed without cane and spats.

An array of more than two hundred shelved shaving mugs bore their one-time owners' names, trades, or fraternal insignia boldly lettered on their sides. Rows of similar mugs once adorned the shelves of many a local shop and bore the names of patrons who came regularly for their ten-cent shaves.

Flat irons, washboards, wooden tubs, and boiling kettles told how earlier housewives did their laundry at home. There were collections of bottles, Gibson Girl plates, milk glass, coin glass, and other glass that rang like a bell when tapped. In ordered disarray there were figures and figurines, ornamental clocks, massive picture frames, charm jugs, candelabra, and ornamental paper weights of endless variety. Unnumbered other items suggested that their days were those of elegant living.

Gathered over a period of more than thirty years, the items mentioned, along with others not named, were in the collection of the late Mrs. Elizabeth Doty. Leisurely wandering through and wondering about this collection gave glimpses of another way of life and made this visitor wish to be a millionaire. Then he could buy the entire collection and admire it until he grew tired, if ever. Items like these tell a thousand stories to those who look with understanding.

🌻 *OLD ADVERTISEMENTS*

NEARLY EVERYONE is interested in newspapers and seeks the latest issue. Headlines are rapidly scanned to see what added alarms, threats, crises, scandals, tragedies, blessings, and brinks the day has brought. Yesterday's paper immediately becomes stale. The ones of last week are practically forgotten.

Strange to say, if these papers are allowed to lie around for about a hundred years, they again become interesting. Their advertisements even become intriguing, though the merchant and his wares are long gone.

This became apparent to the writer during a recent visit to the Illinois State Historical Library. Early files of the Kaskaskia, Shawneetown, and Vandalia papers were being inspected for another purpose when an advertisement attracted more than casual attention. Interest increased when it was observed that the signer was James Ford, legendary character of the Cave-in-Rock area. The scare line, large for that day, said "$100 Reward." At the end of this line was a crude woodcut of a runner with a bundle on his shoulder staff.

Ford's advertisement continued, "Ran away from the subscriber . . . Ben and Reuben, Ben about 40 . . . short and heavy made . . . yellow complexion . . . plays on the violin, with both his ears off close to his head, which he lost for robbing a boat on the Ohio. No doubt he has changed his clothing since he left home." Reuben "has a down look when spoken to, one of his fingers next to his little finger is off at the first joint, which hand is not recollected, and walks lame occasionally, by a pain in the hip."

Perhaps Ben and Reuben made good their escape since the notice of reward continued to appear in each issue of the paper for many weeks.

Similar notices of runaways from Kentucky, Tennessee, Missouri, and

Mississippi were frequent. There was Savage from Williamson County, Tennessee, with "thick lips and a bold look." Next came Charles with "left thumb off at first joint . . . fond of whiskey . . . and large knife scar on left breast . . . fresh."

"Six foot . . . rough, rawboned . . . Brister . . . stutters if interrogated or made mad . . . took pair of old saddlebags when he fled." Pete from Todd County, Kentucky, "has a small piece of one of his ears bitten off and a rather feminine voice."

The sheriff of Jackson County had two runaways, Negroes Bartlett and Daniel, presumably slaves, in the jail at Brownsville. Either could be had by his owner if proper evidence of ownership was presented and costs paid. Otherwise, they would be bound out locally for a period of some months. At the end of that time they would be considered free and released. James was held in a like manner by the sheriff of Jefferson County.

In two notices concerning runaways there is a hint of humor. Ebenezer Capps of Randolph County offered a "Reward of One Cent" for the apprehension of David Ditson, "indentured apprentice." David may have been a white bound boy since he was "of a fair complexion." A similar notice and a like reward was offered by another man living at Raleigh, in Saline County.

Slaves and apprentices alike appear to have been somewhat dissatisfied with their lots.

Other advertisements also were interesting. "Good Kentucky Whiskey" was $1.75 a gallon. One merchant had "allum, alspice, hyson, tea, straw bonnets, rosin, fuller, Bandanna handkerchiefs, and Russian diaper" (which doubtlessly was used as its latter name indicates). He could also supply such strange items as "bombazet, bombazeen, sarconet, jaconet, linen, mull muslin and Canton crepe," as well as "hand and tenant saws." Another had "Genuine Garden Seed."

An advertisement appearing March 8, 1823, states that "AFRICA, the most beautiful and well blooded stud horse brought from Virginia . . . acknowledged by all who have seen him to be the finest and most elegant horse ever brought to the state" had arrived at Mt. Pleasant in St. Clair County.

On March 29, 1823, an advertisement in the Vandalia paper literally screamed,

ROBBERY! ROBBERY!! ROBBERY!!! $300 REWARD

The bank at Vandalia had been robbed. The robbery had occurred "between seven and half after eight" (meaning between 7:00 and 8:30) on the twenty-sixth. A news article told the story in about seven inches of column space on page two. No other mention was found in later news columns, but the reward notice continued to appear until July 26. One wonders if the robbers were caught.

❦ SOUTHERN ILLINOIS WENT "A BORROWING"

SOUTHERN ILLINIOS, like almost any other section of the country, has borrowed much from older settled places. Excellent illustrations of this practice are furnished by some of the borrowings made from a small region about Lancaster, Pennsylvania, the area where the Pennsylvania Dutch or "plain people" live. A similar listing of other borrowings could be made for different regions from which numbers of our earlier settlers came.

When the first arrivals from the older states reached the Illinois Country to make their homes, they came carrying "Kentucky" rifles. Actually, these were not Kentucky rifles. This weapon, the first strictly American firearm, had its beginning in a Pennsylvania gunsmith's shop about 1700. From this original shop in Lancaster their making was taken up by craftsmen in other shops. Made entirely by hand and often with only those tools that the workman himself had fashioned, they were marvelous productions.

These rifles once were considered an essential family possession. Now they are a collector's item. It was with these firearms that the pioneer defended himself against the Indians and killed the game that was the first source of the family's meat supply.

As soon as overland trails were opened to Illinois, immigrants began to arrive on Conestoga wagons, another Lancaster product. The making of these wagons began about 1750 and continued for more than a hundred years. In these staunchly built vehicles thousands of settlers moved along the Cumberland Road to Illinois and on to the West. Also known as "prairie schooners" they rolled onward across prairie and desert over the old trail to Sante Fe, and on to the Pacific. These were the wagons used by the "stogie" smoking teamsters to haul freight over the Goshen and other early Illinois trails. So far as is known, the last one of these wagons in southern Illinois rotted away some years ago. The last of the men who drove them were old, old men a lifetime ago. Again, we borrowed something good.

Kentucky rifles and Conestoga wagons are not all that the Lancaster region gave us. It was in the same locality that the cradle-manger scene began as a Christmas decoration. The custom of reproducing the Nativity scene was brought to this country by the Moravians and practiced in Pennsylvania, as it still is. We borrowed it from them. They also passed on to us the symbolic Easter bunny and the coloring of eggs for Easter.

A bronze marker on the front of a building in Lititz, near Lancaster, tells us that the baking of pretzels in America began there in the 1850's. They still are a popular product, being sold at roadside stands and in bakeshops over the area. They are given to babies to help them teethe and are served along with ice cream for dessert. Beer and pretzels complement each other.

Many books have been written to tell of the cooking of the Pennsylvania Dutch. Their region popularized the drying of fruit and the making of apple butter. The pies they make are famous, especially the one they call shoo-fly pie. Pennsylvania Dutch who immigrated to Illinois brought their cooking skills and no one regrets this borrowing.

The Lancaster area gave us several other things. It was there that a German named Mannheim Stiegel established his glass works and began to make the glass that all collectors want—finely designed, delicately colored, and having a distinctive ringing sound.

A thousand of our superstitious signs and bits of folklore go back to the Lancaster people. They did much to popularize Groundhog Day and the custom of putting charms above the barn doors to protect livestock from danger and disease.

This list of things we borrowed from that one region could be expanded to include many others. Some even hold that moonshining first became a popular practice there.

🌣 GYPSIES ARE A STRANGE PEOPLE

SOME RECENT incidents have made us Gypsy-minded. A band of the trailering nomads met in southern Illinois at Red Hills State Park were later encountered at a Washington, D.C., trailer court. The same large, marked woman who told my fortune at Red Hills was reading palms in her "ofisa" across the street from the Congressional Library. Interest was renewed a few weeks ago when two women and their children came out of St. Louis on the Illinois Central bound for Birmingham, Alabama; even more recently, a woman in Gypsy dress was seen buying a flight ticket at the St. Louis airport—far cries from traveling in the plodding caravans that moved over dusty country roads. The accumulation of incidents brought memories of other Gypsies.

The gaily colored to drab horse-drawn vehicles making up their picturesque caravans are gone from the dusty highways of southern Illinois, but Gypsies have not vanished. It is only that they now travel by less spectacular conveyances—like Cadillacs, Chryslers, and house trailers. As horses disappeared from the highways, so did their panelled, carved, and colorful wagons.

Older persons will recall these swarthy, sharp-eyed, queerly dressed, and altogether strange people as they went about the countryside by day and sat beside their campfires at night.

Gypsies are the oldest world nomads. References indicate that they were present in ancient lands and times. Their speech is basically Sanskrit, a language that flourished in northern India five thousand years ago. This should indicate that they came from there. No one seems to know just when they began to wander or why they did so.

Now they are scattered from Lapland to the tip of Africa, from India to Ireland, from Canada to the southern end of South America, and even over Australia; thus, they are the "wanderingest" people on earth.

About the year 1400 they appeared in Western Europe. Spanish records indicate that they were in America as early as 1580. Before 1700 they were in Brazil, and shortly thereafter they were in the French settlements along the Gulf of Mexico. The first Gypsies of record along the Atlantic seaboard came to Virginia on the ship *Greenock* in 1715. Since then thousands have come to wander back and forth, tinker, tell fortunes, steal, play confidence games, trade in horses and now in automobiles, and to gather and spread the folklore of all lands.

The dress of Gypsy men became conventional many years ago, and the gaudy attire of the women is little changed. Their lustrous black hair, parted in the middle and drawn back tightly, still is worn in braids that often have brilliant ribbons or even strings of coins plaited in them. The women always have enormous earrings worn in pierced ears. No Gypsy woman is well-dressed without heavy bracelets and a necklace, often made up of two or more bands of linked gold coins. Even when bedecked with all this jewelry and wearing voluminous dresses of brilliant orange, green, and scarlet, and with gaily colored handkerchiefs tied over their heads, they were sometimes shoeless.

By day the men tinkered, traded horses, doctored farm animals, or coppersmithed, and they were skilled at all of these enterprises. Anyone who could best a Gypsy horsetrader was an expert.

Their women spent the day on rounds of fortunetelling, "blessing" or "removing the curse" from money if the opportunity presented itself, plying their confidence tricks, begging, and picking up almost anything they could escape with. Children, poorly clad and unkempt, went about peddling and begging.

Bands of them still go about; perhaps they always will. They continue to live apart and are little understood; they are a unique example of a primitive people whose contact with civilization has not eliminated them. Perhaps the poet was right when he said, "And the Gypsy blood to the Gypsy blood over the wide world ever." Another one who said, "Only the hearthstone of old India will end the march of Gypsy feet," also may have been right.

Anyway, if opportunity ever again comes, pay a casual visit to a Gypsy camp and have your palm read, but keep your hand on your pocketbook, and skip the "money blessing" feature.

❀ HOW A HABIT GOT STARTED

THERE MIGHT BE one more smoker today if an inquisitive six-year-old boy had been able to withstand the lethal powers of a grandfather's clay pipe, its soggy cane stem, and a fill of crumbled tobacco found in a cloth bag decorated with the picture of a green frog. There may have been one more chewer if a companion had not splashed a sluice of cold water into the face of an unsuspecting ten-year-old swimmer, thereby causing him to swallow a liberal quid of Star tobacco. Just one vigorous sniff of a brown powder from a stone jar left on the mantel by an old lady settled my snuff question for all time.

These incidents together, however, did not settle one other question. Why do people use tobacco and how did the practice ever get started? The following is part of what was learned in trying to find an answer.

When Columbus came to the islands of the New World, men from his ships went ashore to greet and make friends with the natives. In accordance with age-old custom, they took along gifts and the natives who met them exchanged offerings to show their good will.

Among the gifts from the natives were "certain dried leaves" that gave off a pleasing fragrance. Though these leaves were presented with above-average ceremony, the Spaniards failed to realize that they were of any special significance and rather ignored them. Perhaps they were disappointed that the gifts received did not include the spices of the Indies and at least enough gold and silver to indicate that the new land was rich in those metals. Little did they know that the leaves they ignored would some day be worth their weight in silver, as the basic product for America's first great business.

Somewhat later two of Columbus's men, Rodrigo de Jerez and Luis de Torres by name, were sent into the interior of Cuba to find the ruler of Cathay and extend to him the admiral's friendly greetings. On this mission they met natives smoking rolls of the special leaves and blowing on the burning ends between puffs, just as some cigar smokers still do. De Jerez and de Torres took some puffs and were pleased. The former liked it so well that he immediately became the first tobacco addict among white men in recorded history. Other sailors, acquiring the habit, passed both it and the plant on to other countries and people. In a surprisingly short time its use became worldwide.

In politics momentous decisions are said to be reached in smoke-filled rooms. Even centuries ago, no council of war or state in America was complete without the formal use of pipe and tobacco. Today, a cigarette or cigar is offered as a gesture of friendship or to woo favor, but the natives were doing the same when Columbus came to America.

Because certain mystic qualities were ascribed to tobacco, the church once banned its use. Nevertheless, one high churchman found a way to justify evasion. He declared, "I need it because of the dampness and my catarrh."

Tobacco has had many a virtue assigned to it. The Indians thought its use would lessen hunger, dull fatigue, slake thirst, and ease pain. Men still say the same. Wounds and injuries, snakebites and insect stings, boils and open sores had their quids of tobacco applied. In some quarters, the practice persists.

It also was believed that smoking would help to cool those who felt themselves too hot and give warmth to those chilled. Even yet, men say the same. Indians believed that smoke blown upon an area of pain would ease the misery; there are still those who believe that earache may be relieved by blowing tobacco smoke into the ear, especially if it is done through a cane stem. In earlier days here people sought to ease the baby's colic by blowing smoke on its stomach. Water in which tobacco had been boiled once was rubbed on the navels of children to rid them of worms. There are those yet who think that blowing tobacco smoke on rose bushes will keep the bugs away. (As a temporary measure that may be true.)

Tobacco has had many a name applied to it. It has been the "soverane herb," the "witching weed," the "silver weed," and "herba panacea." At the other extreme, some have called it the "filthy weed."

Though tobacco and its uses remain, the cigar store Indian has become a museum piece. The cigar store "Indian" might be a fair maiden, a turbaned Turk, a Negro, a kilted Scot, or an Indian brave with a handful of cigars. All alike were made of pine. It is claimed that there once were a hundred thousand such figures.

By strange coincidence the last one of them I saw in real service was standing in front of a store in Pocahontas, Illinois, about thirty years ago.

🌿 MARTHA ANN AND DAVID
GO FOR A RIDE

YOUNGSTERS SEEM to have gotten in early with ballooning in this country. A fifteen-year-old boy, Edward Warren, made the first ascension in America near Baltimore, Maryland, on June 24, 1784. It was ten years after this before a Frenchman named Blanchard completed a second ascent.

Perhaps the most widely circulated account of a balloon ascension in America tells of an unplanned one that Martha Ann Harvey, eight years old, and her brother David, three, began near Centralia on September 17, 1858, three years after "Professor" Silas M. Brooks had made the first Illinois ascent at Chicago on July 4, 1855.

Balloons then were rare in Illinois. Newspapers rated them as first-class sources of stories and used such terms as stupendous, sensational unrivaled, glorious, daring, and mysterious to describe them. With terms like these they announced that Brooks, "that greatest of American aeronauts," would make an ascent at the Illinois State Fair being held at Centralia on September 14-17, 1858. The flight was to be on the afternoon of the seventeenth.

Brooks was indisposed on that day, and the ascent was made by his helper, Samuel Wilson. All went well. The balloon rose from the fairgrounds, quickly reached a height of about two miles, and drifted about. At Central City it paused about fifteen minutes; Wilson whiled away the time reading newspapers that were to be tossed out when he was aloft. When he tired of staying over Central City, Wilson dumped ballast and rose, as he tells us, to a height of about three miles. From there he could see the Mississippi River and steamboats on it. He also tells of watching a glorious sunset.

As night came on, his balloon cooled slightly and began to descend. When it sank low enough, Wilson cast out a long rope with a grappling iron on it. The iron caught in a tree and the farmer, Daniel Harvey, and his son, who had never "seen the elephants," hastened to help him. Other members of the family and the neighbors flocked in.

With all holding the balloon by attached ropes, Wilson clambered out of the basket. Harvey climbed in, and with others holding the balloon, made a controlled ascent. When he had been hauled down, Harvey placed three of his children in the basket and gave them a similar ride. In the meantime Wilson had turned aside to answer the questions of some women standing nearby. Before doing so, he asked them to securely anchor the balloon.

When the balloon was lowered to unload the children, Mr. Harvey helped his older daughter from the basket first. This suddenly decreased the load and caused the balloon to give such a surge that it tore loose from the grasp of those holding it and from the fence to which it had been tethered. It sailed away among the stars with Martha Ann and David aboard. Martha Ann cried out, "Mother! Let us out, Mother! Let us out." In a short time the balloon was out of sight in the darkness, and the calls for help could no longer be heard.

An alarm was quickly spread. Mr. Wilson rode one of farmer Harvey's horses into Centralia to spread the alarm by railroad and by wire. An extra of the local paper appeared the next morning telling of the children's plight. Some time during the day, news arrived that they had landed safely on the farm of a Mr. Atchison, not far from Centralia.

Before daybreak on the morning of September 18, Mr. Atchison had arisen early to look at Donat's comet, then visible in the sky. He forgot all about the comet, however, when "an immense specter arising from a nearby tree" rather appalled him, particularly when he heard a childish voice calling for help. Martha Ann was happy to be down, and David complained of being cold.

Fragments of this story that were passed in turn to their children still are repeated in the Centralia region. A full account is in the transactions of the Illinois Agriculture Association for 1858–1859, and in numerous papers over the nation.

❦ REPLACEMENTS FOR THE OLD

PREVIOUS ARTICLES have been about our vanishing landscape, our changing environment. Almost always nostalgic comment has been made about once familiar objects, now seldom or never seen. Likewise, vanishing customs, strange beliefs, and abandoned practices have been mentioned, again with a bit of nostalgia.

The vanished objects mentioned have varied widely. They have included such things as rail fences, wall sweeps, corduroy roads, ash hoppers, high-top button shoes, splint bonnets, peg-top trousers, and top buggies. Lizards, sidesaddles, ox teams, windmills, log wagons, and the "surrey with the fringe on top" have slipped away to join the objects mentioned earlier. Older persons can readily add to the list.

Along with these material objects there also has gone much of the once familiar lore about ghosts, witches, signs, superstitions, remedies, and odd beliefs. Personal narratives and tales, often tall ones, that made up conversation around the open fireplace when lantern-carrying neighbors came "to set until bedtime," also have passed from circulation.

Many of these objects, practices, and beliefs passed so quietly and naturally that their departure was unnoted. One day we simply looked and they were not here. Strangely, however, they seem to have left no vacant spaces. Other things came to fill their places and to keep the environment crowded.

Persons seventy-five years old can recall when several of the space fillers, now considered indispensable, came into general use. Perhaps they have caused the greatest turnover of this kind in any period of equal length in history. The writer remembers vividly the coming of the first telephone to the village of Texas City, with the curiosity and comment it aroused. "How does it work?" was explained by "The wire is hollow." Today, in puzzlement, he dials a number, half a continent away, afraid to ask questions, and feels obligated to listen while some fifteen-year-old boy or girl clearly and accurately explains just how it works.

Then the radio came with its crystals and "cat whiskers." These first ones were followed by Armstrong, Hazeltine, and other named circuits made up of a weird collection of tuning coils, variable and fixed condensers, and tubes filled with queerly arranged grids and filaments. From a table littered with these assorted parts, plus long-nosed pliers, soldering irons, copper wire, bits of tape, tinfoil, phone jacks, wooden panels, formica if it could be had, and other articles too numerous to mention, the daring amateur assembled his own set and was happy when he heard KDKA at Pittsburgh, or Atlanta with its boast that it covered the country "like the dew covers Dixie." Now it is television, with sight, sound, and even color.

These are only some of the wonders that a single lifetime has brought. In addition it has seen the automobile become commonplace. Along with the automobile there has come a system of paved and improved highways to lift us out of the mud, then airplanes to complete the lift.

Mechanical refrigeration has eliminated the springhouses that some oldsters have known. It also has eliminated the practice of hanging milk and butter in the well or setting the jars and crocks of milk in tubs and troughs of cold water, sometimes of wrapping them in wet cloths, even in wet tow sacks, so evaporation would cool their contents. Ice cream and frozen desserts, then rarities, have been made common by home refrigerators.

Washing machines have replaced the wash kettles that hung on a pole in the backyard or sat on the kitchen stove. The wooden tubs, washboards, and sadirons went with the kettles.

Oldsters also can remember when rural free delivery of mail came and it was no longer necessary to go to the post office for the scant mail. That was before the deluge of "Boxholder" and "Rural Route Patron" advertising. Perhaps this partially explains why more than half the world's mail moves in the United States.

These same people saw the coming of the phonograph with its two-minute wax cylinder records telling of "Uncle Josh at the County Fair," or of "The Preacher and the Bear," all listened to through a device resembling a physician's stethoscope. Now it is magnetic tape and hi-fi or stereophonic long-playing records.

More fortunate oldsters will recall seeing "The Great Train Robbery," the first full-length movie, silent of course. With varied feelings they have seen the boom and decline of the movies, as well as the practical passing of the circus and showboat.

This same generation has seen bathrooms, bicycles, scooters, motorcycles, and beatnik haircuts come in numbers. It also has seen the advent of plastics and synthetic fibers, and amateur photography. It has seen the coming of tractors and bulldozers, grain combines and cotton pickers, weed killers, insect destroyers, and a myriad assortment of other sprays for almost all purposes.

Then there are the wonder drugs, antibiotics, the assembly line, rural electricity, and the atom bomb.

Don't feel too sorry for oldsters—they've seen many things come and many others go. They've seen two ways of life.

Index

Shawnee Classics

SHAWNEE CLASSICS A Series of Classic Regional Reprints for the Midwest